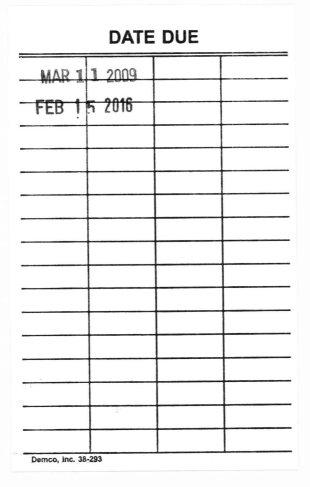

DATE DUE

MAR 1 1 2009		
FEB 1 5 2016		

Demco, Inc. 38-293

STROM

STROM

The Complicated
Personal and
Political Life of
Strom Thurmond

JACK BASS AND

MARILYN W. THOMPSON

PublicAffairs
New York

Published in the United States by PublicAffairs™,
a member of the Perseus Books Group.
All rights reserved.
Printed in the United States of America.

Images courtesy of The Strom Thurmond Collection, Special Collections, Clemson University
Libraries, Clemson, S.C., except for Essie Mae Washington ... South Carolina State University
Historical Collection, Mark F. Whittaker Library, *Edgefield Advertiser* "exposes" ... Marilyn W.
Thompson, With a long, controversial career ... Doug Marlette, It's just Ol' Strom ...
Robert Ariail, Strom, Jr., at twenty-nine ... Roger Harvell, The ancient senator ... Robert Ariail,
Strom Thurmond's casket ... *The State*, and Essie Mae Washington-Williams ...
Clint Bowie / *The Edgefield Advertiser*.

Book design by Jane Raese
Text set in 12 point Centaur

Library of Congress Cataloging-in-Publication Data
Bass, Jack.
Strom : the complicated personal and political life of Strom Thurmond /
Jack Bass and Marilyn W. Thompson — 1st ed.
p. cm.
Includes bibliographical references and index.
ISBN 1-58648-297-1
1. Thurmond, Strom, 1902- 2. Legislators—United States—Biography.
3. United States. Congress. Senate—Biography. I. Thompson, Marilyn W.
II. Title.
E748.T58B374 2005
328.73'092—dc22
[B]
2005047581

FIRST EDITION

10 9 8 7 6 5 4 3 2 1

To Nathalie Dupree

—J. B.

To the memory of Robert W. Thompson Jr.

—M. W. T.

Contents

The Perfect Strom

As the Senate began its impeachment trial of President Bill Clinton in January 1999, Strom Thurmond presided over the swearing in of Chief Justice William Rehnquist. The ninety-six-year-old senator from South Carolina appeared a bit unsteady in his most public act as president pro tempore of the Senate, a mostly ceremonial position. But he understood that the moment also contained a strong element of irony.

Here was the Congress of the United States sitting in grave judgment to determine whether the president was guilty of "high crimes and misdemeanors" for conduct stemming from a relationship with intern Monica Lewinsky. And here was Strom Thurmond, a man who had taken unabashed pride in achieving a reputation for lechery that could put Clinton to shame, starting the show. A titan of the Republican Party's conservative wing, Thurmond had a clear political obligation to vote "guilty."

But before the trial began, Thurmond had met with a few of his closest advisers and ranted just as he had in the old days. "These conservatives," he complained. "All this judgmental stuff . . . this is personal! It's nobody's business!"

Further, as his advisers were aware, Thurmond harbored a secret that he knew would emerge eventually, one that had the potential to redefine his legacy. Forgiving admirers would likely view this secret as evidence of his determination to do the right thing and to meet his personal obligations. His enemies would see it as the ultimate hypocrisy, living proof that the senator's career as banner carrier for the white supremacist Dixiecrats and his years opposing the civil rights movement were the result of pure political expedience.

Thurmond sometimes ruminated about how the story would break, probably after his death. It would be bigger than anything in his life. If they could do this to Clinton, he would ask, then what in the world would they do when they finally learned the truth about the onetime segregationist's illegitimate black daughter, Essie Mae Washington-Williams? Once, recalled Armstrong Williams, his trusted adviser, and a black man, Strom laughed so hard at the irony that his frail body rocked and tears rolled down his cheeks.[1]

On July 1, 2004, exactly a year after Strom Thurmond's funeral, the name "Essie Mae" was chiseled into the stone base of the seventeen-foot-tall Thurmond statue on the Statehouse grounds in Columbia, South Carolina. It was added to that of his other children—Nancy Moore, J. Strom Jr., Juliana Gertrude, and Paul Reynolds—all borne by his second wife, Nancy. The base of the statue further lists his public career highlights but leaves unmentioned his third-party 1948 bid for the presidency, a campaign that was listed on the inscription of his first wife's tombstone in 1960. Its absence thirty-nine years later on the pedestal of the Statehouse monument symbolizes Thurmond's denial in his later years of the motivating force behind that 1948 campaign, a bitter and forcefully expressed defense of the South's then-entrenched system of racial segregation.

Ms. Williams had come forward six months earlier, at age seventy-eight, to declare at a Columbia press conference covered by major worldwide media, "My father's name was James Strom Thurmond." She was speaking now, she said, because "I decided that my children deserve the right to know from whom, where, and what they have come. It is their right to know and understand the rich history of their ancestry, black and white." She added, "I feel completely free."

Thurmond's family in South Carolina acknowledged her claim. "We have no reason to believe Ms. Williams was not telling the truth," thirty-one-year-old Strom Thurmond Jr. told the press, adding that he felt "good" from "doing the right thing." In the history of the American South, this acceptance of such a relationship by a family approaching the prominence of the Thurmonds was unprecedented. It contrasted sharply with the protracted resistance of Thomas Jefferson's white ancestors to claims made by descendants of his slave mistress, Sally Hemings. Yet these stories had something in common, black relatives seeking to clarify their identity and claim a piece of their heritage.

It was, as Strom had predicted, the inevitable rounding out of his parallel lives of Strom the politician and Strom the searing and sometimes rascally individualist. These qualities mixed together like the fruit in a blueberry-and-peach cobbler to make him one of America's most enduring twentieth-century political figures. Ms. Williams's breaking her lifelong—

up to then—silence confirmed the tales of "colored offspring" that had long circulated within South Carolina's black community and among knowledgeable whites and, with Strom's penchant for young beauty-queen wives and an image he stoked of sexual prowess, provided him with a reputation for ribaldry of almost folkloric proportions. Despite this, and partly because of it, many ordinary citizens loved him. Further, he was the rare politician who seemed to relate to and care about everyday people, certainly everyday white people, and more and more, black constituents as well. A master of retail politics, he spoke the common man's language.

"He took small county politics and applied it on a statewide basis, always ready to help someone," explained Butler Derrick, a Democrat who served twenty years in Congress with Thurmond and grew up in his hometown of Edgefield. "Politics is a matter of addition, not subtraction, and he's the one who wrote the rule on that."[2]

Thurmond's political legacy is found not in the annals of legislative achievement but in his pivotal role in reshaping America's political culture. As the segregationist States Rights Democratic Party—the Dixiecrats—candidate for president in 1948, he won four Deep South states and shook the foundations of the Democratic "solid South," which emerged from the Compromise of 1877, in which Republican Rutherford B. Hayes got the electoral votes of South Carolina and two other Southern states to win the presidency by a single electoral vote. In exchange the South got an end to Reconstruction. This 1948 break in the white South's political psyche opened the path for and accelerated two-party development in the region, in which Thurmond would again play a major part.

After an unprecedented election to the Senate in 1954 as a write-in candidate, he switched parties ten years later to campaign across the South for presidential candidate Barry Goldwater, who had voted against the landmark Civil Rights Act of 1964, which Thurmond also vigorously opposed. The combination of Goldwater's vote against the Civil Rights Act, his pro-military anti-Communism, and Thurmond's party-switching endorsement pulled large numbers of the most racially reactionary white Southerners into the Grand Old Party. There Strom helped build the foundation for a race-flavored "Southern strategy" that would alter politics nationally and change the character of the party of Abraham Lincoln.

In 1968, Thurmond became kingmaker for Richard Nixon, first holding the South for him against California Governor Ronald Reagan at the

Republican National Convention to win the nomination for president, and then thwarting Alabama Governor George Wallace's third-party drive. Thurmond had already led the charge that blocked President Lyndon Johnson's ally, the liberal justice Abe Fortas, from becoming chief justice of the Supreme Court after Earl Warren. As Thurmond foresaw, President Nixon's appointments would begin the Court's movement to the right.

Once, when a staff member included the word "afraid" in a speech, Strom handed the text back to him with the comment, "I've never been afraid of anything." His record in military and political combat validated this boast.

As a child, he had learned how to shake hands from the legendary South Carolina senator and race baiter, Pitchfork Ben Tillman. Thurmond shook hands so long and so often in South Carolina that he learned to detect a glint of recognition in someone's eyes and would greet them with, "So good to see you again." The ordinary citizen would think, "He remembered me."

His political mastery, however, was based not on show, but substance. The four corners of its foundation were: political boldness, which reflects both courage and an unsurpassed instinct for timing; a refusal to keep an enemy, which dissipates opposition; a willingness to take a firm stand on issues, which generates respect; and a record of legendary constituent service, which creates goodwill.

Thurmond's effrontery at pork barrel politics was breathtaking. After voting against almost all federal legislation aimed at improving health care, education, housing, and other domestic spending programs not involving the military, he sought every federal dollar he could get for South Carolina, with accompanying press releases seeking credit for every grant made to the state.

After Lieutenant Governor John C. West, a progressive Democrat, was elected governor in 1970, his staff worked directly with Senator Thurmond to secure grants for pilot programs in housing for the poor, distribution of food commodities, and other programs in which West was interested. West's staff grumbled at times that his office developed the plans and proposals but that Thurmond claimed all the credit. All the same, West found the arrangement satisfactory. It got him what he wanted—funding from a Republican administration for needed social programs.

Ordinary citizens sensed Strom's total commitment to his state and to his office—he held several important ones over the years—and this led them to trust his convictions. A textile worker in overalls once explained he would vote for Thurmond "because he stands up for what he believes in— even when he's wrong."3

Thurmond's political foundation was further reinforced by a quiet and simple religious faith, values placed on family pride and loyalty, and a fierce determination to win. This drive to win was mirrored in his lifelong passion for physical fitness. On his sixty-fifth birthday, he demonstrated his vim, vigor, and vitality by performing push-ups before an audience of reporters in his Senate office. He stopped after reaching a hundred.

Until Alabama Governor George Wallace's presidential campaigns of the 1960s, no one symbolized resistance to civil rights for African Americans more than Thurmond. In the Senate, the former Dixiecrat set a filibuster record when speaking against the 1957 Civil Rights Act. That record still stands. But when the tide of changing laws and national opinion forced the American South to abandon its rigid state-enforced racial segregation, changes in attitude followed. As he would do so often, Strom Thurmond moved with the tide.

He abandoned his ship of "states' rights" opposition to civil rights progress and swam into the mainstream. He voted in 1982 to extend the Voting Rights Act that he had bitterly opposed in 1965. He became a champion of historically black colleges in the 1970s. He supported legislation in 1983 to make the birthday of Martin Luther King Jr. a national holiday. He reached out, politically and personally, to blacks in South Carolina, recognizing that they too had become constituents who should get service from his office. Most of all, this new Strom reflected his recognition that blacks now voted. (In the 1980s, he once strode over to a black journalist, pumped his hand, and whispered, "Tell your people to vote for me.") As always, he adapted to changing political circumstances.

After his marriage in 1968 at age sixty-six to twenty-two-year-old Nancy Moore, a former Miss South Carolina, Strom not only sired four children in less than eight years, but he regained the sense of humor that had seemed to wither in the early 1960s following the tragic death of his first wife, Jean, from brain cancer.

Famously tightfisted, Thurmond treated the public's money as frugally as he treated his own. When he became chairman of the Senate Judiciary Committee, Thurmond personally approved every expenditure—down to buying a box of pencils.

Dennis Shedd, his trusted staff director who would later become a federal judge, never forgot his first presentation as a young staffer in Thurmond's Senate office. Shedd had carefully read and absorbed an in-depth, four-page article in a Sunday issue of the *Washington Post* that analyzed complex issues about nuclear energy. When he came in Monday morning, Thurmond asked him to read the article, written by a noted scientist, and brief him. Shedd saw it as an opportunity to display his brilliance.

A few minutes later, he told Thurmond he was ready, and the senator said to go ahead. After less than thirty seconds, Thurmond stopped him and asked, "Is he for it or against it?"

Shedd explained, "He just wanted to know if the man was for nuclear energy or against it. I learned a very important lesson."

When he became top aide, Shedd told other staffers that in briefing the senator they needed to be prepared to do it in fifteen seconds. "I told them, 'If you can't tell him in fifteen seconds, you don't understand it well enough yet. And if he wants to hear more, or ask questions, be prepared to talk for up to an hour.'"[4]

Given these strengths, then, what were Thurmond's weaknesses, his character flaws? The same qualities that his admirers lauded were seen through a different lens by his political and personal enemies. To them, the focused determination that helped him conquer long-distance running as a young man became the cold calculation he employed in his unending quest for political office. He mastered the art of expediency, shifting with the changing winds and never stopping to apologize to those hurt by his actions.

Sheer vanity drove many of his actions. He loved setting records and achieved two as the nation's oldest and longest-serving senator. In the first days of the Reagan revolution, he boasted that his rank as president pro tempore made him one of the "most powerful men in the wuuullld." He helped pioneer hair-transplant surgery. He often appeared "out of it" because, as one former aide explained, he had such trouble hearing.[5] Thurmond told witnesses sitting too far from the microphone at Senate committee hearings, "Talk into the machine. Talk into the machine."[6] As the book of Ecclesiastes has it: "Vanity, vanity, all is vanity." In South Carolina, his name seems everywhere—buildings throughout the state, highways, schools, a lake, and more. The granite marker over the grave of his

universally admired first wife, Jean Crouch Thurmond, includes two long
engraved lines that identify her as:

The Wife of a Lawyer–Governor–
Presidential Candidate–United States Senator

At Clemson University, Strom's alma mater, the entire floor of one
building is dedicated to the Strom Thurmond Collection and its 8 million
pieces of paper. A former staffer in his Senate office said that "everything—even napkins from a reception" was collected and sent to Clemson.
Full-time archivists organized the material—speeches, correspondence,
newspaper and magazine articles, and endless photographs. During
months of cataloging photographs, an archivist said that eleven cubic feet
of them were discarded.

True, as his huge archives showed, Thurmond's career was more complicated than almost any other modern-day politician. It ran the gamut from
Roosevelt New Dealer and progressive Southern governor to Dixiecrat
segregationist, from first successful Senate write-in candidate to champion
of the filibuster. He survived a party switch, abandoning the Democratic
Party once and for all in 1964 to emerge a few years later as kingmaker for
Richard Nixon. He swerved radically from being the leading Senate opponent of civil rights to a supporter of Martin Luther King Day, somehow
convincing himself and his electorate that he had never based his positions
on racial animosity, only on the principles of states' rights. He challenged
George Wallace and helped dismantle the liberal Warren Court.

His personal life was equally complex. He had a penchant for young
wives and a lifelong reputation for ass-pinching licentiousness. He groped
female reporters and members of the Senate with such abandon that most
avoided riding with him on the Senate elevators. Rumors of "colored offspring" followed him throughout his career.[7]

Most of his life played out on a national stage, but he was a signature
product of the complex Old South state that sent him to Washington. He
was known by a single name—Strom—that conjured up a multitude of
images: the decorated war hero who crash landed in a glider behind enemy
lines on D day; the virile governor who impulsively stood on his head for
Life magazine; the elderly father with burnt orange hair plugs whose young

children wore T-shirts pleading "Vote for My Daddy"; the frail, tottering old senator showing up for work from his room at Walter Reed Hospital.

In the end, it was only fitting that he go back to South Carolina. He lived 100 years, and he was buried in the town where he was born.

PART ONE

Brave Beginnings

CHAPTER 1

The Boldness
of an Edgefield Man

On the outer wall of a building next to the Ten Governors Café, at the southeast corner of the courthouse square in the small town of Edgefield, a large mural boasts that Edgefield has produced "more dashing, brilliant, romantic figures, statesmen, orators, soldiers, adventurers, and daredevils than any other rural county in America." When W. W. Ball, the knowledgeable editor of the *News and Courier* in Charleston, wrote this in 1932 it was not exaggeration, but mere observation.[1] Strom Thurmond absorbed all of this—a little place, but with outsized figures—through his pores.

Located on a Cherokee trail that ran from present-day Asheville, North Carolina, to nearby Augusta, the Edgefield village of 2,500 still reflected a frontier culture during Strom's youth. "The whole atmosphere you grew up under was that you had to fight to get ahead, and whatever's necessary to do, you did," he recalled.[2] Strom and his two brothers, growing up after the turn of the century, were accustomed to seeing men take target practice in the town square, shooting bottles off store railings. "They were mean people—but of good honest character," younger brother Allen George Thurmond once described Edgefield's citizenry. "They were good about helping each other, but they would also shoot you. They would fight for what they believed in."

A half century later, two crusty farmers in overalls ruminate with cheeks stuffed with tobacco along Edgefield's busy main street, their eyes fixed on passing cars like tennis fans watching a rally at center court.

After quietly watching an unfamiliar dented Dodge with Georgia license tags, one spews a stream of brown tobacco juice onto the sidewalk and turns to the other with a joke.

"Hey," he says, pausing long enough to wipe with rumpled handkerchief the sweet juice in the corner of his mouth. "J'you hear the one about Strum and the 'bortion bill?"

"Nope," says the other, his eyes never leaving the road.

"Well . . . Strum's up in his office, up thar in Washington, one day and the secretary comes in and sez, 'Senator, thar's a lady on the phone wants to talk to you.' Well, Strum's kind of busy, doncha know, and he looks up from his desk and growls, 'What she want?' The secretary says, 'Well, senator, sez she wants to talk to you 'bout the 'bortion bill.' Strum didn't even look up. Just as natural as anything he yells out to the secretary, 'Just tell her to pay it and I'll reimburse her.'"

If "Strum" had been there, he would have chuckled with them, relishing as he always had the off-color references to his sexual prowess. He left his hometown, for the most part, in 1947, when he moved to Columbia as Edgefield's tenth homegrown governor.[3] But his presence was still felt in the county seat of 2,500 that had shaped his view of the world and was where his political career began.

From Roosevelt New Dealer to death-sentencing state judge, from liberal governor to Dixiecrat candidate, from choosing young wives to stories of "colored offspring," from party-switching Democrat to Republican savior for Richard Nixon, from civil rights antagonist to supporter of a Martin Luther King holiday, from a D day crash-landing in a glider behind German lines at Normandy to a liberator role at Buchenwald, from a direct challenge of George Wallace to assaulting the Warren Court, and from a death-house seduction to patting journalist Sally Quinn's ass, Thurmond lived and survived with the boldness of an Edgefield man.

Miss Hortense Woodson, for decades the keeper of the flame of local history in Strom's hometown of Edgefield, knew him since he was a little boy coming into church with his father and his mother. "He hasn't changed," she once told a writer for the *New York Times Magazine.* "Everything he's done has been done to the fullest. There's no halfway doings about Strom."[4]

Blood ran thicker and honor ran hotter in Edgefield, a county more Faulknerian than Yoknapatawpha, with a history marked by personal conflicts and seared by political violence. When 4 percent of all indictments in South Carolina were for murder, in Edgefield it was 8 percent.[5] An early twentieth-century merchant remembered eighteen bloody murders committed in front of his store.[6] Courage and impetuous action led to both romance and tragedy. As Thurmond once explained, his own father probably would have been elected governor except "one time he had to kill a man."[7]

Walk across the square and you will see, facing the stately courthouse in which Senator Thurmond's portrait hangs, along with one of his father, John William Thurmond, a life-size statue of Strom himself. Sculpted by Maria Kirby-Smith, an artist with Edgefield connections, local wags have called it "Strom's last erection" ever since it went up in 1984. (Fifteen years later, another statue joined other South Carolina luminaries on the Statehouse grounds in Columbia—men such as John C. Calhoun and James F. Byrnes, Wade Hampton and Pitchfork Ben Tillman—all defenders of their respective eras' racial status quo, which meant slavery for Calhoun and rigid segregation for the others.)

The otherwise unremarkable statue of Strom standing on the courthouse square in Edgefield, his right arm extended as if giving a speech, incorporated a cockroach on Thurmond's left rump, hidden beneath his overhanging suit jacket, an addition, the artist told a fellow sculptor, after Strom's sister confided to her the senator was disappointed that his trousers "lacked a sufficient bulge." After a Columbia newspaper ran a story about the bug, the statue became a tourist attraction until Bettis Rainsford, the entrepreneurial Harvard-educated chairman of the statue committee whose Edgefield roots precede the Revolutionary War, sent in a construction worker with a blowtorch to remove the metal pest.

Just as Thurmond remains part of the town's humor, part of its folklore, and part of its glory, so his life symbolizes its past. The town's future is less certain, and his death and its aftermath are still being absorbed. When Essie Mae Washington-Williams visited on May 8, 2004, she returned to a town frozen in time. Welcomed for the first time to the white side of town, she met relatives on both sides of her family and visited her father's grave. Bettis Rainsford served as her guide.

She displayed "class," he remarked of her dignified manner. The two local weekly newspapers gave page one coverage to her visit, complete with two-column photographs, one including her daughter, Wanda Terry. "Strom Thurmond's Daughter Visits Edgefield," read the banner headline in the *Citizen-News*. The *Edgefield Advertiser* ran the headline, "Essie Mae Visits Edgefield," above an understated account that detailed her full day of activities, including her visit with Stella Dorn, a black woman in her nineties who had known Essie's mother and said how pretty she was. Everyone was on their best behavior.[8]

The Southerner's deep-rooted sense of place is reflected in the invariable first question asked of a stranger in Edgefield. "Whar' ya from?" If the answer is New Jersey or Chicago, the likely response is, "Oh," followed by a silence that may reflect suspicion or simply disinterest. If the visitor is from Texas or Tennessee, however, the questioner may tell of a friend or relative who moved there. If the stranger is from anywhere in South Carolina, the local might ask, "Who's your daddy?" And the response could set one's social rank. South Carolina's late poet-philosopher James McBride Dabbs compared the process to two strange dogs sniffing one another.

Among deep-rooted white families in the state, one traditional indication of status has been the presence of many area blacks sharing the same surname. This indicates that one's forebears were prosperous slave owners. Modjeska Monteith Simkins, a black woman who became known as "the matriarch" of the civil rights movement in South Carolina and married the son of a man who had been one of Edgefield's top black political leaders during Reconstruction, said she was always greeted on the street in her native Columbia as "cousin" by one of the city's most prominent white attorneys.[9]

Around the corner past the Thurmond statue and the courthouse and adjoining the aging three-story hotel that was once the finest boarding house along the well-traveled Dixie Highway sits the home of the *Edgefield Advertiser*, the state's oldest newspaper, established in 1836. When Thurmond was born in 1902, the *Advertiser* was the voice of literate thought and culture in frontier territory, reporting on the latest trends in everything from Paris fashion to social and economic developments in Washington, D.C. The *Advertiser* served as the community's public-spirited conscience. Its motto proclaims: "We will cling to the pillars of the temple of our liberties and if it must fall we will perish amidst the ruins." William Walton Mims, the editor for sixty-six years, from 1937 to 2003, lives by that motto. His father and grandfather were editor and publisher for a combined sixty-three years before him. When Thurmond was elected in 1954 to the U.S. Senate as a write-in candidate, Mims ran a full front-page replica of the ballot, with an arrow pointing to Thurmond's name handwritten on one line. For years, a framed copy of that front page hung prominently in Thurmond's Washington office, a memento of that campaign and, perhaps, of their alliance. Over time, their relationship would change dramatically.

"I don't know anything good about him," Mims told the authors of this book in 1998. "My view of Thurmond is he is Satan's agent for South Carolina. He is my mortal enemy."[10]

When the Thurmond statue was unveiled in the square, some remarked on its slightly reddish hue, and Mims was heard to remark that this was due to Thurmond's being such a Communist.

A gentlemanly eccentric whose soft voice belied the terror of his pen, Mims would closet himself in a dark, cluttered back office to write long, rambling editorials intended to expose Thurmond's villainous ways. Many townspeople long dismissed him as "a nut," but few questioned his honesty. On October 14, 1970, using his largest headline type to display "BIGGEST SCANDAL IN COUNTY'S HISTORY," Mims linked Thurmond and county planners to a "shocking" affair that "has the elements of conspiracy and the appearance of a fraud against the best and long-term interests of this county." He was contesting the location of a new $5 million county water and sewer system. Soon thereafter, his newspaper suffered a total advertising boycott.

After having sought unsuccessfully to pry loose the plans for the system from federal agencies, Mims became outraged when he learned that instead of covering all of Edgefield County as a federally designated "redevelopment area," the system would be concentrated in the southern part of the county.

The majority black and poor white population in economically depressed northern Edgefield County would be neglected, Mims contended, and the main water line would be located near land owned by Thurmond's brother and moneyed supporters, with primary benefit going to the neighboring and more prosperous Aiken County trade area.[11] Thurmond fired back that Mims owned land in the area of Edgefield County he wanted to include.

Butler Derrick, a state legislator before his election to Congress in 1974 and a son-in-law of Mims at the time of the dispute over the water system, said funding for the project included revenue bonds, which required that it initially serve the area of greatest population density. An oversized trunk line to draw water from the Savannah River was installed, Derrick said, to allow expansion into other parts of the county, which he said has occurred. Derrick said Thurmond wasn't involved in the "so-called boycott."[12]

In 1972, Mims ran as a write-in candidate against Thurmond in what the senator called "a scurrilous campaign." Mims printed large headline type down the length of his front page accusing Thurmond of having

"COLORED OFFSPRING WHILE PARADING AS A DEVOUT SEGREGATIONIST."[13] He was, of course, writing about Essie Mae Washington-Williams, though her name was not known to him. There was no attendant article. The editor repeated his charge in a sworn deposition given to back his case in a federal restraint of trade lawsuit filed against the local businessmen who had boycotted his paper. Mims said he could substantiate the "colored offspring" charge with taped conversations he had had with Edgefield blacks who knew the details of the birth. The line of questioning was dropped abruptly.

After securing a lawyer from the prestigious Arnold & Porter law firm in Washington to represent him in what would become a six-year court fight, Mims won a judgment of $151,500 in damages in a restraint of trade verdict against the local businessmen. Adding $101,333 in attorneys' fees and costs produced a total award of $252,833.

Mims's attorney, David Bonderman, said that he "never saw any evidence of Thurmond's involvement in the Mims dispute, although it is obvious that the ringleaders were all Thurmond supporters." Mims, however, believed that Thurmond's Washington office directed the boycott efforts by telephone. Mims said his attorney advised him against making Thurmond a named defendant in the case because "all the jurors will have voted for him in elections, and they won't go against him." Mims said he was offered $450,000 to consolidate his newspaper with the *Citizen-News*, then owned by Bettis Rainsford, whom Mims viewed as "Thurmond's commissar in Edgefield County."[14]

Mysteriously, Mims's large two-story home on the Dixie Highway burned to the ground, his newspaper did not regain retail advertisers during his time as editor, and almost all the veterans for whom he supplied subsidized room and board were withdrawn from the hotel he owned next door to the newspaper office.

Thurmond was known for refusing to keep a political enemy, and Mims acknowledged the senator had called him. But the editor refused Thurmond's entreaties, saying, "I'll never forgive him until he apologizes to the people of Edgefield County."[15]

By the time of Ms. Washington-Williams's historic visit to Edgefield, Mims had retired, living alone in the otherwise closed hotel. His daughter Suzanne, divorced from Butler Derrick, took over the newspaper in 2003, in less than a year restoring it from a circulation of roughly 400 to more than 3,200, a few hundred behind the *Citizen-News*. Suzanne Mims Derrick had returned to the basics of country weekly journalism, with community news from throughout the county and objective coverage of town news, and had begun to regain some advertising. She looked forward to returning to profitability.

Her father, in his mid-nineties a bit hard of hearing but with a clear mind, had little to say about the public confirmation of the existence of Thurmond's biracial daughter. A week after her visit to Edgefield, he said, "I spent a long time finding the truth. I spent years working on it. He fought me and I fought him. It doesn't matter now."[16]

WALTON MIMS'S UNIVERSE centers on Edgefield, the town and the county, and despite his antagonism toward Thurmond, he shared fully the currents of piety, ferocity, and love of home that ran through the man. In a gentle voice that reflects his gentrified upbringing, Mims explained:

> Unless you understand Edgefield from way back, you won't understand Thurmond. Edgefield had had a religious theme. The great Southern Baptist Convention was conceived here in the central Savannah River area by Dr. William Bullein Johnson, pastor of the First Baptist Church here, who became its first president.
>
> And there was, thereafter, a long succession of brilliant, devoted, old-fashioned type preachers. They had an intellectuality about them that was unusual. . . . And then you had [William] Travis and [James] Bonham, the heroes of the Alamo. The way I understand it, they revived in this country a patriotic fever, and these people from the Old Edgefield District, they exemplified, they brought to light what had been the character of our people since the Revolution. The background there was religious and patriotic.
>
> The most brilliant lawyers—and this is really what formed the nucleus intellectually and religiously and almost every other way—the most brilliant lawyers began to gravitate to Edgefield in search of the Holy Grail, because there was *something here*. There was something here that you just didn't find anywhere else.[17]

William Jennings Bryan Dorn, the silver-throated Third District congressman for twenty-six years from neighboring Greenwood County, whose own Edgefield roots run deep, explained:

You would never understand Edgefield and the background that goes through all these people unless you understand the violence, the emotionalism of the people. They fought duels. George McDuffie was a congressman from this district one time, and he was always into a duel. Preston Brooks was a congressman. He whipped the "H" out of Senator Sumner on the floor of the Senate. That brought on the Civil War probably as much as anything. They said it was inevitable, and it probably was, but one of the immediate causes of the Civil War was Preston Brooks whipping Sumner.

And then you would have big shootouts there, like Abilene and Dodge City, occasionally in Edgefield. I even remember yet hearing the old-timers talk about it.

It had a lot of anti-Negro feeling. Edgefield has been noted for that kind of violent politics. As for Senator Thurmond's seeming radicalism on the race issue, it was not radical for Edgefield. That's the tradition of that area and the heritage of those people . . . Ladies didn't vote. In those days, with no women involved, things would get so hot they had bodyguards at the political meetings and all this kind of doings.[18]

Talking about Edgefield's history, Strom himself once said, "Back in Edgefield County everybody would fight." With a laugh, he added, "Fighters and lovers."[19]

As Thurmond indicated, the passion in that history spilled over into sex—and sex scandals. Francis Pickens, a wealthy Edgefield planter who served as congressman and ambassador to Russia before becoming South Carolina's Civil War governor, protested sharply before the Civil War about a woman's claim that he had fathered her illegitimate son. He supported the woman and child financially despite his expressed doubts about being the father, but said, "If a man's character depends upon maids or low women, he would indeed be damned in this world as well as the next."[20]

Fellow Edgefield District planter James H. Hammond had formally "taken" this woman's claim, but as governor he maintained a discreet silence when charges were made against him that he had seduced four nieces, the daughters of his brother-in-law Wade Hampton II. To do otherwise would have compromised the honor of his four nieces, he said, once the charges were made public by their father, then countercharged that that was precisely what Wade Hampton II had done by exposing the incident. In a letter to another brother, Governor Hammond said he believed the people of South Carolina would be with him: "They would not mind it a pin's worth if it was known I had seduced all of Hampton's daughters."

South Carolina legislators didn't impeach Governor Hammond. Although the nieces' incident exiled him for a while from state politics after his term ended, Hammond was subsequently elected by the legislature to the U.S. Senate.

Sexual liaisons also crossed racial lines, including among the elite. Hammond, for example, openly maintained a slave mistress and in his diary noted telling a legitimate son to take special care of a specific slave because he was the son's half brother.[21]

Sameera Thurmond, a black woman from San Francisco, has spent much time visiting Edgefield, conducting genealogical research at the Old Edgefield District Genealogical Society. She was able to trace one side of her biracial family ancestry to a great-great-grandfather, George Washington Thurmond, Strom's grandfather. (She had developed an interest in genealogy after watching the television miniseries of Alex Haley's *Roots* in the late 1970s.) George Washington Thurmond fathered two sons by a slave woman, Elizabeth Doolittle. The two black children were named George Washington Thurmond, after himself, and Thomas Jefferson Thurmond, after his brother, respectively.

These young black men both married and moved to nearby Augusta, Georgia, with Thomas marrying Mimie Chism, Sameera's great-grandmother. As did most of the couple's fourteen children, Robert Gilbert Thurmond, Sameera's grandfather, moved north, in his case to Morristown, New Jersey, where he worked as a janitor at the post office. His son, Sameera's father, John Clark Thurmond, worked as a chauffeur, butler, and cook for a white physician. Sameera received a college degree and later attended law school. When she learned of Essie Mae, Sameera called her and they developed a telephone friendship.[22]

Before the Civil War, some free persons of color in Edgefield—roughly 1 percent of the African American population and usually of mixed racial parentage—married whites. South Carolina did not adopt laws against interracial marriage until after Reconstruction.

But of course the end of slavery did not mean an end to white-black sexual liaisons. Lucy Holcolme Pickens, a Texas beauty less than half the age of fifty-five-year-old Francis Pickens when she married him, was joined in Edgefield after his death by her brother and a male friend of his. Both men took former slaves as lifelong partners, who bore them children. The children grew up in the Pickens family mansion in Edgefield and played with neighborhood white children.[23]

During Reconstruction, blacks achieved a brief political parity and held many offices in Edgefield, creating social and economic opportunities. They became attorneys, clerks, business partners with whites, bakers, and shopkeepers. The period was by no means peaceful, however, with gangs of white bushwhackers attacking and killing black men in widespread violence throughout the county.

Many black families moved into Edgefield, for reasons of both opportunity and safety. When Edgefield whites regained power after Reconstruction ended, however, occupational choices for black men again became restricted to traditional agricultural roles, as sharecroppers or laborers. By 1880, residential segregation created black sections in Edgefield, with many households headed by females, who found work as domestics. These poor sections of town received little in the way of public services and would remain intact and behind at the end of the twentieth century.[24]

A FEW BLOCKS EAST of the courthouse square, the weight of history is felt in the quiet of Willowbrook Cemetery, behind the First Baptist and Trinity Episcopal churches. Hortense Woodson, the Edgefield historian, lived across the street from the cemetery for most of her ninety-four years. She died in 1990. On her tombstone, not far from the oversized Thurmond family plot, is engraved the full text of her four-stanza poem, "The Spirit of Edgefield," written to be sung to the tune of "The Bells of St. Mary's."

The final stanza reads:

> Old Edgefield, dear Edgefield
> Thy children all love thee,
> Thy great men, thy good men,
> Wherever they be,
> Turn back to the scenes oft
> Remembered in story
> Thy children all come back,
> Come back
> To thee, thee.

With 150 Confederate soldiers, generals, other local heroes and villains from multiple generations, and the intermarrying families of ten governors, and seven of the governors themselves buried there, with its faded Confederate battle flag flying from the pole erected decades earlier by the Edgefield Chapter of United Daughters of the Confederacy, the cemetery serves as Strom Thurmond's final resting place.

By virtue of some of the martial imagery, and the cemetery's inhabitants, the faint echoes of Edgefield's violent past are heard here, too. Marking the grave of Preston Smith Brooks (a great-great-grandfather of the sculptress Maria Kirby-Smith) is a marble obelisk extolling that he "Will Be Long, Long Remembered as One in Which the Virtues Loved to Dwell." His crippling assault in 1856 on Massachusetts Senator Charles Sumner (believed by South Carolina congressman Bryan Dorn to have helped precipitate the Civil War) was made in response to Sumner's speech casting dishonor on Brooks's aged Edgefield relative, South Carolina Senator Andrew Pickens Butler. Brooks delivered approximately thirty blows to Sumner, enough for him to remark that he "wore out my cane completely." Brooks resigned his seat after scandal ensued, though he was immediately reinstated in a special election with barely a dissenting vote.[25]

Buried next to the crowded Brooks family plot is General Matthew Calbraith Butler. The handsome co-leader with General Martin Witherspoon Gary, the "Bald Eagle of the Confederacy," in the violent Redshirt campaign of 1876, Butler was a man who, after a foot was blown off by a cannonball in the Civil War, would later return to battle with one foot, mounted on his horse. He eventually became a U.S. senator.

Francis Pickens, the early Civil War governor, is interred in the adjacent plot. Beside his marker is that of his spirited daughter, Frances Eugenia Olga Neva Pickens, born March 14, 1859, in St. Petersburg, Russia, while Pickens was ambassador. Known to all as Dushka (Little Darling—spelled phonetically in Edgefield as "Douschka"), she is celebrated in Edgefield as "the Joan of Arc of South Carolina." At age seventeen, she rode sidesaddle on her horse from nearby Oakley Park at the front of 1,600 Redshirts who soon would terrorize blacks and help steal the election for Wade Hampton III, the "redeemer" governor who ended Reconstruction rule. (A man so physically powerful that he wrestled bears in the swamps that bordered the Hampton Mississippi Delta plantations, he was a leading general in the Confederate army and namesake for Scarlett O'Hara's little boy.)

M. C. BUTLER'S PORTRAIT adorns a wall at Oakley Park, Martin Wither-spoon Gary's five-columned, two-story plantation home on the edge of town that today serves as the Redshirt Shrine. An upright display case there exhibits one of the original red shirts, made of homespun cloth dyed with pokeberry juice. At the bottom of the same case sits an authentic car-petbag, a suitcase made of carpet in which the stereotypical Yankee inter-lopers carried their belongings when they joined turncoat Southern scalawags and the freed slaves during Reconstruction. In the words of United Daughters of the Confederacy tour guide Amelia Reese in 1998, this period was "worse than the war for the people."

Organized racial violence by Edgefield County whites became wide-spread in 1876. In July at Hamburg, the site of present-day North Augusta, a confrontation occurred between black militia and a white mob. After two blacks and one white were killed by gunfire, forty black militiamen surren-dered. Five black political activists were picked out and executed to avenge the death of the white man. It became known as the "Hamburg Massacre."

Ben Tillman, who as a teenager was not drafted during the Civil War be-cause he had lost an eye in an accident, had become a leader in the white rifle clubs that organized and participated in the violence. He later wrote that Generals Gary and Butler had agreed to pursue a policy of "terroriz-ing" local blacks "by letting them provoke trouble and then having the whites demonstrate their superiority by killing as many as was justifiable."[26]

On September 17, Butler's men had killed more than 100 blacks at Ellen-ton when joined by Tillman and roughly forty men under his command. The arrival of federal troops saved other blacks from being massacred.

Two of Tillman's men, however, were selected to execute Simon Coker, a black state senator from Barnwell. Upon being informed that he had only a few minutes to live, Coker replied, "Here is my cotton house key; I wish you would please send it to my wife and tell her to have our cotton ginned and pay our landlord rent just as soon as she can." Asked if there was any-thing else, Coker said he "would like to pray" and dropped to his knees in prayer.

Tillman described what happened next: After a few moments, one of his men said, "'You are too long.' . . . The order 'aim, fire,' was given with the negro still kneeling." Tillman continued, "It will appear a ruthless and cruel thing to those unacquainted with the environments. . . . The struggle in which we were engaged meant more than life or death. It involved everything we held dear, Anglo-Saxon civilization included."[27]

On election day, Martin Witherspoon Gary's Redshirt patrols prevented blacks from voting in Edgefield. Yet the vote there exceeded by 2,000 the voting age population as recorded by the 1870 census. Without Edgefield's fraudulent vote inflations, Hampton would have lost to incumbent Republican Daniel Chamberlain.

In a two-tier campaign, Hampton had personally pledged to protect the rights of the freedmen. At the same time he approved units of black Redshirt supporters, he also allowed implementation of Rule 12 of Gary's thirty-three-rule "Plan of the Campaign," which stated, "Every Democrat must feel honor bound to control the vote of at least one negro, by intimidation, purchase, keeping him away or as each individual may determine how he may best accomplish it."[28] Gary's all-white Redshirt supporters spread the use of violence, intimidation, and fraud beyond the confines of Edgefield. More than a century later, one observer concluded that no Southern county regained white domination with "more fanaticism and brutality than Edgefield."[29]

Hampton's contested victory provided a key element in the Compromise of 1877. Political control returned to white Democrats, with an understanding that the states rather than the federal government would gain the right to set policy on racial matters. That understanding would later reverberate powerfully in Strom Thurmond's 1948 Dixiecrat "states' rights" campaign rhetoric.

Tillman would emerge as the state's new political leader, beginning as the spokesman for aggrieved farmers. But the farmers' revolt in South Carolina never shared the radical goals of the larger Populist movement, which in other Southern states often involved a biracial coalition. Tillman's virulent racism precluded that possibility.

Elected as governor in 1890, he established two land grant colleges, Clemson for men and Winthrop for women. He used his influence and his control over the state legislature, which then elected U.S. senators, to displace the aristocrats Wade Hampton and M. C. Butler, his former allies, from the U.S. Senate. Tillman had himself succeed Butler.

The historian Francis Butler Simkins, Tillman's faithful biographer and an Edgefield native who grew up next door to the Thurmond home, considered Tillman's act against Hampton "a ruthless violation of cherished traditions."[30]

A crude, profane, one-eyed man, a demagogue on issues of race, in the Senate Tillman defended lynching, the ultimate weapon for controlling blacks after their loss of political rights to vote or serve as jurors had reduced them again nearly to bondage. He articulated in terrifying language that classic fear of the white South—black male sexuality. "Whenever the Constitution comes between me and the virtue of the white women of the South," he told the U.S. Senate in 1902, "I say to hell with the Constitution!"

Tillman vividly described a mythical Southern woman raped by a black man, "her chastity taken from her and a memory branded on her brain as with a red-hot iron to haunt her night and day as long as she lives." Then, arguing that such a rapist had "put himself outside the pale of the law, human and divine," he raged, "Kill! Kill! Kill!"[31]

A popular speaker on the national Chatauqua circuit, Tillman has been rumored to have told Thomas Dixon the story that became his best-seller 1905 book, *The Clansman*,[32] from which D. W. Griffith made *Birth of a Nation*. That film glorified the Ku Klux Klan and helped create a searing national image of the black man as the lustful beast described in Tillman's speeches.

After retiring as president of Morehouse College in Atlanta, Benjamin Mays, the mentor of Martin Luther King Jr., told a story of the film's power. Mays grew up not far from Bryan Dorn in Greenwood County and as a child hid under Dorn's grandfather's house during a race riot. As a student at Bates College in Maine, Mays said, he faced little discrimination. But he told of having to run for his life after an audience watching *Birth of a Nation* left the college town's only theater.[33] The film, which President Woodrow Wilson showed at the White House in 1915, stimulated a rebirth of the Klan.

Tillman dominated the 1895 state constitutional convention that effectively disfranchised blacks and extended the white electorate. Presiding over it was another Edgefield governor, John Gary Evans, a nephew of Martin Witherspoon Gary. (Evans received strong support from Edgefield's State Representative John William Thurmond.)

Evans won the election as a handsome, thirty-one-year-old bachelor. On a trip to Connecticut, he attended Sunday worship services at an Episcopal church, where a message scribbled on a card was passed to him. It said,

"Sir, you are sitting in my pew." It was signed by David Plume, a wealthy manufacturer, who stated the amount of his annual dues.

Evans sent back a reply: "You are paying too damn much," and signed it "John Gary Evans, Governor of South Carolina." After the morning services, Plume introduced himself and invited Evans home for dinner. There he met and fell in love with his host's daughter, Emily Mansfield Plume, whom he married after his term as governor ended.[34]

The fighting spirit of Edgefield men never dulled. At the rear of the Oakley Park Redshirt Shrine, a well marks where 108 of them gathered to go fight in the Spanish-American War. Twenty-eight of them returned. Inside the house, dominating a wall in an upstairs room is a large wooden seal from the city of Havana, Cuba, where John Gary Evans served as provisional mayor. In 1941, two years before his death, Evans gave Oakley Park, which he had inherited, to the United Daughters of the Confederacy. They restored it as a memorial and museum.

In December 1881, approximately 5,000 Edgefield County blacks, roughly one-fifth of the black population at the time, migrated to Arkansas. This organized response to political and economic repression after Reconstruction remains the largest mass exodus in South Carolina history.

Government land in Arkansas was available at a price of eight acres for a dollar. There were no fence laws to prevent free range for livestock, and farm laborers received cash wages. The people who migrated to Arkansas, says the historian Orville Vernon Burton, "left Edgefield County not out of despair, but out of a faith that somewhere in America they could find a home where they could realize the hopes of equality and prosperity they had conceived during Reconstruction."[35]

Not until a century later did Edgefield blacks regain a full role in local politics, only after the federal courts finally restored the Reconstruction amendments to their original intent. Despite accusations of corruption, historical evidence indicates that local black Reconstruction leaders had been neither inept nor corrupt. Men such as Paris Simkins and Lawrence Cain, who served as legislators, sought economic as well as political rights for blacks, created schools with state funds, and helped the black community through private donations to build their own churches, the only social institution they could control.[36]

The fierce intensity with which white Edgefield struck to end Reconstruction and regain power suggests the extent to which they felt little control over their destiny during this black political dominance. Historian Joel
Williamson, himself a native of the South Carolina Upcountry (the half
of the state above the point—the fall line—where rivers become navigable
through the gently sloping Lowcountry to the Atlantic coast), argued that
whites such as those in Edgefield were suffering from a "rising confusion
of identity."[37]

As their society seemed to crumble, they tended to turn their loyalties
toward the family. Religion also became more important. Another response to the South's fragmentation during Reconstruction, Williamson
has contended, was an intensely personal politics. As an Edgefield man,
Thurmond would personify all of these elements in a public life that
stretched into the next millennium.

Historian James G. Banks, who in 1970 at Kent State University wrote a
dissertation on Thurmond, saw him as shaped by Edgefield's history and
culture and described him at his core as "an exceedingly simple man,
fiercely individualistic, combative, paternalistic, a citizen soldier who
merges the intensity of the evangelical gospel preacher with the fundamentalist values of a simpler time."[38]

South Carolinian W. J. Cash, in his 1941 classic, *The Mind of the South*,
described the region as a "tree with many age rings, with its limbs and
trunk bent and twisted by all the winds of the years, but with its tap root
in the Old South."[39] His words provided a poetic description of Strom
Thurmond.

CHAPTER 2

"I Have Good Genes"

WHEN STROM THURMOND WAS SIX YEARS OLD, his father hoisted him into a horse-drawn buggy on a Sunday afternoon and set off for the home of Senator Pitchfork Ben Tillman, six miles down the road. The boy had never met the senator and, as he would later tell it many times, he sensed even then that he was about to encounter an uncommon man.

Will Thurmond, by then Tillman's personal lawyer and campaign manager, had tried to prepare the youngster. Tillman was known for his outrageous temper and profane language, and the eye patch he wore could be unsettling to children. Strom's father told him that when they pulled into the Tillman farm he should jump down and offer a handshake.

Tillman was waiting when they arrived, so Strom hopped off the buggy and said, "I want to shake your hand." Strom then stood there holding Tillman's hand until the old senator barked at him, "You said you wanted to shake. Why the hell don't you shake?"

Strom hesitated for only a moment and, as he later told it, "I shook and I shook, and I've been shaking ever since."[1]

From even before he climbed out of the buggy at Tillman's place, Strom had been learning from his father how to court the average citizen of feisty Edgefield. Will Thurmond was already an established political leader—though his career had stalled—when his wife gave birth on December 5, 1902, to the son who would eventually carry out his own thwarted political ambitions. They named him James Strom Thurmond, after his maternal grandfather, but never called him by his first name.

Will Thurmond grew up on a farm in the Colliers community in western Edgefield County, between Stephens Creek and the Savannah River. The Thurmond family had come to the Edgefield District from Virginia's Albemarle County in 1784, and Will's father, George Washington Thurmond, owned a few slaves and farmed cotton and corn. When Will was born in 1862, George Thurmond was off fighting in the Civil War, his third war—he had already battled Cherokee Indians and Mexicans—and

had lived with a first wife in Galveston, Texas, before meeting and marrying Mary Jane Felter in New Orleans and carrying her to Edgefield. When
the Civil War ended, family lore has it that Corporal George Thurmond,
one of only two men left alive in his infantry company, was present in tat-
tered uniform with Robert E. Lee for his surrender at Appomattox, then
walked home penniless and maimed—he'd lost an arm—from Virginia.
He stopped long enough in Columbia to see the devastation General
William Tecumseh Sherman's troops had visited on South Carolina's capital city, half of it burned to the ground. Strom remembered hearing that
his grandfather was a tough outdoorsman who "could drink liquor and
work out in the open" and had all his teeth when he died in 1904 at eighty-
four.[2]

Will Thurmond rode by horse to a country academy to get his schooling, studying extra at night with his mother. He saved enough money to
spend a semester at South Carolina College in Columbia, a breeding
ground for state political leaders. He returned to Edgefield, worked as a
teacher, and spent nights studying law at the office of John Sheppard, an
Edgefield attorney who served a few months as governor. When the self-
taught Thurmond wrote his bar examination, the state supreme court cited
it as the best of the year. Strom Thurmond called his father "the ablest
lawyer I ever knew."[3]

Once Will Thurmond became a lawyer, entering politics was irresistible.
He offered for the job of town attorney and won the votes of all three
councilmen. Building on his contacts, he was elected in 1894 to the state
House of Representatives. As a legislator, he nominated Tillman for the
U.S. Senate and worked ardently to elect him to the seat held by aging
Edgefield Confederate hero M. C. Butler.

Edgefield had divided into what were called the Tillmanites and the
anti-Tillmanites, and Tillman's enemies also became Will Thurmond's enemies. He was serving informally as Tillman's man back home, obediently
soothing riled tempers and stepping on toes on the senator's behalf. Thurmond's enemies referred to him derisively as "Pussyfoot Bill." As one of
his contemporaries described it, the title recognized Thurmond's ability to
"slip around quietly to arrange things. He'd move around the way a cat
slips up on a rat."[4] When he ran in 1896 for solicitor (the judicial circuit
prosecutor), he easily defeated the incumbent.

On a March morning in 1897, a confirmed Tillman hater named Willie Harris came to town apparently looking for a fight. Folks had seen him reeling from whiskey, loitering outside the courthouse and talking tough with his drinking buddies. One witness heard him say, "I've got a good knife and a Colt's pistol in my pocket."[5]

When Will Thurmond—as was his routine—left the courthouse and headed toward the small white cottage that housed his law office, Harris planted himself in his path and began taunting him. As a witness later described it during a coroner's inquest, Harris asked Thurmond, "Weren't you elected by the Tillmanites? Didn't Bennie send word to elect you?" Harris persisted, walking beside the lawyer and bellowing so loudly he could be heard across the square, finally calling him a "low, dirty scoundrel." His honor assailed, Thurmond then pulled a pistol and shot Harris, hitting him square in the center of his chest, killing him instantly. Thurmond declared he shot in self-defense even before Harris's body was carted away.[6]

The Thurmond family version of this event has Will Thurmond shooting Harris only after going inside his law office and being threatened. Newspaper accounts portray Thurmond pulling his pistol outside his law office and firing in plain view of a handful of spectators.

Edgefield's traditional hypersensitivity to matters of honor aside, South Carolina had long outlawed dueling, and Thurmond's behavior as a sworn officer of the court initially shocked many. The *Edgefield Advertiser* branded the killing "one of the most deplorable homicides in recent years. Both of the men were young and well-liked and the cause of the difficulty was so trifling as to make the results all the more pitiable."[7]

The outraged Harris family pushed for prosecution. Thurmond felt sure he would be cleared, though he recognized the case's political implications. In early April, with the trial scheduled for August, he announced in a statement to the *Advertiser* that he would not prosecute cases until his own name was clear and that he would pay for an interim prosecutor. "While I sorely regret said unfortunate occurrence," he wrote, "I feel perfectly justified before God and man in what I did, and do not believe that I will be blamed in the least when the facts are known."[8]

The courthouse was packed for his August 2 trial for murder. Proceedings began promptly at 9:30 A.M. Seated behind the defendant was young

Eleanor Gertrude Strom, who had recently become his fiancée. A delegation of distinguished citizens from as far away as Columbia attended as character witnesses.

To defend himself, he hired two law firms connected to Ben Tillman, one that included Thurmond's mentor, former Governor John Sheppard, and another that of Tillman's nephew, James H. Tillman. Assisting the state attorney general in prosecuting the case was M. C. Butler, the Confederate hero whom Tillman three years earlier had replaced in the Senate in a bitter campaign. Although witnesses conflicted in testifying whether or not Harris was armed, the *Advertiser* characterized Thurmond's testimony as "very clear and emphatic in stating that Harris did throw his hand on his hip pocket as if to draw a pistol and that he firmly believed he was in danger of losing his own life unless he protected himself." After a parade of character witnesses testified that J. William Thurmond was a noble man of good character, Sheppard spoke to the jury in a presentation that the *Advertiser* called "magnificent."[9]

The jurors, all white males, as all juries were at the time, listened politely to all the testimony, retired late in the day to deliberate, and returned thirty-five minutes later to clear his name, an exoneration that the *Advertiser* noted was "according to general expectation."[10]

Will Thurmond's marriage in 1899 to Gertie Strom helped further restore his reputation. Her father, James Harrison Strom, was a country doctor and state legislator who owned thousands of acres of land in upper Edgefield County. Dr. Strom had sent her to Augusta to buy herself a custom-designed trousseau.

The Stroms descended from a family of Palatine Germans that was transported by sea to Charleston under the Bounty Act of 1761, given a modest sum for supplies, and forced to relocate in the sparsely settled northwestern part of the present-day Edgefield County area along the Savannah River—a buffer against feared Creek Indians.

The marriage between Will and Gertie linked the two politically dominant families in the county, with the Stroms traditionally reigning over the upper half of the county and the Thurmonds presiding over the lower. As Strom himself would say, "There was a big connection there—the Thurmonds and the Stroms both. They practically covered the county in influence in one way or another." As a child, he found the political union fascinating and once asked his father if he married Gertie because she came from such a prominent clan. "He said he married her because he loved her," Thurmond recalled years later.[11]

While Gertie was pregnant with Strom, Will Thurmond had launched a race for Congress, campaigning for a month in the Third District's seven agricultural counties. The last black officials in South Carolina were voted out of office that year, with none to reappear as legislators until 1970. Race, however, wasn't an issue in Thurmond's campaign.

Edgefield residents considered Thurmond a strong candidate from the moment he entered the race. The *Advertiser* endorsed him as a "just and reliable" man who "considers duty more sacred than holding a public office" and "would work for the poor man." Letters to the editor praised him.[12]

The stump meetings between Thurmond and his two opponents were unusually civil, without the traditional name-calling and fistfights. (The candidates of this era still stood on tree stumps to declaim to their audiences, the tradition from which the term originated.) Thurmond's opponents were both distinguished legislators. Except for blacks who could swear under oath that they had voted for Wade Hampton in 1876 and had voted Democratic in all subsequent elections, only white men voted in the Democratic primary to elect the next congressman. Reflecting the Progressive spirit of the period, Thurmond called for free trade, trust-busting, rural mail delivery, and federal aid to local governments.

No one mentioned the Willie Harris episode, and it didn't seem to hurt Thurmond in Edgefield County, which he carried. But he lost badly elsewhere, finishing last.

Years later, he told his children his version of the Willie Harris episode and offered this bit of fatherly advice: "Never kill anybody. It will hurt you all your life." Will Thurmond never again sought elective office. Instead, he channeled his political energies back into working on Tillman's behalf as a local troubleshooter while developing a lucrative law practice.[13]

His legal skill and finely tuned political instincts paid dividends in the courtroom as he established a reputation as the man to see for anyone facing legal trouble. He had an uncanny ability to pick a sympathetic jury and taught Strom that helping others could help himself. It was a lesson Strom would take to heart.

When an Edgefield man died, the town's citizens would soon see Will Thurmond's wagon loaded with food or supplies roll down the street to the widow's home. In lean times he gave away crops from his fields and offered his name as collateral on loans. Local children thought of him almost as a Santa Claus figure, handing out candy as he walked home every afternoon. According to his children, Thurmond showed his appreciation to the family's domestic help by giving them Christmas trinkets and sending a buggy of food and supplies when they were sick.

When Strom was four, his father moved the family to a four-acre tract about three miles from the center of Edgefield proper. One of the grandest homes in Edgefield County graced the property. A white two-story with wide wraparound porches and tall windows that looked out on pecan and peach trees, it was a country gentleman's dream, with heart-pine floors and fireplaces in every room. Thurmond paid $5,000 for the new homeplace, a considerable sum at the time.

He owned another fifty acres or so in nearby tracts of farm and pasture land. He wanted to be closer to the land, to instill an appreciation for it in his children, and to have them learn the virtues of farm work. "He wanted us to see how hard it was to make a living on a farm," Strom said.[14] During their school years, the three boys would rise early to turn the cows out to pasture, with homework and farm chores filling their afternoons.

Strom became the milker. His three sisters—including the twins, six years younger than Strom—often gathered round to taunt him, and he would turn an udder in their direction and squirt, sending them away shrieking. But he was also the first to call the children together for a ball game or swimming lesson, and his sisters regarded him as a substitute father whenever Will Thurmond was traveling.

Even as a child, Strom displayed an obsession for cleanliness and order. He liked to organize the family storeroom, stacking canned goods by size. He would get in a bad mood if he couldn't brush his teeth after eating. (In the U.S. Senate, he kept a toothbrush in his suit pocket.)

At harvest time, the Thurmond children helped pull river-bottom yellow corn and picked cotton, working beside black farm laborers. Strom's brother Allen George remembered that their paternalistic father taught them to respect the black workers—"darkies" as he called them—and tend to them in times of need. His sister Mary recalled, "If they needed food or clothes, he'd send them down to Reel's store and tell them to get whatever they needed."[15]

Will Thurmond owned another thousand or so acres in the county, worked by sharecroppers. Thurmond furnished fertilizer and cottonseed, a mule and plow, credit to purchase necessities, and shelter. The sharecrop-per's family provided the labor. Sharecropping had developed throughout the rural South after the Civil War, when the freedmen refused to work in labor gangs as they had as slaves. The system provided them a degree of autonomy, but little opportunity for economic independence. Strom would regularly ride in the buggy with his father on trips to visit the share-croppers, absorbing Will's lessons along the way.[16]

Strom often accompanied his father by train to the state capitol in Co-lumbia, where oil paintings of Tillman and John C. Calhoun, the cham-pion of nullification, decorated the walls. He peered over the brass rails of the General Assembly to watch the heated legislative debates. He watched his father's every move, the way he offered the same strong handshake to a black laborer that he gave a white landowner. His father sometimes sat as a special judge on the state supreme court, and he introduced Strom to all the justices. Back in Edgefield, he watched his father work his magic in the courtroom and saw his fearlessness there, once telling a hostile witness, "If you want to fight, let's fight," and offering to settle the dispute outside the courtroom. In his Senate office, Strom Thurmond prominently displayed an enlarged photograph of his father. He told a visitor, "He was my idol. I tried to imitate him as much as I could."[17]

Already well aware of Strom's interest in politics, Will Thurmond took him in 1912 to a stump meeting in Edgefield that featured Governor Cole Blease, a rousing race baiter, and his opponent in the gubernatorial race, Ira Jones, an able but staid chief justice of the state supreme court. The event left an indelible impression on the boy.

Thurmond later recalled:

They put up a platform for them to speak on and brought a big pitcher of water. Jones, he made a good talk, a literary talk. But he just didn't stir the people. Well, Cole Blease was a fiery kind of fellow and a great orator. You could see people who were not really the thinking people who were carried away by his speech. I could see then the influence that he was going to have over the state for being such a good speaker. . . . After hearing him speak, I knew that I was going to run for governor. And I was going to learn to speak, and I would never let a man do me like Blease did Jones that day.[18]

Blease won the election.

STROM'S MOTHER, GERTRUDE, was a pious and stern woman known for delivering wonderful prayers and her devotion to attending Edgefield's First Baptist Church with her children every Sunday. Strom was often charged with hitching the horses to the carriage for the ride into town.

When he was eleven, Strom marched to the front of the church and asked the preacher to baptize him, which for Southern Baptists meant full immersion in water, usually in the church baptismal pool. Gertrude was proud. Strom said years later that she shaped his life in religious and spiritual matters as profoundly as his father shaped his political instincts. Baptists believe that the baptism, involving as it does repentance and the acceptance of Jesus as one's personal savior, means the forgiveness of later sins.

At the time of Strom's childhood profession of faith, many Southern Baptists tended to treat man's relationship with God as a direct and highly individual experience, not unlike that of Jews. Although he attended church on Sunday mornings in his younger years and was active in a youth group known as the Royal Ambassadors, prayer for him tended to be a private matter. Years later, in the Senate, he became a regular member of organized weekly prayer breakfasts. His key aide Harry Dent said Thurmond "never missed it. He kept it on his calendar as a highest priority." He surprised fellow senators at one breakfast early in his Senate career when he delivered a thoughtful, moving talk about Abraham Lincoln. Dent did some special research on that one, entitled "The Long Road to Faith."[19]

Dent said religion fit into Thurmond's "overall framework of virtues. He lived by his perspective of right and wrong."

BACK IN EDGEFIELD, Senator Ben Tillman had been looking for ways to reward Will Thurmond for his years of loyal service. He saw a chance twelve years after Will Thurmond lost his bid for Congress. After Woodrow Wilson—who had spent part of his boyhood in Columbia as a Presbyterian minister's son—regained the White House in 1912 for the Democrats, Tillman recommended Thurmond for a vacant post as U.S. attorney in South Carolina. The White House found him unsuitable because of the Willie Harris slaying. Tillman dug in his heels. Over stiff opposition, he split the state into two federal judicial districts. The western district was designed for Thurmond. When Wilson balked again, Tillman exploded and exerted political pressure to get his way, writing to the attorney general that Thurmond had to "crawl around on his belly and be kicked around" before he killed Harris.[20]

The nomination went through and Thurmond became U.S. attorney for half of the state, with headquarters in Greenville. He considered relocating the family to a large farm near Greenville, six hours away by a car moving at the era's best pace—fifteen miles per hour. But in the end, the Thurmonds decided not to uproot the children—John William Jr., Strom, Gertrude, Allen George, and the twin girls, Mary and Martha. Their father decided to allow his children to remain in Edgefield, though he would be gone much of the time.

Although the Thurmonds were landed gentry and respected citizens, their rural origins set them apart from the older families of Edgefield who considered themselves the community's social elite. They coalesced around the Episcopal Church, a small brick structure on a hill overlooking the larger First Baptist Church.

But the Thurmonds led a prosperous life. Mary remembered her father taking the girls on trips to New York and Niagara Falls. Under Gertrude Thurmond's strict supervision, the family always had a black domestic staff of at least three members—a live-in cook, houseboy, and gardener, with substitute help when needed.

A typical meal included garden vegetables, meat cured in the family's smokehouse, and hot whole-wheat bread made of grain grown on the farm. There were almost always visitors in the house. Will usually walked home from town with a companion for the evening meal, which was followed by listening to recordings of John Philip Sousa's marches (Will's favorites) or to Gertrude's spirited Bible readings. Many guests stayed overnight, and Strom learned early that this hospitality strengthened the visitors' bonds with his family.

Will Thurmond acted as an adviser not just to Tillman but to political up-and-comers like the young James F. Byrnes, an ambitious court stenographer from Aiken. Byrnes sometimes dropped by the Thurmond family home and spent the night. Eventually, he worked his way to Washington as congressman, U.S. senator, U.S. Supreme Court justice, and secretary of state—before returning home to become governor.

"Our house was like a hotel," Strom recalled. One country cousin lived there for months so he could go to better schools in Edgefield. He became a physician. Grandmother Mary Thurmond lived in the home for years, tutoring the older children in grammar and becoming an important force in the household. She died of pneumonia when Strom was eleven, her body laid out in the parlor.[21]

More than his siblings, Strom enjoyed farm work. When a neighbor went into the army during World War I, Strom and his older brother bought the unharvested crop, hoping to make a sizable profit. William quickly backed out, and Strom bought his interest, then worked long hours in the field. But it was a drought year, with a skimpy return. A frugal teenager, Strom worked Saturdays at a store in town and saved $600 before going to college.

But he also had a mischievous streak, and that same overcharged energy that allowed him to work so hard during the day sometimes kept him out at night. When his father was out of town, he gave his mother fits by sneaking out of an upstairs bedroom window at night to meet girls, according to his sisters. More than once, he was caught sneaking up the back stairs, and a lingering family story tells of Strom hiding out on the roof to avoid his mother's whipping, only to be fetched down by a servant.

He boxed and played football in high school, rode horses bareback, and drove a motorcycle at high speeds on country roads with his hands off the handlebars. He developed a lifelong (and life-lengthening) devotion to physical fitness. But his consuming interest was girls. He was a good dancer and played the field.

WHEN HE FINISHED TENTH GRADE, Strom had the option of continuing to the white high school's new eleventh grade—added just that year by the state legislature—and getting a diploma or going off to college without delay. He enrolled at Clemson, where many of his Edgefield friends were going. Then an all-male military school as well as the state agricultural college, the Clemson campus is nestled in the rolling hills of the state's Upcountry.

The campus is located on part of John C. Calhoun's estate, given to the school by his son-in-law, Thomas Clemson. From their spartan barracks, cadets could look out at Calhoun's graceful white-columned plantation home, Fort Hill, and hear the softly chiming clock from the tower of Tillman Hall, the center of university life.

Strom enrolled in the fall of 1919, not yet seventeen. The rigid routine suited him. Roused at 6:30 by reveille, the daily routine consisted of calisthenics ("taking exercise" is what Strom called it), class work, mandatory chapel, study hall, and military drills before taps sounded at 10:30 P.M. College rules barred mustaches, long hair, cigarettes, drinking, and card playing, and leaving the barracks without permission or behaving irreverently during chapel were grounds for dismissal. Biweekly dances with local girls provided some relief from the grinding routine.

College administrators generally tolerated upperclassmen physically hazing freshmen, and with war veterans returning to school in 1919, Strom's freshman year was rougher than usual. Laughing later over his college experience, he said, "I've had many a broom handle broke over my rear end."[22]

Clemson helped transform the shy but determined boy into a confident, disciplined, and driven young man. Although Strom enjoyed the biweekly dances, earning a notice in the college yearbook as a "ladies' man of the first order," what he wrote years later to a friend's son about to enter Clemson reflected his sense of purpose there: "A great many boys will flit away their time at college, in the pool room, loafing and fooling around. You will be at college only four years. Make every minute count. During the time you are not in classes, I suggest you be on the athletic field or in the gymnasium taking exercise, in the library reading or conversing with ambitious and enterprising men with whom you will form a deep friendship."[23]

At Clemson, he became president of the Calhoun Literary Society, where he debated and learned parliamentary procedure. No professor influenced him more than Daniel Wistar Daniel, a polished orator of national reputation who taught English, brought in nationally renowned speakers, and laced his classroom lectures with wit and country wisdom. Strom practiced public speaking, working for hours at a time to correct an adolescent stammer. Although never a spellbinding orator, Thurmond would eventually become very skilled at reducing political messages to their core and expressing himself with conviction in clear, concise, simple language. At Thurmond's 1947 inauguration as governor, he had Daniel introduce him for his inaugural address.

His competitive drive found an outlet when he trained as a distance runner on the track and cross-country teams. Although Strom was no star athlete, he distinguished himself by displaying an awesome willpower, determination, and unwillingness to admit defeat. At the end of the fall cross-country season in 1922, his senior year, Strom and four teammates decided to find out whether they could run the twenty miles from Clemson to Anderson, South Carolina. The hilly dirt road became paved for only the final two miles. Strom wore new canvas tennis shoes that were too large. By the time he and his teammates reached the paved road, his feet were blistered and his toenails had rubbed off.

"But if I stopped I wouldn't have accomplished what I wanted to, so I kept on," he remembered more than half a century later. "Every time you put your foot down it'd feel like you were driving a nail right in your leg."[24] He went the distance. This tenacity would, of course, become a well-recognized trait in the public Strom.

A FEW WEEKS AFTER attending Strom's graduation from Clemson, his father typed the following letter of "ADVICE from J. Wm. Thurmond to his son J. S. Thurmond":

> *Remember your God.*
>   *Take good care of your body and tax your nervous system as little as possible.*
>   *Obey the laws of the land.*
>   *Be strictly honest.*
>   *Associate only with the best people, morally and intellectually. Think three times before you act once and if you are in doubt, don't act at all.*
>   *Be prompt on your job to the minute.*
>   *Read at every spare chance and think over and try to remember what you have read.*
>   *Do not forget that "skill and integrity" are the keys to success.*
>   *Affectionately.*
>   *Dad*[25]

More than seventy years later, Strom was still signing copies of the document for special friends and associates. And—just as at Clemson—he was still doing calisthenics every morning. Not as many push-ups or sit-ups, but still twisting, bending, and stretching, then riding a stationary bicycle, and still swimming a half mile once or twice a week. He started each day with a glass of prune juice and watched his diet, eating lots of fruit and vegetables and avoiding caffeine. Asked the secret of his longevity and vigor, he would add, "I have good genes."[26]

CHAPTER 3

"The Commendable Efforts
of Mr. Thurmond"

Before his college graduation, Strom considered a military career, but decided to take a reserve commission as a second lieutenant "and be available if war ever came." He believed he could show more initiative in civilian life, "and if I worked hard I could rise faster," he would later explain.[1]

The *Advertiser*, which took note of numerous developments in the prominent young man's life, described Strom's "credible record" at Clemson in a short item about his leaving Edgefield on June 28, 1923, for a job with the AA Fertilizer Company in Carteret, New Jersey, a state that must have felt as foreign to him as New Delhi. He would only be gone for two months.

He returned to South Carolina and accepted a job teaching agriculture and coaching all sports in McCormick, the sleepy county seat twenty-six miles northwest of Edgefield. Strom hit it like a buzz saw. A rare male teacher in the eleven-grade, two-story, red brick school for white children, a natty dresser with a penchant for tight-fitting suits and wide-brimmed hats, he stood ramrod straight after marching into his classroom and lectured with enthusiasm on the intricacies of pig farming and peach-tree pruning. He developed his best students into a special livestock judging team. He piled them into his automobile and raced down country roads while holding forth from behind the wheel not just about fruit trees, poultry, and livestock but on values like sportsmanship and temperance. Female students and their mothers swooned over the slim, muscular young bachelor with intense eyes, slicked-back hair, and an unabashedly flirtatious manner.

In a letter to the weekly *McCormick Messenger*, he offered "to teach any white adults who have had poor opportunities for an education the fundamental principles, even the alphabet itself ... at any time, day or night, when not engaged in my duties at the high school." He wrote monthly columns for the *Messenger* on such subjects as the pleasures of growing fruit

(with detailed instructions on choosing varieties for planting), the importance of good seed in growing vegetables, and the proper spray schedule
for peaches, plums, and cherries.[2]

He wrote an article defending football as an activity that builds a good
physique, teaches boys to be "aggressive and persistent"—lessons essential
to achievement—and provides training for "quick thinking" and "alert-
ness of action."[3] In the 1923 season, his McCormick team lost 19–6 to
heavier, more experienced Greenwood, a much larger town, which the previous year had won 66–0. Everyone was noticing him.

When Strom took his outclassed boys' and girls' basketball teams to
play against the bigger high school in Edgefield, he gave his charges a special treat—a sampling of high society in the larger town. After tea at the
Dixie Highway Hotel, they went to a lavish dinner at Gertrude Thurmond's table, followed by a party at Miss Addie Sue McGlendon's where,
as recorded in the *Advertiser*, "progressive conversation and dancing were enjoyed until a late hour."[4]

During this time, Strom lived at the family home, enjoying hearty meals
and the company of his father's frequent important visitors from around
the state. But he did nothing to undermine the "ladies' man" reputation he
had earned at Clemson. One of the area's most eligible bachelors, he had
no intention of getting married anytime soon. A half century later he explained, "I wouldn't be tied down, because I felt sooner or later I'd end up
in statewide politics. So I could make more contacts; if I'd had a wife it'd
hold you back. Have to come home every night, or you'd have to be in by a
certain time, or take your wife out. I felt that being unfettered that I could
make my own schedule and wouldn't inconvenience anybody."[5]

After two years, Edgefield lured him home to teach, with the *Advertiser*
predicting he would be "a valuable factor in this county." When Edgefield's
county farm agent, an important figure in the rural county, died, Strom took
up the slack. He wrote long informational columns about poisoning boll
weevils, controlling corn blight, and preserving eggs. When local farmers
produced a surplus of chickens, he arranged to ship fryers by train "somewhere up north" and saw to it that farmers got paid in cash. "An indefati-
gable worker and efficient painstaking teacher," the *Advertiser* called him.[6]

Strom's life did include moments of frivolity—and escape. Traveling the
country back roads, young Strom's romantic escapades with a bevy of
women admirers quickly became fodder for small-town gossip and wild

speculation. In keeping with the times, it was not unusual for young white males from the most Bible-thumping families to "cross the tracks," as the saying went, to explore their sexuality in secret with forbidden black women. Bruce Elrod, a Thurmond family historian, recalled his grandmother telling stories about fine young white men meeting compliant black girls for sex at a spot on the South Carolina map called Cleora, between Edgefield and Aiken. Enabling these adventures were the Brunson sisters, two little old ladies with a big house full of bedrooms who tended to be "fairly open-minded," he said. "Men would come to the Brunson place by the back door, slip a little change to the sisters, and buy themselves use of an upstairs bedroom. No questions were asked."[7]

THE *Advertiser* REPORTED in its October 7, 1925, issue that Strom left Edgefield for Florida to seek his fortune in a real estate boom, adding, "We wish Mr. Strom success in his new field." Five days later in an unknown house in Aiken County—16-year-old Carrie Butler gave birth to a light-skinned baby that she named after a sister, Essie Mae.

Bettis Rainsford observed, "The fact she went to Aiken was no accident," that by going away the event would receive little notice in Edgefield. Noting Bill Thurmond's reputation as the "big fixer" around Edgefield, Rainsford surmised that Senator Thurmond's father "paid somebody well to get that child out of here and off to Pennsylvania."[8]

Carrie Butler and an older sister each had worked one day a week in the Thurmond household, helping out with the cooking. A slender five foot seven with a walk that caught men's eyes, she wore a white uniform when she worked as a domestic. Willie Adams, who was born in 1914 and grew up on a tenant farm on Will Thurmond's land near his home outside Edgefield, knew Carrie by her nickname of "Tunch" when she worked for Strom's mother. "Tunch was brown-skinned, with short hair and a pretty face," Adams said.

Her father, Jasper, was born in 1855, a slave on the plantation of aging United States Senator Andrew Pickens Butler, who died two years later. As a matter of convenience, freed slaves often adopted the surnames of their white owners. Carrie's mother, nineteen years younger than Jasper, was born free. Carrie spent much of her early life in "old Buncombe," a black section of Edgefield dating back to slavery and situated behind the grand homes facing Buncombe Road, a state highway that developed from a Cherokee Indian trail that stretched from present day Asheville (Buncombe County), N.C., to the river port of Augusta. Carrie lived with numerous siblings on then-unpaved Brooks Street. Relatives of hers still live there. Others among her extended family of Butlers moved to the northeast.

Earlier, Carrie had lived with relatives, named Oliphant, in Augusta, Georgia, where better education was provided for black children. Frank Roberson, a local black school administrator and historian, located her there as "Carrie Oliphant" in the 1920 census. Old-timers told him of seeing her attend fund-raising events at Bettis Academy, a private junior college for blacks in rural Edgefield County named for a black clergyman who organized some forty churches to provide financial support.

After she had returned to the old Buncombe community in Edgefield, where Adams lived after moving to town, he recalled seeing Strom's sister Mary leave groceries at the house where Carrie lived, and of Carrie going with "Miss Mary" and her twin sister to sit inside the drug store, where other blacks weren't allowed, or to sit with them downstairs at the movie theater, where all other blacks entered through a side door that led to the balcony.[9]

When Essie Mae was born, her mother could barely manage to feed and clothe the child, according to taped accounts editor William Walton Mims conducted with black Edgefield residents who were aware of her birth. Neighbors, some barely able to feed their own families, had to rally around to help the child survive her first months. These neighbors knew of Thurmond's connection to the child and considered shameful his failure to offer financial help. Longtime civil rights leader Modjeska Simkins, who later knew about the circumstances of the girl's birth, shared the outrage. Although Simkins did not make a public issue of Essie Mae's existence, she found Thurmond's behavior in the episode outrageous. She considered him the supreme political opportunist.

Essie Mae Williams has said she believes her mother had a loving and long-standing relationship with Thurmond, that she was not the product of a one-night stand. Others familiar with the relationship have confirmed that it endured over many years, although there were other men in Carrie Butler's life, including a husband, Willie Clark, who sired a son with her. (Williams has said that this half brother was not Thurmond's child.)

Six months after her birth, arrangements were made for baby Essie Mae to move to Coatesville, Pennsylvania, a rugged steel-mill town about thirty miles west of Philadelphia, where one of Carrie's sisters, Mary Washington, and her husband, John, became her surrogate parents, providing a caring home and a surname. Like many other blacks from Edgefield, the Washingtons had moved to Coatesville to work in the steel mills, hard work that provided a steady paycheck. For almost every town in the South there developed a corresponding destination point in the North or Midwest, where migrating blacks could connect with friends and relatives in their shared quest for a more prosperous and freer life. Coatesville was Edgefield's unofficial northern sister city. By the time Strom returned to Edgefield in 1926, the fatherless black baby had been conveniently whisked out of town.

Given the overwhelming power whites held over blacks at that time, in that place, and in that household, it is hard to imagine a young black servant thinking she had the right of refusal or, should it have occurred to her, insisting upon it. Nevertheless, in South Carolina, where miscegenation was forbidden by law, the age of legal consent for sex was fourteen years old at the time Thurmond impregnated Carrie Butler, sixteen years old when her baby was born.

STROM SPENT 1926 TEACHING IN RIDGE SPRING, a hamlet nestled along the road to Columbia, and he continued to win accolades. Back in Edgefield in 1927 as a teacher and coach, he also became an organizer and president of the Baptist Young People's Union, the denomination's youth group. He traveled the county, visiting all the rural Baptist churches, meeting people, and accruing what would prove to be valuable political capital.

Thurmond helped develop Summerland, a six-week summer camp for bright farm boys, teaching academic courses and the latest agricultural advancements. He went to the Lions Club and to churches, getting them to raise funds for $12 scholarships—and further expanding his contacts. Over four years, enrollment at Summerland grew from fourteen to 200. Thurmond publicized the program by writing articles in nearby county newspapers and one Sunday feature in the *Augusta Herald.*

Strom continued his courtship of the press, inviting editors not only to visit Summerland to write stories but also to speak to the boys. He often dropped by the *Advertiser,* sometimes bearing gifts that got a mention in the paper's society column, such as: "The finest peaches of the season that we have seen were presented to us by Strom Thurmond, having been plucked from his orchard."

It was really Summerland that laid the groundwork for Strom's political career. He became a hit with his students, firmly established himself with the rural population, made more appearances in the local papers, and gained an appointment to the Edgefield School Board. "I made a lot of friends working with those boys," he later recalled. "I wrestled with them and I played with them and ran with them. But I was interested in young people, and it turned out to be very helpful politically."[10]

One year at Summerland, he told almost 200 boys that he would call each of them by name, "and if I don't you can send me through the belt line." A former student vividly remembered Strom calling off the names one by one, row behind row, without a miss. Afterward, a teacher told him that "Strom Thurmond could run for governor with that kind of talent."[11]

In 1928, he announced he would challenge the incumbent county superintendent of education, W. W. Fuller, whose wife was Thurmond's cousin. The *Advertiser* reported that Fuller had won the respect of teachers by "paying them promptly in cash." But Strom knew as a school-board member that Fuller's poor fiscal management kept the county in debt and that he provided little leadership. "I kind of hated to run against old man Fuller," Thurmond remembered, "but he'd been there a long time; all he did was hunt."[12]

Strom had ideas and ambition. He wanted school building improvements, a literacy campaign, and a health course to teach all students that "if you don't have a healthy body you can't do anything." And, as he had always believed in fiscal responsibility, he felt certain he could control the district's finances.

But his personal ambitions went far beyond improving Edgefield County's schools. Larger goals had begun to come into focus. He believed the superintendent's job could help him establish a record on the first rung of a ladder to higher office. "Back then, you couldn't just get out and run for governor," he said a half century later. "You had to work your way and develop a reputation. You had to prove yourself." The superintendent's job gave him time to study law after hours in his father's office and at home.

Strom said his father's only advice was "if you want it, go after it," and that he then stayed out of the race. Strom had developed his own contacts and organized an army of volunteers who fanned out across the county, delivering flyers and praising Strom. He went house-to-house himself, knocking on doors and shaking hands. And, of course, being Will Thurmond's boy didn't hurt him.[13]

He delivered his first political stump speech from a platform at the Colliers community, a long-awaited rite that must have conjured up all his boyhood images of fiery Cole Blease and Ben Tillman. He began by quoting Thomas Jefferson, "I believe in education of the masses, not the classes," then vowed to serve as "an inspiration" to the hundreds of pupils who would come under his supervision. Strom won 1,312 votes to Fuller's 802, a landslide victory in the Democratic primary, the only election that mattered.

The November general election ballot listed only the Democratic nominees for state and local office. Some local Baptist leaders urged voters to abstain in the presidential election in protest against the Democratic nomination of New York Governor Al Smith, an urban Catholic "wet" candidate, a proponent of repealing prohibition. But open support for Republican Herbert Hoover in the era of the Democratic "solid South" was generally regarded as unthinkable. Among South Carolinians who voted, Al Smith won with 92 percent.

Only whites voted in both the Democratic primary and the general election, the majority black population in Edgefield remaining political objects rather than participants in an era in which white supremacy reigned without challenge. This public policy was implemented by Tillman and sanctioned by the U.S. Supreme Court in the 1898 *William v. Mississippi* decision, which approved the use of the sort of poll taxes, literacy tests, and residential requirements that were designed to keep blacks from voting. Edgefield whites embraced segregation as the way things were intended to be and would remain, as dependable as the sun rising in the morning and setting in the evening.

At twenty-six, Thurmond was the state's youngest county superintendent of education, responsible for both black and white students. The school system he took over in the summer of 1929 was typical of rural public education in a state that ranked at or near the bottom in every measurable educational standard. Black pupils, many of them relegated to dilapidated one-room schoolhouses, outnumbered whites by two to one. One-room schools for blacks outnumbered those for whites by more than five to one. Whites generally attended larger schools. Edgefield County spent $5.35 per year for each black child's education and $63 for each white child. School terms for whites were almost twice as long. White male teachers earned a respectable $1,530 a year and white women teachers, $826. The typical black teacher earned less than $300. Only white children received bus transportation to school. These numbers, buried in the state superintendent of education's annual report, reflected the state and regional norm—and raised no alarm.

Thurmond was, for the most part, an energetic and effective superintendent. "I was trying to prove myself as a superintendent," he said later. "I always felt if you did a good job, then you would be appreciated and it would help you for the next position you occupied." He got the school board to raise taxes and pay off debt, equalized taxes and expenditures among the local school districts in the county, and pared expenses to produce a surplus.[14]

In January 1930, he launched a countywide "Write Your Name" campaign against adult illiteracy. The program took particular aim at the 3,289 blacks—almost 30 percent of the county's black population—that the 1920 census had revealed could neither read nor write. It was designed to reduce to as few as possible the number of people who would sign an "X" for the 1930 census. Thurmond urged blacks to come out to "Moonlight Schools," for which he hired sixty-nine black teachers to work overtime for $1 a night, an amount that a proficient cotton worker might earn for a day's work. Lessons were held three nights a week in schools and churches during nine-week sessions. Separate classes were set up for the county's 140 illiterate whites.

Within a month, the *Advertiser* reported that more than one-fourth of the county's illiterates were being taught to read and write their names "through the commendable efforts of Mr. Thurmond." A black teacher wrote, "Our county superintendent is leaving no stone unturned in helping us to eradicate illiteracy in our group. He has been instrumental in helping to obtain efficient teaching faculties and is urging every colored teacher to support the work."[15]

By the end of the campaign, 798 black adults had learned to write their names, 648 had learned basic reading, and all who attended had received, at Thurmond's insistence, lessons in hygiene and "good principles of living." In the 1930 census, black illiteracy in the county dropped by more than one-fourth, from 29 percent to 21 percent. A young black principal years later told his children he could "get what he needed from Thurmond."[16] Thurmond was already beginning to attract the attention of the state Department of Education in Columbia.

He also launched an innovative program in which the state health officer and local dentists went into the schools to examine children and treat defects. Although Thurmond's recollection years later was that all children—black and white—participated, a faded clipping from *The State* reports, "Examination of 1,500 white school children of Edgefield County began Tuesday under direction of Dr. Ben Wyman, state director of county health work, assisted by a staff of seven county health officers, six nurses and two inspectors in addition to local physicians."[17]

But Thurmond did talk about health care for all children in 1932 to Modjeska Simkins. She first met him when she represented the South Carolina Tuberculosis Association, in charge of their "Negro program." She traveled the state, trying to get health education into the black schools.

She had found most white school officials insensitive, often rude, and seldom more than condescending. But in Edgefield, she found Thurmond courteous and sincerely interested in her pleas. She applauded his effort to bring doctors and dentists to rural schoolchildren whose parents couldn't afford preventive medicine. When they finished talking, he walked Mrs. Simkins to her car. Although she already knew the young politician's personal secret, she was heartened by his political outlook. Heading back to the capital, she thought the leadership of the state could be looking "up and out" with men like Thurmond on the rise.[18]

Strom moved the superintendent's office next door to his father's law office, and he secluded himself there at the end of each day, studying law through the LaSalle University Extension Course, a course prescribed by the state supreme court, and by reading *Thurmond's Key Cases*, a respected reference book compiled by his father. He studied for three years, his father tutoring him. "It was just like having a full-time law teacher," Thurmond remembered. "He saved me hours of looking stuff up because he could answer it right there."[19] Strom had also learned much from sitting in the courtroom, watching his father try cases.

In late 1929, however, the elder Thurmond suffered the first of a series of debilitating heart seizures that would lead to his death five years later. He called on Strom to help in his law practice, even before his son had taken the bar exam.

The first time involved a hearing before the state supreme court. Will Thurmond got the court's permission to allow Strom to argue the case. Strom won it and two others in the trial courts before passing the three-day bar exam in 1930. He bragged that he tied for the highest grade with J. Robert Martin, a Harvard Law School graduate from Greenville who later achieved a reputation for fair-minded toughness as a jurist. Martin ultimately issued many of the state's major desegregation orders on his way to becoming chief judge for the U.S. District Court of South Carolina.

Thurmond had studied in his father's office with a friend from Mc-Cormick, J. Fred Buzhardt (the father of a future key aide to Senator Thurmond). They were close and later practiced law together, in Edgefield and McCormick. Buzhardt recalled Strom had "more girl friends than you could shake a stick at," big-busted women who would come to the office and sometimes wait hours for him to finish his work and take them out.[20]

After passing the bar exam, Thurmond practiced law with his father while simultaneously completing his term as county superintendent of education. After Strom won an acquittal for a murder defendant in one of his first cases, the *Advertiser* characterized his jury argument as "very eloquent and effective."[21]

In 1932, Edgefield County's state senator, a friend of Will's, announced he wasn't seeking reelection. Strom, twenty-nine, went down to the courthouse and paid his $15 filing fee to run for the office. Although much younger than the typical senator, who had usually served first in the South Carolina House of Representatives, Strom seemed to be headed for a free ride. He was becoming ever more well-known, had proven himself energetic and progressive, yet tight with the purse strings.

Until the Supreme Court's "one man, one vote" reapportionment decisions ruled it unconstitutional, South Carolina functioned under a "little federal" system. The forty-six-member state Senate provided for one senator from each county. A 124-member House was based on population, but with at least one member from each county. This system assured rural domination of the legislature in the overwhelmingly rural state, even as the state's urban areas grew. State senator was also a powerful local office. The senator at that time chaired each county's legislative delegation—controlling county government, filling many local offices, and writing the county budget, or "supply bill." Legislators then logrolled this local legislation with an unspoken understanding of "I'll vote for yours and you vote for mine."

As the filing deadline approached, opposition came from an unexpected source, Benjamin Ryan Tillman Jr., Pitchfork Ben's son. The younger Tillman shared his father's reactionary racial views, but they were very different men. He had a reputation as a heavy drinker and had outraged Edgefield in a bitter and public divorce case in which the state supreme court had to settle custody of his children. Furthermore, he had grown up, for the most part, in Washington, D.C.

Thurmond, running as a "Progressive Democrat" in a year that the Great Depression reached crisis status, pledged to reduce spending, cut legislative salaries, and provide more state support for public education. He had already been selected as a delegate to the 1932 Democratic National Convention, which gave him de facto support from the party organization. He trounced Tillman in the August primary, 2,350 to 538. He was now for all intents and purposes the senator-elect from Edgefield County.

A week later, Strom went to Chicago and joined in nominating New York Governor Franklin D. Roosevelt for president. As was well known at the time, Roosevelt had spent time at Warm Springs, Georgia, for therapy after being stricken with polio. While there, he would drive around in one of his custom-designed cars, stopping for long talks with farmers. He developed empathy for and a real knowledge of the South, its people, and its problems. Since the Civil War, only Grover Cleveland and Woodrow Wilson had served as Democratic presidents, and an enthusiastic Thurmond returned home to campaign. "I think our whole delegation was impressed with Roosevelt," Thurmond remembered. "He had a grasp of what needed to be done for the farmers, and at that time farming was the main industry in South Carolina. I was impressed with FDR because he was a man of action and I felt he would get things done."[22]

Thurmond organized a Saturday afternoon Democratic rally in downtown Edgefield. Hundreds of schoolchildren paraded, and an overflow crowd filled the courthouse. One speaker, J. E. Stanfield of Aiken, called Edgefield "the cradle of liberty" in South Carolina and referred to the role "that Edgefield leaders had played in ridding the state of Republican tyranny in 1876."[23]

Roosevelt won South Carolina with 98 percent of the vote.

Meanwhile, the self-confident, twenty-nine-year-old Thurmond prepared a set of proposals to present to the legislature, but a serious case of influenza that lingered for ten days kept him in Edgefield on January's opening day. In his letter of resignation as county superintendent of education delivered to Edgefield's citizens on that same day, he appealed to the schoolchildren to remain committed to their education and to try and prepare themselves for service and a useful calling.

Confined at home and restless, he sent a letter to *The State*, which printed his six-point legislative program. It included Strom's proposals for a 50-percent cut in legislative salaries, to $200 a year, reorganization of state government to reduce costs, and slashing appropriations—"for our people are simply not able to pay high taxes." He further proposed school consolidation as a means of reducing expenses.[24]

When Thurmond arrived to take his seat in the Senate, the seventy-five other freshman lawmakers had already settled in. Many of the newcomers, mostly country lawyers and prosperous farmers elected by their neighbors to keep a careful eye on state spending and to see that the "right people" ran things at home, had begun to discover the generosity of lobbyists with access to good bootleg whiskey and easy women. Others joined all-night songfests in local cafés or simply enjoyed the lavish display of food at evening receptions. Except for the more worldly delegation from Charleston County, with its wide-open port city, the newcomers explored an atmosphere that for them was both unfamiliarly exotic and hedonistic.

In Columbia, the western wall of the granite Statehouse still bore—as it bears today—ten brass stars to mark where it was struck by small cannonballs fired across the Congaree River by General William Tecumseh Sherman's artillery. Sherman had pounded the city, where the initial Ordinance of Secession, written by an Edgefield lawyer, was signed in December 1860 (in the First Baptist Church, site of Strom's July 2003 funeral service).

A deep skepticism about executive authority in state government lingered from South Carolina's colonial past, when the governor was appointed by the king of England. Power had become vested in the legislature, which was no longer necessarily the preserve of the state's aristocracy and was often criticized by opinion leaders as weak-willed, stubborn, and small-minded. Charleston editor W. W. Ball observed of the state's politicians: "Nothing is so much abhorred . . . as an idea. And if the idea happens to be new they faint."[25]

Thurmond's arrival in Columbia coincided with the beginning of a shift in state political power to Barnwell, a county seat fifty-seven miles southeast of Edgefield. Senator Edgar A. Brown and Representative Solomon Blatt, both lawyers from Barnwell, had razor-sharp minds, and they practiced what Brown preached when he explained to new members, "There's no education in the second kick of a mule," literally meaning "don't make the same mistake twice."

A stalwart Democrat and a close friend and political ally of James F. Byrnes, the lean and bespectacled Brown had already made an unsuccessful run for the U.S. Senate in 1926. As chairman of the Senate Finance Committee for more than four decades, he would hold a tight grasp on South Carolina's purse strings and earn the sobriquet "Bishop from Barnwell" from his habitual promise to "give prayerful consideration" to entreaties for support of legislation. In his 1949 classic, *Southern Politics in State and Nation*, political scientist V. O. Key likened Brown's role in South Carolina to that of a prime minister.

Across the lobby, Sol Blatt was the son of a Jewish immigrant peddler who saved enough to open a store in the Barnwell County village of Blackville and send his boy to the University of South Carolina and its law school. Blatt was just beginning his climb to Speaker of the House. He would hold that position for thirty-three years, setting a record unmatched by anyone in any legislature in the United States. At a political barbecue the previous year, his hosts had realized they had failed to provide chicken for their Jewish candidate, serving only pork along with the traditional side dishes. "That's all right," Blatt told them, "We'll just call it goose."[26]

Over the years, Thurmond's career would often intersect with these men, who together became known collectively as the Barnwell Ring, a term Brown would one day define as "two old men who sometimes agree and sometimes don't."[27] One observer said they spent the state's money like it was their own, dominating like-minded rural colleagues. Although fiercely conservative and generally resistant to change, they were practical men, and open to persuasion.

THURMOND HAD VISITED THE LEGISLATURE several years earlier, hawking his father's *Thurmond's Key Cases* for $5 a copy. One senator remembered that he "wouldn't take no for an answer. You had to pay him five dollars just to get rid of him."[28]

Perhaps with this memory still in some minds, and already with a shared awareness of Strom's love of the spotlight, some of his new colleagues eyed him warily, and Strom confirmed their skepticism by quickly introducing his bill to cut legislative pay in half and to prohibit extra pay for an extended session. His efforts failed, raising hackles among those forced to vote against it, but it got Thurmond some good press. He also joined four other senators as part of Governor Ibra Blackwood's official party to attend Roosevelt's inauguration. Later in the year, he returned a $260 voucher to the state comptroller, with a note that he had voted against extra pay and refused to accept it.

Politically astute blacks like Modjeska Simkins carefully—and hopefully—watched Thurmond's early stances, only to find inconsistencies when it came to matters involving race. He publicly supported more money for Negro education, then introduced an unsuccessful bill to ban Negro employment in the Capitol complex. He voted to exempt Ku Klux Klan property from state taxation.

A supporter not only of Roosevelt but of the new president's New Deal, Thurmond sought to shift the tax burden to the wealthy, proposing to end state property taxes and offset the loss with taxes on income and intangibles (stocks and bonds). The legislation didn't pass, but it added to his developing liberal reputation. Speaking out for a bill that would outlaw locking employees inside mills as a means of keeping them on the job, a common practice at the time, Thurmond called himself a "friend to capital but more a friend of labor."

Thurmond became a major supporter of Governor Olin D. Johnston's proposal for a state-developed, state-owned electric power project. The project would dam the Santee River and divert its flow to the Cooper River, create two major inland lakes for recreation, and generate low-cost electricity, much of it to be sold to rural electrification cooperatives. The project would be financed in part by federal funds and create thousands of jobs.

Johnston was a hulking, determined former textile worker who managed his way to the University of South Carolina, where he played tackle on the football team, and worked his way through the university's law school. He remained forever loyal to his roots. Unlike Governor Eugene Talmadge in Georgia, who in the 1934 textile strike, the largest walkout in American history, called out the National Guard to suppress the strikers, Johnston supported the South Carolina workers. The strike ended only after five workers in the village of Honea Path were shot to death by armed guards working for the textile mill, whose superintendent was mayor of the town.

Even when selected to represent the Senate in a mule race challenge to the House at the state fairgrounds, Thurmond was determined to win. "I know mules, so I picked a long-legged one whose ears laid back," he explained years later.[29] He shipped in the speedy mule from Aiken, a horse racing center. His genial House counterpart, Frank Hampton, saw the contest as a joke to promote bonhomie and showed up at the starting line with an underfed, overworked ice-wagon mule.

"When they said 'go,'" Hampton remembered, "Strom's gone. I can still see that fellow taking off on that mule. Strom took it all so serious."[30]

Strom pursued the opposite sex with equal diligence, developing a "shady reputation" among the ladies of Columbia's Junior League, one former senator remembered, because of his flirtation with a woman who ran a snack stand in the Statehouse. "He was a little heavy-handed and redneck with the women," the former colleague recalled. "He might have fit right in with the morals of today, but back then he was considered a Casanova."[31] Marshall Williams, later state senator for many years from Orangeburg, who double-dated with Thurmond, said, "I always had to drive because Strom needed both hands in the back seat."[32]

Roy Powell, a former gubernatorial aide to Olin Johnston who also sometimes double-dated with Thurmond, remembered him as "persistent" with women; Powell so admired Strom's "eye for beauty" that he got the governor to appoint Thurmond a judge in the annual Tomato Queen beauty contest, the kind of role that would become a pastime for Strom, regularly including a kiss on the mouth for each winning contestant.[33]

Busy professional schedule and mischievous personal life aside, Strom headed back to Edgefield each Thursday when the Senate adjourned until it reconvened on Tuesday, picking up the bulk of the workload in the law practice with his father, whose health continued to deteriorate. Will was too weak to attend son Allen George's graduation from medical school in 1934. A year later, he sent Strom to accept an honorary degree for him at the University of South Carolina spring commencement.

J. William Thurmond's life slipped away a few weeks later on a Sunday afternoon. By sunset, the *Advertiser* would report, the Thurmond home was besieged by a "stream of sorrowing people from all walks of life who came to pay their respects." The newspaper devoted half the front page to his obituary and funeral coverage.

Editor Mims remembered the funeral as a show of the older Thurmond's statewide political reputation and the growing influence of Strom.
"When Mr. Thurmond died, Strom Thurmond sent wires to all the digni-
taries and prominent people everywhere in South Carolina," Mims said,
"and as I recall, the street was literally lined with these nice black cars,
these status symbols, with, I think, in one or two cases, chauffeurs."[34]

The county commissioners ordered that a portrait of Will Thurmond
hang in the courthouse to serve as "an inspiration to present and future
generations." The oil portrait, still there today, is of a heavyset, robust man
with piercing eyes. Strom would always consider him "the smartest man I
ever knew."[35]

Strom assumed more of the workload at the prospering law firm. With
his growing influence in the legislature, the firm had already been attracting handsome retainers from such state-regulated corporate clients as
Southern Railway and Security Bank. Years later, such payments to a
lawyer-legislator would have raised ethical questions, but not in the 1930s.

In reviewing Thurmond's years as senator, Roy Powell said, "Strom always impressed me as an effective senator. He tended to his chores. He
looked after his county. He never forgot a friend."[36]

AMONG THEMSELVES, blacks in Edgefield noted Carrie Butler's regular
late-afternoon visits over many years to Thurmond's law office. By then
she lived nearby with relatives on unpaved Brooks Street in the town's well-
defined colored section.

Willie Adams, again using Carrie's nickname, said, "Tunch would go to
Thurmond's law office late in the afternoon, and the door would then be
locked."[37] Modjeska Simkins said those visits were well known among
blacks in Edgefield.[38] Adams also said he saw Carrie on one occasion at a
drugstore soda fountain, where blacks were excluded, with Strom's sister
Mary. On another occasion he saw Strom delivering groceries to the house
where Carrie lived. (The real taboo among whites at the time was not in
having such relationships, but in talking about them. Even if "everyone"
knew, silence prevailed.)

The daughter fathered by Thurmond seemed only a memory. By this
time, she was quietly growing up alongside John and Mary Washington's
son Calvin. The 1930 census recorded the family as living in South

Coatesville, the father working as a laborer at the nearby Lukens steel mill. Ten-year-old Calvin was the only one in the family who could read and write, the census indicated.

Thurmond's secret seemed safe enough in the first half of the twentieth century. "Back then," Adams said in an observation that also functions as a summary of the impact of the civil rights movement, "a black man couldn't talk about a lot of things, but I've seen the change, and now a black man can talk."[39]

In Columbia, Thurmond won appointment to the Senate Education Committee and became known among teachers as a champion of public schools. He introduced bills to expand the school term from six months to eight, to increase teacher pay by 10 percent, and to provide a system for renting textbooks at a modest fee. He pushed for compulsory school attendance. As chairman of the Senate Public Works Committee, Thurmond pushed hard to fund a new classroom building at Winthrop College, the state's publicly funded school for women. Thurmond served on the Winthrop board of trustees, which named the new building for him, an unusual tribute to so young a public official, and one he enjoyed. It was the first public facility to bear his name. Finally, in his role on the Education Committee, he became concerned about Communists infiltrating South Carolina's schools and pushed for a law requiring teachers to take a loyalty oath before being hired.

His loyalty oath bill was apparently linked to his becoming state councillor in 1935 of the Junior Order of United American Mechanics, essentially an American nativist organization opposed to immigration. The Junior Order's motto was "Put none but Americans on Guard." Their creed was "One Language, One School, One Country, One Flag." In this role, Strom traveled around the state making speeches. He mentioned the "disturbance and discord growing out of the Communistic propaganda among the ignorant and unthinking people." He blamed growing crime on "illegally entered foreign born and those that have no other reason to be in this country than to accumulate a competence and go back to their native lands."[40] His strident position reflected the odd mixture of progressive and regressive thinking that defined his politics.

In insular Edgefield, Thurmond had known little of immigrants. Had he even gotten to know Sol Blatt better, he would have discovered a World War I doughboy who deeply loved his country for the freedom and opportunity it gave at least one immigrant's family.

THURMOND WAS REELECTED without opposition in 1936, a testament to his formidable influence. He returned to Columbia in 1937 amid talk of his becoming a candidate for lieutenant governor in 1938. But fate intervened on a sweltering August day in Newberry, forty miles northwest of Columbia, where alumni of Lutheran-affiliated Newberry College were gathered for a reunion. State trial judge Carroll Johnson Ramage, whose four-county judicial circuit included Edgefield County, spoke for the occasion under a blazing sun. Moments after he finished, he dropped dead of a heart attack.

The legislature elects judges in South Carolina, and speculation over who might be Ramage's successor began almost immediately. Ramage had been a close friend of Will Thurmond, and Strom served as a pallbearer and delivered a stirring eulogy.

Although he seemed to have given little thought to serving as a judge before Ramage's death, Thurmond understood clearly the political opportunity that had opened up before him—a circuit judge holds court in every county in the state over a six-and-a-half-year period. "I decided I'd better take that and try to do a good job at it," Thurmond remembered, "and then I'd make friends going around traveling as a judge over the state. And that would be a good foundation if I cared to resign and later enter politics for governor or the United States Senate."[41] A lieutenant governor, ostensibly a much more prominent position, did little more than preside over the Senate. Despite his earlier vote for a failed bill prohibiting members from filling offices elected by the legislature, Strom announced his candidacy almost immediately after Ramage's funeral.

Opposition came from George Bell Timmerman Sr. Considered one of the state's leading lawyers, he had served as solicitor for the circuit and once practiced law with Will Thurmond. They had remained friends until the end of Will's life. Timmerman was currently chairman of the state highway commission, where he strongly supported the politically powerful highway administrator, Ben Sawyer, in a raging battle with Governor Johnston. Timmerman was the early favorite.

Strom approached the election by treating the 169 voters in the legislature (other than himself) with the same door-to-door intensity that had earlier won him his first elected office. "I ran into Strom on Broad Street in Charleston," said Robert Figg, a former legislator who became one of Thurmond's key advisers a few years later. "He said, 'I've been all over the state and talked to everybody in the legislature.' Well, it wasn't too long before I saw him in Charleston again. I wouldn't be surprised if he didn't make three swings across the state that fall and talked to everybody in the House and Senate."[42]

Sol Blatt considered his candidate Timmerman a shoo-in until he witnessed Thurmond's relentless campaign. "What he used to do was find somebody in the House who lived maybe eight or ten miles out in the country. Strom Thurmond would go right out to his house, probably in the afternoon, and then the fellow would invite him to eat supper or spend the night and he'd do it. He did that in many, many places. And every time he spent the night at a house, he got a vote. George Bell Timmerman handled it differently. He'd approach a fellow in his place of business. He didn't play the political game as it should have been played. But Strom was as good as I've ever seen."[43]

When the General Assembly convened in January 1938, Thurmond politicked until the last moment, then took a seat in the visitors' gallery with pencil and paper to tally the vote. His House colleague from Edgefield nominated him. The lieutenant governor asked if there were other nominations. Silence. After a murmur of surprise rolled across the floor of the chamber, Edgar Brown moved that the nominations be closed and that Thurmond be elected by acclamation. Blatt said later of himself and the other Timmerman supporters, "We took a count, and he didn't have anything like enough votes to win."[44]

Contemporary political reporters theorized that Governor Johnston quietly threw his support to Thurmond, who had essentially remained neutral in the bitter highway battle (Johnston eventually called out the National Guard to occupy the state highway department). Statehouse reporters simply missed the story of Thurmond's unflagging and effective pursuit of votes. The *Anderson Independent*, however, correctly called his victory "a political upset of major proportions, which stunned even those who usually feel that they know what is going to happen."[45]

Thus, at thirty-five, Strom Thurmond was elected circuit judge without opposition to become the youngest jurist in the state of South Carolina.

CHAPTER 4

Circuit Judge
James Strom Thurmond

STROM THURMOND LOOKED BACK on his years as a judge as "the easiest, nicest job I ever had, just from the standpoint of health and respect. Everybody respected you."[1]

Although Strom admired the job, his record wasn't universally admired. Harry Ashmore, a fellow Clemson graduate who went on to become a Pulitzer Prize–winning newspaper editor in Little Rock, Arkansas, was a reporter in Greenville at that time and covered Thurmond as a judge. "Strom was a competent and, in a way, absolutely honest judge," Ashmore recalled, "but he was totally humorless. I couldn't see much signs of compassion. And he didn't seem to me the kind of a person who could dispense justice without kind of an arbitrary, doctrinaire view of whatever the case was. I never detected any signs of race bias in his court, but segregation was absolute in South Carolina in those days. There was no challenge to it."[2] Historian Joel Williamson grew up in Anderson, South Carolina, and regularly attended court as a teenager in the 1930s, as he found watching trials more entertaining than movies. "I saw J. Strom preside and thought it was terrible," he recalled six decades later. "He looked arrogant. He looked in a rush. From my point of view, there seemed to be no heart. There was no warmth. There were other judges who impressed me. In my young eye, he was the worst one."[3]

Lawyer Thomas A. Pope, Speaker of the state House of Representatives during Thurmond's last two years as governor and never a political ally of Thurmond, also found his performance on the bench unimpressive. "I thought Strom was the weakest circuit judge we had since Reconstruction," Pope said. "I said that to Judge [Eugene] Blease [chief justice of the state supreme court], and he said, 'Well how about' . . . and named one other judge, from Orangeburg. That was his only comment. Thurmond didn't know the law very well."[4]

Pope believed Thurmond's lack of formal legal education limited him. The training under his father prepared him to try cases but deprived him of the intellectual stimulation of class discussion and gave him little background in broader concepts of legal theory. Thurmond would often call attorneys into his chambers to persuade them to quietly work out a settlement. Before issuing important opinions, he would call his friends, particularly Robert Figg (whom Pope called the most brilliant lawyer in the state) for legal advice. Later, as a U.S. senator, Thurmond seemed to have little grounding in constitutional law.

Of course, what would eventually become a kind of never-ending campaign went on uninterrupted. Figg remembered being asked by Thurmond, who was holding court in Charleston, to go with him to the YMCA for exercise during a recess. "He shook every hand in the place and said, 'I'm the judge and I'm running the court down here, but I want you to remember me because one day I'm going to be running for governor.'"[5]

As a judge, Thurmond denounced the activities of masked night riders. When charging the grand jury at the opening court term in Greenville in January 1940, he responded to a letter from a lawyer there urging him to speak out against the Klan (which had been active in the area).[6] After reading the state statute outlawing masked threats or assaults in the courtroom, Thurmond asserted, "I am not in sympathy with any such doings. Anyone convicted need expect no mercy at my hands." Such incidents, he added, "are in my judgment the most abominable type of lawlessness."[7]

Political opponents later charged that Thurmond set an all-time reversal rate by the state supreme court, but he conducted his own research on the issue to refute the charge. In the early 1960s, a political scientist at the University of South Carolina analyzed the reversal rates of all state circuit court judges over a period of several decades since a previous study published in the *USC Law Review*. He submitted it to *Law Review* editor Colden Battey, but when Law School dean Robert Figg reviewed the article, he handed it back to Battey and said, "You don't think I'm going to print this damn thing, do you?" It was never published. Battey believed Figg did not want to embarrass the judiciary and especially not Senator Strom Thurmond, then a U.S. senator, whose reversal rate as a judge was the only one that exceeded 50 percent.[8]

Some of the cases in which he was reversed suggested more compassion and sense of justice than his critics perceived. For example, he ruled in fa-

vor of a textile worker in a workmen's compensation case against Judson
Mills in Greenville. The man, a weave room worker, collapsed and died after working a full shift in 85° heat. Thurmond agreed that temperatures in
the mill were too hot and decided the man's family should collect compensation. The state supreme court reversed him, saying the decision had been
based on "conjecture and speculation." No liability was found against the
company.

In another case involving two young men arrested and imprisoned for
loitering in a vacant lot in Greenville, Thurmond ruled there was no cause
for their detention and arrest. The supreme court again overturned him.
Lending support to his critics, however, other reversals involved applications of the law to complex matters, financial and otherwise.

Without question, Thurmond continued to use his time as a judge to
lay the foundation for his larger goal. In charging the grand jury on his
first visit as a judge in Charleston, he congratulated the state for nominating Charleston Mayor Burnet Maybank for governor. He referred to Maybank as "one of the cleanest, most able and most public-spirited men in
South Carolina" and envisioned "a new era of great progress for the state."
The News and Courier also quoted the judge commending the city for its
"hospitality, charm and culture."[9]

Meanwhile, newspaper notices and stories reported Thurmond speaking to such groups as a church Sunday school, the Exchange Club in Columbia, the Knights of Pythias in Anderson, and the Lions Club in
Charleston. He attacked the national crime rate and blamed it on corrupt
politicians, a "breakdown of parental responsibility," and, once again,
"foreigners." And at a time when violence against Jews was intensifying in
Nazi Germany, a Jewish alderman introduced Thurmond at a Charleston
civic club, where he repeated his hard-line stance on immigration, saying
the United States should not, under any circumstances, let the guard down
for a wholesale immigration of foreigners.[10] He also urged a state system
of supervised parole, especially for young offenders. "I had just as soon
send them to a college of crime as to the reform school," Thurmond said,
"for there they are placed in contact with seasoned criminals and learn the
new art of crime."[11]

Thurmond remained active in public affairs. He joined a small delegation from South Carolina and Georgia that went to Washington to urge fa-
vorable action on the proposed $21 million Clarks Hill power, navigation,

and flood control project that would border the western boundary of Edgefield County. (In 1988, Congress renamed it the J. Strom Thurmond Dam and Lake.) And he remained active in the Junior Order of United American Mechanics, attending a national meeting in Philadelphia.

He resigned as a Winthrop College trustee after criticism about dual office holding by a legislator, but he was present at a banquet there for South Carolina newspaper editors, addressed the graduating class of the Winthrop Training School, established a $1,000 loan fund for home economics students at the college, and attended the ceremony at Winthrop naming the new home economics building for him.

When the afternoon newspaper in Anderson published a fortieth anniversary edition, Thurmond wrote a letter to the editor praising it as "one of the finest editions of any newspaper that I have ever read." He praised "your progressive city" and suggested, as the only civic improvement he would make, "the elimination of noise" from automobile horns.[12]

IN THE SUMMER OF 1939, while Strom Thurmond accumulated political capital as a traveling circuit judge, Carrie Butler Clark left Edgefield and her husband behind and moved to Coatesville with her young son, Willie Clark. She stayed briefly with her sister Mary Washington and her family, which of course included her daughter, Essie Mae. Carrie soon moved to nearby Chester, Pennsylvania, leaving her son in Coatesville for the fall semester. Just as in Coatesville, many blacks from Edgefield had moved to Chester for industrial jobs. In Chester, Carrie soon moved in with a man, a native of Virginia, who supported her and Willie. Essie never lived with her mother, but she did retain a close relationship with Willie (who would work thirty years for Scott Paper Company, then endure dialysis after kidney failure until finally dying of a heart attack).

How and why Carrie left Edgefield is unknown. What is known is that Strom was a circuit court judge with plans to run for governor. Did he suggest that Carrie move north to avoid any political pitfalls regarding their relationship that could occur in a statewide campaign? Did he finance her move or provide funds for transitional support? Or did she choose to leave on her own, to start a new life where she could be near family and friends, live in a more open society, and meet her daughter? These questions remain unanswered.

Although the vast majority of his cases involved petty crimes and minor civil disputes, Thurmond did preside over four death penalty cases. He would recall these publicly four decades later. As chairman of the Senate Judiciary Committee in his role as senator from South Carolina, he held hearings in 1981 to bring back the death penalty for a number of federal crimes. He cited his experience as a state trial judge.

"I am convinced the death penalty is a deterrent to crime," he said. "I had to sentence four people to the electric chair. I did not make the decision; the jury made it. It was my duty to pass sentence, because the jury had found them guilty and did not recommend mercy. But if I had been on the jury, I would have arrived at the same decision in all four of those cases."[13]

The first of these cases came to trial in February 1940. J. C. Hann, a twenty-seven-year-old white textile worker from Pickens County, had killed his ex-girlfriend, slitting her throat with a razor so deeply that he nearly decapitated her. At his trial he blamed the victim for his suffering from a case of gonorrhea, which interfered with his plans to marry another woman. He testified that the former girlfriend's taunts about his predicament enraged him. (Penicillin, which cures the disease, had not yet been discovered.) Although he begged for mercy on the witness stand, the jury found Hann guilty without recommendation of mercy.[14] The Associated Press reported that before Thurmond imposed the automatic death sentence, Hann made no statement when asked by the judge if he had anything to say, then sat down quietly beside his mother. The state supreme court rejected Hann's appeal. He was executed in Columbia on February 7, 1941.

The other three cases involved black men, each of whom was threatened by lynch mobs after their arrests. The first defendant, a Saluda County sharecropper named George Abney, was indicted on a Monday in July 1940 for the murder of his employer's wife. Thurmond that same day appointed Billy Coleman, a lawyer just out of law school, to defend him. The trial was held on Wednesday, and Thurmond sentenced Abney to death on Thursday.

Coleman had known George Abney since they were boys. Abney's father had sharecropped on land owned by Coleman's father. Coleman had played and hunted rabbits together with George's older brother; George had been almost like his little brother.

Coleman recalled four decades later that Abney was suffering from an advanced case of syphilis and that the white farmer for whom Abney worked as a sharecropper, instead of taking him to a physician, took him to a black root doctor who prepared a foul-smelling concoction of "scummy, green, slimy stuff like what you would get off the top of a stagnant pond." The farmer's wife brought a bottle of it to Abney's house and, assisted by Abney's wife, tried to hold him down and force him to swallow a dose.

Abney went berserk, grabbed his shotgun off the wall and killed both women. He then walked six miles into Saluda, where the local magistrate noticed "a darky on the street with a shotgun" and arrested him. Abney was mumbling incoherently. When the women's bodies were found, he was rushed from the local jail to the state penitentiary in Columbia to avoid a possible lynching.

Coleman recalled that he wanted the jury to understand his wretched client's half-deranged condition, that the actions of the employer's wife were a provocation and she had no business there. "But back in 1940, you couldn't say that," Coleman said. "It would have been dangerous to say anything like that. You're talking about white people and black people. I'd have been run out of town if I'd said that." He expressed remorse for being unable to save Abney's life but believed that even if he had succeeded, a lynching was likely.[15] "I did the best I could, but in those times it just wasn't good enough," he said.[16]

On September 6, 1940, Abney was electrocuted.[17]

The next case involved George Thomas, a black man in the coastal town of Georgetown who was accused of raping a young white woman just before Christmas of 1940. Thurmond said later that the victim was "a very fine lady who was a clerk at the ten cents store and was walking home after dark and this fellow ran out, pulled her into a vacant lot, and raped her."[18]

After Thomas's arrest, an angry mob of armed white men gathered at the jail and demanded the sheriff turn over the prisoner. The sheriff stalled for time until a National Guard unit was mobilized and mounted a machine gun on a second-story balcony. By then the mob had grown to 300. After the victim identified Thomas as the attacker, officers took him by back roads to the state penitentiary in Columbia for safekeeping. White vigilantes roamed the black neighborhoods of Georgetown for several nights, forcing residents to remain inside their houses, before the National Guard could restore order.

The state supreme court scheduled an extra term of court for late January and assigned Thurmond to try the case. A lawyer retained for Thomas by the National Association for the Advancement of Colored People (NAACP) requested a change of venue and reported his own life had been threatened, but prosecutors presented testimony from attorneys and others that Georgetown County would give, as one put it, "as fair a trial" as any man could find in the world. Thurmond turned down the request to move the trial elsewhere.[19] "There's tension in every case you try, no matter where you try it," Thurmond said when asked in 1981 why he had so ruled.[20]

Two months before the trial began, Justice Hugo Black of Alabama had written for a unanimous Supreme Court that racial discrimination in jury selection "not only violates our Constitution . . . but is at war with our basic concepts of a democratic society and a representative government."[21]

In Georgetown County, where almost two-thirds of the population was black, Thurmond began the jury selection by announcing to the jury panel: "We are about to enter upon the case of the State against George Thomas. George Thomas is a Negro, so it will be unnecessary to inquire as to [any kin] relationship to him, since all jurors at this term of court appear to be white." The jurors were also all male, because at that time South Carolina excluded women from jury service.[22]

Thomas maintained he was innocent, testifying that he had come home drunk several hours before the attack, eaten supper and fallen asleep, and stayed home until morning. His wife and son corroborated his story, and seven other witnesses supported his testimony as to his whereabouts during the day of the assault.

The victim, however, identified him as her attacker, and a policeman testified that he found burrs and grass in the front of Thomas's underwear after his arrest. The jury deliberated little more than an hour. It found Thomas guilty of rape, with no recommendation of mercy. Judge Thurmond imposed the automatic death sentence.

When the defendant appealed, contending he had been denied a fair trial because the judge refused to move the case out of Georgetown, Thurmond had to describe local conditions in a report to the state supreme court. He made no mention of the lynching attempt or the rioting following Thomas's arrest. He said Thomas had been sent to Columbia "due to the congested condition at the county jail."[23]

The *Georgetown Times* reported that the courtroom was packed throughout the trial and traffic was barred from passing by the courthouse. A special detachment of thirty-five state policemen stood guard. Governor Burnet Maybank sent a representative with authority to order out a National Guard contingent on duty a few blocks away.

Thurmond's report said that "only a few people attended court," that the presence of the national guardsmen had no connection, "directly or indirectly," with the trial, and that nothing out of the ordinary occurred. Based largely on the judge's assessment, the supreme court found his refusal to move the case justified. Thomas was electrocuted on February 20, 1942.[24]

The next man Thurmond sentenced to death was seventeen-year-old Sammie Osborne, a sharecropper in majority black Barnwell County, then a backwoods region of blackwater swamps, modest farms, and pine forests. As elsewhere in the state, blacks neither voted nor served on juries.

Osborne sharecropped for a white farmer named William Walker, a contentious fifty-eight-year-old man who wore a pistol strapped to his side when going into the fields. Young Osborne had already exhibited an independent attitude and a quick temper. When Walker forced him at gunpoint to work in the fields on Saturday despite Osborne's claim of an injured foot, the teenager responded later that day by placing a crude cardboard sign on a stick near the house where Walker lived alone. "Please come on," the sign read. "Bring sixteen at a time down here in the house. Please come on. I like bad man like you to come." The sign had Walker's name written on it and the word "Hell," twice, at the bottom.

Although Osborne would later testify he intended only to scare Walker and keep him away, the prosecution contended it was a challenge designed to lure the landowner into an ambush. Still, knowing enough to anticipate trouble, Osborne spent that Saturday night at the other tenant house on Walker's property, occupied by an eighteen-year-old friend. Osborne slept with his friend's loaded shotgun next to the bed.

Walker found him there the next morning. Osborne told police that Walker, armed with a pistol and stick, entered the house and started beating him while he was still in bed. Osborne said he grabbed the shotgun and shot the older man, whose body was found with the pistol and stick beside it.

After the shooting, Osborne walked barefoot to his father's house, six miles away. His father drove him fifty miles to the state penitentiary in Columbia. A posse was already out looking for him.

When Osborne returned to Barnwell County a month later to stand trial, local powers Sol Blatt and Edgar Brown had agreed at the request of Walker's relatives to serve as prosecutors. Osborne stuck to his story throughout—in interviews at the penitentiary, with the prosecutors, and at the trial—that he had killed Walker in self-defense.

As in Georgetown, Thurmond denied a motion for change of venue after a heated hearing before an overflow crowd. The prosecution relied on Osborne's taunting note to show that the killing had been a premeditated ambush, not self-defense. Of course, the note had challenged Walker to come to Osborne's house, not his friend's, but there was no question that an impudent young black man had killed the white man on whose land he lived.[25] Thurmond remembered Osborne as a "very vitriolic, stubborn and hard young man . . . who was looking to challenge somebody.[26]

The jury found him guilty, made no recommendation of mercy, and Thurmond sentenced him to die. The state supreme court, however, ruled on appeal that Thurmond had incorrectly explained the law of self-defense to the jury. At a new trial in the same courthouse before a different judge, another all-white jury took fifteen minutes to again find Osborne guilty, and he was again sentenced to death.

By the time of his electrocution, two years after Walker's death, Osborne spoke as the electrodes were placed on his head. "I'm ready to go," he said, "because I know that I am not guilty."[27]

Almost forty years later, eighty-six-year-old Sol Blatt told David Bruck, a lawyer in South Carolina specializing in death penalty cases, that he was afraid an innocent man had died. "The Osborne case always did worry me. It still worries me."[28]

Despite Thurmond's strong belief that the death penalty deters crime, the murder rate for South Carolina in the 1940s was two to four times that of the rest of the country, even though the state executed people at a far greater rate. During his four years as governor in the late 1940s, a total of twenty-one men were electrocuted, all of them black.[29] Thurmond later insisted, "I didn't know what color they were. I never did ask what color."[30]

As JUDGE, HOWEVER, Thurmond's most heroic moment came when he was called upon leaving church on a November Sunday in 1941 to intervene in an Edgefield County shoot-out that left two men dead, another dying, and a fourth wounded by gunfire.

CHAPTER 5

The Judge's Women

OF ALL THE WOMEN with whom Strom Thurmond was ever romantically linked, none was more deadly than Sue Logue. The trial judge believed the murder that sent her to the electric chair was "the most cold-blooded . . . in the history of the state."[1] It also generated enduring lore, legend, and myth about Thurmond.

Although Thurmond's long-standing reputation as a womanizer had become a lively source of gossip in Edgefield, the most salacious rumor was that for some years he had been carrying on with Sue Logue, who had zealously campaigned for him in his race for county school superintendent. She and the handsome young candidate had often been seen driving around the country distributing flyers, and they traveled together to meetings of the Baptist Young People's Union. Strom approved her hiring by the neighborhood school board, on which her husband served—a decision that enraged many in the local community. Married women at that time were generally excluded from teaching jobs, and another applicant had a college degree. Sue, who taught the primary grades, had never attended high school. Sue's reputation for sexual prowess was such that men told stories of her reputed vaginal muscular dexterity. The lore of Edgefield for the rest of Thurmond's life included the whispered story of the pair having once been found in flagrante delicto in the superintendent's office.

The dispute that escalated into violence began in 1940 with an argument over a calf kicked to death by a mule and ended with nine people dead. In the Edgefield County crossroads community known as Meeting Street, the relationship between the neighboring Logues and Timmermans resembled the fabled Hatfields and McCoys. Although the calf controversy led directly to the confrontation that culminated in Davis Timmerman shooting Wallace Logue, the suspicious Logues also believed Timmerman was involved in some way in Sue's bitterly fought loss of her teaching position for the 1939–1940 school year. During the summer of 1940, when Timmerman campaigned unsuccessfully for a seat on the county commission, Sue, Wallace, and George Logue all had threatened to kill him.[2]

The lingering quarrel between slightly built, forty-three-year-old Davis W. Timmerman and forty-nine-year-old J. Wallace Logue over compensation for Logue's calf turned into a raucous and violent confrontation at Timmerman's Store on September 30, 1940. It began when Logue, his thick-necked, barrel-chested neighbor, demanded more money than previously agreed to for the calf, and escalated when Logue grabbed an ax handle from a rack and swung at Timmerman. He stepped aside and deflected the blow with his arm so that it grazed his head, bloodying his lip. Timmerman grabbed a revolver from a drawer beneath his cash register. Two shots hit Logue, a bullet in the heart area of the chest and another through the top of his head.

By the time of Wallace Logue's funeral, his widow and his unmarried brother, George Logue, had begun plotting revenge. Sue lived with her mother-in-law and George in a farmhouse about a mile from Timmerman's Store. Joe Frank Logue, thirty-three and a city policeman in Spartanburg, attended his uncle Wallace's funeral on October 1, 1940, then visited his uncle George and aunt Sue. He was loyal to them because they had helped care for him after his father's death. Sue vowed that night, "I will kill Davis Timmerman or see that he is killed."

Timmerman was charged with murder, his trial scheduled at the Edgefield courthouse. Before the trial, Joe Frank made several trips from Spartanburg—a two-hour drive each way—to consult with his Edgefield County relatives. Each time, Sue and George Logue repeated their vow to kill Timmerman or have him killed. Their resolve only intensified after a jury acquitted Timmerman in March 1941 on a plea of self-defense. "Well, they told lots of lies today," Joe Frank heard Sue Logue say, "but it won't do them any good."

The Logues first took their plan to Fred Dorn, a devoted sharecropper. A few weeks later, a black hired hand of Timmerman's was killed by a single rifle shot. The killer was never identified, but suspicion centered on the Logues and Fred Dorn.[3]

In April, as the Logue-Timmerman feud was escalating, Essie Mae Washington visited Edgefield with her mother, Carrie, whom Essie had met only two years earlier when Carrie moved to Pennsylvania. She showed up one day in her sister's home in Coatesville. After the two sat and talked for a while, Carrie walked back to the kitchen. There she asked the thirteen-year-old girl washing dishes if she was Essie Mae. More than six decades later, Essie recalled, "I said, 'Yes, and who are you?' And she said, 'I'm your mother.'"

They saw little of each other after Carrie moved shortly after that to nearby Chester, but they rode the train together to Edgefield in 1941 to attend a family funeral. Carrie Butler also saw it as an opportunity for her daughter to meet her father.

Carrie's relationship with Strom remained sufficiently intimate that she walked over to his office as state circuit judge, his former law office near the courthouse square, to arrange the meeting. Carrie then returned to help Essie pick out her best dress, after telling her, "I'm taking you to meet your father." That's all she said.

Essie, halfway through her sixteenth year, recalled more than sixty years later that she had no idea who the person was, but was thrilled to know that she indeed had a father. She walked several blocks with Carrie to his office. Carrie let Strom know they had arrived, and he asked from his office that they sit for a few minutes in his waiting room. Her mother had talked to Essie about her birth father. "She had told me the story but never that he was white." When Strom walked out of the office and Essie saw him, she recalled, "I was totally surprised."

Strom showed no surprise, Essie later recalled, and greeted them in a welcoming manner. Her mother introduced Strom to Essie as her daughter; his first words—directed at Carrie—were, "That's a very pretty daughter you have."

After a moment of silence, she responded, "Well, she's yours, too." He laughed pleasantly and complimented Essie on her high cheekbones, a family trait among Thurmond women. Essie did offer a clear physical resemblance to the judge. She had nice features, light honey-brown skin, bright eyes, and a warm, engaging smile. Her impressive manners and grooming reflected the fine upbringing she had found in her young aunt's home and in the integrated schools of Coatesville. He began asking his daughter about herself. The shock of meeting her father soon dissipated. "Things became clear. I was very impressed with him. I was impressed with the way he carried himself, and very elated to finally meet him." The attention of the prominent white man made her glow.

"We talked for almost an hour, with him asking what my interests were," she continued. "He always gave advice about food and nutrition and exercise. He wanted to know if I planned to go to college and what I wanted to do with the rest of my life." He recommended that she consider South Carolina State, the historically black college in Orangeburg. "I thought it was a good idea because I wanted to go away from home, and I already had a lot of relatives there."

But, she recalled, "He never called my mother by her first name. He didn't verbally acknowledge that I was his child. He didn't ask when I was leaving and didn't invite me to come back. It was like an audience with an important man, a job interview, but not a reunion with a father."[4] Soon after the visit, Strom's sister Mary Tompkins, who lived in Edgefield, drove down to a house on Brooks Street where Essie was staying and brought "some funds to help us out." Essie left Edgefield soon afterward by train, understanding their secret should remain intact.[5] (Sixty-three years would pass before she again visited Edgefield.)

From that first meeting, however, Essie believed that her mother and father had an ongoing relationship and that "they cared for each other." If not for that family funeral, the father and daughter might never have met. "Had my mother's sister not died," Essie said, "I might never have come down."[6]

That July, the whole Edgefield Logue clan drove to Spartanburg to visit Joe Frank Logue and his schoolteacher wife. On that trip, Sue took Joe Frank aside: "Joe, I want you to get a man to kill Davis Timmerman. You can do it, and you have got to help us get the man."

Joe was reluctant. They talked for twenty minutes, and Sue pleaded, "We haven't had any luck in getting somebody to kill Davis Timmerman. We've raised you, fed you, taken care of you and all your brothers and your sister, and sent them off to school. You've got to help us. Get somebody to help us. We will pay the man $500."

Joe Frank later said he told her killing was wrong and wouldn't bring her husband back. But she said, "Davis Timmerman has told lots of lies on me, and I'm going to get rid of him one way or the other. Fred Dorn never could get close enough to him to kill him; every time he went down there in front of the house in those woods he would get up and go in the store, or a car would come along, or something, and you have just got to help us."

When this did not work, Joe Frank said she threatened him that if he didn't help them, "Something will happen to your mother and your wife." He believed the threats were real because he knew "what they would do, what they had done."[7]

Days after Sue's offer to pay, followed by the threat, Joe Frank approached Clarence Bagwell, an itinerant laborer, on a Spartanburg street. Joe Frank asked him, "Clarence, some parties want you to bump a fellow off; will you do it for them?" Bagwell said he would think about it. A week later they saw each other again, and Bagwell asked how much was in it for him.

"They'll pay $500," Joe Frank said.

"I'd kill everybody in Spartanburg County for $500, as broke as I am," Bagwell responded.

Joe Frank explained the details—Timmerman killing his uncle, the trial and acquittal, the widow and brother wanting Timmerman killed. He described the section of Edgefield County where Timmerman lived.

Joe Frank next saw Sue and George on August 2, while on vacation visiting his mother in Edgefield County. As soon as Joe Frank walked into their house, George asked, "Have you found the man?"

"Yes, I think I have."

Sue asked, "How much will he do it for?"

"For the $500."

Every day that week, Joe Frank saw Sue and George and heard them talk about having Davis Timmerman killed. They wanted it done immediately.

After Joe Frank returned to his job, George came to see him again in Spartanburg.

"The man hasn't backed down on you?" he asked. "We've been waiting on you. When will he be ready?"

"Right away," Joe Frank said. Soon afterward, Joe Frank brought Bagwell to Edgefield County for a scouting mission. Joe Frank showed him where his aunt Sue and uncle George lived, explaining that they were the ones who wanted him to kill Davis Timmerman. They then cased Timmerman's Store and his house, then returned via the Greenwood Highway to Spartanburg.

On September 15, a Monday, an anxious George again showed up in Spartanburg and approached Joe Frank on the street. "We want it done this week; we want him killed," he said. Sue was safely stashed in Albany, Georgia. "Tell the man not to worry; we'll have the money ready for him."

The next day, Joe Frank bought a pistol at a pawnshop. He saw Bagwell and told him everything was set. On Wednesday afternoon, they met at 2:30 P.M. at Spartan Billiard Parlor on North Church Street. Bagwell said he would get a taxi and meet Joe Frank on the outskirts of Spartanburg on the Woodruff Highway.

Joe Frank borrowed a black Ford two-door sedan from Pierce Motor Company in Spartanburg and picked up Bagwell a mile outside the city limits. Driving toward Edgefield, they each took swigs from Bagwell's bottle of Canadian Club whiskey.

As they approached Timmerman's Store, Joe Frank stopped the car, moved to the backseat, and lay down on the floor. Bagwell continued to the store, got out, and asked how far it was to Edgefield. Timmerman's wife was on duty. She gave Bagwell directions to Edgefield, but noticed him get back in the car and head in the opposite direction.

The men decided to wait a bit until Mrs. Timmerman would be inside the house cooking supper. They stopped in Saluda for cold soft drinks, then headed back toward Timmerman's Store. Pulling off onto a side road, they parked for thirty to forty-five minutes, and again pulled out the whiskey.

As the sun set, Joe Frank lay on the back floor under a raincoat, and Bagwell drove back to Timmerman's Store. He left the motor running and walked inside.

Timmerman was standing behind the counter when Bagwell walked in. Bagwell asked for a Coca-Cola. None were cold, and he then asked for a pack of cigarettes.

As Timmerman turned and reached up to get the cigarettes, Bagwell steadied his pistol on the counter. Bagwell didn't want to shoot him in the back and said, "Turn around." As Timmerman turned, Bagwell told him, "I come here to get you."

Joe Frank heard five shots fired in rapid succession. Bagwell got back in the car and drove toward Saluda as Joe Frank climbed into the front passenger seat. In the scramble, they barely avoided a wreck with a horse-drawn wagon, then continued toward Spartanburg, arriving around 9:30 P.M. Bagwell took the pistol with him as he went on his way. Joe Frank returned the borrowed car and went home to his wife. The next day, he returned to duty as a policeman.

Two nights later, Bagwell became anxious about getting paid, telling Joe Frank, "I want you to go down and get my money from your uncle and aunt." They agreed to meet Monday morning, and Bagwell warned, "Don't bring any cops."

On Sunday, Joe Frank went back to Edgefield with his wife and brother. When the visitors arrived, George took Joe Frank aside. "The man did a damn good job," he whispered. Back of the barn, George handed over $500 in five, ten, and twenty dollar bills, saying, "That's the best money I've ever paid in my life." Sue joined them on the front porch. With calm satisfaction, she said, "Well, Joe, the man did a good job." Off and on during the day, George and Sue cautioned Joe Frank not to discuss the killing, and especially not to tell his wife.

The next morning, Joe Frank picked up Bagwell at the Montgomery Sandwich Shop and handed him the money. They drove north, crossed the North Carolina line, and rode around Lake Lanier. At the edge of the lake, they used a hammer to batter the pistol into pieces that they threw into the water.

Joe Frank drove back to Spartanburg and went on duty. Saturday afternoon, George approached him on North Church Street, warning, "They're raising the devil down there. They've turned it over to the FBI. Tell the man he had better go to Chicago and get away from around here." A reward had been offered.

But Bagwell remained in Spartanburg and presumably drank good whiskey for a while. He had a fight with a girlfriend, who then went to the sheriff's office and told Chief Detective O. L. Brady that Bagwell had killed someone. She didn't remember where, but it was a place with a "field" in it. It could have been Fairfield or Chesterfield or Edgefield. A quick check narrowed it down.[8]

After Bagwell's arrest, Mrs. Timmerman identified him, and he confessed, implicating Joe Frank Logue. A Spartanburg policeman confirmed he substituted for Joe Frank the day Timmerman was murdered. The sheriff's office located a witness who saw Joe Frank and Bagwell together on the Asheville Highway after the murder.

Joe Frank was arrested on a November Sunday and transported to Newberry County, where Bagwell was being held. One of the lawmen present at the jail was a cousin of the Logues. He was Edgefield sheriff Wad Allen. Joe Frank at first denied knowledge of the murder, saying, "I know nothing about it and have no statement to make." He claimed that he had worked on the day that Timmerman was killed.

Sue and George visited Joe Frank the next day at the jail, before his transfer to the state penitentiary in Columbia. They pressed him to keep quiet, but he decided to tell the truth after he talked with his attorney, Edgefield state Senator B. E. Nicholson III—whose father had once practiced law with Strom's father. After getting Sheriff Allen to pledge to protect his wife and mother, on Saturday Joe Frank gave and signed a full confession, explaining the role Sue and George had played in the murder.

The next morning, all hell broke loose. Sheriff Allen went unarmed with his deputy, W. L. Clark, who was armed, to the Logue house to arrest his cousins. Allen assumed they would come out peacefully, but as they were entering the house, George Logue and Fred Dorn, the faithful sharecropper, ambushed them with gunfire. Bullets from Logue's pistol killed the sheriff and wounded Clark. The deputy feebly pulled his gun and wounded Logue in return. Although a blast from Dorn's shotgun sent him reeling, Clark was able to draw his pistol and fatally shoot Dorn. Clark crawled away from the bloody scene and flagged down a passing motorist who carried him to Edgefield. Rushed to a hospital in Augusta, he briefly rallied after treatment by two physicians—one of them Strom's brother, Allen George—but died two days later.

WORD SPREAD QUICKLY in Edgefield as church was letting out. Strom Thurmond heard about the horrible standoff at Sue Logue's house. Sue and George had barricaded themselves inside, warning approachers to beware. By early afternoon, several hundred people had converged around the property. Many were armed—including a few Logue family friends who went inside as reinforcements.

There are several versions of what happened next. One is that Judge Thurmond realized there was no other law enforcement in the county left to take charge, got in his car, and headed for the farmhouse.[9] Another is that because of his known relationship with Sue, he was urged to go in the belief he could talk some sense to her.

Charles Simons, later a law partner and confidant of Strom Thurmond before becoming a U.S. district judge, was present at the scene. Then in his mid-twenties, he knew Deputy Clark as a fellow townsman from Johnston. While others waited cautiously, Simons saw Thurmond walk onto the porch and heard someone inside yelling out, "Don't come in, Strom, or we'll have to kill you."

Simons saw Thurmond remove his suit jacket, unbutton his vest, and turn his pants pockets inside out to demonstrate he was unarmed. He asked to speak to George and Sue Logue. A voice called out that George had left the house and Sue was not feeling well. Inching forward, Thurmond insisted on speaking to her and was finally told to come to the back door. There he found himself staring at a shotgun held by a Logue family friend. Strom talked his way inside, where he learned that George was indeed gone and Dorn's body had been removed. Then, he met privately with Sue, agitated and afraid to surrender. He held her hand and persuaded her that it was best. "You better let me take you to the penitentiary," he told Sue, who soon consented to go with him.[10] Protectively walking by her side, he escorted her safely through the hostile crowd. Simons watched it all, and more than fifty-five years later he said, "Now that takes guts!"[11]

Contemporary accounts pay tribute to Thurmond as a hero determined to prevent further bloodshed, taking grave personal risk. Hortense Woodson would later write, "Judge Thurmond was accorded widespread commendation for his courageous act."[12]

THREE WEEKS AFTER Strom escorted Sue Logue from her family farmhouse, and eight months after his visit from Carrie Butler and Essie Mae, the Japanese bombed Pearl Harbor. Judge Thurmond responded by sending a telegram the next day directly to President Roosevelt volunteering for active duty. As a judge he was exempt from military duty, although a new state law would allow a leave of absence.

His political enemies later contended that he volunteered at least partly to get away from the sensational atmosphere of the Logue case, so lurid and notorious that it would be written up in the April 1942 issue of the pulp magazine *Official Detective Stories*. Whatever the timing with the Logue case, however, for Thurmond to volunteer immediately was consistent with his record as a man of action imbued with a certain Edgefield tradition. He was an intense patriot with a deep belief that a man must be willing to defend his conception of freedom. And though he had resigned from the Army Reserve in 1937, his correspondence shows he planned to go on active duty soon after the expected war was declared. His subsequent volunteering for the most dangerous type of combat duty clearly demonstrated his desire to be part of the fight.

By the time Thurmond got orders on April 8, 1942, to report to active duty as an army captain assigned to a New York base, Clarence Bagwell, Sue Logue, and George Logue had all been convicted in Lexington County for the murder of Davis Timmerman, without recommendation of mercy. Joe Frank Logue testified as a key state witness.[13]

Randall Johnson, a black man who supervised "colored help" at the Statehouse and often served as a driver and messenger, drove Sue on Christmas day from the women's penitentiary to the death house at the main penitentiary in Columbia (where she and the two men were housed in separated cells during final appeals). In the backseat with her on the drive to the death house, Johnson said many years later, was Thurmond, home on leave. They were "a-huggin' and a-kissin' the whole way," said Johnson, whom Thurmond later considered a trusted driver when he became governor.[14]

The state supreme court, the U.S. Supreme Court, and the governor all turned down appeals. Sue Logue, George Logue, and Clarence Bagwell all died in the electric chair on January 15, 1943, with Sue going first. She became the first woman ever electrocuted in South Carolina. With the first 2,300-volt surge at 6:18 A.M., her body jerked and lifted off the chair, and an oversized face mask fell off, "revealing contortions and bulging eyes" as smoke rose from burning flesh. She was pronounced dead three minutes and fourteen seconds later.[15]

In the fall of 1930, Sue had become pregnant, which could have led to a loss of her teaching job. Without mentioning it to fellow teachers, she called Dr. A. R. Nicholson, seeking an abortion. Abortions were then illegal in South Carolina, and he declined on both ethical and legal grounds. Soon afterward, Sue "botched" an abortion attempt, suffered an infection, and called Dr. Nicholson for help. He treated her and signed a death certificate that the female infant lived a few hours and died of premature birth. Burial followed in a family plot that today is beside hers in the East View Cemetery, with a one-word marker that says, "Infant."[16]

Joe Frank Logue was tried separately soon after the electrocutions. An Edgefield County jury found him guilty for his role in the murder, without recommendation of mercy. The state supreme court denied his appeal. On the date of his scheduled electrocution, his head was shaved. An hour before time was to run out, Governor Olin Johnston commuted his sentence to life imprisonment.

Joe Frank worked for years as a trusty for the State Law Enforcement Division (SLED), training and "running" the bloodhounds, achieving a lasting reputation for catching many runaway criminals and escaped convicts. Joe Frank's wife visited him on weekends at his cottage near the dog kennel, and he conducted Sunday morning religious services at a penal institution. He eventually received a parole but briefly continued to work for SLED until a severe auto accident. Returning to his wife's home at Cross Anchor in Spartanburg County, he preached at several churches and sold automobiles and Bibles.[17]

In whispered "graveyard" talk—the kind of stories not to be told to outsiders—the word around SLED was that Joe Frank said his aunt Sue was the only person ever seduced on the way to the electric chair.[18]

CHAPTER 6

"So Many Narrow Escapes"

THREE WEEKS AFTER HIS RAPID PROMOTION from major, Lieutenant Colonel James S. Thurmond climbed into glider No. 34 of the Eighty-second Airborne Division late in the afternoon of June 6, 1944—D day. The initial wave of American infantry forces had waded ashore on the beaches of Normandy twelve hours earlier under withering fire from German defenders. Thurmond was one of three officers from his civil affairs unit who volunteered to go in behind German lines. He welcomed the chance to see action. Years later, when asked why he volunteered for such a dangerous assignment, he said, "I gave up my judgeship position temporarily to come into the war and fight, not just sit behind a desk."[1] Until D day, he had been chair-borne rather than airborne, handling routine legal matters and once getting a bit of notice for defending a private trying to recover $310 worth of repossessed furniture.[2] There is evidence, however, that Thurmond prevailed in his determination to become part of the D day assault despite objections from higher officers. Almost six decades after the event, Columbia lawyer Alva Lumpkin, who served as an infantry officer at the time, said that General "Wild Bill" Weaver of Texas—whom Lumpkin knew—refused Thurmond's request to participate in the D day attack because he was not assigned to a combat unit. Lumpkin said that Thurmond finally found a glider officer who let him sit aboard a supply glider.[3]

At 6:52 P.M. (1852 military time), tow planes moved the glider contingent out from Greenham's Common, an airfield near Newbury. It took more than an hour for the 150 or so motorless aircraft, each towed by a C-47, to form as a column in the air over England. They crossed the English Channel, passing the coastline of France above Utah Beach at 2100 (9 P.M.). They approached the point where the planes would break the tow lines and return to base, the motorless craft gliding on, each with five paratroopers and a land vehicle ready to strike behind the German lines.

Minutes later, the column came under antiaircraft fire. The pilot of the lead plane delayed cutting his glider loose. Ground fire intensified, and the gliders were released over enemy territory deeper than planned. Glider No. 34 headed for an apple orchard near St. Mère-Eglise, seeking cover at dusk from the leafy trees. The flimsy craft bounced from one apple tree to another, falling apart as it came to a halt.

Thurmond suffered cuts on both hands and another jagged wound on a severely bruised left knee, yet he and the four paratroopers were able to walk out of the wreckage. He helped them release their jeep and then joined Major Bernard P. Deutsch, another civil affairs volunteer, whose glider had come down nearby. The men immediately came under enemy small-arms and mortar fire.

Deutsch and his crew set up a protected area for the wounded and injured. Thurmond borrowed a vehicle and surveyed other nearby gliders, assisting injured troops in getting to an assembly point. Thurmond and the men from his glider then set out to locate a Fourth Infantry Division command post to effect a rendezvous point with American ground troops.

He soon radioed Deutsch that a tentative rendezvous had been established at a crossroads near Blosville. With directions from friendly civilians, they proceeded under less intense enemy fire, carrying the wounded in vehicles that were transported in the gliders. They remained surrounded by German forces, with small-arms fire continuing from all directions and shells falling in the vicinity, while they dug foxholes in ditches and under hedges and trees. They set up patrols to defend the position throughout the night.

Thurmond received medical treatment at an aid station, and a doctor suggested that he rest. The Edgefield man said he didn't want to rest, telling the medics just to put antiseptic on the wounds and bandage them.

The next morning, they realized the enemy still surrounded them. At one point when Thurmond was walking beside him, an Eighty-second Airborne flight surgeon's head was blown off by a German shell. After establishing radio contact with division headquarters, which was also surrounded, Thurmond's detachment moved from one place to another throughout the day, constantly under fire and seeking the protection of ditches, hedges, and foxholes.

They moved into six different positions. At about 7 P.M., it was determined that the detachment, loaded into six vehicles, could be saved only by somehow getting through to division headquarters. From there, an infantry patrol was dispatched to lead the detachment by secondary roads. Three times within a quarter of a mile, intense machine-gun fire from both sides of the road forced the column to stop. The men took cover in the ditches and returned fire.

Whenever enemy fire lessened or stopped, the column dashed on, reaching division headquarters shortly after 9 P.M. Although the enemy remained on all sides and snipers were abundant, friendly troops surrounded the division headquarters. The next morning, after the Eighty-second Airborne took control of the town of Cretteville, Thurmond and another officer entered the town, conferred with the mayor, and saw to the feeding and care of refugees. They held a ceremony to raise France's tricolor flag.

The remainder of Thurmond's civil affairs unit landed in France the next day. Their job was to assist in establishing local government to organize the region behind the Allied forces and to maintain law and order, but not to set up a military government in France.

On June 26, Thurmond and another officer slipped into the port city of Cherbourg to make arrangements for their civil affairs unit to move in. While riding in a jeep with a driver, they came upon and captured four German paratroopers.[4] Guarding the Germans with their own pistols, Thurmond had two of the prisoners lie across the hood and the other two on the backseat.[5]

In a letter a couple of months later to a South Carolina friend, who released it to the Greenwood *Index-Journal,* Thurmond wrote there were "so many narrow escapes that it is a miracle to me that any of us who landed by glider are still alive."[6]

Thurmond's heroic adventures abroad had attracted a following back home in South Carolina, where newspapers carried occasional items about his accomplishments. On November 28, 1944, he was awarded the Bronze Star "for heroic achievement in action" June 6–14. A two-column photo of Thurmond, wearing an infantryman's metal helmet and standing at attention while receiving the award, ran a month later on the front page of *The State.*[7] It was the best free advertising a gubernatorial hopeful could imagine.

Thurmond's unit accompanied combat troops, and he participated in the Battle of the Bulge. "It was rough," he remembered. "That's the coldest I have ever been in my life." He saw little additional direct combat action in Europe. On one occasion as he was walking down a street, he decided to cross to the other side. Moments later, a bomb fell where he had been walking.[8]

In April 1945, near the war's end in Europe, Thurmond's unit, having crossed France and Belgium, entered Germany. He was near Leipzig when the first American troops entered the nearby Buchenwald concentration camp. Thurmond arrived shortly thereafter, totally unprepared for and astounded by what he witnessed.

More than a half century later, he recalled:

Men were stacked up like cordwood, ten or twelve feet high. You couldn't tell whether they were living or dead. We thought nearly all were dead, but we found some still alive. So we had the medics come in and examine them . . . and they received treatment. And some were saved. Most of them died.

I found the Germans were killing these people in three different ways. One was to starve them to death. The only food they received was a bowl of thin pea soup once a day. . . . Most of the people I saw . . . were killed that way.

Another way that some of them were killed, agents of the Germans in charge suggested to them that they go down and cross the fence, that they might get out. And when they did, they'd shoot them and kill them.

The third was a booth like a telephone booth, and they would have those people walk in the front of the booth. And there was a door in the rear of the booth where a big SS guard had a mallet. And when they came and sat down in that booth, they'd crush their head. I saw the mallet that was used and saw the blood splattered all over it.

I had never seen such inhuman acts in my life. I couldn't dream of men treating men in such a manner. It was awful. And I was told that the wife of the commander there was fond of tattooing, and if anyone had tattooing on them, they'd take the tattooing off and enough skin with it, and she would make lamp shades out of it. I did not see those, but everything I saw was distressing. And when I look back upon it, I cannot realize now how cruel anyone could be in treating other people.[9]

Although Thurmond had heard of death camps where people were gassed and had heard of the Buchenwald camp, he wasn't aware of what went on there. "I didn't dream of such terrible circumstances taking place," he said.

When asked the effect his firsthand experience with the Jewish Holocaust had on his political philosophy, he said, "It's very difficult to say what effect it has on anybody, but it's an experience you would never forget."[10]

THURMOND SERVED A MONTH in the Philippines as the war against Japan was winding down, but the medals he received came from his role in Europe. They included the Purple Heart, French Croix de Guerre, Belgian Order of the Crown, five battle stars, and a dozen other decorations in addition to the Bronze Star. The publicity kept his name alive politically. He had been reelected in absentia by the South Carolina legislature to another term as judge.

Thurmond demonstrated on the battlefield the characteristics that would mark his political career. A man of bold action rather than reflection, he made swift and decisive tactical moves based on instinct and intuition. He never looked back, and he fought to win.

He later told a story of Secretary of State James F. Byrnes meeting General George Patton in Europe and commending him on his legendary record of leading Allied forces there. When Byrnes said he must have done a fine job of planning, Patton replied, "No, I didn't plan it. [Omar] Bradley planned it. I executed it."

Byrnes said that Patton added, "I couldn't have planned it. I don't have that kind of brain. Bradley couldn't have executed it, either."

Thurmond admired General Bradley, but he called General Patton "probably the best we had because he was so aggressive."[11]

When he was discharged on October 19, 1945, at Fort Bragg, North Carolina, Thurmond seemed to have in mind the message his friend Bob Figg sent in a letter after reading about Strom's glider landing. Figg wrote, "You better get back to South Carolina and run for governor when the war is over!"[12] Thurmond got a ride from Fort Bragg to South Carolina with Jules Brunson, later a physician in Camden, who remembered, "He told me then that he was going to run for governor, and we stopped at two or three places along the way for him to shake hands."[13]

A month later in Abbeville, Thurmond held his first term of court. Before leaving town, he attended a rally honoring veterans. Pork barbecue, the traditional cuisine of South Carolina politics, was served.

CHAPTER 7

Progressive Outlook, Progressive Program, Progressive Leadership

THE SOUTH CAROLINA that Strom Thurmond returned to after the war looked the same. Segregation remained in place, but beneath the surface a nucleus of black leadership was developing. It would use the federal courts to unlock the doors of political participation closed a half century earlier. Soon enough, the evolving politics of race would become a central element of Thurmond's career for the remainder of the century.

In the South Carolina legislature, Sol Blatt and Edgar Brown had consolidated their power, with Blatt entrenched as Speaker of the House and Brown as powerful chairman of the Senate Finance Committee. As chieftains of the so-called Barnwell Ring, Brown and Blatt took care of Barnwell County, the state, and themselves. They also served respectively as trustees of Clemson College and the University of South Carolina, where as patrons they were first among equals.

Barnwell County had a second representative, Winchester Smith, and Blatt got him named chairman of the House Ways and Means Committee, from which the all-important state appropriations bill originates. Smith's brother, a tombstone rear admiral whose qualifications for the job were reflected by his campus nickname, "Snuffy," for hillbilly comic strip character "Snuffy Smith," thereby became president of the University of South Carolina.

On a cold January evening in 1946, Blatt was at home with family and a handful of close friends welcoming Sol Jr. back from the war. As the dishes were cleared amid the sounds of laughter and reminiscing, Mr. Speaker rose to escort his guests to the living room. A knock on the door interrupted the conversation.

As all the invited guests watched, an annoyed Blatt walked to the door wondering who might be calling. He opened it and there stood a smiling Strom Thurmond, newly returned to his circuit judgeship. "We invited him in, asked him to sit with us and have some of the food there or have some dessert," Blatt later recalled. "He declined and sat there for a moment or two in the presence of all those people and said that he was going to run for governor and wanted my support. I told him how sorry I was, but I could not support him. And that made him mad, and then he told me, 'I'm going to Edgefield. I'm going home.' Well, I thought he'd gone and that was the end of it."

As Blatt strolled to his law office the next morning, the county sheriff alerted him that Thurmond was still in town and had gone to call on Edgar Brown. "Well, Senator Brown told him the same thing. He wouldn't support him," Blatt remembered. "So he exploded and condemned us very severely and made the statement that he didn't want our votes. And I remember I made the statement, 'Who ever heard of a man coming to a home and visiting with people whose votes he didn't want?'"[1]

Blatt and Brown had already pledged their support to Governor Ransome Williams, an uninspiring man elevated from lieutenant governor to fill an unexpired term. Olin Johnston, like Burnet Maybank before him, had left the governor's office at midterm to run successfully for the Senate, Johnston defeating six-term octogenarian Ellison D. "Cotton Ed" Smith.

Thurmond also called newspaperman Harry Ashmore, then the new editorial page editor of the *Charlotte News*. Ashmore had covered the South Carolina legislature before the war, and Thurmond asked him to take a leave of absence and manage his campaign. "I politely said I didn't think I was ready to abandon the career I had started," Ashmore recalled. "I didn't say what I really thought, that he would really have been a bad choice for governor because of his sort of rigid, doctrinaire approach to any question that came up. And I thought politicians had to do some trading."[2]

IN EARLY APRIL 1946, little more than a month before announcing his campaign for governor, Thurmond attended a judicial conference in Philadelphia and sent word in advance to Essie to meet him at his hotel. Thurmond and Essie had corresponded during World War II but had not seen each other since their meeting five years earlier in Edgefield. Strom,

Essie, and Mary Washington, the aunt who raised her—this was the only time she would ever meet Strom—gathered in the hotel lobby.

By the 1940s, Coatesville's black children went to a segregated school in their early years, but the small percentage who made it to high school became part of the integrated Coatesville High School. Essie was among a small group of ambitious blacks who became part of the graduating class of 1945. She excelled in school, took part in numerous extracurricular activities, and fancied a career in nursing. Her goal, however, meant that she would have to leave the comforts of small-town family life and move to New York City. In the days of segregated hospitals, Harlem Hospital was one of the only places a black woman could get a nursing education. (After she worked during high school as a hospital volunteer in Coatesville, her supervisor recommended her for nurse's training there, but blacks were not accepted.)

Meanwhile, the call for civil rights rumbled at low volume across the American landscape. The NAACP, which had mobilized around the Coatesville Zach Walker lynching in the early twentieth century, found itself experiencing rapid growth in the early 1940s as it pushed for a federal anti-lynching law and elimination of the all-white primaries of the South and continued developing the strategy to push for equal education. Luminaries like First Lady Eleanor Roosevelt helped the cause with moving speeches about the need to end racial discrimination. "The minute we deny any rights of this kind to any citizen, we are preparing the way for the denial of those rights to someone else," she told the American Civil Liberties Union (ACLU) in a Chicago speech in 1940. A year later, as part of this building crescendo, a new South Coatesville branch of the NAACP began holding rallies at Coatesville's Tabernacle Baptist Church.

As Essie Mae Washington grew to adulthood, the black community of Coatesville knew that this polished young lady came from prominent Southern stock. An elderly neighbor of the Washingtons on Coatesville's Newlinville Road said she was told point-blank by Mary Washington that Strom Thurmond was the girl's father, sharing her displeasure that the girl had come to Pennsylvania with nothing. Although Thurmond had yet to burst onto the national political stage, many of the Washingtons' neighbors, from Edgefield, were familiar with the Thurmond family name. Some learned from Essie's aunt Mary that Strom Thurmond was the girl's father and had provided almost no support. By rearing the girl from infancy to adulthood in a more socially progressive culture, however, Mary and John Washington had vastly improved Essie's educational opportunities and unleashed her from the social stigma of being fatherless, the child of an unwed black woman in the Jim Crow South.

Strom already knew from Essie's letters that after her graduation from high school, she had entered the rigorous nursing program at Harlem Hospital in September 1945. But she may not have communicated in her letters that she hated living in the noisy, crowded city. Essie longed for quieter surroundings. She was, by her own self-description, a small-town girl. Furthermore, she had already decided that a nursing career wasn't for her, withdrew from the training, and set her sights on college. By the time she met her father in Philadelphia, she was enrolled in two education courses at New York University. She supported herself doing stock work for an exclusive dress store in Manhattan.

In Philadelphia, he renewed his suggestion made five years earlier that she explore admission to South Carolina State Colored Agricultural and Mechanical College, the all-black state-supported school in the sleepy town of Orangeburg, South Carolina. He also gave her some money.

On April 29, Essie wrote the judge from her apartment on West 111th Street. "Judge Thurmond," she began. "I wish to let you know that I received the telegram. Thank you very much. I'm getting along as well as ever. School is fine; finals will be this month. I haven't heard anymore from A&M about my acceptance as yet. I hope to as soon as possible. I will let you know when I do. Until then I am, Sincerely yours, Essie Mae."[3]

At some point, in his characteristic handwriting, Thurmond scribbled her last name—"Washington"—on the bottom of the letter and filed it away in his official papers.

AT A PRESS CONFERENCE, Thurmond announced his candidacy on May 15, 1946, calling for "a progressive outlook, a progressive program and a progressive leadership." He proposed expanding and modernizing public schools and colleges, with better-paid teachers. He linked educational opportunity to economic expansion. He advocated better pay for working people and expanded programs "of public health, public welfare, and assistance to the aged, the blind, and our dependent children." Thurmond had returned from the war with his New Deal liberalism intact.

He entered an eleven-man race, a returning war hero with a solid record of public service. At the opening stump meeting on June 11 at Winnsboro, Thurmond heard another candidate charge that the state was being run by a "ring." Detecting the scent of its emotional appeal, Strom dropped in a line that South Carolina government "is under domination of a small ring of cunning, conniving men," a thinly veiled reference to Brown and Blatt.

By the time the corps of candidates reached Barnwell on June 25, Thurmond had already begun explicitly attacking the "Barnwell Ring," declaring on June 19 at Conway that he "would gladly accept the challenge of opposition from that crowd," and adding, "it will be interesting to see whom they lavish their money on in this race."

In Barnwell, Winchester Smith gave $50 to gubernatorial candidate Roger Scott, a rural populist with a gift for barnyard invective, whom a reporter once described as looking "like a man who stuck his finger in a light socket." Scott, who would precede Thurmond as speaker, was told to raise hell with the Barnwell Ring, to take the edge off of Thurmond. When Smith congratulated him afterward, Scott offered to do an even better job at the next stop in Allendale.[4]

Presiding over the stump meeting, Edgar Brown had asked the crowd to give each speaker "a good hand, regardless of what he might say." Thurmond got booed, as expected, when he attacked "the ring and its henchmen" for blocking "reforms the people want." But in spite of the Smith and Brown attempts to upstage him, Thurmond continued to dominate media coverage, emerging as the courageous crusader against the "Barnwell Ring." He then lured Blatt and Brown into a response.

Fellow candidate Marcus Stone, a lumberman from Florence who had attempted to defend the Barnwell leaders, accepted a challenge from Thurmond to debate the "ring" issue. Stone then withdrew at the request of Blatt and Brown, but he released letters from them asserting with pointed detail that Thurmond had sought their support before formally entering the race.

Thurmond called the letters "a lot of baloney," denied he had sought their support, and said they didn't want a debate "because they are scared of what I'll say." The voters would have to decide whom to believe, a war hero and former judge—he had left his judgeship to campaign—or two men known only as powerful politicians.

Thurmond led the first primary—including 92 percent of the vote in

Edgefield County, where he had campaigned with the same vigor and thoroughness as in his first race for county superintendent. The one outspokenly white-supremacist candidate, state Senator John Long of Union, received only 6 percent of the vote. Thurmond made one bare mention of race, saying, "I will never sign a bill to mix the races." A brief Associated Press item on the first primary took note that "ten Negroes voted in Spartanburg," despite Democratic Party rules limiting balloting to whites, and a smaller number attempting to vote in Columbia had been turned down. The story added that "South Carolina, alone of the southern states, bars Negroes altogether from voting in a primary."[5]

In the runoff, Thurmond attacked his opponent, Florence physician James McLeod, for being insufficiently supportive of President Roosevelt at the 1944 Democratic National Convention. Thurmond won the runoff with almost 56 percent of the vote—139,821 to 106,749—to become the first Edgefield governor since Pitchfork Ben Tillman.

In a profile of the governor-elect, the Associated Press reported: "His energy and determination amazes his associates. His campaign this summer was so arduous . . . he had to exchange drivers each week—so fast was the pace and hard did he strive to become governor."[6]

When a distant relative of Thurmond's was asked during the campaign what job he would get, he replied, "If Strom's elected governor, I wouldn't work for the state of South Carolina for anything on earth. He would work me to death. He believes in working all the time, and he can't understand how other people don't have the same ideas."[7]

The national AP story added that Thurmond "makes up with earnestness what he lacks in finesse. He is not a finished public speaker and appeared ill at ease in many of his campaign appearances."[8]

Three months after the runoff, during the week of his forty-fourth birthday, Thurmond attended the Southern Governors Conference in Miami as a guest. He promptly set off a lively discussion after he asked the group to endorse American foreign policy as directed by Secretary of State Byrnes. Either because he was not yet a governor or because they chose not to delve into foreign policy issues, the Resolutions Committee rejected Thurmond's suggestion.

With a raw January wind blowing, Thurmond, standing beside his mother, took his oath of office in front of the South Carolina Statehouse, swearing on the Bible he had carried with him throughout World War II.

More than a half century later, his inaugural address is remarkable as a progressive and realistic assessment of the state's needs, a 15,000-word document of reform that set the direction of South Carolina government for much of the next four decades.

Thurmond read a condensed version. He was not a polished orator, often coming across as uncomfortable in his campaign speeches, but the text of the address, like many of his best speeches, reflected the craftsmanship, knowledge of government, and first-rate mind of its draftsman, his friend Robert Figg. Later named dean of the University of South Carolina Law School after arguing the state's losing case for maintaining segregated schools (the South Carolina case of *Briggs v. Elliott* in *Brown v. Board of Education*) before the U.S. Supreme Court, Figg advised a succession of governors.

In his inaugural speech, Thurmond declared, "We are on the threshold of a new era," and he called for ending the poll tax, a tariff on voting that had effectively kept blacks from participating, and developing a system of permanent voter registration. He advocated a state minimum wage (one of his few proposals never adopted), stronger child labor laws, and "working conditions which make for health, decency and the welfare of our workers," including temperature controls and cafeterias in textile mills.

He called for reorganizing and consolidating the unwieldy system of overlapping state agencies; a commission of top lawyers to revise the outdated state constitution and submit changes as constitutional amendments on which the public would vote; a system of county governments; and enforcing the existing state constitutional ban on dual office-holding.* He advocated industrial development; protection of natural resources from polluters; control by laymen of the State Board of Health; free treatment for sufferers of venereal diseases; and mandatory premarital blood tests.

He sought $5 million in increased liquor license fees and taxes; proposed a ban on all liquor advertising; and added that if the legislature had a better plan, "I will sign it."

---

*Thurmond won the fight to end dual office-holding. One way it worked in practice was that Blatt gave up his seat on the USC Board of Trustees, but not his voice. He was replaced by Sol Blatt Jr. Thomas Clemson's will provided for a system in which the legislature named part of the board, which then elected a self-perpetuating majority of "life trustees," one of whom happened to be Edgar Brown.

He proposed an eight-point educational program that included free text-books and expanded vocational education, and recommended "federal aid for education, with the proviso that states maintain control of the schools."

In calling for "more attention given to Negro education," Thurmond asserted, "The low standing of South Carolina, educationally, is due primarily to the high rate of illiteracy and lack of education among our Negroes. If we provide better educational facilities for them, not only will much be accomplished in human values, but we shall raise our per capita income as well as the educational standing of the state."[9]

Blatt stepped aside as Speaker, and Thurmond ignored tradition—actively supporting Bruce Littlejohn of Spartanburg in a spirited campaign against Tom Pope of Newberry. Littlejohn won.

LESS THAN A MONTH AFTER TAKING OFFICE, Thurmond got a call from the city editor of the *Greenville Piedmont*, telling him that a black man accused of murdering a white taxi driver had been taken from jail by a mob of white men and killed. Although there had been no lynching in South Carolina for fourteen years, Thurmond called for vigorous prosecution that resulted in state and local police working with FBI agents. (The state was still a focus of national attention for its handling of a case the previous year in which a police chief had beaten and blinded a black veteran just returned from World War II.)

Willie Earle had been arrested after the fatal stabbing and robbery of Greenville taxi driver Thomas W. Brown. A deputy sheriff followed clearly outlined shoe tracks from the abandoned taxi to the dying Brown. He arrested Earle at his mother's home in the Pickens County town of Liberty, twelve miles from Greenville.

The deputy discovered a recently washed Boy Scout knife with blood-stains in Earle's pocket, and bloodstains on a freshly washed jacket. The twenty-four-year-old "fit . . . perfectly" the description of the assailant that Brown gave during a brief period of consciousness before dying at a hospital. Earle's mother said her son had come home drunk and told her that he had taken the bus.

After Earle's arrest on a Sunday night, eight taxis and another automobile assembled at about 4:30 A.M. on a bridge near Greenville, then took off for the Pickens County jail, the adjacent county where Earle was being held. More than thirty men woke the jailer, one of them pointing a shotgun at him, and demanded he turn over the Negro. Earle was forced into a car and driven to the countryside, where his battered corpse was later found on a nearby road.

The ensuing police-FBI investigation resulted in the arrest of thirty-one white men, twenty-six of whom made confessions, some naming the individuals who slashed and tortured Willie Earle and then killed him with a shotgun as he lay on the ground.

One confessor told of arriving at the scene after Earle had been driven down a country road. "I could hear licks like they were pounding on him with the butt end of a gun. I also heard the Negro say, 'Lord, you done killed me.'" The confessor said that one man yelled out, "Don't beat that nigger with that gun and get blood on it." Another man then pointed at Earle with the shotgun and pulled the trigger.

As with the lynching itself, Thurmond's response to the arrests was vigorous and decisive. In addition to Greenville solicitor Robert Ashmore (editor Harry Ashmore's cousin and later a congressman), Thurmond brought in Solicitor Sam Watt of Spartanburg, a prosecutor who had convicted 471 of 473 persons brought to trial the previous year. "We in South Carolina want the world to know we will tolerate no mob violence," the governor said.[10]

Thurmond got many letters of support. James McBride Dabbs, South Carolina's poet-philosopher who would serve as president of the biracial Southern Regional Council, wrote, "We who look to the future are proud to follow your leadership."[11]

With its thirty-one white defendants, this was the biggest lynching trial in the nation's history. Presiding was state circuit judge J. Robert Martin, at thirty-eight already known for his no-nonsense toughness. None of the defendants testified before the all-white male jury composed of textile workers, a farmer, a mechanic, a salesman, and a divinity student. In charging the jury, Judge Martin told them "not to allow any so-called racial issues to enter" into their deliberations, an unequivocal instruction to work toward a verdict that would not just be justice as usual. Because of clearly insufficient evidence, he had already dismissed charges against several defendants. After seven hours of deliberation, the jury acquitted the remaining twenty-eight.

Obviously displeased, Martin turned his back to the jurors and dismissed them without thanks. Then he slammed his Panama hat on his head and stormed out of the courtroom.

The *Atlanta Journal* termed the outcome "a ghastly farce" but acknowledged that mob murders of four blacks the previous year in Georgia's Walton County "were never brought to even the semblance of a court trial."[12] The *New York Times* said in an editorial that the outcome "hurts the United States" as the story would be told abroad. Yet Thurmond garnered praise. The editorial pointed out that Thurmond and other officials "did their utmost to bring Earle's slayers to justice" and that they received support from local press and ministers "and a strong body of public opinion throughout South Carolina." The editorial concluded, "There has been a victory for law, even though Willie Earle's slayers will not be punished for what they did. A precedent has been set. Members of lynching mobs may now know that they do not bask in universal approval, even in their own disgraced communities, and they may begin to fear that some day, on sufficient evidence and with sufficient courage, a Southern lynching case jury will convict."[13]

In response to a letter applauding his handling of the matter, Thurmond asserted, "I think great good was accomplished by having the accused arrested and tried even though the jury acquitted them. I believe that position will assist in the future in preventing lynchings."[14] There have been no lynchings in South Carolina since the murder of Willie Earle in 1947.

ROUGHLY HALF of Thurmond's ambitious program passed the legislature, but insiders were giving far more attention to a pair of federal lawsuits, one aimed at desegregating the University of South Carolina Law School and the other at ending the all-white Democratic primary.

In the 1944 Texas case *Smith v. Allwright*, decided while Thurmond was preparing for D day, the U.S. Supreme Court ruled the white primary unconstitutional. South Carolina responded by repealing all its election laws, a legal ruse to convert the Democratic primary into a "voluntary association" over which the state ostensibly had no control.

Meanwhile, the state's few scattered local chapters of the National Association for the Advancement of Colored People had organized as a statewide "conference of branches." The NAACP was quickly developing strong leadership and emerging as the state's dominant civil rights organization. The national organization sent in its first-rate legal team, headed by Thurgood Marshall.

In South Carolina, Marshall found a sympathetic federal judge in eighth-generation Charlestonian J. Waties Waring. A repentant former white supremacist,* Waring began following the Supreme Court's new direction with gusto. (Early in his term, Thurmond found his mailbox crowded with angry letters from constituents about the judge, his "Yankee" wife, and their march toward destruction of the Southern way of life. Thurmond responded to the rising political storm by displaying rancor toward the judge.)

On July 12, 1947, from his seat on the bench in Charleston's courthouse, Waring issued rulings in both the law school and the voting rights cases. In response to the NAACP's legal action, which sought admission of blacks to the USC Law School, Waring accepted the state's plans to open a law school in September at all-black South Carolina State College.

In the voting case brought by George Elmore, a Columbia taxi driver-businessman turned away from the polls in 1946, Marshall argued that the repeal of state primary laws made "no difference" because the Democratic Party was still "exercising a governmental function." Waring agreed, naming other Deep South states that allowed blacks to vote in primaries.

"I cannot see where the skies will fall if South Carolina is put in the same class with these and other states," he declared. "It is time for South Carolina to rejoin the Union. . . . All citizens of this State and Country are entitled to cast a free and untrammeled ballot in our elections."[15]

---

*Waring's social equals in Charleston blamed his conversion on civil rights to his marrying a liberal Yankee after divorcing his first wife. His biographer, Tinsley Yarbrough, attributes Judge Waring's developing sense of racial injustice to his experience in the Isaac Woodward case. Woodward, a World War II veteran returning to his wife in Winnsboro in February 1946 after his discharge as an army sergeant, was arrested in Batesburg after exchanging harsh words with a bus driver in a dispute arising from Woodward's need to use a restroom. He was knocked unconscious with a billy club and then punched in the eyes, leaving him permanently blinded. After charges brought by U.S. Attorney General Tom Clark, Waring presided over the trial of the police chief who administered the beating. An all-white jury deliberated only thirty minutes before finding him innocent. The Woodward case played a key role in President Truman's decision to appoint his President's Committee on Civil Rights (Kari Frederickson, "'The Slowest State' and 'Most Backward Community': Racial Violence in South Carolina and Federal Civil-Rights Legislation, 1946–1948," *South Carolina Historical Magazine*, April 1997, p. 184).

Thurmond, in Salt Lake City to deliver a National Governors Conference speech on military preparedness, avoided comment on the voting rights case. He met the next month, however, with a group of black leaders—including state NAACP president James M. Hinton and political activist John McCray, editor of the *Lighthouse and Informer* in Columbia—to talk about improving conditions at the John G. Richards Industrial Training School for Negro Boys, an institution for juvenile offenders. Thurmond said afterward their proposals had merit.

In September, he outraged realtors in the state by declaring, in a speech officially welcoming delegates to a regional convention, his support for rent controls and denouncing "profiteering real estate owners" who withdrew rental units and sold them "ridiculously and exorbitantly overpriced." The president of the National Association of Real Estate Boards retorted that Thurmond's speech sounded like a release from "the international office of the Communist party." Thurmond replied, "I said what I meant. I meant what I said."[16]

OCTOBER 1947 BECAME A TIME of serious transition for Thurmond, politically and personally. On October 2, 1947, in Louisville, Kentucky, he participated in a panel discussion and delivered a short radio speech entitled "Let's Look at '48." What he said reflected a philosophical peak, and a commitment to the Democratic Party, from which he would rapidly descend. He asserted that the "ineptitude of the Republican leadership in the present Congress" provided a timely warning to the American people "not to trust their economic future to the tender mercies of the Republican Party."

Thurmond concluded by declaring, "We who believe in a liberal political philosophy, in the importance of human rights as well as property rights, in the preservation and strengthening of the economic and social gains brought about by the efforts of the Democratic Party . . . will vote for the election of Harry Truman and the restoration of Congress to the control of the Democratic Party, and I believe we will win."[17]

Later in the month, the President's Committee on Civil Rights issued a report, "To Secure These Rights." It chronicled the nation's tragic history of civil rights, and called for federal laws against lynching, against discrimination in employment and voting, for legislation to end the poll tax, and for strengthening the civil rights division in the Justice Department to enforce such legislation. In essence, it proposed undoing the Compromise of 1877, in which the federal government had tacitly ceded to the states control of issues involving race. Several months would pass before President Truman responded. In reaction, Strom Thurmond would perform a backward somersault with a reverse twist.

But matters of the heart would take immediate priority.

CHAPTER 8

"My Darling Jean"

Strom first met Jean Crouch in the fall of 1941 when her father, Horace, took her high school class on a field trip to observe a session of Judge Thurmond presiding at the Barnwell County courthouse. An Edgefield native, her father was a cog in Barnwell's Democratic political organization as elected county superintendent of education and well aware of Thurmond's ambitions. He took his daughter up to meet the judge. Strom told Jean that she had "pretty eyes." She never forgot this encounter. She was fifteen.

A blue-eyed tomboy with long, dark hair and a magnetic smile, captain of the Williston-Elko girls basketball team, she returned to high school to chalk up every imaginable accolade. She would be class valedictorian and winner of the Solomon Blatt Medal for Expression before heading off to Winthrop College. Strom next saw her there briefly in the spring of 1946, when he attended a college function. She was the most popular girl in class and one of the prettiest.

Late in 1946, as governor-elect, Thurmond visited Horace Crouch at his home in the village of Elko to talk about state educational problems. On the wall he spotted a portrait of the strikingly attractive young woman with silken hair and deep-set eyes whom he had seen on campus a few months earlier. He coolly asked who it was. "That's my daughter, Jean, whom you met some years back at court in Barnwell," Crouch said. "She's a senior at Winthrop."

Thurmond learned she was studying commerce (a major designed to train young women in secretarial skills, for their own career or to teach to high school students) and wondered aloud if she might like to work in the governor's office. He was told she would soon be visiting Columbia for a South Carolina Education Association meeting. "Maybe you can talk with her then," her father said.

Thurmond was as persistent and creative in his pursuit of women as he was in his politics. He made it a point to address the coordinating council at the SECA event. As Winthrop's senior class president, Jean was among a group of college students on the program. She planned to teach the next year in Sumter, forty-five miles east of Columbia.

Before she left town, Thurmond boldly asked her if she wanted to change her plan and work awhile for the new governor. A few weeks later, he mailed a "Glad-to-have-seen-you" postcard from Miami, sent from the Southern Governors Conference there. It was heady stuff for a college coed.

Thurmond was mesmerized by the young woman, but he was also driven by a political calculation. He had achieved his boyhood political ambition to be governor despite a confirmed reputation as a skirt chaser, too much the man in a hurry to let a steady, monogamous relationship slow him down. Now he realized that a wife, a reliable social companion and a hostess at the Governor's Mansion, would be a political asset. And at age forty-four, he felt it was time to reform his ladies'-man reputation and start a family. The only issue was finding the right woman. (As a soldier he had sat awake at night, pondering whether marriage would enhance his chances of becoming governor.) He sensed something special in this girl with the pretty eyes, that she in particular would be a great asset. That she was less than half his age bothered him not at all.

His moment of glory, inauguration as governor on the Statehouse steps on January 21, was soon to arrive when Strom cooked up a scheme to lure Jean there to witness it. He called Henry Sims, president of Winthrop. As Thurmond related it, "I told President Sims to send a group of seniors down here if he wanted to, and we would take care of them at the inauguration. And I said, 'You might send the president of the senior class and some representatives.' He didn't know that I kind of had my eye on the president of the senior class."[1]

Thurmond said it would be "a nice experience" for the young women, and Sims conveniently agreed it was "a fine idea." A month after that trip, another carload of Winthrop girls drove down from the Rock Hill campus to attend an event in Columbia and visit the governor's office, Jean Crouch again among them. Governor Thurmond learned from an aide that she was there and invited her to have lunch at the mansion with him and his sister Gertrude, whom he had installed as official hostess.

Jean hastily accepted the lunch invitation, before any of the other girls could blurt out that she had already eaten lunch. With its fine furnishings and staff of black domestics, the Governor's Mansion must have offered a dazzling show of opulence to a country-bred, small-town girl. The meal began with a chilled raw oyster cocktail. Jean despised oysters and had to force herself to eat it. She then ate a full-course meal while silently praying for digestive peace. When the other girls teased her about the governor's attentions on the return trip to Winthrop, Jean smiled and said nothing.

In March, Thurmond invited her to the American Legion horse races in Columbia, specifying, "Bring along a friend, a girlfriend." Strom used the occasion to appoint Jean as the host Miss South Carolina for Charleston's annual Azalea Festival in April. The governor was there to crown the queen of the Azalea Festival. He planted the usual kiss on the queen, and kissed Miss South Carolina for good measure. She beamed—and made a mental note about his delight at crowning beauty queens. Strom next saw her on several official trips to Winthrop, a college now getting more attention than usual from a governor.

With his increasing interest in Jean, the governor explained to her that a position in the governor's office automatically limited personnel to purely official relationships, and he offered to place her in a state agency job. Jean retorted, "What are you hunting, a secretary or a playmate?"

He told her, "Come on down. We'll expect you."

She thought it over and announced that she would fill a secretarial vacancy on his staff. Thurmond initially interpreted Jean's decision to mean that she was indifferent toward him. But she later told him, "I knew if you saw me every day you couldn't forget me."

She reported to work on July 1, two weeks before her twenty-first birthday. She was soon asked to join lead secretary Wilma Smith as the second secretary in an entourage to accompany Thurmond to the National Governors Conference at Salt Lake City.

One evening in Salt Lake, Jean had sat in her room typing a speech while the governor and a bachelor aide escorted the attractive daughters of Governor Earl Warren of California to a rodeo. She teased him the next day about his date. Thurmond sensed her irritation—and that she was interested in him after all. That night they sat and talked for two hours. The governor's attention to Jean intensified and that evening their relationship turned a corner.

Wilma Smith, who had adored Strom Thurmond since he taught her seventh-grade class at Ridge Spring, remembered that the conference had planned "all these things for the ladies to do while the men were in meetings. But Jean did not go to a single thing for the ladies. She just stuck with Strom."[2]

The office staff no doubt noticed that the governor soon decided it was dangerous for Jean to walk the three blocks from the Statehouse to the apartment she shared with two former classmates. He frequently arranged his schedule to be free to offer her a ride to her door. But sealing a relationship with a confirmed bachelor proved to be difficult for Jean. Finally, she drew the line. She told him that her "boyfriends" found the competition a bit stiff, that if he really liked her, that was one thing. Otherwise, no more rides home.

Taken aback, Strom mumbled something about their both knowing soon what they should do. On September 9, Jean confirmed in a letter to her parents an informal but definite understanding between her and Strom that they would marry. She wrote that they would be driving to Elko Saturday night:

I suppose you all know we're really serious now. We've thought and thought about it. We know what we want. He'll always be *so* good and kind to me, *so* we're going to do what will make us happy for always. Please don't think for a minute that I'm swept off my feet 'cause I know what I'm getting into. He's Governor now, but that will last only three years. Marriage will last a lifetime. . . . He doesn't know I've written you all this—he just said let's go down Saturday and talk to my folks. . . . Please think hard and realize that I'd always regret not marrying him 'cause he'll always love me to death just as I do him.

On Saturday, Strom made his proposal formal by calling Jean in after lunch so he could dictate a letter for her to type. Written to "My Darling Jean," and with a touch of dry humor, it began:

You have proved to be a most efficient and capable secretary, and the high caliber of your work has impressed me very much. It is with a deep sense of regret that I will have to inform you that your services will be discontinued as of the last day of this month.

. . . you can serve humanity best, perform duties that will be more worthwhile to the State, and most especially make the Governor happier, in the new duties which I desire you to undertake.

. . . I must confess I love you dearly and want you for my own. I didn't realize that a girl could attach herself so to a man and could twine herself around his heartstrings as you have done. It seems to have been no special effort heretofore to fight off love, but in your case, I have made a complete failure in the attempt and frankly admit that your charms have won me— heart and soul. . . .

Anticipating an early reply and hope that it shall be forthcoming as quickly as possible as upon your answer will depend my future happiness.

Again assuring you of my deep love and expressing the hope that the time is not too distant when we can be joined as one and live happily for-ever.

Jean closed her shorthand pad and left, soon returning with the letter neatly typed for signature. The governor read it and looked fondly but firmly. "I didn't say 'twine herself,'" he said with feigned seriousness. "I said 'entwine herself.' Please fix that."[3]

With no change of expression, Jean departed. She let the governor cool his heels until the end of the day, then handed him the corrected letter. And her typed acceptance: "My dearest Strom, Yes! My love always, Jean."

STROM, FEARLESS HERO AT NORMANDY, governor of the state of South Carolina, perhaps the most famous bachelor in all of the South, fidgeted nervously that Saturday evening as Horace and Inez Crouch listened cautiously to his request for their daughter's hand. The age difference bothered them, and Mrs. Crouch suggested that they wait awhile and get to know each other better, but Strom insisted they knew each other well enough. Finally, he found his politician's instinct to close a deal in his favor and said, "Well, as long as you haven't voiced any objections, I'll conclude that at least you don't object."[4]

The media discovered Strom's young love interest before their engagement could be formally announced. *The State* ran a three-column front-page photo of the pair seated together in the governor's box at Carolina Stadium for a football game. A headline over the photo stated, "The Governor Takes a Pretty Girl to the Game."[5]

It did not take long for Thurmond to confirm that he and Jean planned to marry. The press quickly fell in love with her. "This striking young lady is a tall brunette with laughing blue eyes and an infectious smile that gives her an unaffected charm," the AP wrote in a typical dispatch. "South Carolinians will find their new First Lady, though youthful, poised and intelligent as well as pretty and talented."[6]

They wed in November in a quiet ceremony at the Governor's Mansion, then left for a two-week honeymoon in Miami and Havana. They returned to view the coverage given by *Life* magazine. Its three-page spread included a full-page shot taken the day before the ceremony, with Thurmond clad in tennis shorts, standing on his head. In the background leaning on a bicycle was a smiling and shapely Jean, dressed in shorts and a sweater.

The caption read, "Virile Governor demonstrates his prowess in the mansion yard day before wedding. He asked the photographer to feel his muscles and observed, 'Why, I can stand on my head,' and promptly proved it. Then the Governor noticed his fiancée's sweater and commented leeringly, 'If I could look that good in a sweater, maybe I'd put one on!'" But the display of prowess backfired. The entire state clucked over "Strom standing on his head," and the photo would come back to haunt him politically, fodder for his enemies to make him look foolish.

His sense of political drama and of the first couple as public figures undiminished, Thurmond issued an invitation for the entire state of South Carolina to come meet their new first lady at a Sunday afternoon reception at the mansion. As many as 10,000 people showed up, some driving several hours from the small villages where Strom had made his name, to wait in a line that sometimes extended for five blocks. Most were visiting the lavish Governor's Mansion for the first time. Jean, clad in her flowing ivory wedding gown beside Strom, greeted them at the door.

Jean would charm those South Carolinians skeptical about the age difference between her and the governor. She was gracious, displayed poise and judgment, and was the kind of woman who seems to radiate an inner beauty and strength. She assessed the strengths and weaknesses of his staff, served as a sounding board, and gave sound political advice. Even Strom's enemies in the Barnwell Ring enjoyed Jean's presence and sought out her company. She quickly learned protocol and management skills for running the social operation at the Governor's Mansion. Just as Strom's mother had, she grew used to last-minute notices to put together dinners for impromptu visitors. Adopting Strom's ordered ways, she kept the cupboards meticulously organized and took pride in her ability to throw together a delicious meal in minutes. She bought him new clothes that made him look more dignified. She put an end to his crowning beauty queens. She filled an inner void, making Thurmond feel more whole. And the first couple of the state projected an image that was modern, vigorous, and loving; riding horseback, swimming, and playing tennis together.

But even Jean's warmth could not entirely melt away Strom's sometimes cold practicality. He ordered twin beds for them to sleep in and, after it became clear that the marriage would produce no children, once pointed out bluntly that this was her fault and not his. On New Year's Eve, Strom in a gesture of love conveyed to Jean two tracts of real estate worth $20,000, the equivalent of almost two years of a governor's salary, "in order that you may have some income of your own." It included two filling stations rented to Gulf Oil and two rental houses. In a letter, he expressed hope "that you can keep it rented on a satisfactory basis."[7]

Early in 1948, Strom invited the twenty-four-year-old rookie Columbia bureau chief for United Press to the mansion for lunch. Eugene Patterson, who would succeed the fabled Ralph McGill as editor of the *Atlanta Constitution*, vividly remembered Jean's making him feel welcome. "She kept up a playful whispered commentary to me about Strom, who looked more like her father than her husband," Patterson remembered half a century later.

"Have you noticed he wears the same color tie every day?" she asked. I had not. The tie was a plain one, without figures, in a shade between red and maroon. "It goes with whatever suit he decides to wear," Jean said, "so he sees no need to complicate the matter."

Later she giggled as the governor started squeezing lemon on his fish fillet. "He loves lemon, but watch his face," she whispered. Sure enough, Strom licked the lemon slice and the astringency of the thing caused his face to draw up and pucker into a comical grimace. "He looks just like a big old baby when his face does that," Jean laughed.[8]

CHAPTER 9

"Dear Sir"

A WEEK BEFORE THURMOND'S MARRIAGE to Jean, a studious coed at South Carolina State College in Orangeburg sat down to type the governor a simple—but telling—letter. Addressed to "Governor J. S. Thurmond" and dated October 31, 1947, it began "Dear Sir" and stated, "This is to acknowledge receipt of your loan received on Saturday, October 25. Thank you very much." In carefully rounded, strong penmanship, it was signed, "E. M. Washington."[1]

In accordance with her father's suggestion and her own desires to branch out from Coatesville, further her education, and still be near relatives, Essie had enrolled at the college in August 1946, soon after her father's hard-fought victory in the Democratic primary runoff.

Essie Mae Washington has said that Thurmond took care of her tuition and expenses. Essie was older than most of her classmates, who had graduated from South Carolina's then eleven-grade school system. Essie, seven when she enrolled in first grade, later missed a year of school at Coatesville when a vermin epidemic forced her school to close for a full academic year. Add her year in New York, and she started her freshman year just shy of her twenty-first birthday.

Although other students at the all-black college could claim blood links to prominent whites, ties to white families were often well understood but not openly talked about, and so it was with Essie's relationship to Strom. She knew it was a source of gossip but would not discuss it. M. Maceo Nance Jr., a student at the time who later served almost two decades as president of SC State, recalled, "At the time, it was accepted belief on campus that the top assistant to the president of the college was the son of a white trustee. For her to be the daughter of the governor was not viewed as any big deal."[2]

Thurmond began attracting national attention as a new breed of Old South Democrat, surprisingly progressive in his views, including some civil rights issues. Although it was within the context of segregation, he talked often about the need for better Negro education, including the theme in his inaugural address. Already he had navigated the state through a national firestorm over the Willie Earle lynching. For many black leaders in the state, he was a breath of fresh air.

The excitement of change and progress permeated campus life when Essie arrived in Orangeburg. Because returning black veterans found themselves restricted to segregated schools after World War II service and combat, enrollment at SC State soared with discharged soldiers taking advantage of the GI Bill.

One returning veteran was future federal judge Matthew J. Perry of Columbia, a tall, handsome business major with a deep baritone voice. Perry enjoyed a short-lived career as a campus ladies' man before meeting and settling down with another coed, his future wife, Hallie Bacote. (In Timmonsville, a small town in the tobacco-growing Pee Dee region, Bacote's family maintained friendly relations with white relatives.) Perry briefly dated Essie Washington, the quiet young woman from faraway Pennsylvania. It was "a casual kind of thing," he said. "I found her attractive. I was a young man just returning from the war and looking over all the young ladies."[3]

Perry later became chief counsel for the NAACP in South Carolina. His voice, engaging smile, and courtly manner combined with intellect, perseverance, and legal skill to win him wide respect. He litigated case after case that desegregated schools, state parks, and other facilities and successfully defended students and others involved in protest demonstrations, in some cases breaking new constitutional ground on appeals that he helped argue before the U.S. Supreme Court. Through a mutual friend in Columbia, he maintained a long-distance friendship with Essie. And ultimately his life's path would change because of her father.

During the brief period that Perry dated Essie, "She indicated in some fashion that the then governor and his family were interested in her welfare and her education at SC State. . . . She described it as a longtime relationship." Perry said he had no personal knowledge of her visiting Governor Thurmond in Columbia, although he saw Thurmond's official car drive up at SC State and he was aware of campus speculation that Essie was Thurmond's daughter. "From time to time, the sitting governor would surface on campus, but he was the ex-officio chairman of the board of trustees. A couple of times, I think I saw the car drive up," Perry said.[4]

Occasional Thurmond sightings on the all-black campus became the stuff of legend. With students gawking from the sidelines, the governor would arrive by chauffeured car, cruise up the long driveway, and stop in front of the office of President Millard F. Whittaker. By prearrangement, Essie would have been notified of his arrival and pulled out of class or summoned from her dormitory to walk over to the administration building. The school president would allow the governor and the girl to talk privately in his office. Essie Washington later revealed that these friendly visits involved the delivery of financial assistance for her schooling, always handed over by Thurmond in cash.

Emma S. Casselberry, who served as Whittaker's executive assistant, remembered: "Governor Thurmond would come to campus, for some other reason, and ask to see 'this girl from my hometown.' I would call the dean of women and ask that she have Essie come to the president's office, and she and Thurmond and Mrs. Thurmond would meet for fifteen minutes or so in private in an anteroom. He would come once or twice a year."[5]

The gossip surrounding the visits eventually attracted a reporter from *Ebony* magazine, who came on campus to confront Essie and ask if Thurmond was her father. She denied it. Before Essie acknowledged in December 2003 that she was Strom Thurmond's daughter, she had adamantly denied his paternity for years to those few journalists who sought her out on the subject. The answer was always that her mother and her aunt had worked for the Thurmond family, as indeed they had, and that he remained a friend of the family. She would say, "There is no substance whatsoever to these rumors. People believe what they want to believe. . . . My mother and my aunt worked for the Thurmond family. I guess this is how it all got started. He visited me one time [at SC State], one time, that's all. He had to go down to the president's office, and he was interested in how I was doing, so I went over and talked to him there."[6]

Of course, there were other reasons for the governor to check in on conditions at SC State. As student Matthew Perry and others were aware, he was an ex-officio board chairman during a turbulent time in the school's life. The creation of the "separate but equal" law school on campus was very much an ongoing concern.

In Judge J. Waties Waring's courtroom during the NAACP efforts to integrate the state university law school, a chief witness for the state had been SC State president Whittaker, the enabler of Thurmond's visits with

Essie. Under questioning by Thurgood Marshall, Whittaker had to acknowledge that the legislature's creation of an unfunded law school for
blacks had amounted to nothing—the "school" had no professors, no law
library, no classrooms. Whittaker testified that he saw little hope that SC
State could offer by the fall of 1947 a law program for black residents that
would be comparable to the white program at the University of South
Carolina.[7]

Waring's ruling that USC did not have to admit John Wrighten, the
plaintiff in the case, to its law program and that SC State should create by
September a law program "on a complete parity" with USC left President
Whittaker frazzled and in what he believed to be an impossible bind. He
scrambled to hire a law school dean, Benner C. Turner from the North
Carolina College of Law, as well as two law professors. A vacant classroom
was found in Wilkinson Hall. The law school's first-year enrollment included five full-time and four part-time students.[8] (John Wrighten refused
to attend until the following year, when a law school building and library
were provided.)

One of the first students to enroll was a slim, smart, good-looking veteran from Savannah, Georgia, Julius T. Williams. Within a short while, he
and the governor's secret daughter had become a romantic item.

THE RELATIONSHIP between Essie Mae Williams and Thurmond was
consistent with patterns of the few other acknowledged, high caste parent-
child interracial relationships in the South. Justice John Marshall Harlan,
who wrote the famous dissent in *Plessy v. Ferguson*—the 1896 Supreme Court
case that established the "separate but equal" doctrine and provided the
basis for the South's segregated society for the next six decades—maintained some relationship with a half brother, Robert, whose mother was a
slave. Harlan's father attempted to provide the justice's half brother with a
college education, and Robert became a successful businessman.[9]

One of Essie Mae's closest friends at SC State recalled another young
woman student there, whose white father maintained her family on the
edge of a large farm away from the house of his white family. When the
young woman became engaged to a fellow SC State student, the father insisted on meeting the young man and giving his approval.[10]

The historian Joel Williamson, a South Carolina native who became a
leading authority on miscegenation, said the pattern is that the woman

tends to be a light-skinned domestic and there has been miscegenation before in the family.[11] In his biography of author William C. Faulkner, *William Faulkner and Southern History*, Williamson tells the story of the "shadow" family that descended from Faulkner's grandfather, the "old colonel," William C. Falkner. (The grandson changed the spelling of the name to Faulkner, and surviving members of his family in Oxford, Mississippi, use both spellings.)

The daughter, Fannie Forrest Falkner, was named by Colonel Falkner, and she attended Rust College in Holly Springs, Mississippi, then the state's most prestigious private black college. It was sponsored by the Northern Methodist Church and provided a quality education. The man she married, Matthew Dogan, later became a college president in Texas, and Williamson reports that family tradition asserted that Colonel Falkner paid Fannie's college bills and frequently came to see his daughter in Holly Springs.

Ironically, Fannie Falkner and her mother had moved into the household of Richard Thurmond in Ripley, Mississippi, before Fannie's enrollment at Rust College in 1885. Thurmond later shot and killed Colonel Falkner, ostensibly over a business dispute involving Thurmond's losing investment in Falkner's railroad. An adult sister or half sister of Fannie's still lived in Falkner's house in Ripley after his wife had left him, and Williamson theorized "that the situations in both Falkner's and [Richard] Thurmond's households had something to do with the obvious hatred of Thurmond for the Colonel" and for the jury's failure to convict Thurmond. Richard Thurmond had moved to Mississippi from North Carolina.[12]

ALTHOUGH ESSIE GENERALLY IGNORED the campus rumor that Strom Thurmond was her father, her reputed linkage to the governor may well have helped her move among the campus's highest social strata. According to some familiar with her behavior, this gave her a strong sense of entitlement. Others say there was no such behavior. Emma Casselberry said, "Essie didn't make any display. She got no special treatment. . . . I heard that anything she wanted, she just called [Thurmond]."[13] Essie would show up occasionally in Columbia, according to observers, and received exceptional treatment for a black person of the time. With some resentment, Thurmond's driver, Randall Johnson, the same man who drove Army Major Thurmond and Sue Logue to the death chamber, recalled being asked by Thurmond to pick up Essie at the train station in Columbia and drop her off for shopping trips at Tapp's, then the premier downtown department store. Johnson, the longtime superintendent of "colored help" at the state capitol, said Governor Thurmond had confided to him, "You're somebody I can trust."[14] He also had orders to deliver her to a side entrance of the Statehouse, which she would use to slip through to the governor's office. On one such visit, Essie remembers Strom's pretty wife, Jean, poked her head in the door and waved.[15]

Lonnie Hamilton, who went on to become chairman of Charleston County Council, remembered as a freshman at SC State wanting to go for a weekend evening drive, a rare treat, with some friends who had a car. Unfortunately, they had little gas and no money for a fresh tank. Essie happened to pass by, joined the group, and told them, "My father would provide the money." Asked where he lived, she replied, "Columbia."

They all piled in, drove to Columbia, followed her directions, and ended up at the Governor's Mansion. She went inside, and Lonnie said to the other guys, "I guess her father must be janitor at the Governor's Mansion."

One of them told him, "Her father *is* the governor."

Hamilton said that she returned with gas money. He told this story only after Thurmond's death and Essie's subsequent announcement. "Back then, it was something you knew better than to talk about," he said.[16]

When asked about this incident, Essie Washington-Williams said, "I've never heard that story before."[17]

Thurmond once asked Essie, "What's it like to have the governor as your father and not be able to talk about it?" Essie did not find this inquiry offensive; it was in keeping with their, perhaps unspoken, arrangement. (After breaking the silence more than half a century later, she said he never told her to hide their relationship. "I didn't talk about it because I chose not to talk about it," she said. "He said it was 'up to you.' He left that to my discretion. The help I got from him was well worth it."[18]) But she clearly understood that she needed to keep it secret, to protect him, and her relationship with him—he was, after all, both her father and a source of continued financial support.

Thurmond over the years referred to these payments as "loans," but there is no evidence that Essie was ever expected to repay them. This was their code, a cover to avoid the appearance of direct support, should the payments be uncovered. The "Dear Sir" letter that she wrote to Thurmond at the Statehouse was perfunctory, but it offered clear evidence of the governor's financial support. Not realizing that much later it would help unlock Thurmond's deepest secret, his aides filed the one-page letter in his official correspondence.

DIGNIFIED, DEPENDABLE, and with good grades, Essie was accepted into the elite Delta Sigma Theta sorority, forming lifelong attachments. Most of the Deltas had some special talent in music or dance or art, but Knoetta Goodwin Judkins remembered, "The sorority was looking for young ladies who had great potential and grade-point averages—the intelligent young ladies."[19] Essie's individual photograph is conspicuously missing from the school's yearbooks, but she does appear in a 1948 group sorority photograph. She was attractive, always neatly dressed and well-coiffed, and—like most of her sorority sisters—had a light complexion. The Deltas generally regarded Essie as a quiet and private person but "willing and cooperative to do what needed to be done," as one of them recalled. Mrs. Curtis Torrey of Fayetteville, North Carolina, who as Rosa Lee Rainey was vice president of the Deltas in 1948, added that Essie was "an unselfish person" and had "ladylike qualities. We accepted her."[20]

Some of Essie's sorority sisters had heard of her alleged relationship with Governor Thurmond. Julie Washington Nance, the daughter of the college's business manager and later wife of the college's president, did not live in the women's dormitory but remembered, "I heard my parents talk about it, who her father was."[21]

WHATEVER KINDNESSES HE SHOWED TO ESSIE, Thurmond's reputation in the state's black community had begun to deteriorate by late 1947. Thurmond's rhetoric on racial issues had become more polarizing, a development much discussed among the politically astute students at SC State.

Essie found that Julius Williams did not share her kind feelings for Thurmond. This became clearer as her relationship with Julius grew closer, as she continued to rely on Thurmond for help and his public profile began to undergo a dramatic change.

CHAPTER 10

Dixiecrat

For DECADES, a favorite item on the breakfast menu at Cogburn's Grill in Columbia was the Dixiecrat—a dark-brown link sausage rolled in a slice of plain white bread. A *Charlotte News* headline writer coined the term "Dixiecrat" for the States Rights Democratic Party, Strom Thurmond's presidential vehicle in 1948, and the menu item at Cogburn's—earthy, simple, and wrapped in something as pure white as bleached flour, symbolizing the appeal of the Dixiecrat splinter party.

The 1948 presidential campaign transformed Thurmond's image from progressive governor of South Carolina to reactionary national champion of white supremacy. Thurmond forever denied that he had run a racist campaign.

"When I ran for president as a States Righter," he explained years later, "some people considered that a racist fight. But it wasn't that. They misconstrued the whole thing. It was a battle of federal power versus state power. That was my fight. That was the way I viewed it."[1]

Here's what he said in a nationwide radio hookup on the eve of his defeat by Harry Truman: "Don't forget that the so-called civil rights program would bring about the end of segregation in the South, forcing mixing of the races in our hotels, in our restaurants, in our schools, in our swimming pools, and in all public places. This change in our customs is not desired by either the white or the colored race."

"To bring all this about, the federal government would set up a super-police force with power to rove throughout the states and keep our people in constant fear of being sent to a federal jail unless we accepted the decrees turned out by a bunch of anti-Southern bureaucrats in Washington."[2] The rhetoric during the campaign had been even stronger.

Southern progressives lost a champion they could have used. The forces who would push back against the civil rights movement discovered a national leader. And it would take three decades for Thurmond's image to begin to recover.

Thurmond had never before exploited racial politics. Until 1948, the term "states' rights" barely existed in his political vocabulary. His leadership in prosecuting the white mob that murdered Willie Earle, his ultimately successful effort to repeal a state poll tax, and his concern about improving educational and economic opportunities for blacks provided a foundation for leading his state and region into a new era. Had he continued in that direction, a man of his political skill, determination, and energy might well have helped the dawn rise on the "New South" a few years earlier.

Instead, he helped generate forces that over the next half century moved his state, his region, and his country in different directions—sometimes sideways, sometimes backward. The role of defending white supremacy was one he chose. Perhaps, as racial issues increasingly moved to the forefront of public life, he reacted viscerally to his internalized Edgefield County heritage, hearing again the echoing hooves of the Redshirts. That Edgefield heritage would have included the ruling class's paternalistic attitude toward blacks—learned directly from his father—that allowed for concern for their welfare but not for them to clamor for change or power themselves, and a desire to protect his beloved South from change, an impulse that should not be underestimated among a certain sort of Southern gentleman. Or maybe for all his talk of constitutional principles and "states' rights," Thurmond always acted according to what worked best politically at the time. Here, expediency, learned behavior, and something like principle may simply have melded.

At that time, a governor could not succeed himself in South Carolina (Olin Johnston was elected twice, but not in succession), and any political future for Thurmond meant a seat in the U.S. Senate. Johnston and Burnet Maybank had both run successfully for the Senate at midterm as governor, Johnston defeating decrepit "Cotton Ed" Smith and Maybank taking the seat vacated when President Roosevelt appointed James F. Byrnes to the Supreme Court.

Despite press speculation that he might run in 1948 against Maybank, Thurmond had pledged during his gubernatorial campaign to serve a full term, and his eye clearly was on Johnston, who would be up for reelection in 1950 when Strom's term would also be up. As a champion of organized labor, Olin D. Johnston would be a target for fiscal conservatives. Johnston as governor had called the special legislative session in 1944 that repealed the primary election laws to keep blacks from participating in the Democratic primary. His championing of white supremacy helped win him a Senate seat that year.

Although Thurmond was eyeing the Senate, he was also responding to events. In his own words from more than three decades after the Dixiecrat campaign, "I did not run for president just to get in line for the Senate. I ran for president because I felt very deeply that Truman would not represent what I felt was the best type of government for this country. I ran to give people a choice."[3] He added that he defended segregation as law and custom, and "it was the thinking of the people I represented."[4]

After Judge Waring struck down the white primary in the summer of 1947, U.S. District Judge George Bell Timmerman Sr., Thurmond's old opponent and the father of Thurmond's lieutenant governor, issued a stay order, temporarily delaying its implementation. But a three-judge panel of the Fourth Circuit Court of Appeals in Richmond unanimously upheld Waring. On December 30, 1947, Chief Judge John J. Parker wrote for the court, "No election machinery can be upheld if its purpose or effect is to deny the Negro, on account of his race or color, an effective voice in the government of his country or the state or the community where he lives."[5]

In the ensuing months, Thurmond supported the state Democratic Party efforts to somehow discourage blacks from voting—the next stratagem was a loyalty oath that required voters to pledge fealty to white supremacy. Eugene Patterson reported it all for United Press. Much to the surprise of Associated Press veteran Alderman Duncan, Patterson's dispatches included quotes from the NAACP's James M. Hinton and activist black editor John McCray, leaders of the virtually all-black Progressive Democrats.

Duncan, a tall South Carolinian with big blue eyes and an affinity for Panama hats, walked up the three flights of a downtown building to Patterson's UP office. Winded, he put one foot on the windowsill, pushed back his hat, and stared for a moment at his youthful rival. He said he'd noticed Patterson was quoting Negroes and was curious as to why.

Patterson told him he'd been taught to cover both sides of any story and guessed he would go right on, no matter what AP did. Duncan took his foot down, stood erect, and looked at Patterson with genuine puzzlement. Finally, he said, "Gene, do you think niggers should vote?"

"Yes, Dunc," Patterson said, "I guess I do." Duncan shook his head, thunderstruck, and walked out.[6]

This was South Carolina when President Truman finally responded to the 1947 report of the President's Committee on Civil Rights, "To Secure These Rights."

On January 7, 1948, Truman promised in his State of the Union address to present a comprehensive civil rights program. Two months earlier, presidential adviser Clark Clifford had presented him with a strategic political memo, "The Politics of 1948." He predicted Truman would face two opponents, former Vice President Henry Wallace as a liberal third-party challenger and New York Governor Thomas E. Dewey as the Republican nominee. The outcome would be decided, Clifford wrote, by the urban black vote in four states—California, Illinois, New York, and Ohio.

To cut the loss of liberals to Wallace and to rally black voters, Clifford recommended a civil rights package to Truman. He dismissed as "inconceivable" any possibility of a Southern revolt, explaining, "As always, the South can be considered safely Democratic. And in forming national policy can be safely ignored."[7] Later, after Thurmond raised the Dixiecrat banner and the president issued an executive order to desegregate the military services, Clifford wrote in a shrewd subsequent memo to Truman, "The Negro votes in the crucial states will more than cancel out any votes the President may lose in the South."[8]

A week after Truman's State of the Union address, Thurmond outlined his progressive second-year program to the General Assembly of South Carolina. He made only a brief reference to Truman's remarks.

Two weeks later, however, forty-eight of the 170 Democrats in South Carolina's one-party legislature denounced the national Democratic Party's advocacy of "ideas flagrantly repugnant to the South." In a letter to state Democratic Chairman William P. "Bill" Baskin, they suggested it was time to "reconsider our position in the national party."[9]

Truman delivered his civil rights program to Congress on February 2. He proposed eliminating the poll tax, making lynching a federal offense, ending segregation in interstate commerce (such as trains, planes, and buses), and creating a statutory Fair Employment Practices Commission (FEPC). "The protection of civil rights is the duty of every government which derives its powers from the consent of the people," the president said.[10]

Thurmond's initial response was guarded in tone. Congressman Bryan Dorn demanded that Southern governors "march on Washington," but

Thurmond wired support to the governors for "holding the line as far as
... possible" in resisting all efforts "to invalidate the practices, customs
and institutions which we in South Carolina cherish." In contrast, Senator
Richard Russell of Georgia compared the president's ordering the FBI to
work with the Civil Rights Division of the Justice Department to the
"Gestapo" of Nazi Germany.

Thurmond was like a man wading into a wide, sloping channel separat-
ing two islands. As the water rose above his neck, he finally started swimming. Once at home on the other side, decades would pass before he began
paddling to a shifting sandbar in midstream.

At a special session of the Southern Governors Conference the next
week in Wakulla Springs, Florida, the strongest castigation of Truman
came from Governors Ben Laney of Arkansas and Fielding Wright of Mississippi. Wright had already declared to the people of his state that "vital
principles and eternal truths transcend party lines" and that drastic action
might be necessary to protect "our institutions and our way of life."[11]

Thurmond's rhetoric intensified as the conference wore on. "The people of the states represented by the members of this conference have been
shocked by the spectacle of the political parties of this country engaging
in competitive bidding for the votes of small pressure groups by attacking
the traditions, customs and institutions of the section in which we live,"
Thurmond asserted in a conference speech. "They talk about breaking
down the laws which knowledge and experience of many years have proven
to be essential to the protection of the racial integrity and purity of the
white and Negro races alike. . . . Their sudden removal would jeopardize
the peace and good order which prevail where the two races live side by
side in large numbers."[12]

Thurmond proposed challenging Truman through the Electoral College, the system by which each state is allotted electoral votes equal to its
representation in Congress and a presidential candidate must win a majority to get elected. This notion from Thurmond implied that there was the
possibility of a third-party effort in the South. Thurmond also authored a
resolution to reconvene in forty days, during which a special committee
would recommend "joint and common action." It demanded that Truman's
proposals not be included in the Democratic Party platform. Thurmond
was named chairman of the special committee. Talk was building of a de-
fection from the party.

But many others thought the issue should be fought within the Democratic Party. For example, Georgia Governor M. E. Thompson called Truman's program "unnecessary" but declared that "for the South to bolt the Democratic Party would be even more unwise."[13]

Elsewhere, the heat was rising. On February 12 in Jackson, Mississippi, some 4,000 political leaders from all eighty-two counties in the state unfurled the Confederate battle flag, sang "Dixie," and sent rebel yells echoing as they adopted a resolution charging that Truman's program "intrudes into the sacred rights of the state." The resolution called for the South to withhold, if necessary, its electoral votes in the upcoming presidential election. Mississippi's newly elected senator, John Stennis, cautiously urged that the fight be kept within the Democratic Party, but in that frenzied atmosphere, he was politely—and effectively—ignored.

The same day the Mississippians were whooping it up, the House of Representatives in South Carolina's General Assembly unanimously adopted a resolution condemning Truman's civil rights proposals as "un-American."

A week later, on February 19, Thurmond's executive assistant in the governor's office, William Lowndes Daniel, encouraged him in a memo to consider "the opportunity" of becoming the South's leader in the segregation fight. "Please do not discount your own ability during this wrangle," wrote Daniel. "I shall be glad to help put you to the front at the opportune moment, if it presents itself. Others will join in a big way. I know that you will be hesitant in considering that you can play on the varsity on such a team, but I can assure you that after all my observations you can. President Truman would not be in the White House today except for having taken advantage of a similar situation when it occurred. If we watch developments carefully, the opportunity may present itself to work wonders with you, also. The difference in these two cases would be that wonders were worked with Truman, who in my opinion just does not have it—you do have it—All you need is the opportunity."[14]

The same day Daniel's memo crossed Thurmond's desk, Olin Johnston got into the fray with a carefully orchestrated snub of the president. Gladys Johnston, the senator's wife, was a vice chairman of the Democratic Party's annual Jefferson-Jackson Day Dinner in Washington at which President Truman was slated as featured speaker. A few days beforehand, she called Democratic National Committeeman J. Howard McGrath, senator from Rhode Island, to ask for assurance that none of Johnston's associates would be seated next to an African American. When McGrath gave no such guarantee, the South Carolina party, which included the Thurmonds, refused to attend. Their table was located near the speaker's platform because of Mrs. Johnston's vice chairmanship. Olin Johnston hired a former heavyweight boxer to attend the dinner and insure that the highly visible table remained empty.

News stories about Johnston's boycott circulated widely and prompted a flood of congratulations from constituents, including a proud letter claiming that "applications for Ku Klux Klan membership are booming and there's a healthy increase in the manufacture of Red Shirts in South Carolina."[15]

On February 23, Thurmond and his committee of governors presented Chairman McGrath with a letter asking such leading questions as whether he would deny that the proposed federal laws dealing with the separation of races "would be unconstitutional invasions of the field of government belonging to the states under the Bill of Rights in the Constitution of the United States?" They left empty-handed. The *New York Times* reported in a front-page story that McGrath "would not yield on a single point as they fired question after question at him." A week after the meeting with McGrath, Thurmond told his state Democratic Executive Committee, "The president has gone too far," adding, "as far as I am concerned, I am through with him."[16]

On March 13, Thurmond's official committee report called Truman's proposal a "betrayal . . . because so many of the proposals are openly and deliberately directed against our traditions, customs and institutions."

In addition to being guided by his political instincts and sense of opportunity, Thurmond began to respond as a man who had deeply absorbed the Edgefield ethos, reflecting an honor easily pricked and a fighting spirit unyielding in defending the white South against those who aroused the region's deep feelings of grievance. At a March 16 rally, he cited a passage from the "To Secure These Rights" report and bitterly complained, "*They* have the idealism and prestige; we in the South are the wayward." With the ghosts of Preston Brooks, Martin Witherspoon Gary, and John C. Calhoun seemingly rising from the ground, Thurmond declared, "No fight was ever won by staying out of it. Our cause is right and just. We shall honor ourselves by pressing it to the end."

A day later, Thurmond asserted that the civil rights report had "gathered dust" until revived because of political considerations. Thurmond's rhetoric intensified yet again. He called Truman's civil rights proposal to Congress "the most astounding president's message in American history" and declared, "We may as well have a showdown once and for all."[17]

He was now openly calling for Southerners to stand together and throw the presidential election into the House. The Constitution provides that if no candidate has a majority of the electoral vote, the House will select from the three top candidates, with each state having a single vote.

Although most other Southern political leaders, including those in Washington, chimed in with attacks on Truman's proposals, few were joining Thurmond's call for revolt. Congressional leaders feared risking the privileges and power of seniority and loss of patronage at home that would come with Democratic defeat. They understood that acts have consequences.

And, unlike Thurmond and the other governors in the provinces, the Southerners in Washington knew Harry Truman personally and many of them believed that his commitment on civil rights was limited. Congressman Frank W. Boykin of Alabama quoted the president as telling him, "Frank, I don't believe in this civil rights program any more than you do, but we've got to have it to win."[18] Truman's record, however, suggests he may have been simply avoiding conflict with a political ally who needed reassurance for voters at home.

On April 19, the U.S. Supreme Court announced its decision not to hear a challenge to the Fourth Circuit's affirmation of Judge Waring's ruling. The Democratic primary in South Carolina would be open to black voters. Thurmond waited two days before commenting, finally saying he was "shocked" by the refusal to hear the case and proclaiming, "every American has lost part of his fundamental rights." *The State*, in an editorial headlined "No Cause for Shock," accepted the decision as a "matter of course" and suggested that Thurmond only spoke out because he "felt called upon to." The afternoon *Columbia Record* asked whether blacks had "won anything by the Supreme Court decision to which they were not entitled."[19]

Thurmond chose to feed the fears of panicky South Carolinians who saw their social order crumbling. He blamed it all on Harry Truman. Thurmond told an audience, "I took Truman's picture off the wall of my office when he stabbed the South in the back. Let's fight this battle to the end."[20]

On April 22, the Mississippi Democratic Executive Committee agreed to nominate Thurmond for president at the Democratic National Convention, to be held in Philadelphia in July, declaring him "a man of vision and courage who thinks and acts and feels like we do." In Columbia, Thurmond said, "I was surprised." Surprised or not, he accepted an invitation to give the keynote address at a Southwide May 10 meeting in Jackson. The day before, a Sunday, Governor Wright had made a 7:30 A.M. radio address specifically aimed at black Mississippians. Even in the bizarre politics of that state, it stood out as a surreal bit of rhetoric and advice. Wright told black Mississippians "to place your trust in the innate, uncoerced sense of justice of the white people with whom you live." Then he warned, "If any of you have become so deluded as to want to enter our hotels and cafés, enjoy social equality with the whites, then kindness and true sympathy requires me to advise you to make your home in some state other than Mississippi."[21]

Thurmond brought his regular speechwriter Robert Figg with him to draft a fiery message, and Jean accompanied her husband as Wright's guests in the Governor's Mansion. Roughly 1,500 delegates showed up from throughout the South, and another 2,000 spectators—almost all of them Mississippians—sat in at the city auditorium. Wright and Ben Laney of Arkansas were the only other governors attending.

The *New York Times* correspondent John Popham wrote that Thurmond "has been mentioned as a likely Presidential candidate on a States Rights ticket." His story reported some Southern states were barely represented in Jackson and quoted Georgia Democratic State Chairman James S. Peters saying "the Democratic party is like religion and nobody is going to desert the party." However, the story went on to quote Thurmond asserting that the South was "tired of being a doormat for Presidential candidates" and—in a direct though perhaps unintentional refutation of Peters's biblical imagery—that it had now been "betrayed in the house of our fathers."[22]

Thurmond went even further. He aroused all the elements of Southern grievance, from discriminatory freight rates to not getting credit for having "cared and provided for the Negroes in our midst." He prophetically added:

Whenever a great section of this country is regarded as so politically impotent that one major party insults it because it is "in the bag" and the other party scorns it because there is no chance for victory, then the time has arrived for corrective and concerted action. When this campaign is over, leaders in both political parties will realize that we no longer intend to be a doormat on which presidential candidates may wipe their political shoes every time they want to appeal to a minority in doubtful states. . . .

We of the South are a proud people. We come from a stock that has never buckled even in the face of defeat or rule by federal bayonet. We meet here today with no apology. We want no one to be mistaken or misled. We are going to fight as long as we breathe, for the rights of our states and our people under the American constitution and come what may, we are going to preserve our civilization in the South.[23]

One by one, he blasted the particulars of Truman's civil rights package. Why did the nation need anti-poll tax laws, he asked, when states like South Carolina were working to abolish them? Why did the country need an anti-lynching law when the crime had practically been eliminated? The proposals to eliminate job discrimination were not only unconstitutional but the beginnings of a frightening police state that would produce more "duress and apprehension" than the mind of man could conceive.

For him personally, Thurmond said, "the Rubicon is crossed, I care not whether I ever hold another public office. As the Governor of a sovereign state, I do not intend that the rights of my people shall be sacrificed on the block of blind party loyalty."[24]

And he made his meaning of "states' rights" absolutely clear. "On the question of social intermingling of the races our people draw the line," he declared, his voice rising and his right hand chopping in a gesture of defiance, "and all the laws of Washington and all the bayonets of the army cannot force the Negro into our homes, our schools, our churches, and our places of recreation and amusement." He would repeat this language as the central theme of his political message later in the year. He went on, "No decent and self-respecting Negro would ask for a law to force people to accept him where he is not wanted."

William Winter, a first-term Mississippi legislator still in law school who would become a leading force for progressive politics in his state, a half century later vividly remembered that day:

I had the feeling that a lot of people must have had in 1861, that we were be-coming swept up in a political hysteria that was just throwing caution to the winds as to what the ultimate result might be.

It was Mississippi and South Carolina again, as in 1860 when they were the first two to take the lead in secession. Again they were the first two to take the lead in seceding from the Democratic Party. I was troubled that this was going to run us into a dead end, that we were getting ready to for-feit our influence in the Democratic Party and in the Congress by what ap-peared to be a very iffy course. I saw it as a move toward isolating ourselves politically.[25]

An argument can be made that the very notion of the Democratic "solid South" was rooted in the states' rights argument, that when the Compromise of 1877 returned political control in the South to white Democrats, it was done with the "understanding" that the region would be left alone for its white leadership to determine how it handled its own race relations. The Compromise simply ignored black Southerners, the benefi-ciaries of Reconstruction. But in a world emerging from a war against to-talitarian regimes and in which fragile nonwhite democracies were beginning to appear, the historic moment had come when all of the Amer-ican people would have to confront their racial dilemma.

As Thurmond made clear, the heart of the matter did involve race and his defense of white supremacy. He used the term "states' rights" in no other context. The argument is based on the one-sentence Tenth Amend-ment of the Constitution: "The powers not delegated to the United States by the Constitution, nor prohibited by it to the States, are reserved to the States respectively, or to the people."

Under the American federal system, the states retain police powers—laws regulating the general security, health, safety, morals, and welfare of the people except where legally prohibited. That said, Article Six of the Constitution states plainly that federal law is supreme when in conflict with state law.

After the Civil War determined that the United States is an indestructi-ble union, the Fourteenth Amendment of the Constitution was ratified. It granted citizenship to black Americans and declared that no state could deprive a citizen of "equal protection" or "due process" of the law. The late-nineteenth-century Supreme Court gutted the Fourteenth Amendment of its framers' intention. Instead of defending the former slaves and their descendants, it became an instrument to protect corporate economic interests. But beginning in the late 1930s, the Supreme Court began restoring the Fourteenth Amendment to its intended meaning. Thurmond may well have viewed this legal trend as a "battle of federal power versus state power," but his words at the time make clear that his primary concern was preserving the South's capacity to maintain racial segregation and white supremacy.

Although, judging partly from the ferocity and especially the consistency of his remarks, Thurmond apparently held a genuine belief that he was acting in defense of constitutional principle, he conveniently ignored that the Supreme Court is the final arbiter for interpreting the Constitution. Yet Thurmond's dogged stubbornness in politicizing the issue would ultimately make a difference. Over time Thurmond, the former judge, would grasp that if the Supreme Court interprets the Constitution, then who the justices are matters.

As THE 1948 CAMPAIGN DEVELOPED, Gene Patterson recognized Thurmond's evident popularity in South Carolina. He remembered, "His wholehearted embrace of racial segregation pleased the bourbons and the boobs alike, of course. But he did not strike one as being exceptionally bright, and the country-cured accent of his uninspired speechmaking paled in comparison to gentlemanly Burnet Maybank with his clipped Lowcountry combination of Gullah and Tidewater brogue and shambling Olin Johnston with the Piedmont mill hand bawl."

"So I asked Wayne Freeman [later editor] of *The Greenville News* to tell me the secret of Strom's charm over the masses." One of the most knowledgeable political reporters around, Freeman rented an office in one of the two rooms of Patterson's United Press bureau. "It's very simple," Freeman told him. "Strom may not be all that smart. But he's a rarity in South Carolina politics. He's honest. He won't steal."26

On May 19, South Carolina Democrats held one of their most infamous state conventions. Thurmond kept a low profile, but his forces controlled the event. They instructed delegates to the national convention to vote for him on the first ballot as a favorite-son candidate and to reject Truman or any candidate who supported the president's civil rights program.

To discourage blacks from voting, the convention adopted an oath requiring primary voters to swear that they "understand, believe in and will support the principles of the Democratic Party of South Carolina"; to support racial segregation in religious, social, and educational activities; and to oppose and work against the Fair Employment Practices Commission. Ten days later, three of the state's most prominent lawyers, who had handled the challenge to Judge Waring's decision, publicly disclaimed having any role in the new Democratic Party oath. The *Columbia Record* disdainfully asserted, "only a member of the Nazi party in Germany could take the oath and mean it."[27] The oath energized white moderates as well as blacks, who challenged it in court.

On May 26, South Carolina's almost entirely black Progressive Democrats responded with their own convention, whose roughly 250 delegates from twenty-six of the state's forty-six counties included two whites. Keynote speaker Arthur Clement of Charleston assailed Thurmond as one whose training and culture had "evaporated like the morning dew" and who had transformed himself into "another wailing rabble-rouser." The group agreed to send a full twenty-eight-member delegation to the Democratic National Convention.

Political turmoil continued in the state throughout June. A grassroots group of racially moderate white activists organized as the Citizen Democratic Party. When Party Chairman Baskin refused their request to reconvene the state convention to reconsider the controversial oath, this group decided to send its own challenge delegation to Philadelphia, including two black college presidents.

In Philadelphia, a week after Republicans nominated New York Governor Thomas E. Dewey for president and California Governor Earl Warren for vice president, Thurmond found little support for a Southwide revolt. On Sunday night, July 11, a caucus that attracted less than one-third of the 600 Southern delegates heard him berate the president, saying, "We have been betrayed, and the guilty shall not go unpunished." Southern opponents failed to come up with an alternate candidate. (Thurmond had joined an unsuccessful effort to draft Dwight Eisenhower, who was four years away from announcing a party affiliation.) The caucus adopted two resolutions threatening nothing worse than a floor fight over the party platform. The *New York Times* reported the next morning that the rebellion against Truman's nomination had collapsed.

At the convention, South Carolina's Progressive Democrats and Citizen Democrats made separate appeals to the Credentials Committee. The black group sought eight of the state's twenty delegate seats to reflect their 40-percent proportion of the state's population.

David Baker, a young lawyer from Columbia, argued two points for the Citizen Democrats. First, the regular Democratic delegation was unlawful because blacks were excluded from participating at the state convention. Second, the oath "has disfranchised all the thinking and intelligent people of South Carolina."

Thurmond spoke, maintaining that the standard delegates "constitute the regular Democratic Party of South Carolina." He threatened a walkout at the convention if the Progressive Democrats got their proportional representation. After Thurmond's testy refusal to answer directly whether precinct meetings were open to participation by blacks, the activist black editor McCray explained that his group hadn't filed protests when excluded from the meetings because, well, they were excluded from the meetings. Although the committee recommended a new rule be adopted to meet future situations "such as have been developed in the South Carolina case," Olin Johnston seconded the motion to seat the official South Carolina delegation, and it passed, 24–3.

Meanwhile, the platform committee adopted a compromise civil rights plank, ambiguously urging, "Congress should exert its full constitutional powers to protect these rights." On the convention floor, several Southerners argued for specific "states' rights" language. They contended the party was repudiating its historic position, but former Governor Maurice Tobin of Massachusetts pointed out that no states' rights plank had appeared in the Democratic National Convention platform since 1928.

Hubert H. Humphrey, the dynamic thirty-seven-year-old mayor of Minneapolis, followed. He made his first impression on a national audience by speaking out for a minority report drafted by the liberal Americans for Democratic Action that would "support our President in guaranteeing these basic and fundamental American principles: The right of full and equal political participation, the right to equal opportunity of employment, the right of security of persons, and the right of equal treatment in the service and defense of our Nation." Humphrey's speech was electric, with applause interrupting him eight times. "To those who say that this civil rights program is an infringement on states' rights,"

Humphrey said to cheers from the audience, "I say this, that the time has arrived in America for the Democratic Party to get out of the shadows of states' rights and to walk forthrightly into the bright sunshine of human rights."

By a vote of 654½ to 582½, the convention adopted the Americans for Democratic Action plank to the platform. In the tumult that followed, half the Alabama delegation walked out (state Representative George C. Wallace remained), followed by the entire Mississippi delegation. Had the South Carolina delegation been inclined to leave, they knew the Progressive Democrats were ready to take their place.

Thurmond still had a bit role to play, seconding the nomination of Georgia's Richard Russell, a patrician who at fifty was the established leader of the Southern bloc in the Senate and now agreed to stand as a protest candidate. Thurmond earlier had released his delegates to Laney, but the Arkansas governor found little support and backed out. After an introduction as "one of the outstanding heroes of the last war," Thurmond was unbending. "We do not wish to take from any American his constitutional rights," he said, "but we do not intend that our constitutional rights shall be sacrificed for the selfish and the sordid purpose of gaining minority votes in doubtful states."[28]

Thurmond returned home from Philadelphia on Friday, with plans to head to Camp Stewart, Georgia, to inspect a South Carolina National Guard unit the next morning. The Mississippi delegation and others had gathered in Birmingham, reconvening the group that had met in May, and Governors Wright and Laney called Thurmond, urging him to attend. He decided to go.

After stopping at Camp Stewart, he flew on to Birmingham. Laney and former Governor Frank Dixon of Alabama had already turned down offers to become the group's presidential nominee. Thurmond had no sooner arrived at the boisterous gathering of 7,000 Confederate-flag-waving, "Dixie"-singing enthusiasts than he was offered the nomination. He had an hour to decide.

Thurmond recalled, "I knew that accepting the nomination would have future political repercussions, but I had little time to make up my mind, and I thought somebody ought to do something, so I finally decided to take the plunge."[29] One can only speculate about whether he thought these possible repercussions involved alienating himself from the Democratic

Party nationally or raising his profile for greater stature at home as a prelude to the 1950 senate race. Thurmond presumably weighed both.

By the time he came to the podium to accept the nomination of the
States Rights Democratic Party for president of the United States, earlier
speakers had warmed up the audience with a statement of principles endorsing "racial integrity" in specific detail, and keynoter Frank Dixon got
caught up in the mood, denouncing civil rights as a program "to reduce us
to the status of a mongrel, inferior race."[30] Thurmond never stooped to
that level of racist language. But he drew a roar of approval even before he
began speaking, and he didn't disappoint his audience. He used notes on
pieces of paper, stuffing each page into his pocket as he finished.

Thurmond biographer Nadine Cohodas tells of showing clips from
Movietone News footage to two top Thurmond aides forty years later,
young men accustomed to Strom's presentation of this campaign as one
based on constitutional principles and not motivated by issues of race.

They watched the film of an energized Thurmond gripping the podium
with both hands and exclaiming, "I want to tell you that the progress of
the Negro race has not been due to these so-called [and here he spit out
the word as if he had bitten into a rotten apple] e-*man*-ci-*paters*—but to the
kindness of the good Southern people." Then, renewing the main theme
from the May speech in Jackson, he jabbed his right index finger at the
crowd to emphasize each point and declared, "I want to tell you, ladies and
gentlemen, that there's not enough troops in the army to force the Southern people to break down segregation and admit the Negro race into our
theaters, into our swimming pools, into our homes, and into our
churches."* The crowd loved it.

Thurmond's aides were stunned. One shook his head in silence. The
other remembered chills running down his spine and said, "I couldn't believe I was working for the same man."[31]

At the time of his speech, Modjeska Simkins read his characterization
of blacks and was outraged. "I said, 'I'm gonna fight Thurmond from the
mountain to the sea. He will not get away with these things he is saying
about my people.'"[32] During this period, Simkins and other leaders of the

---

*Strom pronounced the word as "nigra," which upper-caste whites in the South did not
consider an epithet. Decades later, fourth or fifth generation audio recordings distorted
the sound and to many listeners it sounded like "nigger."

state NAACP set out to get photographs of Essie Washington that could be used against Thurmond politically. A Democratic Party loyalist and experienced photographer was dispatched to follow her around campus. (The pictures were filed away, resurfacing a few years later.)

The *Baltimore Afro-American*, then one of the nation's largest black newspapers, launched its own crusade against Thurmond, charging in early August that his "race baiting" had prompted cross burnings at two black schools in South Carolina. Later that month, the newspaper printed stories and photographs about miscegenation in the Thurmond clan, interviewing blacks who claimed kinship with the governor. Mrs. Eva Thurmond Smith said, "I remember well when Gov. Thurmond used to visit my grandfather, and they used to sit and eat and talk for hours. I remember asking my grandfather why did that white man always visit our home. My grandfather told me they were brothers."[33]

White-owned newspapers ignored these stories, but they circulated widely among South Carolina blacks, who also heard tales in their communities of Thurmond having a "daughter" at South Carolina State College.

Thurmond's decision to lead the Dixiecrat party rebellion was making him a loathed figure among South Carolina's civil rights community and even among some of Essie's fellow students. Julius Williams and other black law students at SC State tracked the progress of civil rights cases and the vitriolic reactions of white political figures in the state.

Thurmond's Dixiecrat campaign led to the only political conversation Essie ever remembered having with her father. At the prodding of fellow students, she asked him once how he could run on a segregationist ticket when the two of them had the relationship they had. She recalled, "He said, 'Oh, that has nothing to do with us. I have to represent the views of the voters.' I said, 'Maybe you could do something about it.' He changed the subject, and I could see he didn't want to talk about it."[34]

She accepted what he said as the reality that then existed and never again discussed political issues with him. This brief episode illustrates what could be viewed as an example of politically motivated hypocrisy, this man who maintained a clandestine relationship with his black daughter while simultaneously proclaiming black inferiority; or it can be seen as an act of pragmatism on both their parts, or a classic example of Thurmond's compartmentalizing his life. Here was a man who relished power, yet risked it by privately recognizing and supporting his black daughter while proclaiming that "all the troops of the army" couldn't break down segregation. Private and public action to him were simply different realms, and any dissonance between the two did not mean that either should be any less fiercely maintained.

THE LEADERS AT BIRMINGHAM sought not to create a third party but to take over the Democratic state party organizations and make the Dixiecrat candidates the nominees of the Democratic Party. They defined the national Democratic Party as simply a federation of independent state parties. They succeeded in four states in getting Thurmond's name on the ballot as the official Democratic Party nominee: Alabama, Mississippi, Louisiana (where Governor Earl Long called a special session of the legislature to place Truman on the ballot, though not as the official Democratic candidate), and South Carolina. Georgia didn't go along, even though newly elected Governor Herman Talmadge was Thurmond's cousin. (Talmadge's mother spent her early years in Edgefield County, her father a much older half brother of Thurmond's father.)

Jean didn't make the trip to Birmingham, unaware that anything significant was happening there. When she was finally alone with Strom after he flew back to South Carolina late that night, she asked, "What about the political repercussions? You're really sticking your neck out."[35]

At the end of their conversation, she said, "I'm sure everything will turn out all right in the end." Having just turned twenty-two, her first political campaign would be as the wife of a presidential candidate.

Time magazine soon featured a sketch of a dour Thurmond on its cover, along with a story that mentioned one of those attending the Birmingham convention was Gerald L.K. Smith, a notorious racist and anti-Semite. Robert Lipshutz, then a lawyer in his late twenties who later became White House counsel for President Jimmy Carter, had been sent to Birmingham to scout around for the Anti-Defamation League's regional office in Atlanta, which wanted to find out if there was any anti-Semitism in the Dixiecrat movement. Lipshutz learned that Smith was in a motel room, confirmed this, and passed the information to *Time's* Atlanta bureau chief.[36] After the story ran, Thurmond explicitly rejected Smith's support. He said, "We do not invite and we do not need the support of Gerald L.

K. Smith or any other rabble-rousers who use race prejudice and class hatred to inflame the emotions of the people."[37] Despite his own rhetoric,
Thurmond clearly was seeking respectability.

And some respected mainstream newspapers believed his past record
gave the Dixiecrats a leader who deserved to be heard. The *Christian Science
Monitor* noted his war record, youthful vigor, and political ability. "His
nomination gives people everywhere pause," the *Monitor* said. "Many of
those whom he earnestly referred to as 'the good people of the South' will
think before writing off a man of Gov. Thurmond's stature."[38] The
Washington Evening Star wrote, "Thurmond's record as a progressive advocate
for a better deal for the Negro of the South entitles him to a respectful
hearing."[39]

Back home, however, *The State* warned that the South's problems weren't
"going to be solved by fiery speeches. . . . This is no time for hotheaded-
ness."[40]

LOOKING BACK YEARS LATER, adviser Figg expressed disappointment
about Thurmond's decision to make the presidential run. "He hadn't
reached the halfway point in his administration of South Carolina government," Figg said, "and for this side issue to come along . . . Strom just
jumped overboard down there."[41]

The Dixiecrat protest went beyond race. It exploited fissures already developing in the Democratic structure in the South. It was fueled by conservative critics of the New Deal's expansion of Washington power and by
new issues, such as ownership of tidelands oil. During the 1930s, the federal
government claimed it owned the mineral rights in submerged coastal areas.
The states most affected—Texas, Louisiana, Mississippi, Florida, and California—protested. The oil companies supported the states, mainly because
their tax rate was much lower than the 37.5-percent federal royalty.

Congress passed legislation in 1946 that affirmed state ownership, and
Truman vetoed the bill. The Supreme Court ruled in favor of the federal
claim in 1947, and would do so again in 1950. Truman vetoed another bill
in 1952. Nationally syndicated columnist Stewart Alsop wrote that Texas
oil interests, specifically naming oilman H. R. Cullen, were supporting
Thurmond's candidacy. Alsop wrote that Cullen's private plane transported Thurmond as he campaigned around Texas. The Dixiecrats denied
the link to the oil interests.

With Fielding Wright as his running mate, Thurmond campaigned with the vigor of a man who expected to win. In the end he carried only the four states in which he was on the ballot as the official candidate of the Democratic Party. He received more than 1 million votes and got thirty-eight electoral votes from these four states, plus a thirty-ninth from a rogue elector in Tennessee.

In one of the major upsets in American political history, Harry Truman won—and Clark Clifford was vindicated. Political analysts later concluded that a switch of some 21,000 votes in Ohio and Illinois from Truman to Dewey would have shifted enough electoral votes that Truman would have failed to get a majority.

Thurmond would always say—and seem to believe—that under such circumstances he could have been elected. He contended that the Democrats wouldn't have voted for Dewey and the Republicans wouldn't have voted for Truman. If no candidate receives a majority of the electoral vote, the House of Representatives determines the winner, with each state having a single vote.

After the 1948 elections, Democrats had a majority in twenty-five of the forty-eight House delegations (Alaska and Hawaii were not states yet)—including the four that Thurmond carried. Republicans held a majority in only twenty. Three states—Montana, Idaho, and Connecticut—had split delegations.

The first round of voting might have given Thurmond 4 votes for the states he won, with 21½ for Dewey. Truman, with 22½, would need only two more states for a majority. In Louisiana, where Thurmond received only a plurality, the House delegation would have no reason to stick with him. In Alabama, whose governor and both senators were national party loyalists, the House delegation would have everything to gain and nothing to lose by backing Truman. Just as in the actual general election, Truman would have won.

At any rate, history is shaped not by what might have happened, but by what did happen. Thurmond's 1948 campaign both foreshadowed the coming politics of massive resistance in the Deep South and broke loose the psychological moorings that tied the region to the Democratic Party. Fidelity to the party would never again be "like religion."

Donald Fowler, the South Carolina political scientist who became Democratic national chairman under Bill Clinton, likens this affiliation with another party to losing one's virginity. It's easier the second time around.[42] From never voting more than 5 percent Republican, South Carolina went almost 50 percent for Dwight Eisenhower in 1952. Unlike before, the presidential candidates for both parties began to campaign in the South. As Thurmond had said, the South was no longer in the bag, although by 2004 the region appeared to many—at least in presidential elections—to be in the Republican bag.

IN SOUTH CAROLINA, the Dixiecrat campaign had immediate—and long-lasting—reverberations. Judge Waring had tossed out the Democratic oath as "absurd," after a hearing at which Bill Baskin was unable to explain its purpose. Waring had alienated whites—one, whose beach cottage next to his was struck by lightning, put up a sign that read, "Dear God, he lives next door"—but he became a hero to blacks in the state.

Freshman Congressman Dorn had called for Waring's impeachment as a prelude to Dorn's brash challenge of Burnet Maybank in the August Democratic primary. In contrast, although Maybank had criticized Waring's earlier ruling ending the white primary, he left it at that. An estimated 35,000 blacks responded to that court order and voted solidly for Maybank—enough to give him a necessary majority in the first primary, even with three other opponents, and avoid a runoff.

Politically astute though he was, Thurmond failed to grasp at the time the full significance of this new patch of blackness in the electorate. In 1949, he accepted an invitation to speak to almost 150 politically active blacks in Sumter, forty miles east of Columbia. There he paid tribute to Davis Lee—an ultraconservative New Jersey editor whose writings Thurmond had quoted in his Dixiecrat campaign—as "one of America's great leaders." The governor also denounced as "agitators" others who were urging his audience to fight for their rights.

John McCray wrote afterward that blacks generally repudiated Lee's writings as "treason" and said the governor "missed an excellent chance to win the race's confidence." McCray added, "Mr. Thurmond, in his own way, spoke from his heart. He believed in what he was saying as firmly as Negroes disbelieved in what he said."[43] Years would pass before Thurmond learned to listen to blacks rather than lecture to them.

CHAPTER 11

Campaign of the Century

WHEN ERNEST F. "FRITZ" HOLLINGS of South Carolina won reelection in 1998 to his final six-year term before retiring from the Senate, he had served thirty-two years, longer than any other junior senator in U.S. history. But Strom Thurmond kept him in that status by remaining the state's senior senator for four more years, during which he set two U.S. Senate records: He became the oldest person ever to serve in the Senate and served longer than any senator.

Although Hollings and Thurmond carefully kept out of each other's political races and worked cooperatively on projects for South Carolina, their voting records, lifestyles, and personalities could hardly have been more different. A handsome, polished Citadel man of generally liberal political sympathies with a thick Charleston accent, razor-sharp mind, deep intellectual curiosity, and a wit sometimes too quick, Hollings in many ways represented the opposite side of the coin from Thurmond. One South Carolinian who knows both men well—and likes them—once said, "what vanity is to Strom, arrogance is to Fritz."[1]

As politicians, they shared one deeply etched experience. Each ran for the Senate at the end of his term as governor—Thurmond in 1950 and Hollings in 1962. And each lost to Olin D. Johnston.

In his own words, Johnston was "of humble origin. I was born the son of a tenant farmer and spent some ten years of my early life working in the cotton textile mills of my home state. . . . I know how to toil with my hands. I am proud of my heritage. It is noble and honorable. I believe in the dignity of hard, honest toil."[2] Like Huey Long of Louisiana, Johnston was "for the man farthest down" and delivered for him, but he lacked Long's overweening ambition and vindictiveness. Five years older and far more introspective than Thurmond, Johnston set aside a daily period of reflection, up to an hour, when his Senate staff knew to leave him undisturbed.

As a cotton mill worker, he persuaded the president of Wofford College to admit him without an accredited high school diploma. Rejected by the

Marine Corps in 1917 because of flat feet and color blindness, Johnston managed to get into the army. He served more than a year in France, returned to Wofford, got his degree, then played tackle on the football team at the University of South Carolina while working his way through USC Law School. It was a different era. By the time Thurmond took him on in 1950, Johnston had served three House terms in the legislature and had run six statewide campaigns, wearing baggy suits and colorful ties. He had already lost one race for governor by 960 votes and had won two; he had lost two senatorial races, to Cotton Ed Smith in 1938 and Burnet Maybank in 1941, and had won one.

Richard W. Riley, President Bill Clinton's secretary of education and the first person to serve two consecutive terms as South Carolina's governor (1979–1987), worked a year for Olin Johnston after finishing law school. A few months into the job, two prominent men from Riley's hometown of Greenville, brothers who ran an architectural firm, came by to see the senator. Young Riley walked into Johnston's office to let him know. Olin thanked him but asked that instead he show in Mr. Jones, a shift foreman from a Greenville textile mill visiting Washington with his wife.

After some time, Riley went back in to remind Johnston that the brothers were still waiting outside. Olin nodded, then said he was taking Mr. and Mrs. Jones to the Senate dining room for lunch. He left the architects waiting.

When the trio returned from lunch, Olin brought the Joneses back into his office for a few minutes before bidding them good-bye, then called in his new staffer. "Dick," he drawled in a voice that rumbled like a slow-moving freight train, "Mr. Jones is my precinct manager at the Parker Mill precinct, and he's been one of my good supporters for many years." Johnston indicated he was now ready to see the two Greenville brothers. "You can tell those two Republican sons-of-bitches to come on in," he said. "They want to see me about getting that contract to design the new post office we're going to build in Greenville."

Herman Talmadge considered Johnston "the dumbest senator I knew," but Bryan Dorn, who perhaps knew him better, said, "Olin was dumb like a fox."[3]

Roy Powell, one of Johnston's closest aides and later a Columbia municipal judge, recalled that Thurmond solicited Johnston's support in the 1946 race for governor. "He came to Senator Johnston, I remember it was in the old Wade Hampton Hotel. He talked to Senator Johnston, Mrs. Johnston and Bill Johnston, the senator's brother—all of us—and he promised the group that if it would support him for governor that he would never run against Senator Johnston. Of course, we all agreed, and the senator, he went touring around the Piedmont and Chester and all around, and Strom Thurmond was elected. But no sooner had he become governor than he began campaigning for the U.S. Senate."[4]

In South Carolina's then one-party Democratic structure, Thurmond and Johnston represented separate factions that went back to the Civil War, descended from seeds planted by the rivalry of Edgefield's revered Matthew Calbraith Butler, reputedly the youngest general in the Confederate army, and Martin Witherspoon Gary, the head of the Redshirt campaign.

Bryan Dorn, a student of the state's politics, explained:

It is rumored that Butler received a promotion to major general over Martin Gary. They kind of patched things up in the campaign of 1876, when they won the state from radical rule, but the feud and jealousy and rivalry continued to simmer underneath and blossomed into General Gary's hatred of the aristocrats. Gary was the patron saint of Ben Tillman. You'll never understand South Carolina politics until you go back to that. Since then, there's always been factions in South Carolina politics. They never had a two-party state, but they've always had two parties within the Democratic Party.

If you study real carefully, you'll find that Jimmy Byrnes kind of gradually inherited the Tillman faction, although it had become sophisticated when Byrnes came along. The other faction was more radical really than Tillman. That was Cole L. Blease. This is the only state, you know, in American history where you had the terms "Bleasism" and "Tillmanism," completely personalized political organizations. Olin Johnston, then, I would say kind of inherited or fell heir to the Blease element, which was the cotton mill boys, the lint heads and their champion, Coley Blease. They would die for him.

Then on into the 1950s, I see Thurmond carrying the banner of the Jimmy Byrnes faction and Olin Johnston the Blease crowd. Again, Thurmond generally getting some of the Byrnes support, which had kind of graduated to the aristocracy, to the textile magnates, the newspapers. So that campaign in 1950 . . . was the last real lineup of those old factions.[5]

In 1950, Byrnes returned home to run for governor. Immediately the front-runner, at seventy-one he initially indicated he would forgo the grueling forty-six-county tour. Byrnes then reversed his position and said he would participate. As a shrewd politician, he understood that no matter how revered he might be, South Carolinians expected their candidates to campaign vigorously. Failure to do so might raise questions about the physical vitality considered necessary for the job.

But a campaign aide also advised that prominent people insisting that he attend the meetings "seem to be pro-Thurmond folks who believe it would be to his advantage and Johnston's detriment for you to make the circuit."[6]

In those days, before the spread of television, the forty-six county-by-county Democratic stump meetings served to introduce the candidates to the voters. Part carnival, part revival, and part theater, the stump meetings linked politics and popular culture. People ate, drank, and enjoyed themselves. They not only heard candidates express their positions on the issues but saw them react to an opponent's jabs, think on their feet, and respond forcefully or with unease to hecklers. Voters could still expect to shake a candidate's hand, look him in the eye, and get a feel for his character. That kind of retail politics has largely disappeared from the American landscape except for the Iowa caucuses and the New Hampshire presidential primary, which remain so important for these reasons.

One of the bitterest campaigns in South Carolina's history, the 1950 Senate race resembled a rolling heavyweight bare-knuckle boxing match— with Strom and Olin slugging away. At the first stump meeting on May 23 in Lexington, Thurmond attacked Johnston as soft on segregation, calling him a "Trumanite" when in Washington and an anti-Truman Democrat when in South Carolina. He called it a choice between "candidates who are following the President and those who are willing to stand up and be counted in opposition to his un-American, Communistic and anti-Southern programs."[7]

He would soon add that as governor, Johnston ran a corrupt "pardon racket" in return for political favors and future support. Johnston initially ignored Thurmond's charges, saying he was running a "Christian" campaign.

Johnston's tactics changed in the final weeks, a period when voters always become more attentive. With Thurmond running out of political ammunition, Johnston switched to a counterattack. He had always understood that he would have to prove to his white working-class base that he wasn't vulnerable to Thurmond on segregation. Simultaneously, he would depend on newly enfranchised blacks accepting his harsh racial stand as a political necessity and responding to his overall progressive record. With Thurmond's hated Dixiecrat image, black voters understood the choices before them. "It was a matter of choosing between a rattler and a moccasin," explained the Reverend I. DeQuincey Newman, who would emerge as the state's top NAACP official and then become the first black state senator since Reconstruction.[8]

JOHN MCCRAY, a statewide black leader and editor of the *Lighthouse and Informer*, said that NAACP leaders and Thurmond's white enemies in the Democratic Party arranged for Essie Mae Williams to be secretly photographed for use against him. The photographs were made available to Johnston's 1950 campaign staff but were never made public. Campaign advisers said years later that such use would have violated a "gentlemen's agreement" not to indulge in smear tactics.[9] They apparently concluded that use of the photographs in that fierce campaign could backfire.

A criminal libel lawsuit against McCray played a significant role in energizing black support for Johnston because organized black voters "interpreted McCray's indictment as a politically motivated attempt by the Thurmond forces to intimidate them and thus minimize the impact of the black vote." After McCray had reported trial testimony that a black man and the white teenage girl whom he was accused of raping had actually had consensual sex, the editor was charged with criminal libel. In June, after McCray won a change of venue, Thurmond ran an advertisement claiming Johnston was in the courtroom when McCray—"identified in the ad as a defamer of white womanhood and an enemy of Strom Thurmond"— asked for and received a change of venue from Greenwood County, home of the prosecuting solicitor, the alleged rape victim's father. The *Greenwood Index-Journal*, which published the advertisement with its implication that Johnston had somehow intervened on behalf of McCray, followed with a front-page denunciation by the presiding judge denying any contact with Johnston about the case.[10] This affair ultimately led to McCray's being convicted and sentenced to serve time on a chain gang and the subsequent demise of the *Lighthouse and Informer*.

JOHNSTON HAD NOT ACTUALLY VOTED in the 1948 election because a driving rain kept him from getting to the polls before closing time. But at 11 P.M. that night—a time when the president himself believed he had lost the election—Johnston announced that he would have voted for Truman. That set him apart from South Carolina's other politicians.

Now Johnston sought to distance himself from Truman, belittling him as "the little man in the White House," though he simultaneously argued that the Democratic Party represented a broad coalition in which Southerners had always protected their interests. In a slap at Thurmond, he contended that a third party meant political isolation. He recognized that the Republican Party, which in 1950 still retained a large black base in the South as the party of Lincoln, remained too stigmatized to become a viable option for most whites.

Although a first-term senator, Johnston had already become chairman of the Post Office and Civil Service Committee, which gave him influence among colleagues because the postal service was then an important source of patronage. On the campaign trail he emphasized the power of seniority, often citing nearby federal projects he had helped get funded. With Maybank as chairman of the Banking and Currency Committee, Johnston boasted that for the first time in more than a century, both South Carolina senators chaired major committees. (A sweeping Republican victory in 1946 followed by a huge loss in 1948 had restored Democratic control of the Senate, with large numbers of freshmen from the North and the West.)

Johnston had voted to sustain Truman's veto of the anti-labor Taft-Hartley Bill, which allowed states to outlaw closed-shop union contracts, the so-called right to work laws. When attacked for that vote, Johnston used it to demonstrate that he had influence with the president that helped get increased cotton and peanut acreage allotments for farmers. When Thurmond charged he was a tool of the Congress of Industrial Organizations (CIO), Johnston simply replied he was for the working man.

Johnston and Thurmond also vigorously debated federal aid to education. Thurmond, who had supported such aid in his inaugural speech as governor, now changed his position. He told the South Carolina Education Association, the professional organization for thousands of public school teachers, that federal aid would lead to federal control and become a weapon to force school desegregation. And although Johnston supported a pending federal aid bill that explicitly granted state control over spending, Thurmond maintained that desegregation would be demanded in the future.

Johnston said, "I am not for the races mixing because God did not mix them himself." He supported the education bill because it would allow South Carolina to raise salaries for its badly underpaid teachers, without significant tax increases.

On June 5, 1950, the Supreme Court issued three opinions that weakened the constitutional basis for segregation.* Johnston put Thurmond on the defensive by arguing that the court decisions meant facilities would have to be truly equal and that federal funds would be needed because of a projected shortfall in state tax revenue. "We don't like them," Johnston said of the decisions, "but you have to abide by the Supreme Court."[11] Johnston also pointed out that the state's colleges and universities received federal aid but remained segregated. "I have three children and I want them to go to school with white children," Johnston said near the end of the campaign, emphasizing his commitment to segregation while subtly contrasting himself with the—publicly—childless Thurmond.

Throughout the campaign Johnston had good timing. The Supreme Court decisions diverted attention away from Thurmond's attack on Johnston's gubernatorial pardon and parole record. (Thurmond won a legislative battle to take that power away from the governor and place it in a state board.) Early in the campaign, he charged that Johnston as governor had conducted "an unconstitutional, unbridled and unbelievable pardon and parole spree." Thurmond said Johnston had released 3,221 criminals from prison, including murderers and rapists. "It was easier to get out of the penitentiary," he put it, "than it was to get in it."[12] Thurmond hammered at the issue for a month before Johnston responded.

Johnston defended himself by quoting from a letter written by Secretary of State O. Frank Thornton, who said that state records showed that

---

*In *Sweatt v. Painter*, the court ruled that a separate black law school in Texas was unequal to that of the University of Texas because of the latter's superior faculty, resources, and reputation. *McLaurin v. Oklahoma* outlawed that state's practice of segregating black graduate students in the library, cafeteria, and classrooms. And *Henderson v. United States* desegregated dining cars on trains that crossed state lines.

as governor, Johnston had pardoned, paroled, or commuted the sentences of 671 persons, compared to 714 by Governor John G. Richards from 1927 to 1931 and 1,091 by Governor Ibra C. Blackwood from 1931 to 1935. Johnston further denounced Thurmond's charges as "false and malicious" and countercharged that some of those he released had been named honorary "colonels" by Thurmond. The governor then refused to make public the list of the hundreds of people to whom he had given certificates designating them with that honorary title.

On the campaign trail, Thurmond liked to relate the fanciful story of Johnston rushing back to Washington after the 1948 election to meet Truman's victorious return from Missouri: "He elbowed his way through the crowd, almost knocked down several admirals and generals and pushed Cabinet officers aside. They had to make a special seat in the parade because they didn't know he was going to be there."[13] Thurmond also regularly charged Johnston with violating an oath to support the party when he declined to endorse the States Rights Democratic ticket in 1948.

As THE 1950 SENATE CAMPAIGN MOVED FORWARD, Thurmond added a final link between Johnston and Truman. Thurmond compared the senator to two well-known Southern liberals in the Senate who had just been defeated in Democratic primaries in their states—Frank Porter Graham of North Carolina and Claude Pepper of Florida.

One Thurmond campaign ad showed a cartoon figure, labeled "Southern Voter," who had already scratched lines through Graham and Pepper's names on a blackboard and had started a line through Johnston's name. The caption said: "Attention Harry Truman: Two Down—One to Go!"[14]

Unlike Graham and Pepper, Johnston had a record on segregation that wasn't soft. In fact, Thurmond failed to ride his 1948 momentum all the way to a Senate seat in large part because even though race remained the central issue in 1950, this time two segregationists were running instead of one. Johnston portrayed himself as a team player on the twenty-two-member Southern bloc led by men such as Richard Russell of Georgia and Harry Byrd of Virginia. They had used the filibuster and other delaying tactics to defeat the Fair Employment Practices Commission Bill that spring. Johnston's office churned out press releases depicting him as a central player in the fight, and on the stump he called the bill's defeat "a personal victory." He understood the lesson provided by the defeat of

Graham and Pepper, both FEPC supporters, and displayed photographs of Southern senators with whom he was aligned to defeat the FEPC bill.

Johnston then slammed Thurmond for being "in the same boat" as Frank Graham, who had appointed a black youth to West Point. Thurmond had appointed a black physician in Charleston—Dr. T. C. McFall—to the state medical advisory board, based on a recommendation by the state medical association. State law had specified that the governor's appointments to a state hospital advisory council under the federal Hill-Burton Act should follow the state medical association's recommendations. The appointment of McFall in the summer of 1949 generally received praise, if noticed at all; the *News and Courier* headlined an editorial, "Excellent Appointment."[15] McFall became the first black appointed in the twentieth century to a state board or commission in South Carolina. Johnston charged that Thurmond, like Graham, "broke down segregation" and that Thurmond, like Graham, "is going to be defeated."[16]

Johnston's attacks became more emotional than the voters had yet seen on June 22 at a stump meeting in Marion. "Any man that says I am for the mixing of the races is an unmitigated liar . . . a low down contemptible liar . . . I'm getting tired of this," he shouted. "Someday there might be a break in the situation and some of you know about Olin Johnston and how I will rave when I cut loose."[17]

A day later, Johnston held up a copy of the notorious *Life* magazine photo of Thurmond and commented, "You know you get addled when you stand on your head."[18]

On June 24, barely two weeks before the July 10 Democratic primary, North Korean Communists invaded South Korea. Thurmond initially criticized Truman for not taking a firmer stand earlier against the Communists, but Johnston immediately supported Truman and the United Nations for committing to fight. As usual in a foreign policy crisis, the commander in chief's popularity rose, at least initially, and the opening weeks of the Korean conflict undercut Thurmond's assault on the "Trumanite" Johnston.

Then he returned to McFall's appointment. Johnston called Thurmond a hypocrite for appointing McFall while posing as a hard-line states' rights segregationist and an opportunist for doing so to court the new black voters. On June 26 at the courthouse in Newberry, with both Johnston and Thurmond in attendance, the campaign hit its tempestuous peak. Johnston

waved a copy of the *Lighthouse and Informer*, which had boldly displayed Mc-
Fall's appointment while most of the white press ignored it. Thurmond repeated a charge that Johnston had done nothing to protest the Truman
administration's executive order desegregating the armed forces, that he was
"silent as a tomb." Then he taunted Johnston, sitting in the front row of the
courthouse audience, "If that's not so, Senator, stand up and deny it."

Johnston stood up and yelled, "I want to tell you, you are a liar, for
twenty-two of us. . . ."

As bedlam erupted, Strom looked straight at Olin and said, "I'll see you
outside afterwards." An Edgefield man had felt his honor assailed.

As the meeting broke up, Strom waited outside for Johnston. Johnston
came out and reached forward as if to shake hands. Thurmond grabbed his
hand and pulled him around. Before blows were struck, but just barely, a
Johnston aide and a Thurmond aide, backed up by other supporters,
moved in to separate them.

Walking away, Johnston was quoted as saying, "After the campaign I'll
fix him up. I was a heavyweight boxer in the army and I'll knock hell out of
him with one blow."[19]

To the delight of his core supporters, Johnston next ridiculed Thurmond for a letter he sent to William Hastie, the black former dean of
Howard University Law School whom Truman had appointed governor of
the Virgin Islands. The form letter—which Thurmond sent to all governors after he attended his first national governors conference—invited
Hastie to visit South Carolina and stay overnight in the Governor's Mansion. Hastie sent a letter expressing regret he was unable to accept. Johnston gleefully displayed both letters, while Thurmond lamely brushed it
off as a clerical mistake.[20]

In the final days of the campaign, Thurmond defended his appointment of McFall, saying he had had no choice but to follow the law. John-
ston poured it on. He contended that Thurmond should have asked for
another recommendation until a white doctor's name was sent forward.
Johnston's campaign ran full-page newspaper ads with blaring headlines:
"Thurmond Appoints Negro." Subheads read: "Wade Hampton's Era of
Segregation Ends in South Carolina as Thurmond Replaces White Doctor
with Charleston Negro in Bold Bid to Capture Negro Vote of State! First
Negro Appointed to State Position Since Days of Carpetbaggers and
Scalawags."

Four days before the primary, in Charleston, Johnston declared before an audience of 4,000 at the city's baseball park, "Had I been Governor Thurmond, I would never have appointed the nigger physician of Charleston, Dr. T. C. McFall, to displace your beloved white physician of this community . . ." When the 400 or so blacks protested loudly enough to drown out the rest of the sentence, Johnston thundered, "Make those niggers keep quiet!"[21]

One observer called the senator's crude racist assault on Thurmond's appointment of McFall "a moral low point in Olin D. Johnston's political career . . . yet it cannot be denied that the black physician's appointment proved to be a devastatingly effective weapon in the senator's quest for a second term."[22]

The contrast between Thurmond and Johnston in the 1950 campaign reflects that there have always been two types of racism in the South. One is the "democratic" racism that follows from South Carolina Upcountryman John C. Calhoun's theories based on skin color. In its rawest form, poor whites gained a measure of status based solely on skin color, and blacks were looked upon as subhuman. Johnston's core support came from Upcountry working-class whites imbued with Calhoun's racial theories. Thurmond represented more the "aristocratic" racism that predominated in the Lowcountry plantation region. Also convinced of white racial superiority, those who held this attitude felt somewhat paternalistic toward blacks, whom they regarded almost as children. The aristocrats typically looked down on poor whites, too. Thurmond avoided this strain of the prejudice.

The appointment of the highly regarded Dr. McFall could have opened the door earlier as a first step toward new racial relationships. Thurmond never defended the appointment, however, on grounds of qualifications or that it was the right thing to do. He continued to say he had no choice until citing it many years later as an example of his progressive views on race.

AFTER WINNING MORE THAN 70 PERCENT of the South Carolina vote in his Dixiecrat campaign, Thurmond was perceived as the clear favorite at the start of his campaign against Johnston. William D. "Bill" Workman Jr., then the *News and Courier*'s Columbia correspondent and considered the state's top political reporter, was privately predicting a 57–43 landslide for Thurmond on the eve of the July 10 primary. His newspaper editorially opposed virtually everything (except segregation) that Johnston stood for and vigorously attacked him almost daily. Shortly before the election, it exulted that "J. Strom Thurmond's majority . . . will be overwhelming."[23] Johnston stunned the political establishment, decisively winning with 186,180 votes (54 percent) to Thurmond's 158,904 (46 percent).[24]

If Thurmond had run nationally in 1948 to set up his local 1950 Senate campaign, the effort misfired. Johnston proved capable of neutralizing Thurmond's appeal as a segregationist, and his defense of the national Democratic Party and its economic policies won him support from newly enfranchised black voters who wanted to defeat the Dixiecrat candidate. As Modjeska Simkins put it, "Strom vilified Negroes in 1948 . . . and we swore vengeance."[25] Further, the Dixiecrat campaign cost Thurmond the support of the progressive elements that had helped elect him governor.

Charles Simons, whom Thurmond was about to join in a law practice, was his Aiken County campaign manager and carried every precinct, including the textile town of Graniteville. He believed Thurmond's opposing federal aid to education was decisive, that he lost support of teachers and their supporters.[26]

With a spread of less than 28,000 votes, the *News and Courier* concluded that blacks "apparently supplied the margin . . . of victory." In Columbia's Ward 9, an almost all black precinct, Johnston received nearly 95 percent of the vote, beating Thurmond 1,249–72. Of the half million registered voters in the state in 1950, an estimated 73,000 were black. If the percentage of turnout was the same as in 1948, roughly 50,000 voted.[27]

Looking back almost three decades later, Thurmond thought he made a mistake in attacking Johnston's record rather than running on his own. "I think I had a good record as governor, a progressive record, and had done so much for the people I think I'd have been elected," he said of the 1950 race.[28]

AT EVERY STOP on the county-by-county tour, Thurmond's attacks on Johnston had gotten applause, often begun with vigorous clapping by Jean and her driver, a Presbyterian College student named Harry Dent.

Dent had chosen the small liberal arts college in Clinton over the University of South Carolina, preferring to be a big fish in a small pond. He became student newspaper editor his freshman year and soon thereafter doubled as the school's public relations director. He met Governor Thurmond in 1950, when the college president invited the governor for the campus Political Emphasis Week, an event designed to raise political awareness among the students. Thurmond was impressed with the young man, and Dent received an invitation the next day for lunch at the Governor's Mansion.

Dent remembered "being scared to death. I was just a boy from St. Matthews and grew up in the back of a house where we didn't have any etiquette and all that kind of stuff." He took a seat for lunch as servants were setting the table. Someone explained to Dent that the servers were prisoners, this one a murderer and that one a murderer.

Dent was still worried about etiquette when the governor came in and sat down. Thurmond cleaned his plate in minutes, talking as he chewed. "We got right into it," Dent remembered. "He ain't got no etiquette, so I felt much relieved. I said, 'Man, I can handle this.'" Thurmond wanted him to drive him and Jean across the state. "I said, 'Yes, sir, I'll do that.'"[29]

During the campaign, Strom and Jean usually rode in different cars, with Dent driving her. Strom would go early to each courthouse, and Jean and Harry would hit Main Street, distributing brochures. With Jean only a few years older than Harry, the two of them formed a close, platonic relationship, almost like a brother and sister.

Jean had demonstrated during the 1948 campaign that she would support fully her husband's political life. She proved adept at campaigning, accepted its strains, and she and Strom drew closer. In 1949, they wrote regularly when he was traveling without her, Jean addressing him as "My darling husband" or "Hey Sugar!" and frequently signing her letters, "Sugie." Often she went to stay with her family in Elko. When he was on a trip to New York attempting to recruit new industries to South Carolina, she ended a typically chatty three-page letter, "I do miss you so very, very much and love you more every day that passes. Behave yourself and be sweet." He sometimes addressed her in letters as "My Darling Wifey."

While on Army Reserve duty at Fort Bragg in North Carolina, he seemed frustrated, writing, "I do love you so much. Sometimes I may not express to you my deep love, but it is simply that I am rolling over in my mind the hundreds of important matters and responsibilities of State and otherwise."[30]

WHEN THE RETURNS CAME IN on election night, young Harry Dent felt devastated, but Thurmond took it all in stride. He noticed the young man's distress and told him, "Harry, never look up a dead horse's rear end."[31]

CHAPTER 12

"Strum Thormond"

A GENTRIFIED COMMUNITY with streets named for all of the state's other counties, the planned town of Aiken presents a sophisticated, tidy appearance that differs from the typical South Carolina county seat. Racehorses are trained there, and the town has a certain charm—though with some pretensions. With an interstate highway running nearby and a four-year campus of the state university, it is far more cosmopolitan than neighboring Edgefield to the north, its mother county more than a century ago.

Strom and Jean Thurmond settled in easily in 1951, enjoying some of their happiest years. Strom thrived in law practice with Charles Simons and Dorcey Lybrand, smart lawyers and shrewd, well-connected political activists. He would also organize Palmetto Federal Savings and Loan, get it chartered, and become its president.

As governor he had been briefed on the federal government's plan to manufacture raw materials for nuclear weapons in Aiken and bordering Barnwell County. This massive Savannah River Site would displace whole towns. He and his law partners prospered, the law firm quickly demonstrating that it could negotiate more money for farmers and any others whose land was being condemned. The firm took the cases on contingency, keeping one-third of the difference between what the government originally offered and what was finally paid.

Strom often took time off in the middle of the day for tennis or swimming or horseback riding with Jean. As the state's former first couple, their social life was full. Strom began experimenting for the first time with implanting plugs of hair into his balding scalp. The Thurmonds wanted children, and they talked about adopting.[1]

STROM ENJOYED TRIAL WORK and added to his reputation for cagey thinking for his defense of Mrs. Margie Kennedy, brought to court for the murder of her husband. Although Kennedy lived across the Savannah River in Augusta, Georgia, where the shooting took place, she was a native of Edgefield. She called Strom Thurmond to represent her. He focused on the case with the same intensity he gave a political campaign.

He presented Margie Kennedy to the jury as a frail, terrified woman whose 220-pound husband, a politically prominent former fire chief in Augusta, beat her and refused to give her any money. (The prosecution presented evidence that he gave her no money because she would spend it on whiskey.)

The husband had taught her to shoot a .22-caliber pistol. During one altercation, while he was chasing her from room to room, she grabbed it and shot him three times. When he wheeled around, perhaps to head for a doctor, she fired three more times. Each bullet hit him in the back between the shoulders.

He lingered for a week before dying. Thurmond argued that Mrs. Kennedy was mentally deranged by terror and maltreatment, but he really turned the jury after arranging for a friendly coroner to testify that the husband had already been suffering from kidney trouble, uremia, and diabetes. It wasn't those puny little .22 bullets that killed this great big man, Thurmond argued, after getting the coroner to agree that they were only "secondary causes" of his death.

In that era in the South, when "respectable" white women were placed on a pedestal, they relinquished control over their lives for protection from "others." If a woman who killed her husband wasn't certifiably and quite obviously crazy, there would generally be a community presumption that she took control and gave up his protection because for some reason he "deserved" killing. Her lawyer's job was to be creative and figure out a way for a jury to rationalize an acquittal and walk away with a clear conscience. In Margie Kennedy's case, Thurmond performed masterfully. The jury acquitted. The Augusta newspapers displayed photographs of the grateful Mrs. Kennedy embracing her lawyer, with Thurmond resolutely looking away.[2]

By the summer of 1954, Thurmond's political ambitions had begun to resurface. He invited Congressman Bryan Dorn, always a champion of veterans' interests, to his Aiken home for an American Legion meeting. Dorn had regained his House seat in 1950, two years after his ill-fated challenge to Senator Maybank for the Senate seat. Now Maybank was unopposed in a reelection bid.

Thurmond asked Dorn to step into a back room. "When we got back there," Dorn recalled, "he said, 'You realize that some day both of these seats for the United States Senate will be coming open. Now Bryan, Maybank's seat is yours. You ran for it before. But Johnston's seat is mine.'

"We shook hands on it. We weren't making a deal, but we shook hands on it as though that is the way it would be. It was clear he wanted to eliminate me as a challenger for Senator Johnston's seat."[3]

On Tuesday, September 1, having won the Democratic primary without opposition and facing none in the general election, the fifty-five-year-old Maybank died unexpectedly in his sleep while vacationing at his summer mountain cottage in Flat Rock, North Carolina, apparently of a heart attack.

The legal deadline for the Democratic Party of South Carolina to certify its nominees was three days away. Every South Carolina political figure of note went to Maybank's funeral two days later in Charleston. As the funeral procession left St. Michael's Episcopal Church for the cemetery, a black limousine pulled away and headed at high speed toward Columbia. It was carrying Edgar Brown.

THE SIXTY-SIX-YEAR-OLD BROWN, lean and bespectacled, had served on the state Executive Committee since 1914 and for many years had served as Democratic national committeeman. In South Carolina he was regarded as "Mr. Democrat." He already had a history with Thurmond. His was not the only car that left Charleston and headed for Columbia right after Maybank's funeral. Other members of the state Democratic Executive Committee also sped away that Friday. At 6 P.M. the deadline would expire for the state Democratic Party to certify its nominee for the Senate. The procedure was spelled out in a statute that, coincidentally, Thurmond had helped draft when he was a state senator.

But it was all so unseemly. Fewer than fifty politicians met in the clubroom of the Jefferson Hotel with the legal authority to name a U.S. senator for a full term. A vote to circumvent the law and hold a primary failed by a vote of 28–18. Edgar Brown's state senate buddy, Rembert Dennis of Berkeley County, made the motion to nominate Brown. "I, too, as many of you, favor a primary to get a candidate," Dennis said, but added, "In this emergency we do not have time for a primary under our election laws." The executive committee then voted 31–18 in support of Brown, handing him a Senate seat that voters had twice before denied him, in 1924 and 1938.

The press in the state, led by *News and Courier* editor Thomas R. Waring—an unadmiring nephew of the by then infamous Judge Waring—would light a fire of protest. Governor James F. Byrnes would fan it into a consuming blaze.

Although publicly calling for a primary, Byrnes had let the state executive committee know through a friend that he was interested in the nomination and would submit to a draft.[4] As governor, however, Byrnes in 1952 had actively supported Republican Dwight Eisenhower for president, and party loyalists on the Democratic Executive Committee weren't about to lose face by naming an apostate. This meant they wouldn't have considered Thurmond either, because he also had endorsed Eisenhower.

Other loyal Democrats were waiting in the wings. Thirty-eight-year-old Bryan Dorn drove home to Greenwood after Maybank's funeral believing he had a commitment from friends on the executive committee to put his name in nomination. He expected to get overwhelmed by Brown, but the move would position him to make a write-in challenge against Brown based on principle. Dorn's explanation of events a quarter century later gives a clear impression of his own political thinking:

> I would have announced as a write-in immediately, had my name been put up before the executive committee. The race would have been between Dorn and Brown. As the former runner-up for that seat in the Senate, I would have really charged fraud, chicanery, unfairness and everything. It just automatically would have been a race between Dorn and Brown, and I would have won. There's no question about that.
>
> But when I came back here, I was bitterly, sorely disappointed because my name had not been put before the executive committee at all. Well, I made some statements in the news media that they were wrong, that they should have considered other candidates, and I was the runner-up, all this kind of stuff. But then I came back home.
>
> A friend of Donald Russell [then president of the University of South Carolina and a protégé of Jimmy Byrnes and later governor, senator, and federal judge] came and sat right over here, and he had a statement written, typed up, announcing Donald Russell as the write-in candidate for the U.S.

Senate. And if I would tell them that I would not run as a write-in, he would go get on the phone and call Don Russell and he would announce that night for the U.S. Senate on a write-in. Well, I didn't do it. I just didn't tell them, because I knew that I was the logical one to run. I had made that race [in 1948] and spent all that money—all this kind of doings. I just wasn't prepared to do that that night.

Of course, I had to hesitate because I was a nominee of the Democrats for this seat in the Congress. I could not ignore that. This did pose a dilemma. I didn't want to lose both of them.

I went to church and I told my wife, Millie, to buy me some radio time, and I would announce. I was naive enough to believe that Thurmond would follow his own suggested program and support me as a write-in candidate. Also, I hesitated because I didn't know if I could get the money I needed to get on radio and TV to run an effective campaign. Millie had researched the cost of radio and determined that we would need $15,000 just to make a 15-minute announcement on a statewide hook-up.

I think the fellow at the station that Mrs. Dorn was working through called the other side. They concluded that I definitely was going to run. And so, Thurmond announced Tuesday following all this. I was at a VFW [Veterans of Foreign Wars] meeting in Darlington. They thought that I was going to announce that night. So they told me when I got there that Thurmond had announced as a write-in. He just beat me to it.

I still considered it for a couple of days. I didn't want to be buffaloed and halfway cheated out of it. So I considered it for a while and finally abandoned the idea and announced that I would not run. Jimmy Byrnes and others called me to say if both Thurmond and I ran, Brown would get elected.

Thurmond was pretty slick, you know. He had nothing to lose in that campaign. His stock was low. He was out. He was miserable down there in Aiken. He wasn't in politics, first time in his life. And so, he jumped in there.[5]

Governor Byrnes clearly understood that the public would see the Executive Committee's action as a power grab by Brown, from whom he had become alienated. Although Byrnes had served as best man at Brown's wedding many years earlier and Brown had long supported him, Brown refused to follow him in the Eisenhower campaign. Brown, never known for tact, worsened matters when he referred to Byrnes in conversation with friends as "a little sawed-off S.O.B." after the two had quarreled over some Clemson trustee matter. For Byrnes, a write-in candidate who could defeat Brown would mean a measure of revenge.

Likable William F. "Buddy" Prioleau, who had been a top aide to Thurmond as governor, had joined Byrnes a few hours after Maybank's funeral. He remembered:

I went over to Maybank's house that night, and it was just flooded with flowers, and after we got through taking care of all the U.S. senators and people and taking them all back to the airport, we started figuring out what to do with all these flowers. We flooded all the hospitals, and I really wanted to get away from the house anyway, so I said, "I'm gonna take two or three of these big baskets over to Mrs. Byrnes."

They were at their beach home, over at the Isle of Palms, and I called to make sure it was convenient, and the governor said, "Come on over here. I want to talk to you." So I went over there, and the phone was just ringing and ringing and ringing. And it was people calling, and they were all upset because the Executive Committee already had had the meeting and announced the nominee and closed the nominations.

I guess I was in a terrible plight because I was extremely fond of Edgar Brown, always had been. I knew that he was making a terrible mistake. I'm not gonna say I knew he would get beat.

I'm not sure that without all those phone calls that Byrnes would have taken the active part that he took. But they just poured in. Byrnes and Maybank were so close, and he still was so shook up over the unexpected death and all. As the various ones kept calling, he told them, "I swore that I would never get into another campaign, but I'm gonna get into this one."

He wanted a candidate, and he wanted one right away. There was a lot of speculation about Donald Russell. Russell didn't want to do it. Russell was president of the university, and he was concerned about the fact that if he got into it and was defeated what it would do to the university's appropriation and that sort of thing.[6]

Byrnes then asked Prioleau, "Do you think Strom would do it?"

"At the drop of a hat. He's sitting there in Aiken waiting on you to call him."

"You talked to him?"

"No, but I know him like a book."

"Well, call him and see if he can come up tomorrow."

Prioleau recalled, "I knew how bad he'd been wanting to get in the U.S. Senate. He was making more money than he'd ever made in his life, but Strom is basically a political being. He was destined to get back into public life one way or the other."[7]

Alex McCullough, a top aide to Byrnes at the time, had remained in Columbia during the funeral to take care of matters in the governor's office. He stayed in touch with Byrnes.

I told him we were getting a lot of telegrams and calls saying, "Get somebody to run against Edgar Brown. Don't let him do this." Mr. Byrnes really would have liked Donald Russell to run and urged him to step forward. So I said, "How about showing these messages to Mr. Russell?" And Byrnes said, "Well, don't tell him I said to do it," and he hadn't, really.

So I called Russell and I said, "I've got a lot of messages here that I'd like you to see. People are really upset about this nomination of Brown." I volunteered to take them over to the university [about two or three blocks away], and he said, "No, I'll come by there." He and Mrs. Russell came by and I showed these things to him, and I said, "Gee, if anybody thought that the public was upset, you could sure see it from what we had." It wasn't just stacks of them, but it was enough.

And he read these and looked at me and said, "Yeah, well how do you keep this alive until the general election?" He didn't really have the insides for going into battle like Thurmond did. He really just didn't have the kind of political courage it took.[8]

Russell thanked McCullough and added, "Tell Mr. Justice that I appreciate him thinking about me, but tell him I didn't see Donald Russell's name on any of those letters."[9]

Legal partner Charles Simons remembered Thurmond "getting a multitude of calls" from people asking him to run. Thurmond emphasizes that Byrnes asked Russell to run, not him. "He did not call me and suggest that

I run. I called him and told him I was going to run. I had waited several days and was rather hopeful that some other candidate would announce, but I felt it was essential that someone enter the race and not delay longer."[10]

Thurmond recalled twenty years later:

I called Donald Russell and told him that I was going to run, and he said, "Well, since you are going to run, I won't consider it any further." I called Bryan Dorn and told him that I decided to run, and he said, "Well, if you are going to run, I won't run." I am not too sure though that either one of them would have run because they had plenty of time before I announced. I don't think that anybody could have been elected on a Republican ticket at that time. I wasn't too anxious to run myself on a write-in basis because when I look back over it now, I don't see how in the world I got elected. It was a hard decision for me to make, but I made up my mind after giving time to Russell and Dorn and the rest of them who had been mentioned. And once I made the decision I then was going to run regardless of who ran, and I called them and told them.

Governor Byrnes did announce support for me and he based it mainly on the fact that people were denied the right to vote.[11]

Thurmond recalled that Tom Waring "probably did" urge him to run, but that no other newspaper editors in the state contacted him directly. The *News and Courier* set the tone for the state's press. The morning after the Democratic Executive Committee nominated Brown, an editorial in the newspaper acknowledged his ability, but asserted, "His mandate comes not from the people but from the politicians." Thurmond had said just before the meeting that if the people of South Carolina were denied the opportunity to choose their senator, they "would strongly resent any other procedure, and they would resent it rightfully." After the election, Strom would thank Waring "for the masterful job."[12]

Strom announced his write-in candidacy on September 7. He offered Brown the opportunity to resign and run against him in a primary. The rest of Thurmond's challenge was blunter and more fierce: "This is a fight for principle. It is a fight for government by the people instead of government by a small group of committeemen."

In the campaign that followed, fourteen of the state's sixteen dailies—all but the two in Anderson—supported Thurmond's write-in efforts, as did seventy-three of the state's eighty-six weeklies.

On the day after he announced, the News and Courier headlined an editorial, "Thurmond Is the Man." It asserted, "Once before, when Southerners hunted for a way out of voting for a deal they resented, Strom Thurmond came forward. That was in 1948. He was the states rights candidate for president. He didn't have a chance of election, but he ran anyway, as a matter of principle. Again a principle is at stake. It is bigger than personalities, though we do not hesitate to endorse Mr. Thurmond on his own merits."[13]

Thurmond campaigned with his usual vigor, Jean beside him all the way. Dolly Hamby, one of three female partners in a well-connected and respected Columbia public relations firm, Bradley, Graham & Hamby Advertising Agency, Inc., known in the trade as "the girls," was a tennis player who had played mixed doubles with Strom from his days as a judge. When she learned he was considering the race, she called him and offered to help.

Strom told her he had no money or campaign headquarters. She talked the manager of the Columbia Hotel into providing a private room for Strom and Jean and the whole mezzanine as a campaign headquarters.

Hamby said:

One of his greatest assets was Jean. She laughed at his foibles and called him "Pappy." Jean would say, "Pappy, you remember so-and-so." She always remembered names. At one point in October, Strom all but lost his voice. It was a bare whisper. At a speech before several thousand people at Valley Park, he said, "Jean, you have to talk." She made a great speech.

We'd leave his hotel room at 3 A.M. in the morning to finish taping commercials. And he'd say, "Come on for a walk with us. Jean and I are going for a walk." And he'd raise Cain with you if you smoked. I've never seen anyone who could campaign like Strom. He never stopped.

We did all his ads, all his TV spots. He couldn't read the teleprompter. He was too vain to wear glasses.[14]

Had Brown been less greedy for power and shrewd enough to accept the nomination with a pledge to resign after two years, he might well have become the next senator from South Carolina. Years later, he lamented his poor judgment. "I think that if I had made that statement that night—

that this is an emergency, the nomination has come to me in a dramatic way, but it's not the way to elect a senator for six years to serve all the people—I'll accept it, but I promise you that I'll resign before the next primary in 1956—if I'd done that I don't think that they would have ever come out against me."[15]

Brown's problems were exacerbated by regular help from Washington, help that consistently backfired. For example, the chairman of the Democratic National Committee, Stephen Mitchell of Illinois, implied in a Brown endorsement that South Carolinians were not literate enough to allow for a successful write-in campaign.

The crusading support of the state's press and fumbles from the Brown campaign put Strom in a very good position, but the relentless support of Byrnes for Thurmond may have closed the deal. Byrnes possessed far more political sophistication than anyone else in South Carolina. Prioleau said:

[Byrnes] had the best public relations sense that I have ever seen in anybody. He was an old newspaperman himself—he published the Aiken paper down there. He really was an international figure, and the state was pretty much inclined to say, "Well, gosh, if that's what Jimmy Byrnes thinks, that's good enough for me."

He literally called hundreds and hundreds of people who were real entrenched Byrnes people around the state. His whole theory was . . . "What we've got to do is run an educational campaign. Nobody had ever had to write in. Everybody's got to be tipped off on how to do it."

Byrnes would call friendly editors and suggest ideas for editorials. The *News and Courier* began regularly running front-page directions on how to cast a write-in vote. Near the end of the campaign, the directions included a replica of the ballot with an arrow pointing to the write-in line—complete with a handwritten "Strom Thurmond."

Prioleau continued:

Byrnes was the one who had thousands and thousands of pencils printed up with Thurmond's name on it in big letters so they could spell it right. He was the old pro. He looked into the possibility of "Suppose they spell it incorrectly, but it's clearly visible?" He got rulings in advance on all this sort of thing that nobody else would have thought about.

We ran out of money. Well, there wasn't anybody who could raise money like Byrnes. He could pick up the phone and call three people and have $50,000 in thirty minutes. He was in it deep.

John West, a newly elected state senator from Kershaw County, accepted Brown's request to serve as campaign manager. West recalled that after each Saturday afternoon University of South Carolina home football game that fall, Brown had a reception at his Wade Hampton Hotel headquarters, directly across the street from the governor's Statehouse office.

The first post-game party in September drew a comfortably large crowd of county and municipal political leaders, but the attendance got progressively smaller with each succeeding game. Meanwhile, every night, West and Brown could see the lights on in the governor's office, and they learned Byrnes was on the telephone for hours charming and persuading local political leaders throughout the state.*

About three weeks before the election, Thurmond went into a brainstorming session with Byrnes and Hamby and her associates. "We figured we needed something to get us over the hump," Hamby remembered. "Strom said, 'I could agree to resign after two years.'" Byrnes agreed it was a splendid idea, and they planned to make an announcement a few days later, but, for whatever reason, Strom jumped the gun.

Charles Wickenberg, one of the state's top journalists, was waiting as Thurmond left the meeting. When he asked, "What's new?" Strom replied, "Well, I'm going to resign after two years." Wick had a scoop.

In the history of the United States, no write-in candidate had ever been elected to either house of Congress, and none has since. But on November 2, South Carolina voters took their pencils to the polls, and 143,444 of them wrote in the name of "Strom Thurmond" or "Strum Thormond" or something equally close—enough to defeat Edgar Brown by 60,000 votes.

---

*Almost two decades later, when West was governor, he persuaded Brown to allow legislation to pass—Brown still retained his power as chairman of the Senate Finance Committee and had been blocking it—to erect a statue of Byrnes on the northeastern corner of the Statehouse grounds. West then arranged for Brown to visit Byrnes, who was retired and living in Columbia's Heathwood section. The two men hadn't spoken since 1954, but they sipped bourbon and relaxed and told stories. Mrs. Byrnes joined them. Brown returned from the visit in a genial mood. He told West, "I always did love Maude" (Bass interview with John West, January 2, 1998).

CHAPTER 13

Hard Times

ANOTHER HANDWRITTEN LETTER buried in Governor Thurmond's files, dated June 29, 1950 (a time when starting newspaper reporters in South Carolina were being paid less than $40 a week and first-class stamps cost three cents) was sent from Coatesville, Pennsylvania, where Essie had returned to give birth to her first child, Julius. Her husband had just graduated from law school, and he intended to set up an activist law practice in Savannah, his hometown. The letter addressed her father as "Dear Gov. Thurmond" and stated, "Please let me have a loan of seventy-five dollars. I plan to leave here in about two weeks, so may I hear from you within that time. With best wishes." It was signed "E. M. Williams."[1]

Essie Mae and Julius Williams had married in a quiet ceremony in 1949, his family learning about it afterward, according to Charlotte Johnson, his sister. Pleased by the marriage, Thurmond had visited SC State and arranged a meeting with her to hand over what she later described as an "enormous amount" of cash as a wedding gift.[2] She had told her new husband about her father, and he wanted nothing to do with Thurmond. She stashed some of the money in a savings account.

As a law student, Essie recalled her husband as "very aggressive." Once on a trip to Columbia with a friend, a policeman stopped their car on what Julius believed were spurious charges. He defended the driver—a challenge to the white policeman that resulted in both young men being taken inside a police station. "My husband was hit with a blackjack, his face discolored around the eye when he returned to the car. He wanted to file a lawsuit," Essie recalled, "but the dean of the law school advised against it." More than a half century later, she said in regard to filing the lawsuit, "I felt he should have done it anyway."[3]

Frank Cain, a fellow law student, recalled Julius as "rather quiet, easygoing—he smoked a lot. He was a studious person. He did drink, but it didn't prevent him from pursuing his goals."[4]

Essie dropped out of school in her senior year and returned to

Coatesville for the birth of their first son on February 9, 1949. She returned to join her husband for the remainder of his final semester in Orangeburg, where they lived in a modest off-campus apartment, temporary
housing for married students. The Reverend I. DeQuincey Newman, a
Methodist clergyman who would become South Carolina field secretary
for the NAACP and emerge as the state's foremost civil rights leader, bap-
tized the child. In her book, Essie says she told her father about the baby
during one of his visits to SC State. "He never once referred to the baby as
his grandchild, never asked if he could drive over to our house to see him,"
she later wrote.[5]

She told Jack Bass, however, that she took the infant to Columbia to
visit Thurmond and that she "took him in my arms to see his grandfather,
in the governor's office. He was a beautiful baby."[6]

Julius's 1950 graduating class, which consisted of two students, was the
only class there in which graduates automatically became licensed lawyers
in South Carolina. (Future law school graduates there and at USC would
take a bar exam.) Because of a reciprocity agreement between the two
states, Julius Williams also became licensed to practice law in Georgia, and
he had decided to return to Savannah. He longed for the chance to work
on civil rights cases.

Julius's sister said that Essie never talked about Thurmond, but it was
assumed he was her father. "She'd borrow money from my husband,"
Charlotte Johnson told Thompson in an interview for the 1992 *Washington
Post* article, "saying she was going to get the money back from her father.
She used him whenever she'd get into trouble."

When Julius returned to Savannah to practice law, other black lawyers
understood that Thurmond helped him establish a law office. As the late
Judge Eugene Gadsden recalled years ago, the rumor that Julius Williams
was married to Strom Thurmond's illegitimate daughter was accepted as
fact.

Julius worked actively with the local NAACP branch and worked on a
teacher pay equalization case with Aaron Kravitch, a white lawyer who
handled civil rights cases few others would touch. (Phyllis Kravitch, his
daughter, was appointed by President Jimmy Carter as a federal judge on
the Eleventh Circuit Court of Appeals.) That was one of Julius's few big
cases, however. Essie took a job as a secretary at then all-black Savannah
State College.

Meanwhile, the Williams family was growing, with Ronald arriving a year after Julius, Wanda four years later, and finally Monica, two years after that. One of Essie's vivid memories of segregated Savannah was being forced to move to the back of the bus while she was pregnant with Ronald.[7]

Julius next faced bomb threats because of his NAACP activities. His sister Charlotte had moved to California, and he decided in 1953 to take his family there. They settled in Compton, then a quiet, almost all-black town with affordable housing near Los Angeles. Julius took a job as a drill press operator with North American Aircraft, hoping to save enough money to allow time to prepare for the California bar exam. His sister Charlotte lived in the Crenshaw neighborhood of South Los Angeles, and the two families became close.

But life was hard. Ronald remembered hearing his parents argue about Strom Thurmond. Too young to know the man's significance, he later realized that his mother got financial help from Thurmond during times of crisis, and his father objected to it. "It was a man thing," Ronald said more than four decades later, a resentment by his father that his family needed another man to help out.

But Essie believed the family should use Thurmond's money, and he would send it by cable to Western Union. He sent "a thousand here, a thousand there," as she describes it.[8] One check for $1,000 came just after his write-in victory. In 1956 during a summer vacation in Coatesville, Essie took young Julius, then seven, to Washington to see his grandfather and to view Thurmond's fine Senate office. He gave her cash and had a driver take them to Union Station.

After two years in California, Julius Williams moved back to Savannah to try restarting his legal practice. His drinking had become a problem. Essie took the children to live with her in Coatesville, with her aunt Mary on Newlinville Road, where she had grown up. She got a job in a Veterans Administration hospital.

Ronald, who would become a physician, was happy in the fully integrated elementary school he attended for a few years and flourished academically. His mother wanted to reunite the family, however, and she and the children returned to Savannah, where an activist civil rights community existed near the peak of the South's period of "massive resistance" that her father helped promote. Ronald and his brother, Julius, entered inferior all-black schools, where Ronald found himself assigned material he had mastered two or three years earlier. He found fights and stabbings at his school frightening.[9]

Essie tried to raise her children to be colorblind, but in the segregated South that was tough. On a family road trip one day with her four children, Essie and the two young girls went into a diner to order food while the boys waited in the car. When the girls, then about five and seven, climbed up on lunch-counter stools, a white server greeted them with an icy stare.

Glaring at Essie, the server said, "We don't serve colored." The mother gathered up the children and walked out.

Essie tried to ignore such insults and to apply Christian principles to her dealings with obnoxious white folks. Her daughter Monica remembered her as "a walking epistle of forgiveness. She doesn't put up with stuff easily, but she definitely chooses her battles."

Like many black children her age during that era in the South, Monica remembered being oblivious as a little girl to the signs for separate "colored" water fountains and rest rooms in the local department stores. She pushed the limit until one day her mother, fearing an ugly confrontation, sat down and told her, "Monica, you're a Negro!" [10] It took a while for that to sink in.

When the effort to integrate the Savannah public schools under the Supreme Court's 1954 ruling in *Brown v. Board of Education* moved into high gear, U.S. District Court Judge Frank Scarlett, who heard a case brought by the NAACP, was earning a reputation as one of the most recalcitrant, obstructionist, and reactionary federal jurists in the South. After extended delays in issuing a ruling, Scarlett refused in mid-1963 to order a school desegregation plan because a white parents' group argued that integration would be harmful to their children. The Fifth Circuit Court of Appeals overruled him, writing an order to desegregate that fall and directing him to enter it as written.

W. W. Law, a postal mail carrier and president of the activist Savannah NAACP chapter from 1950 to 1976, handpicked twelve outstanding rising black seniors to integrate the twelfth grade of Savannah High School.

Meanwhile, to improve the quality of her sons' education, Essie found sufficient funds that year to send both to Boggs Academy, a private school in Augusta, Georgia. But after a year, the family could no longer afford it.

She sought funds from Thurmond, whose secretary responded to a letter from Essie in July and suggested that "you call him over the telephone
some night about 9 or 10 P.M." She included his number at home. Whether
the money sought was for the boys' tuition is not clear.

Eight days later, he wrote, "I am pressed for money at this time, but
suggest that you call me over the telephone and discuss the matter with me.
My recollection is, without looking up the note, that there is still some
balance due on the loan I made you last." Their references to "notes" or
"loans" reflected a code to give cover to the money he sent for support. As
Essie later said, her father was "frugal."

In the fall of 1964, young Julius enrolled as a junior at Savannah High
School, where the eleventh grade was added to the twelfth in the school
system's grade-a-year desegregation plan. Ronald remembered his brother
telling hair-raising stories to his parents at the dinner table, including
white students chanting, "John Brown had a little nigger."

Unlike going to the movies in Coatesville with everyone else, the opening to all of the formerly white theaters in Savannah was filled with tension. Ronald Williams said the whole atmosphere caused black families to
"live in fear. You would walk on the other side of the street with your head
down and not look at people."[11]

That fall, the family decided to move back to California. Essie set out
by car with the children, and Julius intended to join them. But as soon as
they arrived in Los Angeles at Charlotte Johnson's house, his sister broke
the news that Julius had died during the cross-country road trip. Essie returned to Savannah to bury him.

PART TWO

The Washington Years

CHAPTER 14

Rambunctious Democrat

Fɪғᴛʏ-ᴛᴡᴏ-ʏᴇᴀʀ-ᴏʟᴅ Sᴛʀᴏᴍ Tʜᴜʀᴍᴏɴᴅ arrived in Washington with a strategic swing vote that made Senate Majority Leader Lyndon Baines Johnson court him. The Eighty-fourth Senate, presided over by Vice President Richard Nixon, consisted of forty-eight Democrats, forty-seven Republicans, and Independent Wayne Morse of Oregon. Strom's shaky party allegiance also made him crucial to every Democratic committee. LBJ's propensity for control and Strom's for independent action would only intensify their philosophical differences, but for now Thurmond had a vote that Johnson needed.

He also had a jump on seniority, thanks to Governor Byrnes's securing the early resignation of interim Senator Charles Daniel, a politically active Greenville construction magnate, to give Strom an edge. Nixon swore Thurmond in on December 24, a few weeks before eight other Senate freshmen took office in January 1955. He got good committee assignments on government operations, interstate and foreign commerce, and public works.

Johnson's top operative, South Carolinian Bobby Baker, had served as the national Democratic Party's emissary to Edgar Brown and delivered cash to his campaign. Alex McCullough, who had managed Thurmond's write-in campaign, moved to Washington to serve as his administrative assistant. McCullough remembered that "Johnson and Bobby Baker immediately began courting Thurmond because they weren't at all certain whether he was going to vote with the Democrats to organize the Senate or not. The senator learned to take these things at face value—about how happy they were to see him and so on."

Thurmond was also understood to be no ordinary freshman senator. As a former governor and presidential candidate who had just run an unprecedented successful write-in campaign for the Senate, "He wasn't regarded lightly," said McCullough. "Anybody that's in politics who sees somebody get elected on a write-in vote to the United States Senate—they knew there was a reason."[1]

Thurmond quickly set to work on constituent services, working through federal agencies to push through special requests, and demonstrated his independence on a range of votes. "Pretty quickly after the Senate was organized," McCullough said, "Lyndon Johnson seldom gave Thurmond any attention except to send a threat that he was never going to get on that Armed Services Committee if he kept on voting the way he was, something like that."[2] Johnson, the Texas senator whose domineering personality became the stuff of legend, quickly realized that Thurmond would not be influenced by intimidation.

In his classic book, *Gothic Politics in the Deep South*, political writer Robert Sherrill described his first visit to Thurmond's office, where the senator was leading one of his weekly staff meetings. "They are a combination pep talk, lecture on Politics 301, and sermon," Sherrill wrote. "He was telling the youngsters on his staff about how the Constitution does not allow the federal government to monkey with religion. He ended by saying 'There's just so much power, and you've got to decide where it will be put: in the states or up here.' It was, I discovered, a perfect key to his view of the world . . . of metaphysical absolutes where love and hate and jealousy and power and truth are not limitless, but bounded; where qualities and impulses can be weighed by the pound. It is a world of pure blood. It is a world of one Eden, one Hell, one Heaven, one Right, one Wrong, one Strom."[3] All of Washington would soon be introduced to this worldview, this rhetoric, and this Senator.

From the beginning, Strom hovered over his staff. He advised them to avoid coffee and fatty foods, encouraged perfection in their work, and organized weekend staff bicycle rides through Rock Creek Park. Strom and Jean would lead the way, with panting staffers trailing them. "The secret of strength and health is proper eating, proper exercise and reasonable sleep," he told a reporter soon after his arrival—as he would continue to tell reporters almost a half century later.

Thurmond organized his staff like a military outfit. If anyone drifted in after 9 A.M., their name went on a late list, which the senator reviewed. One staffer said, "If you were repeatedly late, you got talked to, and nobody was late after that." He demanded a twenty-four-hour turnaround for constituent letters and decreed that a telephone should not ring more than twice.

Constituent service was always a priority. By 1989, his office had worked on 523,340 requests. He had posed for 10,600 pictures with school groups and office visitors—and in his remaining thirteen years before retiring, the numbers only grew.[4] Graduating high school seniors, college graduates, beauty queens, and newly elected civic leaders in South Carolina got letters of congratulation. What the staff called the "C and C's"—congratulations and condolences—occasionally got absurd. One young couple once got a letter from Thurmond congratulating them on the birth of their first child, and the infant received one congratulating him for having such fine parents. Washington staffers got tested after special training to sign his signature on photographs and routine correspondence.[5]

Thurmond arrived between 8 and 9 A.M., sometimes after a prayer breakfast. He began each day in the office by checking an obituary list compiled by staffs from his state offices—Aiken, Charleston, Columbia, Florence, and Greenville-Spartanburg. He personally called several of the families, then underlined in red everyone whose family he wanted to get a condolence letter. All of his correspondence included some variation of the phrase, "If there's anything I can do to be of help . . ."

Young Harry Dent had returned from two years as an army lieutenant and dropped out of the University of South Carolina Law School in mid-semester when offered a reporting job in Washington in the fall of 1953 for Sims News Service. A one-person operation, it covered South Carolina news from Washington for newspapers back home. With Jean's prompting, Strom quickly hired Dent as his press secretary.

Lyndon Johnson would work over Thurmond's aides in the Senate cloakroom when he had a problem with Strom. The aides often discussed these visits and the sticky issues prompting them with Jean, and many times Thurmond would arrive in the office the next morning saying he had reflected on a matter and changed his mind. "She had more influence over him than any of us had," Dent said. But Jean also protected her husband when his aides pushed for something they wanted to do that she believed was not in his interest. "He'd go home and come back the next morning, and it's dead," Dent said. "It was Jean."[6]

Meanwhile, Thurmond's quirky behavior caused amusement among his Senate colleagues and attracted attention at home. He ordered pounds of South Carolina yellow grits for his personal use in the Senate dining room. Olin Johnston, fellow senator from South Carolina and former in-

tense rival, received a truckload gift of watermelons from a South Carolina farmer and subsequently sent out a press photograph of himself
and his staff posing beside it. When Olin saw the photo published in a
newspaper back home, he found a smiling Strom had squeezed in among
the crowd. Johnston steamed about the extent to which Strom sought
publicity.

Contrary to custom, Johnston and his wife made no effort to introduce
the state's new junior senator and his wife to the social circuit. Thurmond
and Johnston soon reached a truce, with their staffs working together on
home-state projects, but there was never any warmth between the two senators. At twenty-eight, the youngest Senate wife except for Jacqueline
Kennedy, Jean attracted the attention of Patricia Nixon, the vice president's wife. She took Jean under her wing.

After two statewide campaigns and one national, Jean was politically
seasoned. She adapted quickly to Washington's ways—but kept one foot
planted firmly in South Carolina. Strom believed he owed little allegiance
to the Democratic Party—he got elected without its help. But Jean worked
to mend those party ties. The legislative process interested her, and she
regularly attended Senate sessions and developed a friendly relationship
with LBJ, who on many days spotted her in the Senate gallery and waved.[7]
Governor Timmerman once sent a quartet of legislators to Washington to
represent South Carolina on some matter. They included John West, the
young state senator who had managed Edgar Brown's campaign, and
Robert "Bob" McNair, a young representative from Allendale and a protégé of Speaker Blatt. (Little more than a decade later, West followed Mc-
Nair as a progressive governor.)

Jean ran into them at the Capitol and insisted on taking them out to
dinner. Strom was off to an Army Reserve meeting, and she told them,
"There's nobody I'd rather see and be with than this group." Everyone except Jean was drinking.

When she asked West why he wouldn't support her husband, he replied,
"I'd vote for you for anything! I'd even vote for your husband!"

She laughed and said, "You've been drinking." West shrugged and said,
"If I say it, I mean it. I'd even put it in writing."

She reached in her purse and pulled out a notebook. West wrote that he
would vote for Strom Thurmond and signed it. The others all signed it,
too. Months later, West attended a rally for Thurmond in Kershaw

County. Jean saw him, smiled, reached inside her blouse, and pulled out the piece of paper.[8]

When a group of South Carolina newspaper editors came to Washington for a convention, Jean and Strom had a reception for them at their apartment. As neither Jean nor Strom drank, she debated whether to serve alcohol, knowing that many of the newspapermen might expect it. She ended up offering the same nonalcoholic punch that she had in the Governor's Mansion in Columbia.

(By now a brigadier general in the Army Reserve, Thurmond once went with other congressmen and staffers on an overseas trip for their active duty assignment. At the Turkish national military academy, Thurmond reviewed the cadet corps, rejoined the others at a social gathering, and toasted the bravery and fighting record of the Turks. He raised a glass to his lips, gulped half of it, and then choked. After Thurmond spit his mouthful of Scotch back into the glass, the concerned Turkish hosts fretted and the congressional party snickered. A flustered Thurmond innocently explained, "Er-ah, I thought this was apple juice.")[9]

Thurmond's reputation as a maverick preceded him, and he lived up to it. In a system built on the art of compromise and in a chamber with unwritten rules about teamwork and cooperation, his stubbornness or "bullheadedness," as former Senator J. William Fulbright of Arkansas described it, promptly set him apart as a loner and outsider. "He was a rebel on the Democratic side, and he was always breaking up the china closet," said Dent, who by now functioned as the senator's alter ego and soon would succeed McCullough as administrative assistant.

McCullough's interest was in the process of governing, not politics. Dent believed that McCullough, a stern Calvinist, wanted things done his way and tried to tell Thurmond what to do. "Alex just couldn't get along with the senator," Dent said. McCullough remembered, "The thing that bothered me most was that every decision was a political decision."

Dent was not alone. Fred Buzhardt Jr. was to Dent "the greatest friend I ever had." Buzhardt's father and Strom had practiced law together after studying under J. William's tutelage. "Old man Fred and Strom were like brothers," Dent said. "Young Fred was like a son to Strom Thurmond because of that relationship. Fred was brilliant, first honor graduate in law school, a graduate of West Point."[10] He wrote many of Thurmond's speeches and position papers and advised him on committee work. Terrill

Glenn, a law school classmate who at thirty-one became U.S. attorney in South Carolina in the Kennedy administration, remembered young Fred as "absolutely brilliant, but way out on the right."[11] For this reason, Jean had reservations about his advice to Strom.

Thurmond had learned from his father not to punish his enemies but to convert—or at least neutralize—them. If a former political enemy needed a favor, Strom delivered. For example, not long after the 1954 write-in campaign, Edgar Brown called Dent about a matter. "He wouldn't dare call the senator," Dent said. "He thought the senator wouldn't have anything to do with him. I said, 'Hell, let me put you on the phone with the senator.' I put him on the phone with the senator, and he said, 'What do you want?' And he got it done just like that. That's good politics."[12]

SIMMERING IN THE BACKGROUND during Thurmond's first year in Washington was the Supreme Court landmark decision on May 17, 1954, *Brown v. Board of Education*, which ruled that state-mandated, racially segregated public schools violated the Fourteenth Amendment of the Constitution.

The 1954 decision consolidated four cases, one involving the overwhelmingly black Summerton school district in South Carolina's Clarendon County. With the school cases looming and South Carolina defending its "separate but equal" doctrine, Governor Byrnes, a former Supreme Court justice, in 1951 had won legislative approval for a 3-percent sales tax, with revenue earmarked for public education. Byrnes had declared, "We should do it because it's right. For me, that is sufficient reason. If any person wants an additional reason, I say it is wise."[13] Millions of dollars went to upgrade buildings and facilities at clearly unequal black schools. The South Carolina legislature would also quietly repeal the state's mandate for a public school system.

In its decision, Chief Justice Earl Warren wrote for a unanimous Supreme Court: "Today, education is perhaps the most important function of state and local governments. . . . It is a principal instrument in awakening the child to cultural values, in preparing him for later professional training and in helping him to adjust normally to his environment. In these days, it is doubtful that any child may reasonably be expected to succeed in life if he is denied the opportunity of an education. Such an opportunity, where the state has undertaken to provide it, is a right which must be made available to all on equal terms."

He concluded "that in the field of public education the doctrine of 'separate but equal' has no place. Separate educational facilities are inherently unequal." Thus was a blow dealt to the 1886 Supreme Court doctrine laid out in *Plessy v. Ferguson*, which had given states in the South the authority to impose racial segregation.

White Southerners initially responded calmly, but disquiet grew quickly in those areas where the population was majority black, such as Southside Virginia. Senator Harry Byrd Sr., whose "Byrd Machine" ruled the state with an iron hand, began pushing the idea of "massive resistance."

A few months after Thurmond arrived in Washington, the Supreme Court in May 1955 issued its implementation order in the case known as *Brown II.* The Supreme Court said school desegregation should proceed "with all deliberate speed" and directed the lower federal courts to implement the process. Moderate white political leaders in the South felt relieved. They saw endless opportunities for delay and evasion with friendly local judges, who could be expected to emphasize "deliberation" over "speed."

In the spirit and atmosphere of "massive resistance," however, the young editor of the *Richmond News-Leader*, James Jackson Kilpatrick, soon unearthed the doctrine of "interposition," the theory that a state could "interpose" its sovereignty and invalidate a federal law. He argued for "principled" defiance. Upon close examination, this amounted to little more than John C. Calhoun's nullification theory, an issue that the Civil War had clearly resolved. Under the Constitution's supremacy clause, federal law is "the supreme law of the land" in cases of conflict with state law. "Interposition" amounted to legal nonsense.

But Kilpatrick hammered away, promoting the doctrine of interposition in editorials widely reprinted across the South and helping create a climate of resistance. Posturing state legislatures throughout the region passed interposition resolutions, creating false hopes among fearful whites and encouraging defiance.* Alabama Governor James "Kissin' Jim" Folsom compared his legislature's adoption of an interposition resolution to a

---

*At a seminar at Emory University attended by Jack Bass in the spring of 1998, Kilpatrick responded to a question about his role in popularizing the concept of interposition. He said that at the time there was talk of "blood running in the streets" and that he believed then it would be helpful to elevate the public dialogue. He acknowledged, however, that in terms of constitutional validity, he had been wrong.

hound dog baying at the moon, but as blacks in the South began to ask for and then demand the same rights as other Americans, white fears mounted. Folsom's political fortunes rolled downhill.

For three years, Senate Majority Leader Lyndon Johnson and House Speaker Sam Rayburn, both Texans, had achieved an armistice on civil rights among congressional Democrats by appealing to both sides for restraint. Early in 1956, a critical presidential election year, Thurmond led the effort to shatter that armistice.

Under pressure by men of influence at home not to resign, as he had pledged in the 1954 write-in campaign, but to stay in office and do his job, in January Thurmond and an aide visited Governor George Bell Timmerman Jr., who had been lieutenant governor under both Thurmond and Byrnes. Thurmond wanted to know if he did resign, would the governor reappoint him? "I won't do that," Timmerman said, then pointedly reminded them of Thurmond's pledge to allow the people to elect their senator.[14] It was Timmerman's father, of course, whom Thurmond had defeated in the hard-fought race for circuit judge almost twenty years earlier. The Timmermans had long memories.

Knowing he would resign and amid some speculation that Timmerman might challenge him, Thurmond began trying to unify Southern senators to make a declaration against the 1954 *Brown* decision. Most were wary, but Virginia's Byrd worked with Thurmond to arrange a meeting of the bloc of twenty-two Democratic senators from the eleven states of the Confederacy.

Because of the *Brown* opinion's references to contemporary psychology and a footnote referring to Swedish sociologist Gunnar Myrdal's *An American Dilemma*, which focused on the conflict between the "American Creed" and the prejudiced place of African Americans, Thurmond maintained that *Brown* was based on psychology and sociology rather than law and was therefore invalid. As the Supreme Court indicated in *Brown*, however, *Plessy* itself clearly reflected the prevailing "scientific" theories of its day about race. As a lawyer and former judge, Thurmond surely knew that a unanimous Supreme Court opinion is law, whether or not one agrees with it. He also surely knew that attacking the Court would be good politics at home.

On February 6, 1956, in his mimeographed first draft of what would become an elaborate protest statement, termed the "Southern Manifesto," Thurmond condemned the *Brown* decision as a "clear violation of the

Constitution by the Court." He commended states that had approved interposition resolutions and their intention to use "every lawful means at their disposal."

Many of his Southern colleagues resisted a meeting. With its lock on committee chairmanships and the weapons of filibuster—extended debate—and cloture (Senate rules then required a two-thirds vote to shut off a filibuster), the South's Democratic team had the capacity to block legislation or force compromise. They effectively exercised Calhoun's complex theory of the concurrent majority. Most of the Southern senators, understanding both constitutional law and the depth of white fears about the *Brown* decision and the possibility that it could drastically reshape the social structure of the region, sought to promote calm. (Because the late-nineteenth-century Supreme Court also allowed Southern states to disenfranchise almost all blacks from effective voting, their voices went unheard among elected officials.)

Thurmond and Byrd let the others know they might issue the manifesto themselves, with as many others as would sign without a meeting. With that, Senator Walter George of Georgia, the senior Southerner in the Senate, called a meeting on February 8. Senator George himself faced potential strong opposition that year from former Governor Herman Talmadge. (In the end, George withdrew and Talmadge was elected in a campaign in which he quietly began to court black voters.)

On the morning of the 8th, newspapers carried stories of a crisis in Tuscaloosa, Alabama, where mob violence was forcing Autherine Lucy off the University of Alabama campus. She had just enrolled as the first black student. (Seven years would pass before the color line was finally broken there—a day that history would remember because of Governor George Wallace's "stand in the schoolhouse door.")

At the meeting of the Southern senators, Thurmond introduced his second draft, which continued to endorse interposition and escalated the rhetoric by condemning "the illegal and unconstitutional decision of the Court." Senator George appointed Richard Russell to chair a committee that also included John Stennis of Mississippi and Sam Ervin of North Carolina—thoughtful, restrained men—to study and revise Thurmond's draft.

By the fourth draft—this one edited with the participation of Thurmond and Fulbright, a former university president who had little use for

Thurmond—the word "interposition" was gone. Although toned down by Fulbright, the document still condemned the "illegal . . . seizure of power by the nine men composing the Court" and praised "the motives of those states which have declared the intention to resist this invasion of their sovereignty by the Court by every lawful means."[15]

The fifth and final draft, with Senator Price Daniel of Texas taking Ervin's position on the committee, was presented to the Senate on March 12. Nineteen of the twenty-two Southern senators signed what became known as the Southern Manifesto. Eighty-one House members joined them. As majority leader, Lyndon Johnson wasn't asked to sign it, and the two Tennessee senators, Estes Kefauver and Albert Gore Sr., refused.

The final document declared that the Supreme Court, "with no legal basis for their action, undertook to exercise their naked judicial power and substituted their personal and political ideas for the established law of the land." It deplored the court's "clear abuse of judicial powers" and commended "the motives of those states which have declared their intention to resist integration by any lawful means." (The fact that Fulbright signed the manifesto and Lyndon Johnson did not was later given as an explanation for the reason Johnson was acceptable to John F. Kennedy as a running mate in 1960 but Fulbright was unacceptable as his secretary of state.)

Gore called the manifesto "a dangerous, deceptive propaganda move which encouraged Southerners to defy the government and to disobey its laws, particularly orders of the federal court."[16]

After George introduced the manifesto, officially the "Declaration of Constitutional Principles," Thurmond called it "a historic event" in remarks to the Senate. He denounced "outside agitators" who employed "professional racist lawyers" to end segregation in public schools and disrupt "the harmony which has existed for generations between the white and the Negro races."

He declared, "The propagandists have tried to convince the world that the States and the people should bow meekly to the decree of the Supreme Court. I say it would be the submission of cowardice if we failed to use every lawful means to protect the rights of the people."

He asserted, "The white people of the South are the greatest minority in this Nation. They deserve consideration and understanding instead of the persecution of twisted propaganda."

In response, Oregon's Morse said, "You would think today Calhoun was walking and speaking on the floor of the Senate." Thurmond no doubt took that as a compliment.*

Morse acknowledged that the desegregation decision created problems for the South but declared, "I think it is a correct decision, a sound decision, and a decision that was long overdue." He said that the Supreme Court "has at long last declared that all Americans are equal, and that the flame of justice in America must burn as brightly in the homes of the blacks as in the homes of the whites."

If Southerners really wanted "to put themselves above the Supreme Court and above the Constitution," Morse challenged, "let them propose a constitutional amendment that will deny to the colored people of the country equality of rights under the Constitution and see how far they will get with the American people."[17]

The Southern Manifesto meant the overwhelming majority of the South's political leadership was urging defiance. Adlai Stevenson, counting on support of Southern moderates in seeking renomination as the Democratic presidential candidate, dispatched Harry Ashmore, a key Southern adviser, to Washington. Ashmore, by now executive editor of the *Arkansas Gazette* in Little Rock, had questioned Thurmond on a radio program there during the Dixiecrat campaign. He recalled trying "to get him to talk about something other than segregation, and I didn't succeed at all."[18] Ashmore met in Washington with Olin Johnston, who told him, "It's no use trying to talk to Strom. He *believes* that shit."[19]

In Alabama, Judge Richard Rives of the Fifth Circuit Court of Appeals, which soon would become the primary legal battleground over civil rights, walked down the hall of the federal courthouse in Montgomery for a quiet

---

*More than a century earlier, Harriet Martineau had characterized Calhoun as "the cast iron man, who looks as if he had never been born and never could be extinguished; . . . he is wrought like a piece of machinery, set going vehemently by a weight and stops while you answer; he either passes by what you say, or twists it into suitability with what is in his head." James G. Banks, a leading academic scholar of Thurmond, used this quote to characterize him in a paper titled "A Study in Continuity," presented at The Citadel Conference on the New South (Martineau, *Retrospect of Western Travel* [London: Saunders and Otney, 1838]; Banks, "A Study in Continuity," The Citadel Conference on the New South, Charleston, South Carolina, April 1978).

visit with his friend Senator Lister Hill. He explained that changed political realities had forced him and fellow moderate John Sparkman, Stevenson's 1952 running mate, to go along.

After listening intently, Rives said in his usual soft drawl, "Well, Lister,
I think I understand it now. You fellas have just risen above principle."[20]

Throughout the South, the Citizens Council movement had begun to
spread from its 1954 birthplace in the Mississippi Delta. These "responsible people" vowed to act together to stop any move toward desegregation.
They eschewed violence, opting instead for economic intimidation against
blacks who might seek to vote or enroll their children in white schools. Reaction to the Montgomery bus boycott that began in January 1955 and the
emergence there of the young black clergyman Martin Luther King Jr. accelerated the growth and spread of the Citizens Councils into a grassroots
movement providing Southwide links of massive resistance. From East
Texas to Virginia, they stretched across the region, concentrating in rural
counties with heavy black populations. Strom Thurmond became one of
their heroes.

A few months after issuance of the Southern Manifesto, two North
Carolina Democratic congressmen who didn't sign it were defeated. In
Arkansas, Governor Orville Faubus, running for reelection to a two-year
term, was attacked as being "soft" on integration by a segregationist opponent who got 42 percent of the vote.

In 1957, with segregationists lining up to oppose him and the entire
Arkansas congressional delegation on record to resist integration "by any
lawful means," Faubus called out the National Guard to block nine black
children from enrolling at Central High School in Little Rock. He contended he did so because he feared rioting, but no mob materialized. In the
end, President Eisenhower mobilized federal troops to enforce the court's
order. They remained until the end of the 1957–1958 school year.

Faubus later blamed federal authorities and the Eisenhower administration for putting him on the spot in a politically explosive situation. He asserted, "They could sit back and issue a court order that was going to
cause literally hell and destroy many people, economically and politically.
And they would just sit back and fold their hands and let somebody else
reap the storm. Well, hell, it was their storm. A bunch of goddamn cow-
ards for not coming in the beginning and saying, 'This is a federal court

order. We're going to have federal authorities here to see to it that it's obeyed and enforced." Then I wouldn't have been involved."[21]

Ashmore, whose editorial page condemned Faubus for reckless irresponsibility, received a Pulitzer Prize for editorial leadership in the crisis. But Faubus won 69 percent of the vote in the June 1958 Democratic primary, carrying all seventy-five counties. His 1956 segregationist opponent, after being wiped out in 1958, complained ruefully, "He used my nickel and hit the jackpot."[22] Faubus's display of defiance led to four more terms as governor, but the state's image suffered from news coverage of the turmoil. After emotions subsided, he died with a tarnished reputation.

Although Harry Byrd Sr. continued to advocate a "last ditch stand" against integration, Virginia's commitment to "massive resistance" crumbled when white moderates organized in opposition after public schools in several communities were closed in 1958 to resist integration.[23]

Interposition finally played out in 1962 when Mississippi Governor Ross Barnett claimed it gave him authority to defy federal court orders and block James Meredith from breaking the color line at the University of Mississippi. Meredith enrolled, but only after a riot that left two people dead and scores of federal marshals injured. (Barnett's hero status didn't last long; in 1967, he ran fourth in attempting a comeback in the Democratic primary for governor.)

But Thurmond had set his course. On March 4, 1956, Thurmond submitted a resignation letter to Timmerman, effective April 4, the day before the Democratic primary filing deadline. Thurmond said he would be a candidate but wanted to give sufficient notice to others. No one stepped forward. He moved back to Aiken and rejoined his old law firm for seven months. Interim Senator Thomas Wofford of Greenville, a close Timmerman associate, kept the seat warm until after the election, with Dent remaining on board. "The senator gave his word, and he kept it," Dent said, "And people remembered." After taking his respite in Aiken, he ran unopposed and then returned to Washington, resuming his role as a symbol of Southern resistance to change and continuing his fight against civil rights. Although Thurmond would forever deny he had ever engaged in racism, his rhetoric of states' rights always remained attached to the preservation of segregation. He avoided overt race baiting, but for more than a quarter of a century, beginning with the Dixiecrat campaign, he championed with gusto the cause of white supremacy. He also condemned the Supreme Court, calling for the impeachment of Supreme Court justices who had ruled that defendants accused of subversive activities involving Communism were entitled to see FBI and other files. He called the court a "great menace to this country" but denied his opinion was influenced by the 1954 school integration ruling.[24]

He received letters of approval from Stanley E. Morse of Charleston, president of the ultraconservative Grass Roots League, Inc., and W. J. Simmons of Jackson, Mississippi, executive director for the Citizens Councils. Simmons sent a copy of his letter to Morse. Thurmond corresponded extensively for well over a decade with Morse, once getting him royal treatment from the American consul general when Morse visited Seville, Spain.[25]

To Stanley Morse, the "Communist negro drive was started in the United States in 1920" and spread forward until many clergymen, educators, scientists, and others had become "duped . . . to aid the Communist conspiracy." Morse's "Research Department" reported, "the Commies are making sure that [Martin Luther] King operates according to their plans."[26]

The record isn't clear on whether Thurmond took Morse seriously or was merely humoring a friendly supporter, but in response to one letter from Morse on "documented proofs" connecting the U.S. Communist Party with "the Civil Rights Drive," Thurmond replied, "The material which you furnished has been invaluable in exposing the true nature of the Negro demonstrations." Morse's proof of this link included a report that young Americans at a World Youth Festival in Helsinki, Finland, had sung such "un-American" songs as "We Shall Overcome" and "We Ain't Going to Study War No More."[27]

THE 1957 FILIBUSTER was pure Strom Thurmond. It came after Senator Russell orchestrated a successful eight-day filibuster in early July, in which Thurmond participated, that watered down the Civil Rights Bill. In exchange for allowing a bill to pass—the first civil rights legislation since 1875—Russell got two concessions in hard bargaining with Lyndon Johnson. One involved removal of Title III, the bill's main enforcement mechanism, which would have authorized the Justice Department to initiate school desegregation suits and to seek court injunctions against other forms of discrimination. With its primary enforcement mechanism gone, what remained were sections creating a fact-finding Civil Rights Commission and a new Civil Rights Division in the Justice Department that would begin the process of gaining the right to vote for Southern blacks.

The second concession involved amending the bill to require jury trials in contempt of court cases. Civil rights advocates opposed the jury-trial provision, arguing that Southern juries with their record of refusing to convict whites who had brutally killed blacks would never convict a white official charged with keeping blacks from voting.

After several weeks of debate, a compromise amendment allowed a jury trial in contempt cases involving a fine of more than $300 or imprisonment of more than ninety days. As the nation became more aware of issues involving voting discrimination and other forms of discrimination, Southerners in Congress found themselves losing allies.

Thurmond still wanted to fight, but at a caucus in Russell's office on August 24, agreement was reached that there would be no organized filibuster. Each individual could protest as he saw fit, and Southerners would vote as a bloc against the bill.

Three days later, Governor Timmerman said citizens should "demand that their representatives stand up for what is right—or step aside and let there be elected men with political courage who will."[28] Thurmond again sensed a potential opponent in Timmerman. The next afternoon, Wednesday, August 28, Thurmond again visited Russell, who declined to call a caucus meeting unless a majority of the South's senators requested it. Russell believed the South had gotten the best deal available, that a bargain had been struck, and that you played by the rules—written or unwritten. Thurmond requested a speaking slot. The scheduler slated him for 9 P.M. that night, in the belief that even if he droned on past midnight, he would get little attention. Thurmond apparently had already made up his mind to stage a one-man filibuster, taking steam baths for several days to dehydrate his body so it could absorb liquids without his having to leave the Senate chamber for the bathroom—and lose his right to continue speaking.

Thurmond let his staff know he planned to talk at length and took another long steam bath that afternoon. He intended to focus on the jury-trial issue—a provision that also bothered some of the most liberal members of Congress.

Jean expressed misgivings when the staff told her the plan, but she brought Strom dinner and eventually stayed for the duration. Thurmond began speaking at 8:54 P.M.

Senator Barry Goldwater of Arizona briefly spelled Thurmond at one point, reading a report on military manpower policy, an act that helped develop a strong bond between the two men. Senator Paul Douglas of Illinois, a former marine and liberal Democrat who strongly believed in any person's right to a jury trial, sufficiently admired Thurmond's determination and stamina that after fourteen hours, he brought a full pitcher of orange juice—Thurmond's favorite beverage—to the podium. Thurmond downed it all during the day, his dehydrated body absorbing the liquid like a sponge. Dent had arranged to have a bucket placed in the cloakroom in case the senator needed to relieve himself, an arrangement that would allow him to keep one foot inside the Senate chamber and thus not break the rules. Thurmond needed no such relief. Thurmond had hoped that news about his one-man stand would generate pressure on other Southerners to join the filibuster, but Russell held them in line.

Thurmond did not finish until 9:12 P.M. the next night, twenty-four hours and eighteen minutes later, after having read from the Constitution of the United States, the Declaration of Independence, from magazines and books. He drew laughter from his colleagues by concluding, "I expect to vote against the bill." He spoke almost two hours longer than the record set three years earlier by Wayne Morse. Thurmond's record still stands. Minutes after Thurmond sat down, his distant relative Talmadge accused him of "grandstanding."[29] The next day, Russell coldly commented, "If I had undertaken a filibuster for personal aggrandizement, I would have forever reproached myself for being guilty of a form of treason against the South."[30]

The Senate approved the final bill 60–15.

ALTHOUGH SOME OF THESE GESTURES from Thurmond offended his Southern colleagues, they came to respect the stamina, determination, and political skill that they signified. Talmadge would look back on him as "strong-willed and independent, resolute and dedicated. He was the ablest politician in the body. He never let a chance pass to cultivate a voter."[31]

Despite Talmadge's reputation as a committed segregationist, by 1958 he had turned the corner on race. After Ernest Vandiver won the Georgia gubernatorial election as a segregationist candidate that year, he accepted Talmadge's invitation to visit him at his home near Lovejoy, a half-hour southwest of Atlanta. Vandiver walked in to find Talmadge with a group of Atlanta's top black political leaders. Vandiver abandoned his segregationist stance.[32]

Although Thurmond had set a course as a vocal and unmanageable dissident, Jean's magnetic personality helped prevent his political relationships from deteriorating. She continued to attend Senate sessions regularly, read periodicals, kept her husband informed, and remained socially engaged. She not only charmed the prominent but made friends with the elevator operators and the Capitol police and gave tours around Washington to visiting South Carolinians.

But as summer approached in 1959, Jean began to tire easily. Driving one day in Washington, she ran into the back of a truck. It was at slow speed and there were no injuries. Then in August, at home alone in their Foggy Bottom apartment, she collapsed. When Strom arrived home, she was barely able to get to the door and let him in. Another seizure followed three days later.

Jean's physician brother, Dr. Robert Crouch, practiced in the Maryland suburbs and helped her gain admission to the National Institutes of Health in Bethesda. After extensive tests, it was determined she had a nonmalignant brain tumor, and she underwent surgery on September 17 for its removal. She confided to friends that she worried the operation would leave her damaged and a burden to her busy husband.

Jean's condition worsened that fall and she returned, partially paralyzed, to her mother's home in Elko while Strom did two weeks of Army Reserve active duty as a brigadier general. Strom considered resigning from the Senate, telling Jean he would do so if she wanted him to if it would help in any way. "You mean everything to me," he wrote, "and I shall follow the course that is best for you."

The Thurmonds returned to Washington for their twelfth anniversary, but Jean's condition continued to worsen. She told family and close friends, "I've had everything a girl could want. I've experienced more in thirty-three years than most people experience in a lifetime twice as long as mine."

She returned with Strom to South Carolina for Thanksgiving. Although her condition deteriorated further, for Christmas they went to the Greenwood home of Martha Bishop, Strom's sister. But while they were there, Martha's physician husband had to take Jean to his office for special treatment.

Nine days later, as her condition grew increasingly critical, doctors recommended on Sunday, January 3, that she be flown back immediately to the National Institutes of Health on a U.S. Air Force plane. She underwent surgery on Tuesday to remove pressure on the brain, with both her physician brother and Strom's brother Allen George, also a doctor, observing. The surgeon found a "rapidly progressing malignant tumor." Jean slipped into a coma and never regained consciousness.

Throughout her decline, and with this final, terrible diagnosis, Strom Thurmond refused to believe his beautiful young wife was dying. After her last surgery, he kept vigil through the night, along with her parents and other family. She died at 8:35 A.M. on January 6, 1960. When told that she was dead, Thurmond told the doctors, "But this can't be. You can't mean that."[33]

Strom called his close friend and former law partner Charles Simons to meet him the next morning at the nearest train stop in Augusta, where he would be accompanying Jean's body. "It was a cold, dreary, foggy morning," Simons remembered, "just the setting for something like that. Strom got out and was crying like a baby. He was crazy about Jean." Back in Washington, after Lyndon Johnson announced her death, Olin Johnston paid tribute in the Senate to "this sweet and beautiful woman."

At Strom's home in Aiken, his brothers and sisters gathered and discussed whether to bury Jean in Edgefield or Aiken. Strom asked Simons to go to Edgefield to examine the family plot. It was raining. At Willowbrook Cemetery, Simons remembered, "It was so wet, water would cover your shoes. I couldn't see Jean being buried in a watery grave." He returned to Aiken. "They called me in and really put me on the spot. They said, 'Charlie, where do you think we should bury Jean—in Edgefield or Aiken?' I said, 'Well, Jean loved Aiken and Aiken loved Jean. I think she ought to be buried here.'"[34]

She was buried on a plot of high ground at the town's Bethany Cemetery. Lyndon Johnson led a delegation of more than a half dozen Southern senators to the funeral. Harry Dent, who viewed LBJ's presence there cynically, was standing next to Thurmond when Johnson came through the receiving line to express sympathy. The grief-stricken Thurmond told him,

"I hope you're the next president of the United States," then broke down and cried. Dent saw it as a temporary breakthrough for LBJ in a relationship more notable for its antagonism.[35]

For years the engraved tablet over Jean's tomb was mounted vertically on a stone obelisk. Later it was placed flat on the ground, her parents buried beside her.

The full inscription reads:

Jean Crouch Thurmond
July 14, 1926–January 6, 1960
Born Elko, S.C., Died Washington, D.C.
Wife
James Strom Thurmond
Daughter Of
Horace J. And
Inez Breazeale Crouch
Honor Graduate Winthrop College
And President Senior Class 1947
First Lady of South Carolina 1947–51
First Aiken County
Woman of the Year 1953
Included in Volume I
Who's Who of American Women, 1958
One of the Most Beautiful Charming
And Admired Ladies in South Carolina
And the Nation
As the Wife of a Lawyer, Governor–
Presidential Candidate–United States Senator
Her Life Was an Inspiration to Him
And to All Who Knew Her
She Filled an Exalted Place In
Civil and Governmental Life
Both State and Nation, with Dignity
And Grace
Gentle, Loving, Helpful and Friendly
She Was a Gracious Example Of
Womanhood at Its Finest

Her Unselfish Love and Service To
Others Exemplified the Best In
Christian Faith

THE LAST THING Jean Thurmond said to him, Strom told Dent soon after her death, was, "Never let Fred get you alone with his advice because
Fred is a cause man. He loves you, you know, but he's a cause man. But
Harry is your man. His cause is your cause. You can get Harry alone and
talk to him, but make sure that Harry is there when Fred is filling you in
on anything."[36] Dent was a supreme and practical political strategist.
Buzhardt, equally dedicated to Thurmond, was skilled in legal strategy and
driven by ideology. The Dent-Buzhardt duo, Thurmond, and the forces of
history would converge in 1964 to accelerate the development of a two-
party South.

But in the years immediately after Jean's death, Strom Thurmond buried
his grief in his work. After eating his evening meal in the Senate dining
room or at a hotel, he would stay in his Senate office until midnight, before walking back to his lonely apartment. He soon moved into a smaller
unit, one not haunted with memories.[37]

In 1960, Thurmond was reelected with 90 percent of the vote against token opposition from R. Beverly Herbert, a genteel octogenarian lawyer in
Columbia with the perspective of the Southern white paternalist. He argued that Thurmond had failed to make the rest of the country understand what "we have done for the Negro race."[38]

Although Thurmond had supported Lyndon Johnson's 1960 bid for the
presidential nomination as promised, he backed away from the Democratic
ticket of John F. Kennedy and Johnson as too liberal on civil rights. Rumors raged in the South that Thurmond would abandon the Democratic
Party ticket. Thurmond didn't openly endorse Republican Richard Nixon,
who lost South Carolina by fewer than 10,000 votes, but much later acknowledged that he had voted for him.

When Fritz Hollings, then governor of South Carolina, challenged
Thurmond on his position during the campaign, Thurmond pointedly
replied, "I hope Senator Kennedy's pledge at his news conferences to push
for enactment of all points in the 'civil rights' plank in January will serve to
alleviate the Governor's lack of understanding about my refusal to be in

the bag in this election."[39] Thurmond called the civil rights plank "the most extreme, unconstitutional and anti-Southern civil rights plank ever conceived by any major political party."

After Jean's death, his rhetoric grew more strident and his sense of humor even in private seemed to disappear entirely. He continued to link the civil rights movement with Communism. Early in 1962, after Ku Klux Klan members and other thugs in Alabama attacked "Freedom Riders" testing a Supreme Court ruling outlawing segregation in interstate transportation facilities, Thurmond called the civil rights activists "Red pawns and publicity seekers."[40] He saw Communism's influence everywhere. When the Supreme Court in 1962 ruled unconstitutional a government-written, non-denominational, and mandatory school prayer, Thurmond denounced the court for favoring "Communist interests." He said, "It seems the court is helping attain the objectives of Karl Marx 'to dethrone God and destroy capitalism.'"[41]

After his assignment to the Senate Armed Services Committee and promotion to major general in the Army Reserve, he became an increasingly biting critic of the administration's Cold War military preparedness and foreign policy. He soon denounced the "no-win" policy of the Kennedy administration and launched an attack on the "muzzling" of the military—terms he coined.

On muzzling—or suppressing the military from speaking out on the dangers of Communism—Thurmond engaged Senate Foreign Relations Chairman Fulbright in the kind of fierce and ongoing debate that reflected deep philosophical differences. Knight Newspapers' Washington bureau chief Robert S. Boyd summarized statements made by both men and filed this shorthand version of their views:

FULBRIGHT: The principal threat is external—the armed might of Russian and Chinese imperialism. Military men who equate domestic welfare legislation with Communism are out of step with their commander-in-chief. Military men should stay out of politics. They're not the people to teach the public about Communism. We're in for a long struggle on many fronts and cannot hope for quick, dramatic solutions.

THURMOND: The principal threat is internal—Communist subversion and creeping socialism here at home. Much of the Administration's domestic program is socialism, and socialism is Communism. Military men understand the Red menace better than the White House or the State Department. The Administration's foreign policy adds up to "softness" and "appeasement" of Communism.[42]

Thurmond's relentless one-man crusade against the muzzling of military leaders led to a Senate Armed Services subcommittee investigation. Thurmond's enemies accused him of McCarthyism, referring to Wisconsin Senator Joe McCarthy's discredited Communist witch-hunt that had so wracked the nation in the 1950s.

Once hearings began, an FBI agent warned Dent, "Protect your man. Don't let him call anybody a Communist." Then Thurmond received inside information from the FBI that an early witness had known Communist affiliations. Dent and Buzhardt briefed the senator until well past midnight, repeatedly warning him not to use the word. They recognized that such an attack from Strom would only provide fuel for those who would characterize him as a McCarthyite.

Thurmond appeared unmoved, which worried Dent. "Once that brain locks into place," he recalled, "you can't move it." Sticking his finger over his heart, he continued, "What's in here," then pointed to his mouth, "comes out here."

When hearings began, before an overflow crowd in the Senate caucus room, Dent sat next to Thurmond, positioning his foot in easy kicking range of the senator's shin. Whenever he sensed Thurmond on the verge of using the banned word, Dent kicked sharply. "I kicked the senator's shin until it was bleeding," he said, "but we got him through it without calling anyone a Communist."[43]

After hearing sixty-seven witnesses during thirty-six days of testimony, the subcommittee issued a 90,000-word majority report concluding it was "convinced that a system for prior review and clearance of military speeches is altogether proper and desirable." Thurmond felt vindicated, however, because the committee report added, "The record of the hearings reflects that the actual operation of the present system has left much to be desired." Then the White House, while continuing to emphasize the importance of America's civilian and military leadership speaking with one voice, acknowledged there had been inconsistencies in reviewing senior military officers' speeches and that the State Department would begin requiring its reviewers to explain why changes were made. Thurmond, who submitted a 160-page independent report drafted by Buzhardt, won grudging respect for his doggedness.

Unlike South Carolina's major newspapers, which rarely reported critical news stories about Thurmond or criticized him editorially, the *Charlotte Observer* across the border in North Carolina, which circulated in both states, challenged him without reluctance. In December 1962, after the *Observer* criticized Thurmond's lack of any factual grounding for attacking a "secret" Kennedy administration plan to turn over America's nuclear weapons to the United Nations, Thurmond responded. His source, he proclaimed, was a booklet published by the State Department proposing "general and complete disarmament in a peaceful world." After printing Thurmond's rebuttal, the newspaper pointed out that his earlier allegation of a "secret" plan, rather than a published booklet proposing phased disarmament—available to the public for 15 cents—had suggested a subversive plot.[44]

MEANWHILE, SOUTH CAROLINA FACED its first break of the color line, and it would come at Clemson, Thurmond's alma mater. In January 1963, four months after the riot at Ole Miss that left two dead and the same month that George Wallace proclaimed, "I say segregation now—segregation tomorrow—and segregation forever" at his inauguration as governor of Alabama, architectural student Harvey Gantt of Charleston was scheduled to enroll under federal court order at Clemson University as a transfer student from Iowa State.

State Representative A. W. "Red" Bethea, who ran unsuccessfully for governor in 1962 by promising that if a black were ordered into a state-supported college in South Carolina, he would "close it so tight you can't get a crowbar in it," vigorously opposed an unrelated measure to change the name of Clemson College to Clemson University. He changed his mind when a fellow legislator told him, "Red, if we change it to Clemson University, it'll mean there will never have been a black student enrolled in Clemson College."[45]

In a sign of moderation, however, voters gave Bethea only 7 percent of the vote in the race for governor. Donald Russell won the office, giving lip service to segregation by asserting that South Carolina needed the best legal mind to protect it—coded language that moderate white voters and blacks understood meant adherence to law. He received 62 percent of the vote against Bethea and Lieutenant Governor Burnet Maybank Jr.

One of the state's top historians, George Rogers, has written that the central theme of South Carolina history, certainly after the Civil War and end of Reconstruction, had been the quest for stability.[46] Thurmond was no help as state leaders sought to accept the inevitable with as little turmoil as possible. The only member of the state's congressional delegation to take such a stand, Thurmond told the *News and Courier*'s Washington correspondent at the end of December 1962, "I am opposed to Gantt's admission to Clemson. The admission of students is a responsibility for the trustees, and any other action in connection therewith would have to be taken by the executive or the legislative branch of the State government."[47] At Clemson, an alumni group followed with a protest rally, saying, "Integration is Communism in action."

In contrast, outgoing Governor Hollings stood solidly for obedience to the rule of law. Early in January, in his final speech to the legislature, Hollings declared, "As we meet, South Carolina is running out of courts. If and when every legal remedy has been exhausted, this General Assembly must make clear South Carolina's choice, a government of laws rather than a government of men. As determined as we are, we of today must realize the lesson of one hundred years ago, and move on for the good of South Carolina and our United States. This should be done with dignity. It must be done with law and order."[48]

When the Fourth Circuit Court of Appeals then ordered Gantt's admission, Thurmond said it "substituted fiction for fact, and expedience for law." After Chief Justice Warren refused to issue a last-minute stay of the order by the Fourth Circuit Court of Appeals, the *News and Courier* on January 23 approvingly quoted Thurmond's characterization of the case as a "mockery of judicial procedure."[49]

The Charleston newspaper was sure that black activists were seeking "total mingling of the races," something far beyond token integration. "In recognizing racial differences," the editor wrote, "civilized people are only exercising selectivity which nature itself long ago installed without reference to modern sociological theories."*

---

*The biting editorial opposition to integration by the *News and Courier* soon came to a quiet end after editor Thomas R. Waring, selected as a board member of the Southern Education Reporting Service to assure conservative representation, was assigned a dinner seat next to a black college president one evening in Nashville. (The Ford Foundation funded SERS to provide objective reporting of information on the progress of school

A few days before Gantt enrolled at Clemson, Russell set a conciliatory tone by inviting "all the people of South Carolina" to a barbecue at the Governor's Mansion to celebrate his inaugural. More than 8,000 attended, ranging from black maids clad in housedresses and society matrons in furs to NAACP officials and white business leaders.

Attorney General Robert Kennedy called Russell a few days before Gantt's admission on January 28 to inquire whether trouble was anticipated and to offer federal help. Russell assured him that the administration in Washington "would not be embarrassed."[50]

The State Law Enforcement Division (SLED) had heavily infiltrated the Ku Klux Klan in South Carolina after an outbreak of violence a decade or so earlier. When an informant reported plans for a carload of Klansmen from a Lowcountry county to drive to Clemson for disruptive purposes, SLED Chief J. P. "Pete" Strom (Thurmond's distant cousin) had them arrested and jailed for a day.[51] Gantt quietly enrolled in an event the *Saturday Evening Post* would call "Integration with Dignity." Amid a crowd of national reporters, Gantt stood proudly in front of the campus administration building, Tillman Hall, named for Pitchfork Ben Tillman.

Gantt, who remained in the South after graduation and developed an architectural firm in Charlotte, and would later serve as mayor there and lose two close races to Jesse Helms to represent North Carolina in the U.S. Senate, said while at Clemson, "If you can't appeal to the morals of a South Carolinian, you can always appeal to his manners." Perhaps he was referring to events such as Governor Russell's barbecue.

The other side of that famous civility, with its emphasis on dignity, politeness, and form, was an easily pricked honor and combativeness perhaps best summed up by Fritz Hollings, who said that the typical South Carolinian "gets up in the morning, salutes the flag, recites the Pledge of Allegiance, and spends the rest of the day fighting."[52]

BUT THURMOND HAD SET A COURSE he would continue to follow for years, until he was overcome by the forces that he battled. In 1963, as

---

desegregation in the South.) The planner for the event, President Henry Hill of Peabody College, made the seating assignment deliberately. Waring later told him of being initially quite uncomfortable, as he had never been seated before at a meal next to a black person, but that as the evening progressed he found his dinner companion erudite and charming, and he enjoyed the evening (Henry Hill to Bass, fall 1965, Cambridge, Massachusetts).

President Kennedy proposed to end discrimination in public accommodations after viewing the police dogs and fire hoses used against civil rights demonstrators in Birmingham, Thurmond would call it "dictatorship over American business . . . to appease the Negro vote bloc."

Whatever Stanley Morse told Thurmond for over a decade about Communist influence in the civil rights movement would get reinforced by FBI director J. Edgar Hoover's well-documented vendetta against Martin Luther King Jr.[53]

In *Parting the Waters*, King biographer Taylor Branch wrote that after Hoover began wiretapping the phones of King's associates in 1963, before that year's pivotal March on Washington, a recording caught King and an associate sharing concern about the march's coordinator, Bayard Rustin, and his attraction to young boys. Although a gifted organizer and civil rights strategist, Rustin had been convicted in 1953 of a morals charge in California, involving him and two white men in the backseat of a car. King now expressed concern that if Rustin were drinking, he would "grab one little brother." Within hours, a transcript was sent directly to Hoover.

A day later, Thurmond stood up in the Senate and denounced Rustin "for sexual perversion, vagrancy, and lewdness." Thurmond inserted a copy of Rustin's police booking in the *Congressional Record*. His attack attracted little notice in the news media, Branch wrote, "perhaps because it was so distasteful and obviously political."[54]

When Congress passed the Civil Rights Act in 1964, Thurmond would say, "This is a tragic day for America, when Negro agitators, spurred on by Communist enticements to promote racial strife, can cause the United States Senate to be steamrolled into passing the worst, most unreasonable and unconstitutional legislation that has ever been considered by the Congress."[55]

Thurmond said in 1965 that passage of the Voting Rights Act "shows that [Martin Luther] King [Jr.] must always have an agitation objective lest he end up in the street one day without a drum to beat or a headline to make." This sort of rhetoric would continue for another decade. When the Voting Rights Act came up for renewal in 1975, Thurmond called it "unfortunate that the Congress ever enacted such an unconstitutional piece of legislation."

Was Olin Johnston right in thinking that Thurmond simply believed it? Was he simply too obtuse to recognize that blacks in the South wanted the same rights under law that white citizens had? Was it all a charade, the same political exploitation of race that made Alabama's George Wallace a champion of segregation until the political calculus changed and it no longer paid off? Or did Thurmond simply have to experience new relationships himself, to absorb through osmosis that conditions had changed? Or was it some combination of the above?

CHAPTER 15

The Republican Road

THE OUTCOME OF THE 1962 ELECTIONS in South Carolina reflected new political dynamics in the state. Donald Russell's overwhelming victory over Lieutenant Governor Burnet Maybank Jr. in the Democratic primary indicated he could be a strong opponent for Thurmond's Senate seat in four years. Olin Johnston handily defeated Governor Hollings in the Democratic Senate primary, but political journalist Bill Workman challenged Johnston as a Republican in the fall and received 43 percent of the vote.

Grocery chain heir J. Drake Edens of Columbia, Workman's campaign manager, began providing skilled leadership in building a statewide Republican political organization. Growing up, Edens had "heard my daddy cuss the Democrats from about 1935 on," though he did not attend his first Republican precinct meeting until 1960. The next year he helped draft young local business executive Charles Boineau to run for the state legislature in a special election for a vacant house seat. Boineau won, becoming the first Republican to sit in that body in the twentieth century.

An economic conservative and racial moderate, Edens became Republican state chairman. He used a manual produced, ironically, by the AFL-CIO Committee on Political Education as his guide for building the first genuine political party organization the state had seen.

> I went into towns that I never knew existed. I think the toughest county I ever hit was Chester. I tried to set up a county organization and went back to some of the people who had worked for Workman. I remember one night we called an organizational meeting, and I think three people showed up. We had a party rule that required at least six people organize a precinct, and you had to have at least three organized precincts in the county. I probably made a dozen trips to Chester County and finally put an organization together.[1]

The implications would become clear for Strom Thurmond, as the Republican Party philosophy increasingly offered him a more congenial home; it was building a sturdy political organization in South Carolina. Elsewhere in the South, an unknown college professor in Texas named John Tower ran as a Republican and won a special election in 1961 to fill the Senate seat vacated by Lyndon Johnson. A year later in Alabama, veteran Democrat Lister Hill barely survived a Republican challenge to his Senate seat.

Meanwhile, Arizona Senator Barry Goldwater was aiming to make the conservative wing dominate the Grand Old Party, and he had in mind a Southern strategy, first outlined in a 1961 speech in Atlanta to Republicans gathered from throughout the South. "We're not going to get the Negro vote as a bloc in 1964 and 1968, so we ought to go hunting where the ducks are," he declared. Goldwater then spelled out how this could be done, saying that school integration was "the responsibility of the states. I would not like to see my party assume it is the role of the federal government to enforce integration in the schools."[2]

In 1961, Thurmond and Goldwater had identical voting records on every major issue before the Senate. A year later, they appeared together as speakers at a Madison Square Garden rally sponsored by the conservative Young Americans for Freedom where Goldwater proclaimed conservatism "the wave of the future."

As Goldwater began developing what would become his successful campaign for the 1964 Republican presidential nomination, Thurmond continued to be a voice of protest in the Democratic Party. He drew loud applause in January 1963 from a Jaycee (Junior Chamber of Commerce) group in Rock Hill, sounding like a mock Rhett Butler by declaring testily, "I don't give a damn" how the Kennedy administration viewed his party loyalty.[3] For Thurmond, whose use of profanity was as rare as his consumption of alcohol, this was strong language.

That July, during questions devoted to the president's proposed Civil Rights Bill, Thurmond questioned Attorney General Robert Kennedy at length about its public accommodations section. Thurmond asked how many black men from Charlotte would have to attempt to have their hair cut at a barbershop in Fort Mill, across the state line in South Carolina, for it to be covered under the bill. Constitutional scholar Archibald Cox had based that section of the bill on the expansive interstate commerce clause of the Constitution because the Supreme Court in 1883 had struck down a federal public accommodations law based on the Fourteenth

Amendment.* Thurmond was deliberately posing a question that Kennedy could not answer with precision.

After extensive questioning, an exasperated Thurmond handed Kennedy a simple booklet about the Constitution, illustrated with cartoons. "It's written in such a way, such an interesting way, that almost anyone can understand it," Thurmond said. He was serious. (In 1957, he had sent an instructional pamphlet titled "How Our Laws Are Made," to his daughter Essie Mae in California.)

Kennedy replied coolly, "Thank you, Senator, for your kindness and your courtesy." An amused fellow senator told a reporter, "Bobby didn't know whether to laugh or to cry."[4]

Thurmond's bitter opposition to the Civil Rights Bill drew a rebuke from Senate Commerce Committee chairman John O. Pastore. The Rhode Island senator chastised Thurmond for "browbeating" Atlanta Mayor Ivan Allen, who endorsed the public accommodations section of the bill.

A furious Thurmond denied asking any "loaded" questions and said he resented Pastore's accusations.

Pastore replied that Thurmond had asked a question that went something like, "Mr. Mayor, since the enactment of this bill would close many businesses in small towns throughout the South, don't you think that would mean a taking of property by the federal government without due process of the law?"

When Thurmond angrily denied asking such a question, Pastore asked the committee stenographer to read it back.

Thurmond interrupted, shouting, "Well, all right, suppose I did ask the question. I reserve the right to cross-examine these witnesses any way I see fit."

Pastore bristled in response, shouting, "What do you mean, 'cross-

---

*Five years later, however, the most tragic civil rights conflict in South Carolina occurred over the confusion created by the issue Thurmond focused on, whether the 1964 Civil Rights Act covered a bowling alley in Orangeburg because the facility contained a snack bar serving food that traveled in interstate commerce. A federal court ultimately ruled the bowling alley was covered, but only after a confrontation that ended with three black students killed and twenty-seven others wounded by highway patrol gunfire on the campus of South Carolina State College. The 1968 event, which became known as the "Orangeburg Massacre," received little national coverage when it happened (Jack Bass and Jack Nelson, *The Orangeburg Massacre*, 2nd ed. [Macon, GA: Mercer University Press, 2002]).

examine'? This is not a courtroom. These are distinguished people whose presence before this committee is a service."

"I'm only trying to get at the truth," Thurmond asserted.

"Your truth is not my truth," Pastore replied.

At that, the crowd attending the hearing broke into laughter and applause.

Thurmond next accused Pastore of failing to maintain decorum and said he should have stopped the laughter.

"How can I stop it when it's already happened?" Pastore asked. "I didn't know they were going to laugh." With that, the crowd laughed again.

Thurmond accused Pastore of impropriety for condoning outbursts from an audience "full of left-wingers and sympathizers for this bill."

"Mr. Thurmond," Pastore now roared, "I've been around here a long time, and that question you asked was a loaded question." He then banged his gavel and told the crowd it would have to control itself.[5]

As Thurmond's public profile and rhetoric grew more shrill, he continued to attract the admiration of fringe groups. The anti-Communist John Birch Society—whose founder, candy manufacturer Robert Welch, had written that Dwight Eisenhower was "a conscious agent" of the Communist Party—hung his portrait in a place of honor at its Belmont, Massachusetts, national headquarters. In Savannah, Georgia, at the end of August 1963, a Ku Klux Klan unit expressed support for Thurmond as the 1964 Democratic presidential candidate.[6]

THURMOND DID HAVE CONCERNS beyond civil rights issues and domestic anti-Communism: He was an early and persistent advocate within the Armed Services Committee for developing an anti-missile defense system. His advocacy from 1961 onward led to the initial appropriations for research and development of an advanced system, what would eventually emerge as the costly and controversial Star Wars program of the Reagan administration and be reinstated several decades later by President George W. Bush. Star Wars advocates contend that this initiative helped end the Cold War and bring down Communism in Soviet bloc countries. History will have to judge whether Communism and the Soviet bloc collapsed because of such external pressure or from the system's internal failure to hold the allegiance of its people.

Thurmond joined in the national grieving after President Kennedy's assassination on November 22, 1963. He put aside his dislike for the liberal president and praised Kennedy as personable and popular, although he may well have shared the views of Mississippi's James O. Eastland, who had sat for ten years in the Senate chamber in front of John Kennedy. "He didn't know how to put proposals through Congress," Eastland said later of Kennedy as president. "We had him blocked." On the day of Kennedy's assassination, Eastland was driving through Virginia's Shenandoah Valley on his way to Mississippi when he noticed a flag at half staff in a small town, and the same thing a little farther down the road. He switched on his radio, heard the news, turned his car around to head back to Washington, and said to his wife, "Good God, Lyndon's president. He's gonna pass a lot of this damn fool stuff."[7]

Thurmond's initial response—at least for the record—was to express gratitude to the late president for his foresight and vision in selecting as the man to succeed him in office, in the event of such a tragedy, "one of the most experienced and capable leaders I have ever known."[8] The next spring, Thurmond got Johnson to nominate Charles Simons as a federal district judge in South Carolina, an objective the Kennedy administration had thwarted for three years.

But the first big piece of Eastland's feared "damn fool stuff" was coming down the pike—the 1964 Civil Rights Act. Johnson announced it as a top priority, a tribute to the slain president. On its final vote, Goldwater led five other Republicans in joining twenty-one Southern Democrats in opposition. This landmark legislation would have a major impact in transforming the American South. The Civil Rights Act outlawed discrimination in public accommodations and employment and created an enforcement mechanism that would finally lead to meaningful school desegregation. As an afterthought—actually as the result of a joke made by an opponent of the bill—that would later prove quite important, it outlawed discrimination based on gender as well as race. It also established the Community Relations Service to help smooth the transition to integrated public facilities.

One of the great Thurmond legends involves him wrestling with liberal Senator Ralph Yarborough of Texas outside a committee room. Thurmond was attempting to squash the confirmation of Florida Governor Leroy Collins as director of the new Community Relations Service.

Thurmond had reacted personally in December 1963 to a speech that Collins made in Columbia, South Carolina, denouncing bigotry. Although he did not mention Strom by name, Collins, then director of the National Association of Broadcasters, told the Columbia Chamber of Commerce, "How long are the majority of Southerners going to allow themselves to be caricatured before the nation by these Claghorns? It is time the decent people of the South told the bloody shirt-wavers to climb down off the buckboards of bigotry."

Thurmond issued a statement—written in Buzhardt's slashing style—saying, "For one who professes to abhor the emotion of hate, Mr. Collins proves himself singularly adept at verbally purveying this most violent emotion."

At Collins's confirmation, Thurmond engaged in his customary line of questioning for three hours, asking Collins about past statements of his about race that now were embarrassing. Collins explained, "Later events bring a modification of one's thinking."

On July 9, 1964, the last day of hearings, determined to prevent a quorum and thereby stop Collins's confirmation, Thurmond stationed himself outside the committee room door and tried to talk others out of entering. A couple of senators simply walked down the hall and slipped in through a back door.

But Yarborough came down the hallway, shook Strom's hand, and playfully tugged him toward the committee room. It was the mule race of his state senate years all over again. Strom took it as a challenge and went for Yarborough's knees. Both men were sixty-one, belonged to the same Army Reserve unit, and had wrestled as youths. But the heavier and less fit Yarborough said he learned later that Thurmond had judo training in the army. Yarborough knew a fight could lead to a formal censure. With an election coming up, he wanted to avoid that. Yarborough said it was with this thought in mind that he slid down on the floor with his back to the wall. The Thurmond version is that he threw Yarborough to the floor and pinned him there, saying, "Tell me to release you, Ralph, and I will." Either way, the gentleman from South Carolina now had the gentleman from Texas held down against his will.

Yarborough said he told Thurmond, "This is ridiculous. If they get a picture of us here, they'll defeat both of us." But Yarborough understood, "He wanted me to holler 'Quits, I've got enough.' I said, 'Not on your life.'"

Finally, Committee Chairman Warren Magnuson of Washington learned what was taking place, stepped into the hallway, which had become crowded with spectators, and roared, "Stop that! Get off the floor!" By the time press photographers showed up, the men were separated and standing.

At the urging of his press aide, Yarborough soon rushed over to Thurmond's office, grabbed his hand, raised it, and declared, "Strom, you're the champ." Yarborough said several senators later chastised him for not knowing better than to mess with Thurmond. "I wouldn't say they regarded him as crazy," Yarborough said, "They regarded him as kind of a wild man."[9]

Strom was scolded by his aides, but South Carolina constituents called to congratulate him on "showing that liberal." Thurmond staffers claimed that Texans flooded Yarborough's office with boxes of Wheaties.

For Thurmond, this wrestling match was literally his last fight within the Democratic Party. He didn't attend the Democratic National Convention. With Dent and Buzhardt nudging him along, he reached a difficult decision, but one that he had been headed toward publicly and privately for some time now, beginning with the Dixiecrat campaign in 1948, followed by his write-in victory for the Senate against the Democratic establishment in 1954. The South Carolina senator had been speaking out about political realignment since 1961. "After I got up here," Thurmond later reminisced, "I soon found that the Republican Party was more in line with my thinking and the philosophy of the people of South Carolina than the Democratic Party at the national level."[10]

Barry Goldwater received the Republican nomination in mid-July, although he opened grievous self-inflicted wounds on his campaign as early as his acceptance speech when he declared that "extremism in the defense of liberty is no vice, and moderation in the pursuit of justice is no virtue." To many Americans that line cast him as an extremist whose itchy finger they would choose not to trust with a Cold War nuclear trigger. But Goldwater's vote against the Civil Rights Bill, his commitment to a strong military, his ardent anti-Communism, his belief in decentralized government and a market economy, and his "strict" interpretation of the Constitution all resonated with Thurmond.

With their finely calibrated political senses, Dent and Thurmond knew it was time to move boldly. Dent's objective was to build a two-party political system in the South, and Buzhardt fully agreed. They also believed changing parties now was in Thurmond's interest, that he could be vulnerable in a Democratic primary. Dent said, "If Jean had lived there wouldn't have been a switching."[11] Jean was comfortable as a Democrat and recognized that Strom wasn't without philosophically compatible colleagues among his fellow Southern Democrats in the Senate.

After Strom made his decision to switch to the Republican Party, Thurmond and Dent flew to South Carolina and met with key supporters and opinion leaders, letting them in on his idea and listening to their responses. They first visited Walter Brown in Spartanburg, a top assistant to Jimmy Byrnes in Washington and now (1964) a television station owner on whose behalf Thurmond had intervened with the Federal Communications Commission (FCC). Dent made the pitch for switching parties and endorsing Goldwater. He remembered, "Walter just went livid. 'You're crazy, Strom. This young boy isn't even dry behind the ears.' He assured Thurmond there was no way he could get reelected in South Carolina as a Republican."

They next drove to Greenville to see newspaper publisher Roger Peace. Walter Brown had already called him. "He lacerated me," Dent said. "He said, 'Strom, that boy is going to destroy you.'"

The next stop was Columbia, where Bill Workman had moved in as editorial page editor for *The State*. Publisher Ambrose Hampton, a direct descendant of the Redeemer Governor Wade Hampton III, listened intently. Dent remembered, "Ambrose sat there and listened and said, 'That would be one of the most refreshing things I've ever heard of.' That's all he said."

Then they drove across town to see Byrnes. Strom went to the bathroom, and Byrnes said, "Harry, what are you and Strom up to?" Dent recalled, "He had already gotten a call from up there in Spartanburg. He didn't tell me that, but I knew he had."

"I said, 'We're talking about switching parties.' He said, 'Maude, Maude. Bring me another drink. Strom Thurmond is about to commit political suicide.' And then the senator came out from the bathroom. We sat down and Jimmy Byrnes said, 'Now, what you need to do is be an Independent.'"

Bryan Dorn understood the trip to South Carolina as "a smart maneuver. If you're gonna do it, that's about the only way I know that you can do it and get by with it. You call everybody and say, 'What do you think about it? You know my principles are so and so and so.' Every one of them says, 'Well, it takes a lot of courage to do that. If it was up to me I wouldn't do it.' But when he does it, you see, he's got all of them sewed up. Every one of them. They're in on the act. That's just a tactic, and it's a good tactic."

After returning to Washington, Dent thought Thurmond had been talked out of switching. Buzhardt had already written a statement lambasting the Democratic Party. It was ready to go. "I went back and talked to the senator," Dent said, "and talked to the senator some more. And I saw him come back to life. Once he made his decision, there was no changing it."

Thurmond got an appointment with Goldwater on Saturday, September 12. Dent accompanied him, but this time Thurmond did the talking. Dent recalled that he wasted no time, telling Goldwater, "I have three choices open to me. I can keep quiet, I can come out for you but remain a Democrat, or I can come out for you and go all the way to the Republican Party. I'll do what will help you most."

Goldwater, of course, said that going all the way and switching parties would help the most.

"Well, that's along the line I've been thinking," Thurmond said. He showed his statement to Goldwater for his approval. "Don't change one word," Goldwater told him.*

The Arizonan—nothing if not candid—then commented that he intended to present his views forthrightly to the American people. "If they don't want me, I'll just go back to Arizona and operate my ham radio," he said.

Thurmond and Dent recognized immediately that Goldwater felt he had little chance of success. Still, Thurmond asked Dent to call GOP party chairman Drake Edens to alert Republican officials in South Carolina of his forthcoming conversion. Thurmond said he would make his announcement there on Wednesday, September 16, so he could be on hand the next day for Goldwater's rally in Greenville.

Dent telephoned Dolly Hamby, who had handled press relations for Thurmond's write-in campaign, and asked that she arrange to have the televised address broadcast across ten states. Thurmond then flew to Greenville, South Carolina, on Monday for the funeral of industrialist Charles Daniel. Dent was getting the jitters again. He knew that all the big boys of South

---

*Dent's memory of the meeting was far more vivid than Goldwater's, who in a 1982 letter told Marilyn Thompson he didn't remember any direct conversations with Thurmond "relative to his decision to become a Republican." But Goldwater said Thurmond "gave me tremendous support and . . . was the major single factor in making it possible for me to have carried the South." He added, "I think that Strom's becoming a Republican was the major factor in the South being able to switch over from a solid Democratic bloc to a place where Republicanism has been growing ever since 1964" (letter from Goldwater to Marilyn Thompson, circa 1982).

Carolina politics would attend and likely gang up on Thurmond. Dent told Buzhardt, "We're going to get shot out of the saddle. These guys are going to stop him." Although the senator's staff had press and film packets of his address ready to mail across the South, Dent said to hold them.

The senator called Dent in his office early Monday afternoon to ask if the press material had been mailed out. Dent said no and explained, "Senator, I knew those guys would get you and talk you out of it." Thurmond said, "Yes, they talked to me. Put those things in the mail."[12]

In retrospect, Thurmond's switch appears shrewd. It was bold, but not as risky as his aides make out. As Bryan Dorn would also comment, "In time, if not right then, it would have been very difficult for Senator Thurmond to win a primary with a liberal Democrat and the black vote and all that against him, with a Republican sitting off in right field, you know, already nominated. So he was smart along that line. He is a master politician."[13]

In his speech addressing "My Fellow South Carolinians" but aired throughout the South that Wednesday night, Strom was also adroit enough to suggest that he was motivated not by a desire to join his main group of supporters, which would appear opportunistic, but out of a principled frustration with the Democratic Party, which he castigated as evil and out of touch. It is worth quoting at length:

> The Democratic Party has abandoned the people. . . . It has repudiated the Constitution of the United States. It is leading the evolution of our nation to a socialistic dictatorship.
>
> The Democratic Party has forsaken the people to become the party of minority groups, power-hungry union leaders, political bosses, and big businessmen looking for government contracts and favors. . . .
>
> The Democratic Party has invaded the private lives of the people by using the powers of government for coercion and intimidation of individuals.
>
> The Democratic Party has rammed through Congress unconstitutional, impractical, unworkable, and oppressive legislation which invades inalienable personal and property rights of the individual. . . .
>
> The Democratic Party has succored and assisted our Communist enemies through trade and aid at the expense of the American people.
>
> The Democratic Party has established and pursued for our government a no-win foreign policy of weakness, indecision, accommodation, and appeasement.

The Democratic Party, as custodian of government, faltered at the Bay of Pigs and in the Cuba crisis of 1962—at the very moment when victory was at hand—and thereby forfeited Cuba to Soviet domination, subjected our nation to the perils of an armed enemy camp ninety miles from our shores, and opened the doors of the hemisphere to Communist subversion.

The Democratic Party, as custodian of government, has sent our youth into combat in Viet Nam, refusing to call it war, and demanding of our youth the risk of their lives without providing either adequate equipment or a goal of victory. . . .

The Democratic Party has demonstrated a callous disregard for sound fiscal policies and practices.

The Democratic Party, while hiding behind the deceitful gimmick of a darkened White House, has increased deficit spending and squandered, at home and abroad, billions of hard-earned dollars taken from the American people.

The Democratic Party has utterly disregarded the disastrous effects of the resulting inflation on people with fixed incomes, such as retirees, pensioners, Social Security beneficiaries, and those who have their savings invested in insurance. . . .

The Democratic Party has endangered the security of the nation by negative decisions of military preparedness, preoccupation with bilateral and unilateral steps toward disarmament, and by use of the military services domestically as instruments of social reform. . . .

The Democratic Party has encouraged, supported, and protected the Supreme Court in a reign of judicial tyranny, and in the Court's effort to wipe out local self-government, effect law enforcement, internal security, the rights of the people and the states, and even the structure of the State governments. . . .

The party of our fathers is dead. Those who took its name are engaged in another reconstruction, this time not only of the South, but of the entire nation. If the American people permit the Democratic Party to return to power, freedom as we have known it in this country is doomed, and individuals will be destined to lives of regulation, control, coercion, intimidation, and subservience to a power elite who shall rule from Washington. . . .

The man who has gained the Republican nomination for President against all the odds and opinion polls . . . has demonstrated his fidelity to freedom, independence, and the Constitution by his actions and his votes in the United States Senate. I personally know him to be able and responsible. He is an honest man of courage and conviction, who trusts the American people to hold the reins of government and rule themselves. . . .

I do know we have a fighting chance under Barry Goldwater's leadership and that we are welcomed to his banner. I know also that the course for the Democratic Party has been set toward socialism and arbitrary rule. I know further that the Democratic Party's line of succession is Hubert Humphrey and Robert Kennedy. . . .

For me there is no alternative. The future of freedom and constitutional government is at stake, and this requires that I do everything in my power to help Barry Goldwater return our nation to constitutional government through his election to the Presidency. . . .

I have chosen this course because I cannot consider any risks in a cause which I am convinced is right.

For added drama, a tag line of "Strom Thurmond (D., S.C.)" flashed across the screen, changing two-thirds of the way through the speech to "(R., S.C.)."

When introducing Thurmond the next day at the upstate rally for Goldwater, Drake Edens read this epitaph from the tomb of Strom's grandfather, George Washington Thurmond: "He did not tread on the rights of others and he did not permit others to tread on his." The crowd of 25,000 cheered wildly.

In the fall campaign, Thurmond thundered across the South, drawing large audiences and making more than a dozen appearances with Goldwater, including one televised indoor rally in Columbia on October 31. He won 59 percent of the vote in South Carolina, the first Republican presidential candidate to carry the state since Rutherford Hayes's contested victory in 1876.

Elsewhere, Goldwater won only his native Arizona, Georgia, and the three other Deep South states Thurmond had carried as a Dixiecrat—Alabama, Louisiana, and Mississippi. Lyndon Johnson won the other forty-four states and received 60 percent of the popular vote, a landslide victory.

DESPITE OPPOSITION from a few liberal Republican critics, such as Senator Clifford Case of New Jersey, Thurmond kept his seniority after the switch, moving, for instance, from seventh-ranking Democrat on the Armed Services Committee to fourth-ranking Republican.

Important developments followed. After House Democrats stripped Albert Watson of his two years' seniority for endorsing Goldwater, the South Carolina congressman followed the precedent set by Preston Brooks more than a century earlier after his censure for caning Charles Sumner. Watson resigned, ran for reelection in a special election—but as a Republican—and portrayed himself as a martyr "who would not let my people be punished." He won 70 percent of the vote against a credible Democratic opponent. With Thurmond in the Senate and his protégé in the House, South Carolina Republicans now possessed a base from which to exert Southwide leadership in party building.

As keynote speaker at the 1965 state convention, Thurmond argued that the Republican Party in South Carolina should be "selective in offering candidates" rather than challenge Democrats across the board. Party Chairman Drake Edens disagreed, believing that candidate recruitment was the key to party growth and eventually to real two-party competition.

The Voting Rights Act of 1965 eliminated literacy tests in states where less than 50 percent of the voting age population voted in the 1964 presidential election; it required these states to get advance clearance from the Justice Department before implementing any changes in laws affecting voting. In South Carolina the number of black elected officials would climb from eleven in 1968 to 116 in 1974. The act increased and energized black voting strength in South Carolina. Simultaneously, it antagonized a majority of whites, and Thurmond reflected their views. He attacked the measure as vindictive in primarily targeting the states that had voted for Goldwater. "Deep down in his heart," Dent said, Thurmond "felt Lyndon Johnson was getting even. He felt that the act should be for the whole country, and he's never gotten over that."[14] Segregationists had seethed when Johnson declared, "We shall overcome"—the anthem of the civil rights movement—in mobilizing Congress in 1965 to pass the act after a violent confrontation—seen by millions on television—between Alabama lawmen and blacks protesting discrimination in voter registration at Selma.

Democratic politicians in South Carolina suddenly needed black votes to win and were "scared to death" of seeking them. Don Fowler, then chairman of the state's Young Democrats, became the main emissary to the African American community. "I think during that period of time I was the only person who had any status in the Democratic Party who did that, and I did one hell of a lot of it," Fowler remembered. He continued:

I went to black churches when no other white soul would go to black churches. There was a black preacher in Greenville, dead now, who was minister of the McBee Avenue Baptist Church. His name was David Francis, and he invited me to come up and speak to the countywide meeting on Sunday afternoon.

And I called two or three legislators up there (one of them was future Governor Dick Riley and another was future House Speaker Rex Carter), and they said, "Well, I guess you should go, but for God's sake don't get caught."

And I went and made this speech. It was in the basement of this church, and there were 200 blacks. And if I had gotten caught by a reporter, it would have literally been front-page news, not that I was that important, but that there would have been a white guy down there who had any sort of ties within the Democratic Party.[15]

Fowler was entirely comfortable during the three-hour meeting, except for the "fear of getting caught."[16]

In 1966, Fowler remembered, "Among normal, middle-class white people, it was about as popular to be a Democrat as it was to have bubonic plague. Lyndon Johnson was Satan incarnate. We were right in the wake of the Civil Rights Act of '64 and the Voting Rights Act of '65, and Lyndon Johnson and his Great Society were really cranking up. And, in the common vernacular, he was 'doing all these things for the niggers.' I mean that was just the atmosphere. If anybody asked an office holder about the Democratic Party, they would say, 'I'm a *South Carolina* Democrat.'"[17]

Before long, Democratic candidates would be happy to speak in black churches—and Republicans would eventually join them there. Southern black churches have traditionally served as centers of community life, extending their spiritual role to congregational concerns about government and democratic ideals.

Harry Dent returned to South Carolina in the fall of 1965, after Edens stepped down as GOP party chairman, and took over planning the statewide 1966 campaign. Dent was intent on building the Republican Party, and the GOP fielded a full slate of candidates for state and congressional offices, with Thurmond at the top of the ticket.

Dent's move was suggested by political activist James B. Edwards, a Charleston dental surgeon who would later become governor of South

Carolina and President Ronald Reagan's secretary of energy. Edwards made a special trip to Washington to see Thurmond, persuading him that the thirty-five-year-old Dent was the man for the job.[18] Dent's loyalty to Thurmond assured that the party would never undermine his political interests.

Thurmond continued to capitalize on some lucky breaks. After Senator Johnston died in 1965, Governor Donald Russell responded to urging from Lyndon Johnson and, in effect, appointed himself to fill the vacancy. Russell, who had actively supported LBJ's losing effort in South Carolina in 1964, resigned as governor. Lieutenant Governor Robert E. McNair took the oath as governor and immediately appointed Russell to the Senate. This deal outraged Johnston's widow, who thought she or William "Bill" Johnston, Olin's brother, should have been appointed. But for Thurmond it meant that he wouldn't face an opponent of Russell's stature in 1966, and Strom drew attention for being warm and solicitous to him in Washington. However, the new senator wasn't around long. With his "self-appointment" an issue, he lost to Hollings in the 1966 Democratic primary.

In the general election five months later, Thurmond received 62 percent of the vote against hapless challenger State Senator Bradley Morrah of Greenville. His strength at the top of the ticket almost spilled over enough to topple Hollings in his bid for the remaining two years of Johnston's term. Watson also won reelection, but all other Republicans seeking major offices lost. The GOP did gain a foothold in the legislature.

A solid black vote provided the margin of victory for the Democrats. Dent sought to capitalize on the white backlash, playing footsie with the segregationist independents allied with George Wallace. In one instance, Dent distributed Republican campaign literature showing Governor McNair shaking hands with a black man. Although Dent later retreated from that kind of racial politics, it reflected the initial thrust of the Republican "Southern strategy."

Unlike the Republican candidates who had an organized political party to provide them support, Bradley Morrah, the Democratic sacrificial lamb, received "not a dime" from the state or national party. He further believed that Thurmond was "majestically treated" by the press.[19] Although well regarded and an aggressive campaigner, Morrah was little known outside his base. Thurmond refused to debate him—eliminating at least one way in which Morrah might raise his profile. Thurmond increased the margin of his victory by undercutting Morrah with endorsements from Democratic Senators Russell and Talmadge of Georgia and Stennis of Mississippi, all of whom presumably believed that endorsing Strom would help them in their own races.

Morrah had simultaneously run for his established seat in the State Senate, lost it to Tom Wofford, and would never again hold elective office. In the years ahead, Thurmond would delight in the experiences of those who ran against him. They invariably suffered political death.

CHAPTER 16

"And You Refuse to Answer That?"

It is difficult to conceive of a contemporary native Southerner more unlike Strom Thurmond than Abe Fortas. He grew up in Memphis, the home of the blues, a son of lower-middle-class immigrant Jewish parents. Fine music was as important to him as fitness was to Thurmond.

Born in 1910, eight years after Thurmond, Fortas went to college on scholarships and excelled at Yale Law School when Strom was reading law under his father's tutelage. His Yale faculty mentor was future Supreme Court Justice William O. Douglas. Yale was the center of the developing concept known as legal realism that emphasized the importance of facts and treated law as an instrument of social policy.

The nation's major law firms did not hire Jews in those days, curtailing the opportunities for an ambitious lawyer like Fortas. He spent his early years after law school shuttling back and forth between New Haven and Washington, as a junior law school faculty member at Yale and as one of the bright, creative young men who thrived under Franklin Roosevelt's meritocracy and helped shape his New Deal. During this era, he befriended the equally smart, hard-driving, and ambitious young Texas Congressman Lyndon Baines Johnson. (Fortas helped Johnson arrange for a rural electrification project for his constituents.) The two men shared a liberal political philosophy, believing in an active government with "a concern for people." They became trusting friends.

After World War II, Fortas and his former Yale professor Thurmond Arnold formed a law firm. They soon added a third name, New Deal colleague Paul Porter, who had served as Federal Communications Commission chairman and ambassador to Greece. With their intimate knowledge of regulatory law and contacts inside the government, they quickly attracted significant corporate clients and hardworking, quick-witted young associates. Money poured in. But they also believed strongly in civil liberties and were among the few lawyers who became heavily involved—usually charging only expenses—in assisting non-Communist victims of loyalty programs that often based their charges on reports from anonymous, malicious informants.

After President Kennedy's assassination, Fortas was one of the first people President Lyndon Johnson called. He helped draft the new president's first speech to Congress, emphasizing action, liberal programs, and unity. It urged Congress to adopt Kennedy's Civil Rights Bill and his tax reduction plan. As one aide put it, Johnson wanted to "out-Roosevelt Roosevelt,"[1] and Fortas, a valued friend, became a key adviser and confidant. He turned down an offer to become attorney general but met regularly with the president, recommended people for key positions, and helped shape policy.

In 1965, Johnson coaxed Justice Arthur Goldberg to leave the Supreme Court to become America's ambassador to the United Nations and appointed the fifty-five-year-old Fortas to fill the court vacancy. Fortas accepted reluctantly—in part because he made many times more money practicing law and spent accordingly. Johnson announced Fortas's appointment the same day he announced a dramatic 50,000-troop escalation of the Vietnam War. Fortas breezed through his confirmation hearings, and he praised Judiciary Chairman James Eastland of Mississippi for his "fairness and friendliness."

Despite the Constitution's separation of powers among the legislative, executive, and judicial branches of government, former Justice Felix Frankfurter had offered advice while on the bench to President Franklin Roosevelt. But Arthur Goldberg warned Fortas that times had changed. Goldberg told him, "Abe, while Felix did it, according to present reactions, people do not like a Supreme Court justice being too close to a president."[2] But Lyndon Johnson wanted advice from Fortas, who continued to give it freely. Fortas avoided talking about the Court's business while in the White House, but he attended meetings there, helped shape policy, and continued to recommend people for appointment. Fortas's dual role reflected an arrogance, encouraged by his loyalty to Johnson, and a recklessness that as a prudent lawyer he no doubt would have advised anyone else to avoid.

After President Johnson's further escalation of the war in Vietnam—a policy Fortas encouraged—led to public disenchantment with his presidency, Johnson stunned the nation on the evening of March 31, 1968, by announcing in the starkest terms, "I shall not seek, and I will not accept, the nomination of my party for another term as your president."

In a June 13 letter to the president, Chief Justice Earl Warren wrote that he intended to resign "effective at your pleasure." Johnson, who seemed not to realize how dramatically his power had dwindled after his announcement, decided to make Fortas the chief justice and appoint Court of Appeals Judge Homer Thornberry, a former Texas congressman and Johnson crony, as Fortas's replacement. Johnson thought Fortas had the best legal mind he knew, and their philosophical values coincided. The president replied on June 27 to Warren, "With your agreement I will accept your decision to retire effective at such time as a successor is qualified."[3] Had Johnson chosen a solid moderate Republican instead of Thornberry, as some advisers had urged, his slick deal with Warren might have worked. And if Warren had simply resigned, creating an actual vacancy, little basis for organized opposition would have existed.

BY THIS LATE DATE in Johnson's presidency, Thurmond had cemented a commitment to support Richard Nixon for the Republican presidential nomination: The two men had met with Nixon promising to appoint "strict constructionists" to the Supreme Court. Although Nixon supported *Brown v. Board of Education,* he expressed "understanding" of the "problems" involved in desegregation. Thurmond also liked his views on defense and support for strengthening state and local government. Most important, he believed Nixon could win the 1968 presidential contest.

Thurmond's views about the Supreme Court had just been laid out in *The Faith We Have Not Kept,* a thin paperback.[4] It was essentially a compilation lifted from his speeches over the years. One scholar who read the book called it "a study in anti-intellectualism" in which the Constitution becomes holy writ and Thurmond its fundamentalist theologian.[5] Thurmond seemed to blame all of society's ills—"crime in the streets, a free rein for Communism, riots, agitation, collectivism and the breakdown of moral codes"—on the "Supreme Court's assault on the Constitution."

In his view, the "conspicuous" moment when this assault began was in 1954 with *Brown v. Board of Education.* The problem, Thurmond argued, was that the Constitution now could be interpreted as having "whatever meaning could be derived from the words—as long as the meaning fit the political philosophy of five Supreme Court justices." His argument's first problem is that a unanimous Supreme Court had decided *Brown.* Its more basic problem is that the Constitution has always meant what a majority of the Supreme Court decided, as legal realists acknowledged.

The original interpretation of the Fourteenth Amendment, in the 1873 *Slaughterhouse* cases, was itself a 5–4 decision that narrowly limited the protected "privileges and immunities of citizens of the United States." It was a complex case brought by independent white butchers in New Orleans to protest that city's granting a monopoly to a private group with political influence that threatened their livelihood. The Supreme Court's majority limited the Fourteenth Amendment's protection to "the slave race" but gave enforcement power over civil rights, "the rights of person and of Property," to the states, which by then in most of the South had reverted to control by white Southerners. In other words, the Fourteenth Amendment meant little. The four dissenters said it had become "a vain and idle enactment, which accomplished nothing." One wrote, "What was meant for bread was turned to stone."6

A week later, as further evidence of how the justices respond to prevailing contemporary attitudes, the Supreme Court ruled 8–1 that the state of Illinois had the right to refuse Myra Bradwell the right to practice law because she was a woman. Little more than a decade later, in *Santa Clara County v. Southern Pacific Railroad*, a Supreme Court composed of nine white men with backgrounds in corporate law unanimously decided that what the Fourteenth Amendment really protected was the economic rights of corporations.7

Thurmond's argument to the contrary, *Brown v. Board of Education* restored to the Fourteenth Amendment the meaning intended by its framers—to grant blacks as a class the full rights of citizenship equal to that of other Americans. On one point where Thurmond's version of history did match the reality, he acknowledged that the framers designed the amendment to overcome the 1857 *Dred Scott* case.

Chief Justice Roger Taney declared in *Dred Scott* not only that even free blacks were not citizens and therefore lacked standing to sue in federal court but that they were "altogether unfit to associate with the white race" and "had no rights which the white man was bound to respect."

The slave, Dred Scott, thus could not have a federal court decide the validity of his claim to freedom for having lived in a free state before his master moved to the slave state of Missouri. The case, officially reported as *Scott v. Sanford,* also ruled the Missouri Compromise of 1820 unconstitutional, thus opening up all the territories for slavery.[8]

Justice Benjamin R. Curtis, one of two dissenters in the decision, pointed out that free blacks had voted in some states, including North Carolina, at the time the Constitution was adopted. He factually repudiated almost all of Taney's major points.

The "War Between the States," Thurmond wrote, happened because "social revolutionaries refused to stop at the constitutional barrier" the Supreme Court cited in *Dred Scott.*[9] He gave no further explanation of the case. Abraham Lincoln and other "social revolutionaries" then galvanized the Republican Party in reaction to *Dred Scott*—and won the presidential election in 1860. In historian Thurmond's version, their doing so apparently brought on the Civil War. They presumably got at least help from Thurmond's fellow Edgefield townsman, Francis H. Wardlaw, who drafted South Carolina's Ordinance of Secession. (Wardlaw Academy, the private school in Edgefield organized after the local public schools were desegregated, is named for him.)

Whatever Thurmond's shortcomings as a historian, his political instincts were now sharper than Johnson's. When the president announced his Fortas-Thornberry package on June 27, freshman Republican Senator Robert Griffin of Michigan immediately issued a statement that any Supreme Court vacancy should not be filled by a "lame duck" president. Seventeen Republican senators signed his petition.

Thurmond spoke out the next day. He called Fortas unacceptable for three reasons. First was "his long reputation as a fixer and his involvement with many questionable figures." Next came his alignment with "the radical wing of the Court." And finally, Thurmond denounced Fortas's support of decisions that "extended the power of the federal government and invaded the rights of the states, turned criminals loose on technicalities," and gave aid to Communists. Thurmond then attacked the issue that most seemed to bother his fellow Republicans, charging "collusion between President Johnson and Chief Justice Warren to prevent the next president from appointing the next chief justice." For Thurmond, the Warren Court was the enemy, and he understood as clearly as Lyndon Johnson that Abe Fortas would continue its liberal course.

Five days later, Thurmond demonstrated he was warming up to fight, and this time he knew he had allies who could be mobilized. "Those who have wailed about the damage the Supreme Court has done the country now have a chance to let the people speak through their new president regarding the court leadership for possibly the next twenty years," he asserted.

Republican Majority Leader Everett Dirksen was supporting Fortas, but soon realized his followers were slipping away. Johnson had coaxed Richard Russell, who could bring a cadre of conservative Southerners with him, to support his judicial nominees. But that support fell apart after an *Atlanta Constitution* editorial questioned the fitness of a Savannah segregationist whom Russell was promoting for a federal judgeship. Attorney General Ramsey Clark infuriated Russell by delaying the administration's support until he could investigate. Before Johnson could overrule Clark and pacify Russell, the Georgia senator withdrew his support and joined Griffin's group, bringing his followers.[10]

Using language written by Fortas, Senator Abraham Ribicoff challenged as "a novel and radical idea" the claim by Fortas's opponents that a president should be deprived of his constitutional power to fill vacancies because he would no longer hold office after November.

No sitting Supreme Court justice had ever before submitted to questioning by a congressional committee. Two prior sitting justices, Edward White and Harlan Fiske Stone, when nominated as chief justice, had decided it would be inappropriate to testify. They reasoned that some senators would ask about past decisions and that answering such questions would violate the Constitution's separation of powers provision.

Fortas, however, believed that testifying could help his controversial nomination because of his experience with Congress and his knowledge of how Washington worked. The White House agreed. Invited to testify, he accepted.

Led by Griffin, senators initially focused on Fortas's advisory relationship with the president. Fortas downplayed this role so significantly that his biographer Laura Kalman concluded, "He simply lied."[11] But he did disclose enough to illustrate that the relationship was far more than social and included discussions with the president on such issues as the Vietnam War and urban riots. Fortas insisted he never advised on matters that might reach the Supreme Court, but even his supporters were unsettled by his relationship with the president.

When the subject changed to the record of the Warren Court, Thurmond grilled Fortas for two hours with all the subtlety of an attack dog.

He focused on criminal cases and voting rights—repeatedly asking (some fifty times), and Fortas repeatedly declining to answer, questions about specific cases. Each time, Thurmond concluded, "And you refuse to answer that?"

And Fortas repeatedly answered, "Yes."

He maintained his composure, once explaining, "Senator, with the greatest deference and the greatest respect I assure you, my answer must stand. I cannot address myself to the question that you have phrased because I could not possibly address myself to it without discussing theory and principle. And the theory and principle I would discuss would most certainly be involved in situations that we have to face."

An irritated Thurmond said he could not understand, nor would the people, why Fortas could write and lecture about legal issues but couldn't answer his questions.

"Senator," Fortas replied, "all I can say is that I hope and trust that the American people will realize that I am acting out of a sense of constitutional duty and responsibility."

Thurmond replied, "Well, I am disappointed, even more disappointed in you, Mr. Justice Fortas."

"I am sorry to hear that, Senator."

Thurmond's antagonism to the Court's opinion in criminal cases extended to those decided before Fortas became a justice. Thurmond angrily resurrected *Mallory v. United States,* a 1957 case in which the Court overturned the conviction of a confessed rapist because his arraignment was delayed to permit police questioning.

Thurmond by now was shouting. "Do you believe in that kind of justice? Does not that decision, *Mallory*—I want that word to ring in your ears. Mallory! Mallory! A man who raped a woman, admitted his guilt and the Supreme Court turned him loose on a technicality free to commit other crimes."

Wasn't this decision, he continued to rant, "calculated to encourage more people to commit rapes and serious crimes? As a justice of the Supreme Court, can you condone this?"

This public scolding of a Supreme Court justice nominated by the president to be chief justice shocked even Fortas. Reporters saw him look toward Eastland as if expecting he might call Thurmond to order. Eastland appeared to be reading something and did not look up.

Fortas sat quietly for well over a minute. Then, in a measured voice, he replied, "Senator, because of my respect for you and this body and my respect for the Constitution of the United States and my position as Associate Justice of the Supreme Court of the United States, I will adhere to the limitations I believe the Constitution places upon me and will not reply to your question as you phrase it."

Thurmond pushed further, "Can you suggest any way that I can phrase it differently so you can answer it?"

"That would be presumptuous. I would not attempt to do so."

Thurmond got headlines, but Fortas sympathizers showed up the next day as he again faced Thurmond. When asked whether he agreed that the Court's decisions "make it terribly difficult to protect society from crime and criminals [and] are among the principal reasons for the turmoil and near-revolutionary conditions which prevail in our country," Fortas responded with a simple "No." His supporters applauded.[12]

Although Thurmond had forced Fortas to lose some composure with his first day's assault, biographer Nadine Cohodas years later found tucked away in his files a "blisteringly candid memo" from James Lucier, an aide who frequently wrote for the John Birch Society's *American Opinion* magazine and later joined the staff of Senator Jesse Helms. He viewed Thurmond's strategy in the Fortas hearing as "a disastrous mistake" because the line of questioning "did not appear to be a sincere attempt to investigate his views; rather, it appeared to be an irrational attempt to delay and harass." The better strategy, Lucier contended, would have been to show Fortas "a radical and a revolutionary dedicated to remaking society."[13]

Thurmond's *The Faith We Have Not Kept* was released during Fortas's appearance at the hearings, and he quipped that he might send a copy to Fortas. For Thurmond, the confirmation hearings amounted to a political battle aimed at control of the Supreme Court.

He found the ammunition he needed to sink Fortas's nomination a few days later, after Fortas had completed four days of testimony. James Clancy, who represented a group called Citizens for Decent Literature, claimed that Fortas had cast the deciding vote in forty-nine of fifty-two cases in which the material involved was judged not obscene. He charged that the rulings openly invited pornographers to distribute millions of copies "of what historically had been regarded in France as hard-core pornography."

Under prodding from Thurmond, Clancy contended that pornography bred violence, and he brought with him a pornographic film with the title "0-7," which Thurmond arranged for the committee and press to view. Thurmond thanked Clancy "for the contribution you have made to these hearings."

Clancy had been particularly upset because the Supreme Court had issued a one-sentence opinion that he said overruled findings by the lower court that the film, because of its obscenity, was not protected by the First Amendment. In fact, the issue of obscenity was not in the Supreme Court's opinion, which overruled the lower courts because police had lacked a valid search warrant when they confiscated the film.

Furthermore, Fortas had not regularly cast the "deciding vote," because most of the cases Clancy cited were unsigned. In his one signed dissent in obscenity cases, *Ginsberg v. United States,* Fortas had argued that the Constitution allowed states to enact laws protecting children from obscenity. He even proposed that children and juveniles were entitled to protection from panderers who exploited the prurient content of material that was not legally obscene. In another case, he helped devise a formula that made it easier to convict those who marketed obscene materials.

But Fortas, having agreed to testify but not to discuss the work of the Court, could not return and explain these details to the committee. Its members were left with the impression that Fortas was a defender of obscenity. The committee postponed its report on the nominee, allowing itself a week to consider the justice's approach to obscenity and to view "0-7." Congress then adjourned for the presidential nominating conventions before the report was issued.

When the hearings resumed in September, Thurmond got word from Senator Griffin that Fortas had taught a summer law school seminar at American University and that private contributors rather than university funds had paid his salary. Thurmond called the law school dean and suggested he avoid a subpoena by appearing voluntarily before the committee.

It turned out that Fortas had received $15,000 for conducting a nine-week seminar, funded by wealthy businessmen solicited by Paul Porter, Fortas's former law partner. The amount was more than one-third of his Supreme Court salary and far more than anyone else was paid for such teaching. Although Fortas did not know until the dean's testimony exactly who the donors were and the seminar itself received glowing evaluations, he had exercised bad judgment in allowing Porter to solicit funds without restriction. Thurmond maintained the contributors' wide business interests might well become involved in litigation before the court. Although Fortas had routinely disqualified himself from any cases involving former clients, these new facts raised questions.

Thurmond then called the Los Angeles policeman who had been the arresting officer in the "0-7" film case. He brought two pornographic films and 150 magazines for the committee to review. Thurmond, who issued a newsletter, "Fortas on Filth," showed committee members the films and magazines.

Attorney General Clark called Thurmond's action "outrageous." A *Washington Post* cartoon depicted Thurmond standing in a doorway holding a film and inviting a straitlaced man to come inside: "Psst—Want to see some dirty pictures?"

When the hearings ended, Senator Dirksen told White House staffers, "The movies are what the opposition needed to make their position jell." He added that Thurmond "tastes blood." He and Majority Leader Mike Mansfield agreed that the lecture fee was "hurtful" as a secondary issue.

The committee voted 11–6 to recommend Fortas on September 17. Griffin immediately launched a filibuster, which Thurmond and others joined. On October 2, one day after a cloture vote (a vote to cut off debate) failed by fourteen votes, Fortas asked that his name be withdrawn.

Thurmond called it "the wisest decision Justice Fortas has made since he has been on the Supreme Court." Thurmond then suggested he "go a step further and resign from the court for the sake of good government."[14]

Although Justice Fortas declined to take Strom's recommendation, he did resign in May 1969, after embarrassing press attention—fed by Attorney General John Mitchell—was paid to questionable financial arrangements.* After Earl Warren's retirement, which followed soon after, Richard

---

*Less than a month after going on the court, Fortas accepted an offer to consult for the Wolfson Family Foundation, set up by Louis Wolfson, a Jacksonville, Florida, financier whom Fortas had represented as a lawyer. Justice Fortas would be paid $20,000 a year for life, with such payments to continue to Mrs. Fortas if she should survive him. Fortas was aware that Justice Douglas was receiving $10,000 annually as president of the Parvin Foundation, whose head was a casino operator in Las Vegas. Because Wolfson was a former client and Fortas therefore would disqualify himself if any matter involving Wolfson came before the Court, Fortas had reasoned there would be no conflict. But such an

Nixon was able to make his first two appointments to the Supreme Court and begin to turn it away from the direction set by Warren. For Thurmond this would mean fulfilling—and exceeding—a dream, and leaving a lasting mark on American history.

(*continued*) arrangement, with Wolfson's foundation paying an amount equal to half of Fortas's salary as a justice, would have raised obvious ethical questions if made public. Fortas accepted an initial $20,000 payment in the summer of 1968. After Wolfson was indicted for financial irregularities, Fortas ended the relationship with the foundation and returned the $20,000 check in December. Therefore, no income taxes were due on the money, and in a technical legal sense, there was no fee paid. The issue escalated, after the election, with a *Life* magazine investigation. The Nixon administration's Department of Justice became involved, with Attorney General John Mitchell leaking information to the *Life* reporter and others, implying publicly that Fortas had continued to advise Wolfson on legal matters. Fortas had not, but Mitchell's leaks and innuendo resulted in a media feeding frenzy. Fortas resigned, although he had violated no laws. Mitchell would later go to prison for crimes related to the Watergate scandal that led to President Nixon's impeachment by the House and his resignation as president. Fortas's first cousin and confidant Harold Burson believed Fortas would never have resigned had he been chief justice (Bass interview with Burson, op. cit.).

Baby Strom,
produced in a union of two prominent
South Carolina families

Cadet Strom Thurmond
learned discipline and diction
at the all-male Clemson College,
circa 1921–22.

Circuit Judge J. Strom Thurmond
(circa 1940) traveled the countryside
and laid the political groundwork
for a governor's race.

Elected governor in 1946,
Thurmond gained national attention
for progressive views.

Jean Crouch after being named
by Gov. Thurmond as host
Miss South Carolina at
Azalea Festival in Charleston

In their twelve years together, Jean
softened Thurmond's rough edges.

Thurmond's political enemies seized upon a
controversial photo that ran in *LIFE* magazine.

The Thurmonds traveled across the South
in 1948 carrying the banner of the Dixiecrats.

Essie Mae Washington (third from left, top row) and sorority sisters
at South Carolina State College

Gov. Thurmond prepares for an overhead smash against
his executive assistant, William Lowndes Daniel, in the summer of 1947.
Daniel urged him to seize the Dixiecrat nomination.

Kingmaker Strom Thurmond escorts
Richard Nixon at 1968 Republican
national convention.

Strom thunders Dixie's message, 1948.

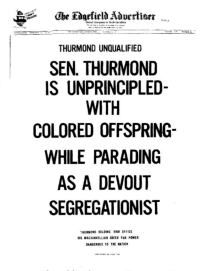

Edgefield Advertiser "exposes"
Strom Thurmond in fall of 1972.

With a long, controversial career and an outsized personality, Strom provided fodder for years of political cartoons. Strom began courting black voters after his candidate lost the 1970 race for governor of South Carolina.

It's just Ol' Strom, Honey.

Strom Jr., at twenty-nine, was in line to become United States Attorney in South Carolina as a result of his father's influence.

The ancient senator hadn't lost his touch.

Strom and
President Ronald Reagan
greet each other in
the White House.

Strom, with hand on daughter Julie's arm while meeting
President Bill Clinton. From left is Julie's husband,
Martin Whitmer, Jr., and Nancy Thurmond

A family portrait:
(Back row, l-r) Paul, Julie,
Nancy Moore, and Strom, Jr.
(front row) Strom and Nancy

Strom Thurmond's casket is carried out of the state capitol in Columbia for ceremonial transport to the funeral at First Baptist Church four blocks away.

Essie Mae Washington-
Williams and daughter
Wanda Terry visit the
Old Edgefield District
Genealogical Society
in May 2004.

CHAPTER 17

"Nixon's the One"

WHEN CONGRESS TOOK ITS BREAK in August 1968 for the national political conventions, Strom Thurmond headed for Miami Beach to hold the South for Richard Nixon. With Lyndon Johnson out, Robert Kennedy killed in May by an assassin, and violent street protests over the erupting war in Vietnam, a raucous Democratic convention in Chicago two weeks later would select Vice President Hubert Humphrey as its nominee.

Thurmond understood that reaction to the civil rights revolution was surpassing party loyalty as a political test in the South. He sensed that Nixon could be the vehicle for shifting the GOP to the right. He also believed that only Nixon could win the election for the Republicans, and a GOP victory would move the country and the Supreme Court to the right.

Thurmond's role as kingmaker in Miami Beach would symbolize that shift. In the fall he slugged it out with Governor George Wallace, whose third-party effort threatened to derail Nixon. Only Thurmond possessed the credibility among Southerners to tell them that a third-party protest was fruitless, that "a vote for Wallace is a vote for Humphrey."

"Strom killed us," said Tom Turnipseed, a key figure in the Wallace campaign.[1]

THE MOST MEANINGFUL EPISODE in Strom's 1966 senatorial campaign occurred by accident. Dent got Nixon, then practicing law in New York, to come to Columbia for a fund-raiser. Dent drove Nixon back to the Columbia Airport at 11 P.M. to meet a corporate jet and return to New York. The plane was an hour late, and the two men sat in Dent's car, talking politics. Nixon expressed reluctance about running for president in 1968 because of a probable challenge from George Wallace, who Nixon believed would siphon white voters away from him on race issues.

Dent remembered the essence of the conversation going something like this:

"George Wallace is going to run, and he's going to mess me up."

"There's an answer to that."

"What?"

"Strom Thurmond."

"Strom Thurmond? How? What are you talking about?"

"Well, he was the States Rights candidate for president back in 1948, and he's known across the South. He's got a bigger image across the South than George Wallace has."

Dent then explained that Thurmond would take Wallace head-on for Nixon and "stiff him."

"You think Strom Thurmond would do that for me?"

"Yeah, I think he'd do that."

In Columbia, Nixon had won points with Thurmond by telling a national interviewer, "Strom is no racist. Strom is a man of courage and integrity."[2] Less than two years earlier—the same month he endorsed Goldwater—Thurmond was named the "least effective" member of Congress in two surveys, one by *Pageant* magazine conducted among members of Congress and the other a poll of Washington journalists. Historian Dan Carter, in his biography of Wallace, would call Thurmond's response to Nixon's words "almost pathetically grateful."[3]

Nixon was seeking his own political resurrection. After serving two terms as Dwight Eisenhower's vice president, he narrowly lost the presidency to John F. Kennedy in 1960. Two years later, he ran for governor of California and lost. The lingering image from that campaign was the exhausted and bitter Nixon stalking into the press room after his defeat, lashing out at reporters, blaming them for his defeat and asserting as his most memorable line, "Well, you won't have Nixon to kick around anymore, because, gentlemen, this is my last press conference."[4]

It was, of course, not Nixon's last press conference. During the Goldwater campaign, Nixon made 150 speeches for the candidate, whose support he would have in 1968. Six months after sitting with Dent in his car at Columbia Airport, Nixon sent an emissary to check in with him. Dent had spoken to Thurmond and reaffirmed that the senator would support Nixon. In the spring of 1968, Governors Ronald Reagan of California and Nelson Rockefeller of New York met with Southern Republican Party leaders in New Orleans. Rockefeller was too liberal and obtained virtually no support, but he did establish relationships by hosting a steak and grits breakfast. Although Reagan did not commit himself to running, his personality and conservatism made the Southerners' hearts throb.

In May, Nixon met with those party leaders in Atlanta, and Dent made sure Thurmond attended. Nixon responded to questions about court appointments (he promised to appoint "strict constructionists"), busing school children for purposes of integration, protecting the textile industry, law and order issues, Communism, national defense, and building the party in the South. Thurmond liked Nixon's answers. He rode in the car with Nixon to the airport and followed up the visit with a public commitment.

As Nixon feared, George Wallace had become the national lightning rod for what became known as "the social issue." Wallace was launching a third-party campaign that would tap into a working-class white electorate, angry and frightened by civil rights and anti-war protesters. He developed new phrases that his listeners would understand as code for racial issues, including "welfare chiselers" and "law and order." Wallace more than matched Thurmond's capacity for the symbolic gesture and was a better speaker. Articulate and quick on his feet, Wallace had first gone national in the winter of 1963, on a tour of major national college campuses that began at Harvard. He avoided overtly racist rhetoric, parried hecklers with a quick wit, displayed some hillbilly humor, and made constitutional arguments about states' rights. Students who had expected a raging demagogue found him engaging.

Wallace had demonstrated a powerful appeal before dropping out of the 1964 presidential campaign when Goldwater sewed up the Republican nomination. In Madison, Wisconsin, an audience had serenaded him with a Polish-accented "Dixie." Opposed by the political, religious, and AFL-CIO leadership of this far northern state and running with almost no money, he stunned the establishment by getting one-third of the vote in the Democratic presidential primary.

Blue-collar workers responded to his message—the same attacks used by Thurmond, but better articulated and with a more populist message that addressed their economic concerns. Wallace attacked the "godless" Supreme Court. He denounced the Civil Rights Bill as a threat to union seniority that "would impose racial quotas," create chaos in the schools, and "make it impossible for a home owner to sell his home to whomever he chose." Wallace didn't camouflage his message with "states' rights" but orchestrated the politics of fear like a maestro.

He followed his performance in Wisconsin with 30 percent of the primary vote in Indiana and forty-seven percent in Maryland. But Goldwater's vote against the Civil Rights Bill ended the 1964 boomlet for Wallace, who made a furtive, unsuccessful effort to get Goldwater to choose him as a running mate.[5]

MORE THAN ANY EXPERIENCE in Thurmond's political past, the 1968 Republican Convention provided an analogy to his glider ride into Normandy. He went to Miami Beach fully committed, and survival depended on making quick and instinctive tactical decisions.

When Nixon arrived by plane late Monday afternoon, Thurmond was there to greet him and ready to warn him of serious problems. The *New York Times* had run a story that morning speculating that if nominated, Nixon would choose as his running mate one of three men—New York's Rockefeller, New York City Mayor John Lindsay, or Illinois Senator Charles Percy. All represented the party's liberal wing.

Buzhardt, who had left Thurmond's staff to return to McCormick and take over his father's law practice, joined Thurmond and Dent in Miami Beach. Throughout the day, Buzhardt and Dent experienced the developing confusion and panic among Nixon's Southern delegates.* The *New York Times* story "went through like wildfire," Buzhardt said. "Boy, all day Monday it was just pandemonium." Dent added that the slogan of Reagan supporters was: "The double cross is on, the double cross is on."

Delegates from all over the South, and some from outside the region, sought leadership from Thurmond. "Up until Monday night, he said, 'I'm

---

*Jack Bass, then the Columbia, South Carolina, bureau chief for the *Charlotte Observer*, and Remer Tyson, political editor for the *Atlanta Constitution*, covered the 1968 Republican convention, Bass as part of the Knight Newspapers team and Tyson for the Atlanta newspapers. The morning after Nixon's nomination, they taped a ninety-minute interview with Dent and Buzhardt, which was interrupted by Nixon's announcement that Maryland governor Spiro Agnew would be his running mate. Publisher Ralph McGill considered the transcript of that interview an important historical document and directed that it be printed in full in the Sunday, August 11, issue of the *Atlanta Journal and Constitution*. It ran more than a page and a half. The account here of Thurmond's role at the convention is heavily drawn from that transcript and from personal observations by Bass at the convention.

standing firm,'" Buzhardt observed. But by late afternoon, when Thurmond left for the airport, Buzhardt continued, "It had gotten to the place where, really, just the senator's 'standing-firm-with-Nixon' wasn't enough."

Meanwhile, California Governor Reagan dropped his coyness and formally announced his candidacy for the nomination. Reagan and his forces had been active during the summer, courting Southern state delegations and siphoning off support. James Gardner, the ultraconservative and ambitious chairman of the North Carolina delegation, began spreading the word that he was for Reagan. He informed Dent of this support at the convention hall as they both entered for the Monday night program.

Working through Brad Hayes, a Nixon campaign staffer and former Aiken County Republican chairman, the Thurmond aides had just gotten confirmation for him to meet with Nixon at 2:30 P.M. on Tuesday. This schedule meant they would meet before Reagan's scheduled appearance at 3:15 before the South Carolina delegation.

On the convention floor, Dent could feel the slippage. Columnist Rowland Evans told him that Ohio Governor James Rhodes said after Reagan's announcement, "It's a new ball game." An insider told Dent that Rhodes planned to throw Ohio's support to Reagan, with Rhodes to become his running mate.

The Nixon convention staff had designated someone to serve as a listening post in each state delegation. About 9:30 P.M. on the convention floor, Dent got a call from John Mitchell, who later became Nixon's campaign manager. Mitchell said that Nixon could meet with Thurmond on Tuesday—or that Monday evening.

Dent interpreted the call as an indication of concern and a desire to meet immediately. Dent, Buzhardt, and Thurmond piled into a cab. Of the ride to the oceanside Plaza Hilton Hotel, Dent would say, "I know Fred was shook, and I was shook. Senator Thurmond doesn't get shook."

Buzhardt said, "There were people coming in to the senator [all day] and saying, 'Strom, you're laying your damn political life on the line. Get your pound of flesh.' We were told this bluntly. . . . These people just don't know the senator. That wasn't his nature." Dent added, "Strom Thurmond wasn't coming there with his hand out. He wasn't going to ask for anything."

When it came to high-stakes politics, Thurmond's strategies incorporated pragmatism and principle. He knew that loyalty to Nixon, a point of honor for Strom, meant there would be no backing down in a fight—this one for the resurrection of Richard Nixon's political life. Thurmond did not ask for anything specific because success would reward him with access to and influence inside the White House—a golden pot of political power that could change the direction of the country.

A little after 10 P.M., Mitchell greeted Dent, Buzhardt, and Thurmond in the lobby, then took them by elevator to the fifteenth floor. From there, they walked up three flights of stairs to Nixon's remote suite. Nixon and Thurmond greeted each other as if it were a casual social visit. Thurmond got his own cup of coffee and took a seat with Nixon on a sofa. The others sat in chairs, joined by Nixon aide H. R. Haldeman. The next minutes were crucial.

Nixon and Thurmond were both seasoned political masters. Both were cool. Each knew without saying, and knew that the other knew, that if Strom Thurmond delivered the South for Nixon, allowing him to win the nomination, Nixon would owe a huge political debt. And if Nixon didn't get elected, the debt would be void.

The important thing, to Dent and Buzhardt, was that Nixon appreciate the level and the risk of Thurmond's commitment and reassure him that the South was important to the campaign. Buzhardt "was personally afraid that Dick Nixon would not understand how far out on a limb Strom Thurmond had gotten without any assurance from him."

Even aside from all the commotion of earlier that day, they had heard reports that Nixon's basic strategy would be to court the urban vote and ignore the South. Dent wanted the senator to "look in Nixon's eyes . . . Strom Thurmond needed to be sure in his own mind that Richard Nixon had not written off the South." Buzhardt added that Thurmond "was saying [to delegates], 'I'm standing with him.' But he didn't want to mislead the people who were coming to him and asking him pointed questions."

The Thurmond strategy was to hold the South as solidly as possible for Nixon, allowing him to lock up the nomination early on the first ballot and not be pressured to make deals on selecting a running mate near the end of the balloting. "We knew the vote count," Buzhardt said. "We knew that if we could hold steady this could be done, and there wouldn't have to be any bargaining." The 356 Southern delegates amounted to more than half the number required for nomination. The South Carolina delegation had committed itself to unanimously nominating Thurmond, who would then step aside and cast the state's twenty-two votes for Nixon. But to mollify a couple of Reagan holdouts, they agreed to switch solidly to Reagan if there was a second ballot.[6] (Nixon would ultimately get 264 of the Southern votes, almost three of every four.)

Dent and Buzhardt briefed Nixon on the extent of slippage and told him about Jim Gardner's move to Reagan, which was news to Nixon. Nixon gave some orders regarding the information, and Dent was impressed that he listened to advice. In Dent's estimation, Nixon understood that his role—in this suite of rooms as on the campaign trail—was that of a candidate with conviction, and he played it well. Although he discussed general principles, Dent said, "He was trying to tell us, 'I do plan to run in the South. I do plan to run strongly in the South.'"

"If Mr. Nixon had not satisfied the senator, if he had said, 'Let's face it. George Wallace has got the South, Strom, and I'm going to have to concentrate strictly on running up north in the big cities, or something else. Now you go on and help me hold the line and that'll be fine,' Strom Thurmond would have gone on and would have helped him because he was committed."

When the subject of a vice presidential candidate came up, Nixon made it clear he would pick his own running mate, telling his guests, "I'm not going to ram a man down the throat of any section of the country." That, Dent said, was "all Senator Thurmond wanted or needed to hear."

As the discussion with Nixon continued, Dent explained, "We said, 'Look, we can't carry your message for you. Senator Thurmond, just one man, can't deliver it. Why don't you tell these people directly?' He said, 'I'll be glad to. I'll answer any question that anybody asks.'" Nixon met twice the next morning with Southern state delegations, six states at a time.

There, Dent emphasized Thurmond's total commitment to Nixon and added that three surveys taken in South Carolina showed him the strongest among all voters of any Republican candidate. Bo Calloway of Georgia introduced Thurmond, who told the assembled delegates, "We have no choice, if we want to win, except to vote for Nixon. We must quit using our hearts and start using our heads." He continued, "I love Reagan, but Nixon's the one."[7]

When Nixon spoke, he began by saying he supported civil rights. As Dent put it, "He said, 'Let me make it straight at the outset, that I am for civil rights and I have supported it and believe in it.'" But Nixon also alluded to the riots that had occurred in northern cities. He said that most of the problems were caused by "extremists of both races" and that a Nixon administration wouldn't act "to satisfy some professional civil-rights group, or something like that."[8] He repeated his position on selecting judges, and he made it clear he would wait until after the nomination to pick a running mate, one who would be acceptable to all parts of the country.

With Thurmond "fully satisfied," the message white Southerners received was clear. Nixon would be "evenhanded" on civil rights, meaning measured enforcement, no new legislative initiatives, and opposition to creative judicial remedies for overcoming discrimination and ending segregation.

Buzhardt said that Brad Hayes continued to be concerned that Reagan might get wholesale switches among the Southern delegates. "He had seen these people's heart beat for Reagan," Buzhardt said. "Reagan gives this really heartfelt, sincere pitch that only he can do. He's a master at it. He comes through personality-wise. He comes through with his philosophical pitch. Real simple, direct answers.

"Goldwater never had what Reagan's got. Goldwater was never able to reduce his positions to a flat inspirational message. . . . Reagan has all these answers down and if you listen to him three or four times they're the same ones every time—pop-pop-pop—and they're word for word. . . . They're worked out where they sound really off the cuff, but they aren't.

"Nixon doesn't give this. If anything, he came across as more sincere."

Later that Tuesday, before meeting with the South Carolina delegation, Reagan met privately with Thurmond in the senator's hotel room. Reagan asked Dent to leave, believing that one-on-one he could persuade Thurmond to support him. Asked a few minutes after the meeting what he told the California governor, Thurmond said, "I told him I would support him next time."* Dent said that Thurmond was unimpressed with Reagan,

---

*The "next time" would come in 1976, after Nixon's resignation and with Gerald Ford in the White House. At the 1976 convention in Kansas City, which Jack Bass attended, Thurmond remained in the background, saying little. Many believed that he wanted to support Ford, the sitting president. Reagan had offended many of the most conservative Southern delegates by announcing moderate Republican senator Richard Schweicker of Pennsylvania would be his running mate to balance the ticket. And Harry Dent was running Ford's Southern operation. In the close contest between Ford and Reagan, which Ford won, Thurmond quietly cast his ballot for Reagan.

finding him shallow, and told Reagan of his commitment to Nixon. "That's something Reagan never understood even though he was told," Dent added.

When slippage for Nixon was reported in the Florida delegation, Thurmond rushed to meet with them at the Doral Country Club, holding a majority for Nixon in a delegation that voted by unit rules, where a majority would determine the full vote of the entire delegation. Elsewhere, he worked to shore up weak spots and to recruit uncommitted delegates.

Thurmond was not alone in holding the South for Nixon. He visited the Mississippi delegation, and so did Barry Goldwater, also a Nixon supporter. Mississippi Republican Chairman Clarke Reed said that Goldwater (who won 87 percent of the Mississippi vote in 1964) meant more than Thurmond in holding that state's delegates for Nixon over Reagan.[9]

The final crisis came Wednesday night, when delegates streaming into the Miami Beach Convention Center saw newsboys hawking a "bulldog" edition of the next morning's *Miami Herald* with a banner headline that Oregon Senator Mark Hatfield would be the vice presidential nominee: "Hatfield Veep Pick."

The story sparked another round of pandemonium among the Southern delegations. If true, it meant to them that Nixon had lied about waiting to make a decision on his choice for vice president. Dent raced from delegation to delegation, insisting the story was false. At one point he spotted Don Oberdorfer, who had written the *Herald* story, as the reporter was walking in front of the Louisiana and Georgia delegations. Dent cornered him and offered a $300 bet that his story was wrong. In the noise of the convention hall, all Oberdorfer knew was that Dent was jumping up and down and saying something about a $300 bet that he couldn't understand. "I thought it was a joke," Oberdorfer said. "I wouldn't bet $300 on anything." Playing on their suspicion of Yankee journalists, Dent yelled through a megaphone to the delegates that Oberdorfer wouldn't bet on Hatfield. Nixon's floor leader at the convention, Maryland Congressman Rogers Morton, stayed busy that evening scurrying with Thurmond from one Southern delegation to another.[10]

John Knight, chief executive officer of Knight Newspapers, which owned the *Miami Herald*, had ordered the Hatfield story. Apparently motivated by vanity, Knight wanted his hometown newspaper to have this scoop. The assignment went to Oberdorfer, an experienced political reporter then in the Knight Newspapers Washington bureau. His source was Gerald Ford, then House minority leader.[11]

Although Hatfield would appeal to the moderate wing of the party, he was a Southern Baptist, and his main sponsor was the Reverend Billy Graham, who joined Thurmond and sixteen other influential politicians to discuss the vice presidential pick with Nixon immediately after the nomination.[12] When Thurmond left the room, he handed Nixon a small piece of paper with columns of names. He named five "acceptables," including Reagan and Congressman George Bush of Texas; two "no objections," one of them Maryland Governor Spiro Agnew; and "unacceptables," who included Hatfield. Thurmond had deposited his veto.

Hatfield might have been selected if John Knight had simply allowed his newspaper to cover the story as it unfolded. It was the drama created by the bogus early leak that made him unacceptable to Thurmond and the South. That would have meant an elevation of Hatfield to president after Nixon's resignation. Instead, Agnew got the nomination, only to resign the vice presidency in disgrace after revelations that he had accepted bribes earlier in his career. The ultimate irony is that Nixon then selected as Agnew's successor Gerald Ford, who had innocently mentioned Hatfield's name to a friendly reporter. And Ford became president.

When Dent went through a receiving line at the end of the convention, Nixon said he wanted him to come to Mission Bay, California, and work for him on the campaign. Dent had always felt Haldeman and fellow Californian John Ehrlichman were suspicious of him. They next tried to block him from seeing Nixon. Dent called Mitchell, who got him in. Nixon agreed that Dent should run a separate operation in the South, "Thurmond Speaks for Nixon-Agnew." Dent flew weekly to New York, reporting to and coordinating with Mitchell each Friday night. Dent said, "Everything worked perfectly."[13]

Thurmond took the message that had worked for him in Miami Beach—that a vote for Reagan was a vote for Rockefeller (because many of Nixon's supporters outside the South would find Reagan too conservative)—and switched the wording for the general election to say that a vote for Wallace was a vote for Humphrey because Wallace couldn't win. In late September, "Thurmond Speaks" saturated the South with television and radio commercials—with the radio aimed at country music stations—in which Thurmond delivered exactly that message. As the former Dixiecrat candidate arguing that the third-party strategy didn't work, he was credible. Tom Turnipseed remembered Thurmond's spots as "very effective" and that Wallace's poll numbers began falling almost immediately. Textile magnate Roger Milliken of Spartanburg, widely believed to be the wealthiest person in South Carolina, led the fund-raising operation that paid for most of the radio and TV spots. "Roger could sit around a table with the other big boys," Dent said, "and tell each one what he needed from them." (The Nixon administration would respond to Milliken's effort with textile import legislation.)

Initially, Wallace had led in the border states of North Carolina, Tennessee, and Florida, as well as South Carolina—states that Nixon ultimately won, with a collective forty-five electoral votes that exceeded his margin of victory. Nixon squeaked by Wallace in North Carolina and Tennessee, where Thurmond's role clearly made the difference, and won more decisively in Florida.

Nixon also had help in the South from a hard-right message delivered by Agnew. Nixon himself attacked busing and endorsed "freedom of choice" desegregation plans. The Supreme Court, in *Green v. New Kent County*, earlier that year had ruled out such plans unless they actually resulted in desegregation. They never did. Under "freedom of choice," no whites chose to attend black schools, and few blacks were willing to face the isolation, intimidation, and hostility that could be expected at previously all-white schools. (Don Fowler got tapes of the Thurmond ads promising freedom of choice in the schools if Nixon were elected and would play them back two years later, with a voice-over that said, "Broken promises.")

Thurmond carried South Carolina with a decisive plurality for Nixon, making it the only state in the South to vote Republican in both the 1964 and 1968 presidential elections. Angry Wallace voters retaliated against Thurmond's opposition to their man by voting for Democrats in local elections. The GOP lost two-thirds of its twenty-five seats in the legislature, including all four State Senate seats in Charleston. Although Wallace won the other Goldwater states from 1964, in addition to Arkansas, Humphrey carried only Lyndon Johnson's home state of Texas, and the other Southern states all moved into Nixon's column.

DENT BECAME A TOP WHITE HOUSE POLITICAL AIDE and got President Nixon to appoint South Carolina textile executive Fred Dent—a distant relative—as secretary of commerce. Buzhardt became general counsel to the Department of Defense. "We put in at least twenty-five South Carolina people in good jobs in the Nixon administration," Dent said. "Nixon believed in the Southern strategy," which to Dent went far beyond issues of race and included full political participation. Thurmond was set to return to Washington as an effective insider, though with some political damage at home.

At a meeting Dent attended with Nixon and Mitchell just after the election, Thurmond told them of his plans to marry Nancy Moore, a twenty-two-year-old former Miss South Carolina. Both Mitchell and Nixon seemed to smirk, Dent observed. He felt Thurmond was making a huge mistake.

CHAPTER 18

"Amazement and Wonder"

W HEN GEORGIA SENATOR Herman Talmadge's son, Bobby, came to Washington in 1968 to spend the summer with his father, he expressed interest in meeting young women. An alert staffer told him to contact a friend of hers in Strom Thurmond's office. "She can introduce you to Miss South Carolina," she told young Talmadge. "She's working there as an intern." Senator Talmadge reminisced, "He came back and said [referring to Thurmond], 'The competition was too stiff.'"[1]

Nancy Moore, born November 1, 1946, was seventeen when she saw Strom in August 1964 at the Grape Festival in York, South Carolina, where he took her square dancing. A Charlotte TV reporter who saw them there recalled that Strom looked "smitten." The next year, after Nancy, nicknamed "Moose," sang and played the piano to win the Miss Aiken and Miss South Carolina titles, he called to congratulate her. They had stayed in touch, but Strom claimed he knew almost nothing about her. "It was just a name," he said. "I called her up and said congratulations."

As *The State* reported, "The new Miss South Carolina," a brownish-blonde with blue eyes and a fair complexion, "is 5'6", weighs 116 pounds and is 35-22-35 for those who keep score." She already had a string of beauty titles. Her mother said, "Even in the first grade she had that curious look of amazement and wonder she has today."[2]

When she and the South Carolina pageant sponsors met in Columbia on the first Saturday in August to drive to Atlantic City, New Jersey, for the Miss America pageant, Strom showed up, and news photographer Bill Barley took a photo of them all. Thurmond had apparently invited Nancy to visit his office in Washington after leaving Atlantic City and to provide a full tour of the nation's capital. Afterward, Thurmond invited Barley to join him for lunch, and then asked if he could drive him around Columbia.

Thurmond rented a car, pulled out a notepad from a pocket and began checking off names. For hours they drove around the city, stopping at residences where Thurmond, the nonstop campaigner, visited supporters. If no one was at home, he left a card with a note.

On Nancy's return trip from Atlantic City, she stopped in Washington, received a full day of activity, and on August 13 sent Thurmond a gushing note of appreciation. She addressed him as "Dear Senator" and thanked him for his "time and hospitality" during "the fabulous 24 hours I spent in Washington." She concluded, "Some day I'll repay you for your kindness."

She also displayed political awareness, reflecting a concern of many white Southerners in the immediate aftermath of the landmark Voting Rights Act of 1965. In response to South Carolina's first 20th century major voter registration drive among African Americans, she wrote, "It is fine for the Negroes to be encouraged to vote, but I do not feel they know what they are voting for or against. . . . There should be a drive for more participation in state and national elections by the white population. This could be vital in the November 1966 [Strom would be on the ballot then] election."[3]

She worked for a month in Thurmond's office as an intern in 1967, an interval between transferring from Duke University to the University of South Carolina. She returned for the full summer of 1968 after graduating with honors and before entering the U.S.C. Law School that fall.

Lee Bandy, The State's Washington correspondent, remembered Nancy delivering press releases to him many times late in the evening in the Senate press gallery. He said, "She would sit down, chitchat, and flirt. . . . All I knew was that she worked for him as an intern. We were all kind of shocked and surprised when they put out a press release announcing their engagement."[4] Strom hadn't met her parents. Her father had moved to Aiken about twelve years earlier to work for the Savannah River Plant.

When Harry Dent and Fred Buzhardt returned to South Carolina from the 1968 Republican convention, they heard rumors about Strom courting the young beauty queen. "People were aghast at the idea," Dent said. "They were saying, 'Can't you stop this? The old man is making a fool out of himself.'" In a "sons-to-father talk," they talked him into staying away from her during the campaign, hoping the relationship would go away.

When Thurmond disclosed his marriage plans after the election, Dent told him it would "ruin you politically, destroy everything you've worked for in your political life. If you do this, just don't plan to run again in 1972. You might as well resign now, like King Edward [VIII, who abdicated the throne in England to marry "the woman I love," an American divorcée, and became the Duke of Windsor] and get public sympathy to offset all the public wrath that'll follow."

The story of what happened next became a much-loved joke among Thurmond intimates, with Dent perfectly comfortable in his role as the butt of it. Dent and Buzhardt met again with Thurmond, stressing the severity of their concerns, and he told them to take their case to Nancy. "If you can talk her out of it, it'll be all right with me," he said. "Go ahead."

Dent and Buzhardt met with Nancy four times over the next two weeks, lengthy sessions in which Dent "went so far as to tell her that if she married him and they had children, those children would be messed up. I almost abused her."

Finally, she broke down and cried, telling them, "I love him. I love him. I love him." Years later, Strom said his two aides' approaching Nancy didn't worry him. "If they could convince her it was the wrong thing to do and she felt it was," he said, "I didn't want her to do it."[5] Dent came away convinced that her love was genuine but said, "I kept telling the Senator, 'Here you are at the apex of your career and you're making a fool out of yourself. You're going all the way back to what you did at the Governor's Mansion by standing on your head.'"[6]

Thurmond was unperturbed. He proceeded to marry Nancy in Aiken a few days before Christmas, joined by a handful of family and close friends. After a one-week honeymoon on Grand Bahama Island, they held a public reception at the campus home of University of South Carolina president Thomas F. Jones. Cake, nuts, and cider punch were served.

Some 1,500 people from all over South Carolina—friends, relatives, acquaintances, and strangers—dressed in their finest outfits and stood in line to shake the senator's hand and meet his new wife on a bright, chilly afternoon in late December. No black people were seen among them. Those attending included Harry Dent.[7]

"The interesting thing about Strom Thurmond," Dent said, "is I don't ever remember in any way the Senator ever rebuking me or Fred. We would always tell him exactly what we thought and it was OK. The marriage turned out to be a big plus. Especially having those kids. And the children turned out great."[8]

Looking back more than a decade after their marriage, Strom said, "Normally, for a man to marry a woman that much younger wouldn't help his career. But I'd been with Nancy enough to know she had her feet on the ground, she was smart, and I just felt she'd make a good wife and mother. So if she felt she was willing to take the chance, well, I was. We both loved each other."[9]

Nancy, gracious and charming, always impeccably dressed, with perfect posture and her long hair in a French twist, quickly became a Washington attraction. She had begun to learn to cook when she was five, and as a new bride in Washington ran a good kitchen. Her favorite meal as a hostess was a roast beef dinner. She enjoyed exercise almost as much as Strom did. They swam together and played tennis. "He wins repeatedly," she told Jack Bass in her first interview as Mrs. Thurmond. They rode horses together. "He's an expert horseman. I love it, but I'm not very good."[10]

The new bride learned early that Thurmond often worked late or brought work home with him.

OVER TIME, RUMORS FLOATED that Strom might retire, with Nancy running for his seat. In response to a direct question from Dent on whether there was any substance to these rumors, Thurmond replied, "I have no plans." (But in 1981 he would tell a *Washington Post* reporter that Nancy would "make an ideal public servant—senator, governor, whatever.")[11]

A top aide said that Nancy "got anything she thought was important, even for him to hire a certain person in the office, to assign a certain person to some responsibility, how to approach certain speeches."[12] Although Nancy influenced Strom, she seldom got involved in major policy issues. "She wasn't Jean Thurmond in any respect," Dent said.

She also never had Jean's staff rapport, nor did the staffers have the same kind of confidence in her judgment. In the early 1980s, Thurmond made a Law Day address at the University of South Carolina Law School, perhaps the school's most important annual event. The prepared text addressed lofty issues, but Nancy edited it and inserted a number of jokes that left the senator's staffers shaking their heads. For example, Thurmond talked about getting up in the middle of the night to do something, then quipped, "but at my age I get up lots of times in the middle of the night." The audience laughed, either with the senator or, his staffers feared, at him.

Although usually in the background, Nancy on occasion played a leading role and demonstrated "presence," that capacity to get people's attention just by entering a room.

Before James Clyburn was elected in 1992 as South Carolina's first black congressman since the post-Reconstruction period, he served for years as executive director of the South Carolina Human Affairs Commission and hosted an annual bipartisan political "roast" that served as a charitable fund-raiser. When Don Fowler got roasted in the mid-1980s, Clyburn invited Nancy Thurmond to serve as "roastmistress." She accepted, prepared carefully, and presided with just the right bite of humor for political insiders.

Clyburn set the tone for the evening when he introduced the head table. Strom sat next to Emily Clyburn, and Jim Clyburn concluded his introduction of Thurmond with a slight pause, then added, "Now Senator, that's my wife sitting next to you, so you keep your hands on top of the table." Thurmond joined in the howling laughter of a knowing, biracial audience.

PERHAPS NO POLITICIAN ANYWHERE could match Strom's reputation for lechery. Washington writer Sally Quinn told of a 1950s reception where: "My mother and I headed for the buffet table. As we were reaching for the shrimp, both of us jumped and let out a shriek. Senator Strom Thurmond, grinning from ear to ear, had one hand on my behind and the other on my mother's. As I recall, we were both quite flattered, and thought it terribly funny and wicked of Ol' Strom." Quinn said her mother had grown up in Savannah, knew Thurmond, and had responded, "Strom, you old devil."[13]

Throughout his career, Strom's notoriety for sexual exploits only grew. Just when and where he said it is disputed—some say at the funeral of Florida Congressman Claude Pepper, who championed the cause of senior citizens, and others after Thurmond began siring children with Nancy— but it has long been agreed that Senator John Tower of Texas once made the earthy remark, "When he dies, they'll have to beat his pecker down with a baseball bat in order to close the coffin lid."

Word got back to Thurmond, who sent an aide out to buy a Sears Thumper baseball bat and deliver it to Tower. Tower placed it on permanent display atop the mantel in the Senate Republican cloakroom.[14] Robert Airail, the talented cartoonist for *The State*, began regularly to sneak a baseball bat into cartoons about Thurmond.

At least one professional woman from South Carolina, seeing Thurmond on a business matter, suddenly found herself grabbed, groped on the breast, and the recipient of a prolonged kiss on the mouth. Women news reporters have shared the experience.

One incident involved a female SLED agent, assigned as a driver for Thurmond in the 1980s. Unlike Hollings, who relied on staff to drive him on official trips in South Carolina, Thurmond for decades called upon SLED.

Allegedly Thurmond called one female SLED driver after both had retired to their motel rooms on an overnight trip. He then asked her to come to his room. When she knocked, he told her to come in, whereupon she opened the door and asked what he wanted; he was sitting on the bed in his underwear, patting the bed and inviting her to come and sit beside him. She closed the door and returned to her room. After her report to her supervisors, SLED stopped assigning female agents as drivers. At least one South Carolina reporter pursued the story, but women agents refused to talk for publication.[15]

At a 1988 Columbia Chamber of Commerce function honoring sixty-year-old Congressman Floyd Spence, Thurmond noted how vigorous and active Spence had become since a double-lung transplant. Thurmond, then eighty-five, quipped he was going to try to find some "different parts" himself to keep going for another twenty years. The audience howled. An editorial in *The State* impishly asked, "Can it be that some parts of the seemingly indestructible Thurmond self-destructed?"[16]

Around this time, the Thurmonds car-pooled activities of their teenage children with their neighbors in Washington's northern Virginia suburbs, fellow Senator Charles "Chuck" Robb and his wife, Lynda, eldest daughter of former President Lyndon Johnson. Strom, by then an octogenarian, drove the van one day when Lynda's mother, Lady Bird Johnson, was visiting.

Lynda remarked to him what attractive children he had. Strom leaned over, placed his hand on her shoulder, and said in her ear, "They could have been yours."

As she and Lady Bird exchanged amused glances, Lynda remembered her visit to the Capitol a quarter century earlier, while still in high school, a year or so after Jean's death. She had run into Thurmond, then almost sixty. He invited Lynda to go bike riding with him that weekend.

She asked permission from her father, the Senate majority leader about to be sworn in as vice president. For the only time in her dating years, Johnson said no.[17]

Maureen Dowd noted in a 1994 *New York Times Magazine* article about Strom that although surrounded by colleagues "edgy about gender politics, Thurmond remains blissfully untouched" by such concerns. Back in South Carolina, two female columnists for *The State* retorted, "The day he does, Dowd, the folks at home will know we've got an impostor on our hands."

The senator once greeted abortion-rights leaders as "lovely ladies." He told one group of witnesses at a hearing: "These are the prettiest witnesses we have had in a long time. I imagine you are all married. If not, you could be if you wanted to be."[18]

It finally seemed to register with him that his behavior might be objectionable, at least in Washington, when a story got out three years after newly elected Senator Patti Murray of Washington state told California Senator Barbara Boxer in 1993 that Thurmond had tried to fondle her on a Capitol elevator. Thurmond denied the charge and, publicly, Murray's press secretary said she "knows what sexual harassment is and that was not sexual harassment."

Thurmond said he was showing Senator Murray "the same . . . gentlemanly courtesies" he had always made toward women. "That includes assisting them through doors, into vehicles and yes—onto elevators."

Boxer said Murray told her that Thurmond put his arm around her, tried to grope her breast, and said, "Are you married, little lady?"[19]

During his 1996 reelection campaign, however, Thurmond actively fed the image of his virility. In a story playfully headlined, "He Is Slipping— It Was Just Her Arm," *The State* reported him grabbing WOLO TV reporter Susan Biggers by the arm—in the middle of an interview—and telling her, "You're a good-looking girl."

On the Clemson campus the same day, Thurmond spotted a covey of coeds and asked: "Any of you girls want a hug?" When three complied, the senator looked around and added, "We'll settle for a handshake for you boys."[20]

Strom considered Nancy not only "wholesome, clean, intelligent, and attractive" but an "excellent writer."[21] She wrote two books, *Mother's Medicine*, a parents' guide, and *Happy Mother, Happy Child*. In 1988, she hosted a South Carolina Educational Television series, *Parent's Point of View.*

Early in 1989, she sought a top job in the Department of Commerce, a $125,000 plum as undersecretary for trade and tourism. It involved travel to many of the world's garden spots. Lee Bandy reported that Secretary of Commerce Robert Mosbacher told a committee staffer, "I don't think she's qualified" but that he was getting "all kinds of pressure from friends of Strom Thurmond." More than twenty senators sent letters of support.

Thurmond had endorsed Senator Robert Dole over Vice President George Bush in 1988, and Bandy initially reported that presidential aides opposed Nancy getting the job for that reason. Strom's top aides believed Nancy influenced him to back Dole because of her friendship with Mrs. Dole, that Nancy would coax ("I hate to say nagging") Strom to get her way.[22]

Former Thurmond protégé Lee Atwater, who had managed Bush's campaign, arranged for Nancy to get hired for the Commerce Department job in a consultant's capacity. But she withdrew as a candidate for permanent appointment in mid-April, after a month and a half of controversy, citing her husband's reelection plans and her learning of the potential conflict with the Hatch Act, which prohibits federal employees from political activity.[23] At that time, Thurmond had no serious opposition, meaning that it might not have been necessary for her to campaign, and a top staff person believed she withdrew because she was in over her head and knew it— and knew that those around her believed she lacked the administrative skills the job required.[24]

Furthermore, although problems in the marriage would not be publicly acknowledged until much later, Nancy had become the subject of Washington rumors. Her behavior seemed erratic.

As relations between Nancy and Strom grew more strained, it became apparent to top staffers there was no longer a real marriage between the two, and in 1991, Nancy announced she was returning to Aiken with her younger children. Their daughter, Nancy Moore, was enrolled at the University of South Carolina, and Strom Jr. followed her there. Paul later won the state 4-A tennis championship as an Aiken High School student. He accepted a tennis scholarship to Vanderbilt University, playing on the varsity team in the Southeastern Conference, one of America's most competitive leagues for college tennis. Julie enrolled at the College of Charleston.

Lee Bandy heard that Strom told Nancy that if she wanted a divorce, she would have to pursue it, because he would not. Although separated, they remained married. Nancy dated other men, but she and Strom still saw one another on his trips home and regularly spoke by phone.

A low point in the relationship came at a Washington birthday bash for Thurmond in March 1993, celebrating his ninetieth birthday. Richard Nixon spoke eloquently. President Bill Clinton and Vice President Al Gore dropped in at a reception. Bob Dole served as emcee, keeping the audience in laughter with one-liners. Congressional leaders delivered tributes.

Nancy attended, escorted by Charlie Duell, the socially prominent and wealthy owner of Charleston's Middleton Place National Historic Landmark. Her efforts to sit at the head table and to speak had been rebuffed by the event's planners as inappropriate.

After Thurmond spoke, soul singer James Brown led a rendition of "Happy Birthday." As the guests remained standing for the benediction by Senator John Danforth of Missouri, an ordained Episcopal priest, Nancy took the mike and started speaking. She extolled Strom's virtues. The guests sat back down, sensing she might ramble for a while.

When she finished, Strom felt obligated to respond. "Not bad for somebody who's separated," he said. Lee Bandy reported that guests left abuzz and discomfited, and he concluded, "The skit writers for *Saturday Night Live* couldn't have written a more bizarre ending to what otherwise was a perfect evening."[25]

CHAPTER 19

"Time for Change"

Strom Thurmond opened the 1969 congressional year by defending "freedom of choice" school desegregation plans and saying he expected future support from followers of George Wallace. Those two issues would dominate the next two years of South Carolina politics.

"I haven't changed my philosophy, and they know it," he said of Wallace's supporters. "I've had their support in the past and think I'll get it in the future."

When Thurmond returned to Washington in January, he seemed completely uninformed about the Supreme Court's decision the previous May that effectively struck down freedom of choice school desegregation plans. Thurmond said in January 1969 that Richard Nixon came out three times in his 1968 campaign for freedom of choice and that he expected the new administration to follow that policy. "What difference does it make if there is desegregation or not if you have freedom of choice and each child has the freedom to choose?" he asked. "That's freedom, isn't it?"[1]

Fifteen months later, Assistant Attorney General for Civil Rights Jerris Leonard told South Carolina school officials in Columbia, "Freedom of choice, for all practical purposes, is dead." He made it clear that the Supreme Court's decision in *Green v. New Kent County* had been the death knell. That decision was rendered May 27, 1968, five days before Thurmond's meeting in Atlanta with Nixon that sealed their pact. Rather than finally reading the court's opinion, Thurmond responded to Leonard's remarks by calling for the removal of "zealots" in enforcement of school desegregation.[2]

Meanwhile, Strom's junior colleague, Fritz Hollings, was beginning to attract attention of his own in South Carolina with a different kind of populist politics. Hollings had won a smashing reelection in 1968 to a full Senate term, beating party-switching Republican State Senator Marshall Parker by more than 150,000 votes, the same opponent he had defeated by less than 10,000 votes two years earlier. Hollings had followed Thurmond's conservative voting line his first two years, even voting with Thurmond against the confirmation of Thurgood Marshall as the first black Supreme Court justice. Hollings now moved to the left, often supporting domestic social legislation opposed by Thurmond.

In early 1969, Hollings's profile was raised nationally by a series of "poverty tours." He accompanied the Reverend I. DeQuincey Newman, state NAACP field secretary, through littered city alleyways and down dusty country roads. Inside weathered shacks, Hollings came face-to-face with severe hunger and malnutrition, children with intestinal parasites, parents who stayed up at night to protect their family from rats. Hollings returned to Washington to tell the disbelievers in a speech in the U.S. Senate, "There is substantial hunger in South Carolina. I have seen it with my own eyes." He acknowledged that as governor, he had helped cover up the problem to present a better image and help attract industry to the state.

Once acknowledged, the conditions could not be ignored. "South Carolina is undoubtedly being hurt by the publicity," declared old guard state Senate leader Rembert Dennis, "but the situation for action is so serious I think our junior senator should be commended for what he's doing."

Thurmond reacted differently. He suggested that it was all a politically motivated Democratic effort to win black votes. He said "friends" had told him there was no great problem, and added that there have always been those who didn't want to work.

"I would like to lose the argument and that there would be no problems," Hollings said the next week while walking through black slums in Anderson, a textile city of 35,000 that had not a single unit of public housing. "But here it is," he said as he stood on a street of unpainted shacks, wrecked cars, and littered yards, with ill-clothed black children scurrying around.[3] The stark focus and congressional testimony Hollings gave to the problem would lead to a massive expansion of the federal food stamp program and creation of the continuing Women's, Infants, and Children (WIC) food supplement program.

Thurmond was in attack mode in the summer of 1969 during Judiciary Committee hearings on authorizing an extension of the Voting Rights Act after its scheduled expiration in 1970. William Want, a Yale law graduate and South Carolina native, monitored the hearings for the U.S. Commission on Civil Rights, where he then worked. More than three decades later, he vividly recalled Thurmond's "vicious attack" on NAACP Washington lobbyist Clarence Mitchell. "He screamed that Mitchell was a liar for saying there had ever been any discrimination in voting against blacks in South Carolina." (When the act had passed in 1965, there were no registered black voters in South Carolina's sparsely populated McCormick County, adjacent to Edgefield.) Want contrasted Thurmond's performance with that of presiding Senator Sam Ervin of North Carolina. Want recalled, "Ervin was just as much against the authorization, but he was witty, gentlemanly, and argued on constitutional grounds."[4]

In an exchange that made the front page of the *New York Times*, Senator Edward Kennedy interrupted Thurmond's verbal attack of Justice William O. Douglas on the Senate floor. It occurred less than a month after the resignation of Abe Fortas and on the day the Senate confirmed Warren Burger as chief justice. Thurmond called for Douglas to resign because he had served at $12,000 a year as chairman of the Parvin Foundation, which helped fund a South American institute to train what Thurmond called "leftwing radicals under the tutelage of such leftist Latin politicians as Juan Bosch and José Figueres."

This exchange followed:

MR. KENNEDY: Mr. President, will the Senator yield, or does he wish to continue? I have some familiarity with the individuals about whom he is talking.

MR. THURMOND: I will be glad to. One of Mr. Figueres' supporters, are you?

MR. KENNEDY: No. I am able to pronounce his name correctly, and I would think that when you are using it in making charges about an individual, it is helpful to pronounce the name correctly, with due respect to an individual.

MR. THURMOND: Some pronounce it "Figueres" and some "Figueres" [placing the accent on different syllables].

MR. KENNEDY: How?

MR. THURMOND: Some pronounce it "Figueres" and some "Figueres." Are you trying to correct my pronunciation in English, or are you holding yourself up as an English teacher? Are you an expert because you went to Harvard? What was your record at Harvard?

MR. KENNEDY: All I was trying to get—

MR. THURMOND: I will not show up your record at Harvard; that is all right.

MR. KENNEDY: I was trying to get the way Mr. Figueres pronounces his name.

MR. THURMOND: I will not go into your record at Harvard.[5]

The news accounts pointed out the apparent allusion to Kennedy's expulsion from Harvard during his freshman year in 1951, after he had a classmate take a Spanish exam for him. Kennedy spent two years in the army as an enlisted man, then returned to Harvard, graduating in 1956.

The *Washington Post* reported only two other senators were present when the heated exchange took place. One of them, Russell Long of Louisiana, whom Kennedy beat for the majority whip job earlier that year, sat smiling throughout the encounter.[6]

PRESIDENT NIXON HAD NOMINATED Judge Warren Burger from the U.S. Court of Appeals for the District of Columbia as chief justice, and he won easy confirmation by the Senate.

Nixon then nominated Fourth Circuit Court of Appeals Chief Judge Clement F. Haynsworth of Greenville, South Carolina, for the slot vacated by Fortas. Although Thurmond readily accepted Haynsworth, he indicated his first choice had been Donald Russell. Lyndon Johnson had named Russell a district court judge in South Carolina after he lost his Senate seat to Hollings in 1966. Insiders disagreed on whether Thurmond was being coy—not his usual style—to spare Haynsworth the taint of his baggage among liberals from the Fortas hearings or whether he genuinely preferred Russell. A highly regarded jurist and Harvard Law graduate, Haynsworth—known for his anti-labor decisions—had been an Eisenhower supporter but had never been overtly political. Thurmond may have believed that Russell, the protégé of Byrnes and a former Democratic senator whom Thurmond had found compatible, would have won confirmation easily and would have provided a sophisticated conservative vote on the Supreme Court.

Haynsworth ultimately failed to win confirmation after bitter opposition by organized labor. His later record and history's judgment indicate he deserved confirmation. An AFL-CIO regional official in Atlanta said that Greenville lawyer John Bolt Culbertson provided information that the wealthy Haynsworth owned small amounts of stock in several companies involved in lawsuits before his court. The appearance of ethical conflict became a major issue in Senate hearings. "Strom Thurmond got our man," the labor official said, "and we got his."[7]

Unlike Haynsworth, Nixon's next choice, Judge G. Harrold Carswell of the Fifth Circuit Court of Appeals, proved inept and a lightweight with a racist past. He lacked support from two outstanding judges on his court, Chief Judge Elbert P. Tuttle of Atlanta and John Minor Wisdom of New Orleans. (Although Tuttle and Wisdom were both Republicans, appointed by Eisenhower, they had been leaders in fleshing out *Brown v. Board of Education* into a broad mandate for racial justice.) The Senate rejected Carswell, too.

Afterward, Nixon declared to the press, "I have reluctantly concluded that I cannot successfully nominate to the Supreme Court any Federal Appellate Judge from the South who believes as I do in the strict construction of the Constitution."[8] When Judge Wisdom's name came up, Attorney General John Mitchell referred to him as "a damn left winger. He'd be as bad as Earl Warren."[9]

Back in South Carolina, the 1970 campaign for governor would provide a clear test of the changing politics of race. Lieutenant Governor John West was a progressive Democrat who had actively fought the Ku Klux Klan as a state senator and had stood almost alone in the legislature in opposing repeal of the state's compulsory school attendance law, part of the official resistance to desegregation. As lieutenant governor he had boldly taken the unprecedented step of delivering an address at a dinner in majority black Clarendon County in honor of NAACP executive director Roy Wilkins. But 1970 was the year of massive school desegregation in the South, and in response to angry reactions among restive whites, West muted his campaign appeals to blacks. At one point he even engaged in a bit of racial rhetoric by attacking the U.S. Department of Health, Education, and Welfare for "social experimentation."

The Nixon administration, having accepted the reality of the *Green* decision, under pressure from Thurmond, still attempted to slow down desegregation. Justice Department lawyers argued in support of Mississippi school districts for more time to desegregate. The Supreme Court, in the fall of 1969, unanimously reversed a lower court delay and declared "all deliberate speed" was "no longer Constitutionally permissible." The Court asserted that every school district was obligated "to terminate dual school systems at once and to operate now and forever only unitary schools."[10]

When the Fifth Circuit Court of Appeals first attempted to implement the Supreme Court ruling by ordering desegregation of faculties, facilities, staff, and transportation by February 1, 1970, but to delay massive student integration until the following September, the Supreme Court on January 14 again reversed the lower court and ordered immediate desegregation. The Fifth Circuit issued 166 school desegregation orders in the next eight months—almost four a week. (Over time, however, as a series of Republican presidents began filling the federal courts with a dominance of "strict constructionist" judges, the initial burst of school integration began to reverse itself. By 1980, four of every ten African-American children in the South attended majority white schools. In the next quarter century, that figure fell by 25 percent.)

But in South Carolina in early 1970, Democratic Governor Robert E. McNair displayed leadership that sharply contrasted with Thurmond's misleading talk about "freedom of choice." McNair told a televised audience in Greenville, where a midyear desegregation order involving extensive busing was being implemented for the combined 58,000-pupil school system for the city and county, the largest in the state, that South Carolina had "run out of courts, run out of time, and must adjust to new circumstances." This story was reported on the front page of the *Los Angeles Times, New York Times, Charlotte Observer,* and *Washington Post,* but on the back page of the then locally owned *Greenville News.* Greenville initiated its plan without disorder, with vigorous support from state senator, and future Democratic governor, Richard (Dick) Riley and his father, Ted, who was the school board's attorney. Young businessman Carroll Campbell, a Republican who after serving in Congress would succeed Riley as a two-term governor, led anti-busing opposition.

The crucial event of the year in South Carolina, however, occurred at the small Darlington County town of Lamar, where an angry white mob attacked school buses carrying black children. Nine days earlier, Congressman Albert Watson had addressed a massive freedom of choice rally at Lamar. West and McNair had spurned invitations to appear.

Watson had told his audience, "*Every section* of this state is in for it unless you stand up and use every means at your disposal to defend [against] what I consider an illegal order of the Circuit Court of the United States."

Lamar was not located in Watson's Second Congressional District, and he had drawn applause when he opened his remarks by declaring, "There are some people who said, 'Congressman, why are you coming over here this afternoon to speak to some of those hard-core rednecks over there?' You know my response to them? 'Those citizens are interested in their children, and I'll stand with them.'"[11]

At the state Republican convention, Thurmond nominated Watson for governor. Watson—with his gift for the kind of fierce and folksy traditional Southern political oratory that somehow tied together religiosity, patriotism, and defiance—was a strong candidate. He wore a white tie throughout the campaign to remind voters of his stand on race.

Watson got all-out support from the Nixon administration in a well-funded campaign. President Nixon's daughter Julie and son-in-law David Eisenhower made trips to South Carolina to join Thurmond in campaigning for Watson. Vice President Spiro Agnew visited twice.

West's campaign manager purchased billboards that read "Elect a Good Man Governor." The violence at Lamar, although never mentioned directly by West in the campaign, became a crucial issue that hurt Watson with white moderates. In the fall, two Watson aides were linked to an attempt to stage a racial confrontation at a high school in Columbia.

The State, with its aristocratic tradition (dating back to its establishment in 1891 expressly to oppose Pitchfork Ben Tillman—his nephew shot and killed the newspaper's first editor and was acquitted), endorsed West, a graduate of The Citadel, the state-supported military college in Charleston that emphasized leadership training and strict discipline. The editor of the newspaper was fellow Citadel graduate William D. Workman Jr., the 1962 Republican candidate for the Senate.[12] And West drew support among both Nixon voters, offended by Watson's redneck racist appeal and its threat to stability, and Wallace voters, many of them traditional Democratic textile workers reacting against the Nixon administration's economic and school policies. Despite objections by Thurmond, almost all the broadcasters in the state ran an ad called "Broken Promises," which used a tape of Thurmond in 1968 promising South Carolina voters that Nixon would permit freedom of choice in the schools. The ad showed Thurmond saying of Nixon, "He will permit the parent or the child to have freedom to choose any school in the community without discrimination. You, not the government, will make the choice." It also showed Thurmond telling South Carolina voters from the same 1968 tape that Nixon had pledged to limit textile imports and that there would be a lower cost of living and lower federal taxes. After Thurmond finished speaking, another voice told listeners, "Don't be misled in '70 as you were in '68."

Thurmond's attorney sent telegrams in 1970 to radio and TV stations throughout the state a week before the election requesting they not run the commercial "on grounds it would be actionable." Contemporary FCC regulations prohibited censorship of political advertising, and Wayne Sawyer, president of the South Carolina Association of Broadcasters, said that a majority of them were "resentful" about Thurmond, with his implicit threat.

Democratic State Chairman Harry Lightsey, Jr. called the ad "both legal and responsible" and said he was "shocked" at Thurmond. "We must conclude the chief reason for his objections is that he now is unwilling for the public of South Carolina to hear his own words and promises of 1968—which we all realize now have been broken. By using Mr. Thurmond's own words of two years ago, we have avoided the possibility of distortion or misquotation of what he actually said."

Thurmond responded, "I have no objection to being quoted. I do object, however, to the use of my picture and voice without my permission." He called the ad "a last-ditch, desperation effort of the Democratic candidate for governor." Thurmond declared the ad "is attempting to convey the impression that I lied . . . when I said that Richard Nixon stood for freedom of choice. His views on this matter have not changed, but it is well known that they have been overridden by decisions of the liberal Supreme Court."

Thurmond added that Nixon has promised to appoint strict constructionists and concluded, "Ultimately, we expect freedom of choice to prevail."[13]

With the schools integrated, "freedom of choice" dead, and promised textile import legislation not yet passed, resulting in layoffs and "short time" (a shortened work week) for textile workers, West pulled support from both Nixon and Wallace voters to add to his solid black majority and won the election by 28,000 votes, 53.2 percent of the major-party total.

For example, West narrowly lost to Watson 433–410 in the upper-middle-income Arcadia precinct in suburban Columbia, which in 1968 had voted 667 for Nixon, 132 for Humphrey, and 69 for Wallace. But West won

ten of the twelve counties in which Wallace had received either a majority
or a plurality in 1968. West's campaign was especially effective in Anderson
County, which Wallace had carried with a majority of 6,419 to a combined
5,043 for Nixon and Humphrey. West won 10,531–5,362. In Columbia's
Ward 9, where all but twenty-four of the 1,904 registered voters were black,
West won 1,006–19, reflecting the almost absolute rejection of Watson
among African Americans.[14] West joined fellow New South Governors
Reuben Askew of Florida, Dale Bumpers of Arkansas, and Jimmy Carter
of Georgia as progressive racial moderates.

In a hotel room postmortem after Watson's defeat, a spy planted by the
West campaign reported hearing Thurmond say, "Well, it means you can't
win any longer just by 'cussin' the niggers,'" a shorthand phrase widely used
in some form by contemporary white and black politicians throughout the
South. (For example, five years later Congressman Andrew Young, former
top aide to Martin Luther King Jr., told a conference of Southern black
mayors, "It used to be Southern politics was just 'nigger' politics, who
could 'outnigger' the other . . . and now that we've got 50, 60, 70 percent of
the blacks votes registered in the South, everybody's proud to be associated
with their black brothers and sisters.")[15] With West's victory, Strom Thurmond understood the new reality.

Strom got immediate reinforcement, first from Dolly Hamby, who had
guided the successful 1954 write-in campaign. She mailed him a four-page
letter on November 6 analyzing how the business community opposed
Watson "almost 100 percent." She added, "The 'racist' charge REALLY
hurt! . . . Strom, South Carolina is much more moderate than many
think. . . . An appeal to race is no longer a vote-getter."[16]

On November 30, a four-page memo on "political implications of the
1970 elections" was sent to Thurmond by Wayne Robbins, a politically astute staffer placed by Strom on the Senate Armed Services Committee.
Through his father's relationship with Nancy Thurmond's father when
both worked at the nuclear research facility at Oak Ridge, Tennessee, Robbins had developed his relationship with the senator. After talking to journalists and political activists in five southeastern states, Robbins outlined a
political strategy that reads like a precursor for the twenty-first century's
"compassionate conservatism."

He wrote about using a "moral pitch," but emphasized, "I do not advocate that we change our basic positions one inch, *but we do need to change our*

way of talking about them" [emphasis in original]. As an example, he wrote, "Let us not allow Senator Hollings to become the champion of the hungry in South Carolina simply because he has written a book on the subject. . . . We should talk more (especially to the press) about our deep concern for poor people. It is needless to concede this position to the liberals."[17]

Additional encouragement for Thurmond to develop a new "image" came from Harry Dent. A few weeks after the election, Dent said in a candid interview with an old college buddy, the editor of the newspaper in Aiken, "We're going to get him on the high ground of fairness on the race question. We've got to get him in a position where he can't be attacked like Watson by liberals as being a racist."[18]

Dent advised the senator to hire a black for his staff—at a time when no member of Congress from South Carolina had a black staffer—specifically recommending Thomas Moss of Orangeburg, the forty-three-year-old state director for the Voter Education Project, a Southwide organization. Moss had invited Dent to represent the Republican Party at a statewide VEP election forum, and Dent was impressed with Moss's quiet competence and the way he dealt with people. He was courteous, patient, and a good listener.

The unpretentious son of a sharecropper, with parents who instilled strong religious values, Moss attended a couple of terms at Morris College, a Baptist-affiliated school in Sumter, South Carolina, where he had been a running back on the football team before being drafted into the army and serving as a combat infantryman in Korea. He returned to Orangeburg and worked in a meatpacking plant, becoming president of a biracial union local to which all but a handful of workers paid dues.

Moss became co-chairman of the voter registration committee for the Orangeburg NAACP chapter in 1968. Under a new state law, he and his co-chairman became deputy registrars. As Republican growth in the state continued, the still all-white, Democratic-controlled legislature had quietly recognized that expanded black political participation was essential to their remaining the dominant political party.

On evenings and weekends, Moss and his colleague roamed Orangeburg County, which stretches a hundred miles across the South Carolina Lowcountry, registering voters on the spot in scattered villages and crossroads communities.

Moss also served on the national negotiating committee for the meat-packers' union, and the next year was offered a $14,000 salary (equivalent to $66,350 in 2003) to cover South Carolina, Georgia, and Florida as a union organizer. He was then making between $8,000 and $9,000 as an hourly worker at the meatpacking plant in Orangeburg. Vernon Jordan, then the Atlanta-based executive director of the Voter Education Project, simultaneously asked Moss to become South Carolina's VEP director for $8,000 annually (equivalent to $37,915 in 2003).

Moss thought about his wife and two children, examined his commitment to the civil rights struggle, and accepted Jordan's offer. In all of South Carolina's forty-six counties, he worked with local legislators to expand the number of deputy registrars.

By the time John West had defeated Albert Watson, 229,000 blacks in South Carolina were registered to vote, and Moss knew their turnout made the difference. Moss's predecessor as state VEP director, James Felder, became one of three blacks elected to the legislature in 1970, the first since the post-Reconstruction era.

Thurmond called Moss in late December and asked him to come work for him.

Moss was a realist who believed changes were needed, patience was necessary, and that "you dealt with the situation as it is." He conferred with fellow black political activists, and they agreed that an opportunity to serve on Thurmond's staff during the Nixon administration would position him to have a positive impact. And his wife approved. He called Thurmond the next day and accepted.

As a meat cutter, Moss had experienced new technology in which automated cutting tools for skinning a cow trimmed a worker's time by two-thirds, leaving a single cut that insured top value for the hide. He clearly understood that new technology would mean jobs that required better-educated workers. He was also aware that financial constraints had forced several of the nation's traditionally black colleges to close.

On Moss's first day on the job in March, Thurmond escorted him to the Senate chamber and introduced him to Senators Walter Mondale of Minnesota, Edward M. (Ted) Kennedy of Massachusetts, Jacob Javits of New York, Henry Bellmon of Oklahoma, and Herman Talmadge of Georgia. Moss never forgot Talmadge's red suspenders.

On the walk from the senator's office, Thurmond asked Moss what issues he thought were important to blacks. Moss told him about the financial plight of black colleges. Months later, Thurmond invited the presidents of the six historically black colleges in South Carolina to come to Washington for a meeting with Elliott Richardson, then secretary of the Department of Health, Education, and Welfare (HEW).

The spokesman for the six, Harry P. Graham, the president of Voorhees College in Denmark, South Carolina, explained the financial challenges facing them. Richardson agreed to make some discretionary funds available to such colleges. (Subsequent legislation created special funding programs to revitalize black institutions that long had provided access to middle-class opportunity.) Before the meeting broke up, Thurmond asked Richardson how many other senators had brought in black college presidents to discuss their special problems with the secretary. "You are the first one, Senator," Richardson told him.

Thurmond instructed Moss to help anyone, white or black, who needed help, but told him to give special emphasis to his "own people." Thurmond later explained, "They would confide more in him when they needed help. He tried to remain in touch with the leaders of his race to find out what they needed, and what help he could render."[19]

Before returning to South Carolina, Moss spent almost a month in Washington, where Thurmond set up an orientation program with visits to a wide range of federal departments and agencies. Moss developed a network of contacts and became acquainted with the details of programs, some specifically designed to help minorities. He met black officials in key agency positions who had South Carolina connections.

In South Carolina, Moss worked primarily out of an office at his home in Orangeburg, regularly spending time in the senator's flagship home office in Columbia and driving around the state. He advised black business owners on how to get technical assistance for establishing regional minority enterprise development centers in the state. He worked with black mayors, who mostly governed hamlets with meager resources. Thurmond then helped them get water and sewer grants and funds for other programs, all of which he announced with great fanfare. These mayors would respond by collectively endorsing Thurmond in his future election campaigns.

Moss escorted Thurmond on visits to black colleges and ceremonial events. He usually made at least one trip a month to Washington, always spending some time alone with the senator. He never advised Thurmond how to vote on a bill, quietly kept him informed about black interests, and sensitized him about black aspirations.

For more than three decades, Moss happily accepted his primary role of helping grassroots constituents, day-to-day requests that he referred to staff specialists for help with Social Security problems, assisting with a son or daughter's military transfer, or resolving a problem with a government agency. He answered all telephone messages before going to bed each night, and he provided a listening post to the state's 30-percent black population. Not once did he feel that Thurmond let him down.[20]

AFTER AN UNSUCCESSFUL RACE for Congress as a Democrat in 1974, Matthew Perry got a telephone call from Thurmond—whom he barely knew at the time—asking that he meet him late that afternoon in Union, a county seat town sixty miles north of Columbia, where the senator would be dedicating a public works project. Perry said he went without "having the slightest idea what it was" that the senator wanted.

Thurmond drove up, accompanied by Billy Wilkins. Someone pointed out Matthew Perry, who later recalled, "He walked over, extended his hand and said, 'Mr. Perry, you have a fine reputation as a lawyer. A lot of people speak very favorably of you.'" Thurmond told Perry he wanted to recommend him to President Gerald Ford for a judgeship on the U.S. Court of Military Appeals. "I was astounded."

The position had six years remaining on a fifteen-year term rather than the lifetime appointment for judges in the national federal court system. Perry was aware there had never been a black judicial nominee from the Deep South, and yet, "Here was a man known as an arch segregationist willing to propose my name to the president."

He told Thurmond he wanted to discuss the matter with some of his colleagues. Perry, chairman of the NAACP's Legal Rights Committee and a member of the national NAACP board and legal committee, was unsure whether to align himself with a "somewhat notorious figure." He consulted with I. DeQuincey Newman and Modjeska Simkins, his law partner Lincoln Jenkins, and a few other friends. Some, like Simkins, warned against it, fearing that the appointment was merely a ploy to remove him from his civil rights work.

"We discussed the historic significance and meaningfulness of it. Some people on the national scene had doubts about whether I should do this—

the court was not that well known. But many felt it could be a breakthrough. It had never been done before and there was a feeling of 'Let's try it!'"

After considering the matter overnight, Perry called back the next day with his acceptance. A few days later, Thurmond escorted him to the White House to meet some of President Gerald Ford's top aides.[21]

Lee Bandy recalled the swearing-in ceremony in 1975 in Washington. It seemed "that the entire African-American community from South Carolina was there. The place was packed. Strom was there. It was a big deal. It really was."[22]

Because some of those present had been Perry's college classmates, speculation arose among knowledgeable blacks in South Carolina whether his having dated Essie Mae had anything to do with the appointment.[23] The two of them had remained friends over the years. Whether Thurmond was aware of the friendship between Perry and Essie is uncertain, but she says she was totally uninvolved in his judicial appointment.

Four years later, in 1979, President Jimmy Carter responded to a campaign pledge and began making the first lifetime appointments of black federal district and court of appeals judges in the South. He sought to name at least one in every state. Attorney General Griffin Bell found it helpful in persuading Southern senators that such appointments would be politically safe by pointing out Thurmond's role four years earlier.[24]

As the Democratic senator in a Democratic administration, Fritz Hollings happily agreed in 1979 to elevating Perry to the district court of South Carolina.

THURMOND WOULD MAKE DRAMATIC CHANGES in addressing issues important to blacks, and Tom Moss quietly and effectively contributed to that change. But Moss wasn't alone. Thurmond developed a dramatically different relationship with South Carolina native Armstrong Williams (no relation to Essie's husband, Julius), who was sixteen when he first saw the senator in 1974. After reading that Thurmond was speaking in nearby Mullins, the black teenager convinced his father, a prosperous Marion County farmer who grew a profitable thirty acres of tobacco and annually raised 2,000 hogs, that they should go hear the senator.

"I'll never forget," Williams recalled. "I extended my hand and said, 'I'm Armstrong Williams and I hear you're a racist.' I thought my father was going to smack me."

Thurmond chuckled and said, "You seem like a bright young man. What grade are you in?"

After Williams told him, Thurmond said, "Well, take my card and when you become a senior in high school, why don't you come work for me and find out whether I'm a racist or not."

Williams called a time or two, and Thurmond would take his calls. At the end of Williams's sophomore year at South Carolina State College in 1979, he knew he didn't want to spend the summer working on the tobacco farm, and he called Thurmond. The senator remembered him and offered a one-month internship. Williams accepted, recalling, "We took a liking to each other."

"I would tease him about whether he was a racist and anti-black or not. My friends all thought he was a bigot. He said he had some archaic ideas and that even if he changed there would be many people on both sides of the aisle who would not really believe it. He asked if I would give him a chance. I said I was young and that he could manipulate me."

In the fall of 1980, after Armstrong had been elected student body president at SC State, he got a call from Thurmond. His wife, Nancy, would be visiting the campus as part of the Reagan presidential campaign, and Thurmond wanted Williams to escort her. He agreed. As the wife of segregationist Strom Thurmond, she received a less than friendly reception on campus. In the dining hall, there were insulting remarks. Some yelled out, "Bitch."

"I was amazed," Williams said. "I never saw such meanness and cruelty in my life. She was in tears. She was really grateful to me, for standing with her. I told her that my father taught me to do what was right."

After Nancy returned to Washington and told Strom what had happened, he called Armstrong to thank him for standing by his wife. "I said, 'It was no big deal, Senator. It was easy. It was the way my parents raised me.'"

"And I said, 'There was a time when blacks were treated like chattel and called racial epithets, and people like you did not take a stand to do what was right, but I never drink from that cup of bitterness and anger, because my father taught me better.'"

"There was a dead silence. I thought I had lost him."

And then Thurmond told him, "I appreciate your honesty." Williams recalled, "He said, 'You're different.' I said, 'No, I'm not different.' And I said, 'No matter what may be in your heart, I'm going to always try to do good.' This is when we bonded."

Thurmond put Williams in touch with Lee Atwater, his protégé who would soon be working in the Reagan White House, with Congressman Carroll Campbell, who soon would be a two-term Republican governor of South Carolina, and with Floyd Spence, the state's senior Republican congressman. These were all savvy politicians who, like Thurmond, understood that the Republican Party needed to moderate its image on the issue of race. The senator told Williams he should take off the month of January and come to Washington as an inaugural intern for the start of the Reagan administration.

Although he worked on Campbell's staff, Williams spent time visiting with Thurmond—going to lunch together, sitting in his office and talking. There was good chemistry between them. Strom Jr. was only seven, and Williams believed that he and the seventy-seven-year-old senator developed something of a father and son relationship. "I was different from him and he was different from me. And he'd say, 'You know, son, there's really no difference between black and white people.'" He remembered Thurmond telling him that people reflected what they had learned and how they had been educated.

After Williams graduated, Thurmond got him a job in the Department of Agriculture. After a couple of months, the young man came to see the senator with a complaint. His superiors had him working only on projects involving blacks and minorities. He said, "They're putting me in a box, stereotyping me."

Williams recalled, "He said, 'Son, you just have to prove your worth. Racism is still alive and well, but I'm going to teach you how to deal with those old geezers because I should know.' He said, 'Just trust me.'"

Williams said he learned from Thurmond how to deal with the media, how to use diplomacy, how to use his Southern upbringing to advantage—the art of being a Southern gentleman. "I was a country boy and didn't know about that etiquette stuff," he recalled.

When he attempted to bring in the controversial black comedian Richard Pryor for a special Department of Agriculture Black History Month program, Williams ran into bureaucratic opposition. "I went to Strom Thurmond and said I could get it to work, that I had creative juices and needed someone to believe in me."

Thurmond told him his idea could backfire and blow up in President Reagan's face. When Williams persisted, however, the senator told him, "If you believe in this so strongly, I'll back you up." Thurmond called the secretary of agriculture and convinced him to allow Williams to move forward. He lined up Pryor, drew thousands of people to the event, got good press, and Reagan had a White House reception for Pryor and Black History Month. Pryor told the *Washington Post* it came about because a low-level Department of Agriculture employee invited him.

Clarence Thomas, another up-and-coming black conservative who was then head of the Equal Employment Opportunity Commission (EEOC), read the article. He contacted Williams, who recalled, "He told me, 'Boy, they don't know how to take advantage of your skills and your savvy. You should come work for me.'"

When Reagan reappointed Thomas as EEOC chairman, Williams got Thurmond to come over and swear him in. Thurmond and Thomas thus developed a relationship that surfaced several years later when Thurmond emerged as a steadfast supporter of Thomas at his contentious and high-profile Supreme Court confirmation hearing. Allegations about the nominee's sexual interests aroused controversy, but Strom no doubt considered such matters irrelevant as a consideration for public service.

Meanwhile, Williams realized that to move up in Washington, he needed a visible patron. Soon after going to work for Thomas, and while living in a "roach-infested efficiency" on Capitol Hill, Williams decided to throw a housewarming party and invite Thurmond to be his guest of honor. Holly Richardson, the senator's personal secretary, called him and said, "Armstrong, the senator's going to be there."

In preparation, Armstrong recited to Thurmond some lyrics to a then popular song from rhythm-and-blues balladeer Barry White: "It's time for change and nothing remains the same. And I've changed." Williams's memory of the words varied a bit from the actual lyrics, but he made the message fit Strom and told him, "You have to learn the words, and it's going to give you some soul." Then he sent out invitations to the housewarming, listing Thurmond as the guest of honor. "Nobody believed that Strom Thurmond was going to show up," he recalled, "but I knew he would. And he knew the words for the song."

As their relationship developed, Armstrong and Thurmond attended events together in Washington. By the mid-1980s, they were regulars when

SC State's football team came up to play rival Howard University, with Armstrong explaining initially to the senator that it was an opportunity to meet his home state's black elite, who would come up for the game. "I explained that they won't want to shake your hand because they don't like you, that what you've got to do is go out of the way, hug them, ask about their families. This old man would shake their hand and greet them, and they'd just melt. And he'd turn around and wink at me."

Williams took Thurmond to eat soul food at the Florida Avenue Grill, where Strom ate collard greens, potato salad, corn bread muffins, bacon, and dressing (what is known outside the South as "stuffing")—all familiar to him. And Thurmond took Williams to White House receptions. "When he'd put oysters in his pocket, I'd say, 'Senator, those things are leaking.' And he'd whisper, 'Well, don't let nobody see it. Protect me.'" Thurmond staffers knew he could stand in front of oysters on the half shell at receptions and eat until the platter was empty. Often he would distribute food from his pocket to aides, including after-dinner mints from the Senate dining room that sometimes had pocket lint on them. He loved to give out peanuts from airliners.

In the years ahead, Williams strengthened his relationship with Thurmond while launching a syndicated radio and TV talk show and a newspaper column that mixed political conservatism with memories of his South Carolina farm boy childhood. He also developed a profitable and far-ranging public relations business in partnership with Stedman Graham, a fellow Nixon administration alum who was well known as Oprah Winfrey's companion.

At President Clinton's first inaugural in January 1993, Williams met Coretta Scott King and said she was amazed that he was involved in so many things. Thurmond was having a reception and asked Williams if he could get Mrs. King to stop by, that it would mean a lot to him. "I asked Mrs. King. A lot of her advisers said no, but in the end she went by and spent about twenty minutes at the reception at his office. And when Mrs. King had her function at the Conservatory Room at the Washington Hilton, I took Strom with me."

Armstrong's mother developed a special affection for Thurmond after her husband died. In the months before his death, he had allowed a Farm Bureau insurance policy to lapse, and company officials wanted to almost triple the premiums to reinstate it. An angry Williams called Thurmond

and told him what happened. "He broke down and cried," Williams recalled. "He felt my anguish and said, 'I'm sorry, son, this is happening to
you.' And fifteen minutes later the president of the Farm Bureau in Columbia, South Carolina, called me and apologized profusely and reinstated
the policy at the old premium. That's what Strom did. It made my mother
love him."

In March 1995, the Washington chapter of the Urban League decided to
give out awards for special friendships between black and white individuals. Williams was asked if they could honor him and Thurmond.

When Williams called the ninety-two-year-old senator, he responded,
"A civil rights organization wants to honor me?" Williams replied, "Senator, they want to honor you." Thurmond canceled a conflicting event.

But when word got out that the Urban League was going to honor the
1948 segregationist candidate for president, protests began to mount. "The
Urban League started calling me to ask if they could give it to us in private," Williams recalled.

"They couldn't deal with the heat. Then they called Strom. He said,
'You talk to Armstrong.' I said, 'Senator, we're not backing down.'"

The event made national news. "The senator and I were walking in, and
he said, 'This is like the civil rights movement. And at my age I'm still in the
thick of things.'" Williams added, "It was fun. Strom and I got our award,
and a few people stood up for him."[25] Others did not, however. The *Washington Post* said Thurmond was as welcome as a "pimple on prom night."[26]

As soon as Essie broke the silence in December 2003, Armstrong
Williams wrote in his syndicated column more about that night at the Urban League function. "Back stage, Senator Thurmond leaned over and
said, 'You know I have deep roots in the black community—deep roots.'"

"His voice softened into a raspy whisper: 'You've heard the rumors.' 'Are
they just rumors, Senator?' I asked."

Later, at an SC State football game they attended together in Orangeburg, "He mentioned how he had arranged for [Essie] Williams to attend
SC State College while he was governor . . . 'When a man brings a child
into the world, he should take care of the child,' said Thurmond, who then
added, 'She'll never say anything and neither will you—not while I'm
alive.'"

Williams added, "Beaming with pride he talked about how she called
him and sometimes took him to task when she didn't agree with state-

ments he made. . . . After nearly eight decades of subverting certain basic and essential facts about her identity, it seems that [Essie Mae] Williams wishes to be honest with herself—and society—about who she is."27

Asked about Thurmond and racism, Williams replied, "Of course Strom had racist thoughts and did things absolutely based on race. There's no question about that. But what shocked me was what a good person Strom was. He's a good man. I trust Strom."

"Every saint has a past and every sinner has a future. We all have a past."

It is a small irony that while Strom Thurmond believed he could not publicly acknowledge the existence of his black daughter, one of his most treasured relationships—in its warmth, closeness, and understanding— was with this young black man from rural South Carolina. Armstrong Williams said, "I've spent so much time hanging out with him; it's like hanging out with your own father."

Williams recalled Strom once looking back at how their relationship developed. "He said, 'The Lord always gives you what you need.' We both needed something at the time. We just clicked. I'm with Strom, and I get a lot of grief for it."

CHAPTER 20

Life in California

W HILE STROM SOLIDIFIED HIS REPUBLICAN BASE and moved toward the center on racial issues, Essie was striving to organize her life back in California. She had four growing children and high ambitions for all of them. The family settled in a comfortable bungalow she purchased on Chesley Avenue in View Park, then a predominantly white South Central Los Angeles neighborhood of palm trees, pastel one-story homes, and close-clipped lawns. Essie would remain there, known to her friends simply as Essie Williams or Mrs. Williams.

For her it meant starting life anew. For tens of thousands of African Americans who had headed west from the South, contemporary Los Angeles promised steady employment and relative tolerance. When she notified Thurmond in Washington of her husband's death, the senator offered to provide support "until the children had grown up," she said in 2003.

Essie got a low-paying secretarial job and began night classes at California State College, where in three years she completed her undergraduate degree. "That's when that help came," she would recall, "and it really did help."[1]

Her son Ronald recalled that Thurmond "never really helped a whole lot, but anything helped when you were living the way we were—close to the cuff. Everything helped." Over time he came to see Thurmond as a "stabilizing force" for his mother, "that he was there to help out if she needed him."[2]

Thurmond called periodically on the telephone and usually arranged to see her on trips to California. "Wherever he was," Essie said, "whether he was making a speech or an appearance, if it was near me, he would make sure that we saw each other. He was good to me and my children."[3]

With her degree, she became a teacher at the Abram Friedman Occupational Center, a comprehensive adult school named for its first principal. The center allowed school dropouts to return and get high school diplomas, as well as to join recent high school graduates in learning vocational skills in such areas as auto mechanics, carpentry, and secretarial work. Essie taught until 1986, when she became assistant principal for counseling, which for ten years put her in a supervisory role over three such schools. She recalled one student who later got a Ph.D. For twenty-two years, until 2002, Essie also taught night classes at Los Angeles Trade and Technical Community College.

"Her attitude toward education was that it was the most important thing you can pass on to your children," said her son Ronald. "A love for learning, that's what she believed."

Melvin Arterberry Sr., a probation officer living across the street, had been the first African American to move onto the block. Essie and her children, he said, "were the second."[4] Before long, however, whites began leaving View Park, fleeing to the suburbs. The neighborhood became tougher.

Ronald, a ninth grader at Mt. Vernon Junior High School, recalled his mother warning her sons to steer clear of gang rivalries. The Crips was the dominant teenage gang in the area.

Always striving upward, Essie concentrated her social life on church activities. Soon after moving into her home, she joined the nearby Congregation Church of Christian Fellowship, which was founded in the 1940s as a multiracial congregation where blacks, whites, and Japanese prayed together. Over time, the 300-member congregation, a majority with college degrees, became almost all black.

The church developed a reputation for its activism on poverty and racial issues. In the 1970s, it supported a busing plan to desegregate public schools in Los Angeles. The congregation also founded on its property a mental health counseling service.[5]

In her early years in the congregation, Pastor Jim Hargett attracted attention for his inspiring sermons and his civil rights activism and personal relationship with Dr. Martin Luther King Jr. After racial riots, the church encouraged dialogue among blacks, whites, and Latinos and began a Head Start program and a food distribution network for the poor.

Essie worked with the Sunday School and later became lay leader in the church, elected by the congregation as the moderator to oversee the church's work. Thelma Mitchell, the church's historian then, recalled it was a time of conflict within the congregation and praised Essie for her leadership. "She was fair; she was articulate," Mitchell said. "She tried to go by the book. She listened to everybody, and she tried to be available. This is where her character came through."[6] The church held a special event to honor her in 1997.

For her part, Essie kept the secret so tightly held that some of her closest California friends did not know the truth until after Thurmond's death in 2003.

Madison Shockley served as pastor in the late 1990s of the Congregation Church of Christian Fellowship and presided over the special event honoring Essie in 1997. A year earlier, however, Shockley had been to Washington and had been invited to deliver the opening prayer to the Senate. He came home and shared with the congregation what he considered "a great irony and sign of progress," he later wrote, with an African American minister escorted to the Senate podium by a former segregationist, Senate president pro tempore Strom Thurmond.

"The service hadn't been over for an hour before one of the church members upstaged my little tale with this simple sentence. 'Well, you know, Reverend, Essie Williams is Strom Thurmond's daughter.' Respecting her privacy, I never considered asking Mrs. Washington-Williams directly."

In a subsequent telephone interview, Shockley said he had heard gossip about Essie being related to Thurmond. "I didn't know what to do with it, so I just left it alone," he said. As he got to know her better and hear her talk about growing up in Pennsylvania, he dismissed the rumor; "the geography didn't add up."

He called Ms. Williams "a pioneer in many ways." She was "not flamboyant—she was quiet, hardworking, dedicated—a woman who speaks up when it is time to speak up." When Shockley finally learned the truth, he saw it as another sign of how "we as a nation continue to live in denial over the continuing legacy of slavery and the everyday impact of race and racism in this country."[7]

ESSIE WAS ALSO ACTIVE with the Los Angeles chapter of the South Carolina State College Alumni Association, a group that held social events and raised scholarship funds for the school. She also enjoyed a good game of pinochle, going to the movies (Denzel Washington was her favorite actor), and regular visits with other members of Delta Sigma Theta, a public-service sorority.[8]

One by one, Essie Williams told her children about their famous grandfather, who at one point in their young lives had come to Los Angeles on business and summoned Essie to bring them to meet him. "We were told we were going to see a friend of hers speak at a church," recalled Monica, who was nine or ten at the time. Their mother had briefed the older children; the girls did not know there was a family connection and simply saw him as a kindly white man with a strange accent who seemed fond of their mother. Occasionally, he would call their house, speaking in his deep Southern drawl. He was the only person to ask for Ms. Williams by her long-abandoned girlhood name, Essie Mae.

Monica took the news the hardest. By age fourteen, she had embraced the Black Power movement and teachings of Malcolm X and wore the black leather jackets that were a uniform of the movement. She used the name Pendaleza, wore her hair in an Afro, and decorated her room with posters of Black Panther leader Huey Newton and Black Power symbols. Televised images of police brutality, of black protesters being hosed in the streets and attacked by dogs, filled her with racial hatred.

Her mother had grown disturbed by her behavior. Deeply spiritual, she "would not tolerate a hateful attitude. She taught love," Monica said.

Essie finally decided it was time to tell Monica about her connection to Thurmond. "My mother sat me down and explained it all to me. She wanted me to see both perspectives of political issues," Monica said.[9] "She started talking to me about love and forgiveness. She told me who the man was I had met at the church. The man who called on the telephone."[10]

The mother told her child that to hate others because of their race or their political views was to also hate "part of yourself."[11]

The news at first devastated Monica. She remembered her father working so hard to push civil rights causes, and Thurmond represented the type of white man she vilified. "I don't remember leaving the house after that. I could not believe it. I was shocked. I had never considered that," Monica said years later.[12]

She recalled staying in her room for days, ashamed to ever admit her connection to her fellow young activists. "I couldn't tell anybody. I wasn't real sure I wanted anybody to know," she said.

PAYMENTS FROM THURMOND, which in 1968 began coming through a family intermediary, continued to arrive regularly. Although Essie maintained her job teaching vocational education for the Los Angeles school district, an exchange with Thurmond's office in May 1973 suggests she had ambitions to work for the federal government. She appealed to her father for help.

> Dear Mrs. Williams,
>
> Thank you for your kind letter of recent date in which you inquired about the progress of your application for a Mid-level position with the Federal Government.
>
> I contacted appropriate authorities and we will see if we can get a status report.
>
> It was good of you to write and with kindest regards and best wishes,
>
> Very truly,
>
> Strom Thurmond

Although apparently no job materialized, Thurmond over the years showered the Williams family with ceremonial trinkets from his Senate office, mementos in glass and silver bought in bulk from the U.S. Senate store. Essie sent Father's Day and Christmas cards and an occasional small gift, like the plaque she sent in 1974 with a poem entitled "Children Learn What They Live."

Meanwhile, Essie usually made annual visits to see Thurmond at his Senate office in Washington. She was among those in whom Strom confided about his intentions to marry Nancy Moore. Essie recognized her father was attracted to young women, and to her the only issue was whether the marriage was something that would make them both happy.

Although many of his written communications with Essie were brusque and businesslike, Thurmond exuded more warmth than he had in any of his previous letters when he wrote in June 1972 to congratulate her on completing a master's degree in education.

> Dear Essie Mae,
>
> This acknowledges receipt yesterday of the invitation to your graduation from the University of Southern California June 8 with a Master of Science Degree in Education.
>
> I am writing to express my congratulations to you upon reaching this milestone in your life. It is an achievement to obtain a bachelor's degree, but to be awarded a master's degree is a still greater feat, and I know your family and friends are proud of this accomplishment on your part.
>
> I understand you are teaching school, so this additional degree should be of added

benefit to you in becoming more competent as well as increase your remuneration as a teacher.

So many people are not willing to pay the price in added work, additional effort and increased responsibility to obtain a masters' degree, and I was pleased to learn about your having done this.

I am forwarding to you under separate cover a graduation gift. Please let me know if it does not arrive within a reasonable length of time.

I wish you success in all of your undertakings and with kindest regards to you and your family.

On the same day, Thurmond sent a letter to Essie's older daughter, Wanda, who had sent her grandfather an invitation for her high school graduation. By this time he had married again, to Nancy Moore in 1968.

Dear Wanda,

Nancy and I were happy to learn of your upcoming graduation and regret that we will be unable to be with you on this happy occasion.

May I take the opportunity to congratulate you upon attaining this milestone in life. I wish you continued success in all your future undertakings, and if I can ever be of assistance to you in any way, please call upon me.

I am forwarding a graduation gift to you under separate cover. If it does not arrive within a reasonable length of time, please let me know.

With kindest regards and best wishes,

    Very truly,

    Strom Thurmond

Meanwhile, Monica mellowed as she advanced through high school, sending an invitation to the Thurmonds when she graduated. She received what appeared to be the standard Thurmond graduation letter, the same or similar to that sent earlier to her sister and each year to thousands of South Carolina high school seniors.

Dear Monica,

Nancy and I appreciate the invitation to your graduation and regret that we were unable to attend.

May I take the opportunity to congratulate you upon attaining this milestone in

your life. I wish you continued success and if I can ever be of assistance to you in
any way, please call upon me.

I am forwarding to you under separate cover a little graduation gift. Please let
me know if it does not arrive within a reasonable length of time. With kindest
regards and best wishes, in which Nancy joins me.

When the gift arrived, Monica opened it to find a silver letter opener
with a gold engraving of Strom Thurmond's name and the seal of the U.S.
Senate. Her mother's message of forgiveness had sunk it. Monica kept the
gift with her throughout her adult life and in 2004—as director of a battered women's shelter, Polly's Place, in Seattle—she was still using it to
open her mail.[13]

In 1975, when her son Ronald began the process of applying for admission to a dozen medical schools at the end of his junior year in college,
Essie called her father on June 16 to seek his assistance. Ronald Williams
was especially interested in a new program at Bethesda, Maryland, the
Uniformed Services University of the Health Sciences (USUHS), which
would mean a free medical education if accepted for the first class in
1976–1977. He wrote his grandfather on June 20 and followed his mother's
directions by marking the letter "Very Personal."

He cited her phone call, pointed out his interest in the 1976–1977 opening class at USUHS and at the Medical University of South Carolina
(MUSC) and enclosed copies of his application and college transcript.
"Because of the difficulty of getting into any of them," he explained, he
would be applying to six California medical schools and six out-of-state
schools. "I would appreciate any additional information you may have on
either of those schools, and I would be grateful for a recommendation
from you at a later date," Williams wrote.

Thurmond responded diligently. He wrote essentially the same letter
the second week of July to the presidents of both schools and also to the
dean of a new medical school at the University of South Carolina:

A young black man, Mr. Ronald Williams, who is originally from South Carolina
but presently resides in California, is applying to be admitted to medical school for
the fall of 1976. For your reference, I am enclosing copies of his resume and college
transcript.

If you are currently accepting students from out of state, and as the federal government is encouraging the education of young blacks within the professions, I feel that Mr. Williams would be a most worthy candidate for admission. He is a very bright and deserving individual and I would appreciate your giving his application your most careful consideration.

With best wishes,

Strom Thurmond

He also wrote Ronald Williams on July 14 to inform him of the letters and to suggest that he write to California Senators John Tunney and Alan Cranston and also appeal to David Packard, a Californian serving as board chairman for the military program. A few days later, Thurmond got responses from the two South Carolina schools informing him they give preference to in-state applicants.

On October 9, Williams again wrote "Very Personal" on a letter to Thurmond, thanking him for his interest and telling him he would follow up on his suggestion to write letters to the Californians. "I am confident that with the assistance of a man of your stature I will be successful," Williams wrote. He enclosed a copy of his application to USUHS, "which I feel aptly summarizes my interests and abilities."

Anthony Curreri, the president of USUHS, sent a courteous, noncommittal response. Handwritten notes on the letter show that Thurmond persisted with a follow-up phone call to Curreri's private telephone line. He kept Ronald Williams fully informed of his efforts, at one point freeing the young man to share "personal information" with William McCord, president of the Medical University of South Carolina in Charleston.

Ronald Williams wrote back on October 9, 1975, again marking the letter "Very Personal." He thanked Thurmond for his interest in getting him into medical school, noting that he was confident "that with the assistance of a man of your stature" he would be successful. Williams said that he had followed Thurmond's advice, writing to the appropriate California senators, and had sent along "personal information" to President McCord at the Medical University of South Carolina.

Thurmond wrote two subsequent letters, addressing him as "Dear Ronald." The first one, dated February 3, 1976, mentioned "Your mother called the other day about helping you all I could. Apparently she did not know that I had already contacted Doctor Curreri." Thurmond added that the competition "is extremely stiff" there, with about thirty-six to be selected from several thousand applicants.

A final letter from Thurmond on July 15 enclosed "a copy of correspondence" from MUSC, presumably notifying him that Ronald had not been admitted.

In the end, Ronald Williams remembers with pride that he was accepted on his own to medical school at the University of Washington, but Thurmond did help him in getting a U.S. Navy scholarship that paid for books and tuition, and Williams later served on active duty as a medical officer. In Washington, D.C., for special training in nuclear medicine at the end of his second year in medical school, he called Thurmond's office and asked to see the senator and to pass on his mother's regards. The staff treated him "as if they knew me."

Thurmond told Williams that he had followed his academic progress. "He said if I ever needed anything to let him know. I never took advantage of the relationship." Williams would move into a career as an emergency room doctor in Morton, Washington.

Thurmond, he said in 2004, "wasn't a direct contributor to anything I did or for that matter, my mother did. We usually did everything on our own. The bottom line is that my mother was never preoccupied with him or with what her life would be like if she had a relationship with him. Just because you're related does not mean that you have to have a relationship with them or live with them or whatever. She did not dwell on it and that caused us not to dwell on it."

"She just kept moving forward. She went on and completed her master's degree, and she didn't pass any bitterness on to her children. She traveled a bit. She had fun with her friends and had a sense of independence."

In retrospect, he always thought it peculiar that the family had to keep Thurmond's secret. "It's ironic to have a relationship like that and I can't tell anybody about it."[14]

Essie's revelation in 2003 brought criticism from some quarters for her having protected him during his many years as a rabid segregationist and outspoken opponent of the civil rights movement. She strongly disagreed with the widely held view, especially among blacks outside the South, that she might have helped the cause of civil rights by "outing" Thurmond early in his career at the height of his segregationist period and his outspoken opposition to advancement of civil rights. She rarely expressed anything other than positive sentiments about her father, his emotional and financial support of her, and how much he helped people, but a month after coming forward about their relationship, she explained that in protecting him she was also protecting herself. To admit her parentage while in college would have revealed her illegitimate birth, and doing so once he developed his segregationist image in 1948, she said, would have been even more embarrassing. "I didn't want people to know he was my father because of his power and his positions on racial segregation, although that did change later. During that period, I didn't want people to know that," she explained. "I wasn't proud of him during that time."[15]

CHAPTER 21

Playing the Game

MORE THAN ANY POLITICIAN OF HIS TIME, Strom Thurmond mastered the art of constituent service and recognized it as the key to political longevity. His principles were simple. Anyone who wrote to him deserved a prompt, courteous response. Those who turned to his office for assistance navigating the clogged federal bureaucracy merited some sort of swift action. Thurmond understood in a way that lesser politicians did not that it was the "little people" who sent him to office—the tobacco farmer waiting for his subsidy check from an unresponsive Department of Agriculture; the war veteran trying to get better treatment at a Veterans Administration hospital; the schoolteacher confused about some new federal policy. Most of these people would never have the courage to relentlessly press a government agency for action, but they came to realize that "Strum" would help them. For Thurmond it was retail politics at its best, building a reservoir of goodwill from which votes flowed at election time.

Staffers in his office worked under rules that were strictly enforced. All requests for help got a response within twenty-four hours. If the individual assigned to a matter couldn't produce a result, the section chief handled it. If that didn't work, the matter went to the administrative assistant, the top staffer in a Senate office. If after all that, a South Carolinian insisted on talking to Thurmond about his or her problem, he returned the call, even if he had never met the person.

"He would say, 'Look, I know that might not sound important to you. That might not sound important to me. But to that person, especially if they take the time to write or call about it, that's the single most important issue in their life,'" recalled a former top aide. "He really didn't have gradations of importance. If he was working on the Fortas nomination, that was important, but getting Mrs. Smith in Duncan her Social Security check was important, too. An amazing thing."[1]

Letters flooded into Thurmond's office, where a staff of junior aides cranked out responses with the efficiency of a textile factory assembly line.

Anyone making the pilgrimage to Washington from the most obscure corners of South Carolina knew they could stop by the senator's office for a sincere welcome and if he was available, a hearty Thurmond handshake.

Once, after succeeding Alex McCullough, Harry Dent had confronted Thurmond about the gall of sending "C and C's" to strangers.

"There was a death that day in the paper of a little five-year-old boy outside Aiken whose father was baling hay, and the little boy got caught up in the hay baler," Dent says. "He got crushed to death. I saw the condolence come across the desk, and I said, 'Watch this.'"

Dent marched in and confronted Thurmond. He told him it was "terrible" to write a sympathy letter to people he didn't know, that it was transparently political. Dent added, "I'm just trying to keep you from hurting yourself." He tore up the letter, threw it into the trash can, and proudly walked out. He said the staff agreed with him. "I said, 'We took care of that. There'll be no more of it.'"

A few weeks later in Aiken, Dent and the local manager went out to breakfast. "There were two old guys that came walking in. And one of them turned to my companion and said, 'Ain't you Senator Thurmond's friend?' He said, 'I run Senator Thurmond's office down here. I want you to meet Mr. Dent. He's the man who runs everything in the Washington office.'

"The man said, 'Well, let me tell you something. My family will never forget Strom Thurmond as long as we live.' Tears welled up in his eyes. He said, 'A couple of weeks ago I was out there in my field and I was baling hay with my little boy. He got caught in that baler and smashed to death.'

"'You know, I got a letter from Senator Thurmond and you know, Mr. Dent, I figured he didn't write that letter. I figure you wrote that letter, but I'll tell you this, Mr. Dent. Me and my family and everyone I know will vote for him as long as we live.'"

Dent said, "It blew me away. I went back to Washington and told the staff. I said, 'The senator knows what he's doing.' I didn't try to give any more advice about bad politics. He was a master."[2]

Strom took many humble visitors to try the signature navy bean soup and corn bread in the impressive Senate dining room, where he offered compelling evidence that big-city life in Washington had not caused him to put on airs. At a 1980 lunch with a South Carolina reporter, he ate ravenously from a vegetable plate while the beautifully coiffed Nancy delicately picked at her salad. Nancy's parents sat silently at the table, while Thurmond told stories about his Senate years. Then, Thurmond asked Nancy to wrap up leftover corn bread in napkins and "take it home to the chillun." Nancy quietly obliged.

Thurmond inscribed the Senate menu for his guest, noting that the day happened to be his wedding anniversary. A few days later, a gracious "thank you" note from the senator's wife appeared in the reporter's mailbox.

In his office, the well-oiled Thurmond constituent machine rarely missed a beat. Always the perfectionist, Thurmond demanded good grammar and punctuation in letters written under his name. Occasionally, however, as with any task involving huge volume, there were minor gaffes.

Shortly after New Year's Day in 1966, Thurmond sent off a letter to his daughter, Essie, in Los Angeles thanking her for a Christmas card sent to his office. Addressed to "Mr. E. M. Williams," the letter read:

Dear Mr. Williams,

This acknowledges receipt of the nice Christmas card you and your family sent me, and I wish to thank you for your thoughtfulness.

I expect to be in Washington for some time now, except for weekend trips to South Carolina, and should be pleased for you to stop by my Senate office whenever you are in Washington.

I hope the New Year will bring you and your family good health and happiness, and with best wishes,

Sincerely,

Strom Thurmond

Thurmond's dutiful staff probably never realized the letter misidentified, as "Mr.," the woman who had been writing him sporadically since his arrival in Washington and who over the years showered him with wistful Father's Day cards and requests for personal assistance. It is also just as likely that the senator never saw the letter, since his sharp eye would likely have caught the error.

Once when Essie wrote, he responded urging her to mark her envelopes "very personal" so that his secretaries would know to bring it directly to his desk. Always, his replies were gracious yet carefully distant, suggesting nothing of their personal tie.

THROUGHOUT HIS CAREER, Thurmond had shown a knack for courting voters with simple favors—a skill handed down from his gregarious father. But his effectiveness at delivering federal action escalated dramatically with Nixon's election, when Thurmond's longtime adviser Harry Dent went to work in the Nixon White House, and he saw the opportunity to use Thurmond's leverage to make the senator South Carolina's "indispensable man in Washington."

The strategy offered a way to counter a growing perception of vulnerability back home. In 1970, Thurmond had pushed Republican Albert Watson for governor. After Watson's decisive defeat by Democrat John West, Thurmond had tried to secure him a seat on the U.S. Court of Military Appeals, but the effort failed after a Senate discussion of Watson's racial record, sending a further message that racial politics had become a losing hand.

Ironically, West's election as governor of South Carolina played into Dent's long-term strategy for Thurmond. West's staff included specialists who combed federal programs and wrote grant proposals for state and local projects in South Carolina. A mayor needing federal funds for a water project, for example, would first call the governor's office. West's staff would do the hard groundwork, assessing community needs, finding a federal program that fit, and sending the grant proposal to Washington.

But with his special entrée to Nixon's Republican administration, it would be Thurmond who guided the proposal through the funding agency. And of course, it would be Thurmond who publicly announced its approval. West was happy with the arrangement. A top federal official told him that South Carolina received more discretionary federal funds than any other state.[3]

Thurmond's newfound White House influence built upon his longstanding relationships with federal agencies. Dent was strongly impressed by this, beginning with his first days of work in the Nixon White House. "One of the first things I did was go to every agency and every department head. I sat down with them to say, 'We're going to need your cooperation.'" Dent made it clear the White House wanted to be informed and credited when appropriate.

When I walked into a Cabinet nominee's office, they would know I previously had been with Senator Thurmond. Every one of them said something to this effect, "Guess who was the first person to pick up the phone and call me when I got here, to say I had his support and ask if there was anything he could do to help? Strom Thurmond." I just heard that everywhere. The senator's got a lot of political sense, and what he did meant that he was going to get everything he needed from that Cabinet member or that agency for his constituents in his state.[4]

When South Carolina interests were at stake, Thurmond fought to win. As a Harvard undergraduate, Edgefield native Bettis Rainsford spent the summer of 1971 as an intern for Thurmond and vividly remembered his effort to get a shipload of South Carolina peaches unloaded in Germany. In those days, Thurmond interns worked as staff assistants and performed meaningful tasks while gaining insights into how government worked.*

Rainsford arrived as angry peach growers in South Carolina, fearing financial ruin, besieged Thurmond with complaints that a Defense Department inspector found their peaches deficient for use on military bases. The inspector ordered that they not be unloaded, and the threat of rotten peaches was imminent.

Thurmond told his secretary to get Secretary of Defense Melvin Laird on the phone, Rainsford recalled. The conversation did not go well. Laird stubbornly backed up the inspector, insisting that he had a job to do. Thurmond clearly didn't appreciate the response. "I've never seen him so agitated," Rainsford said. "He said, 'I'm going to send you a letter' and slammed the phone down."

A short while later, Thurmond called Rainsford into his office, handed the tall young man an envelope, and said, "Take this to the Pentagon and put this in Melvin Laird's hand. Don't give it to anyone else."

A staff driver and car carried Rainsford across the Potomac River to the Pentagon. He made his way to Laird's office, where the secretary's top aide thanked him and assured him that Laird would get it right away.

---

*Thurmond's internships later became patronage offered to children of supporters or those perceived to have political influence—with the interns mostly involved in Washington sight-seeing. In contrast, a senator such as Sam Nunn of Georgia offered four internships a quarter, with the University of Georgia making selections based on merit (Bass interview with Sam Nunn, May 1968).

"No, ma'am," Rainsford said. "Senator Thurmond said I have to deliver it directly to him."

The young aide placed the letter in Laird's hands and scurried back to the Capitol. "By the time I got back to the office," Rainsford said, "the inspector had decided they were good peaches."[5]

Lyndon Johnson's Great Society programs continued to operate after Richard Nixon became president, and federal funds from them poured into South Carolina. Although current observers tend to equate LBJ's Great Society with anti-poverty programs, its reach extended much further. Until undermined by the cost and stresses of the Vietnam War, the Great Society aimed to emulate the New Deal by providing federal funds for a broad range of state and local efforts. Many programs sought to stimulate economic development, and others addressed social needs ranging from education and job training to housing and health care. They involved water and sewer grants and highway funds that local communities could use to develop industrial sites.

The Office of Economic Opportunity was the most visible and contentious symbol of LBJ's war on poverty. Its most lasting legacy was the Head Start program. But the Great Society also included establishment of the National Endowment for the Arts, the National Endowment for the Humanities, and Medicare.

Many of these programs fit the vision that Thurmond had projected more than two decades earlier in his first year as governor, when he supported federal aid to education. The young liberal governor had recognized that the federal government could make a difference in a poor state like South Carolina. But more than twenty years later, with his changed ideology, Thurmond voted against them.

Once these programs were funded, however, he saw to it that South Carolina got its full share. With Nixon's IOU in his pocket, Thurmond could and did deliver, and he made sure everybody at home knew it.

Thurmond's abilities to deliver raised his stock in the African American community, an especially important fact as he faced reelection in 1972 against a new Democratic challenger, Harvard-educated State Senator Eugene "Nick" Zeigler. Zeigler had agreed to take on the challenge after top-tier Democrats—Governor West, Congressmen James Mann and W. J. Bryan Dorn, and former Governor Robert McNair—declined. But Zeigler was more than a sacrificial lamb. The Democrats held hopes that they could capitalize on the growing and almost solidly Democratic black vote and the strength of the new eighteen-year-old voters who, they believed, might view Thurmond as outdated.

Deep into the 1972 Senate campaign, editor W. W. Mims of the *Edgefield Advertiser* stripped the following headline in large type down the length of his newspaper's October 11 front page:

SEN. THURMOND IS UNPRINCIPLED
WITH COLORED OFFSPRING
WHILE PARADING AS A DEVOUT
SEGREGATIONIST

No story about "offspring" accompanied the headline. Mims's headline, which he displayed on a few paid television spots after announcing as a write-in candidate against Thurmond, suddenly brought this long-standing rumor to the attention of white South Carolinians. Except for a report by Jack Bass in the *Charlotte Observer*, the state's mainstream press ignored the story but made reference to a "scurrilous campaign." (Mims had taped interviews with Carrie Butler's former neighbors in the black community who understood that Thurmond was the father of her child.)

The Thurmond campaign quietly asserted that Democratic candidate Nick Zeigler, the erudite lawyer with a classics background, was involved. He wasn't, but at Thurmond's campaign headquarters, in an especially good example of Thurmond's ability to be sometimes pelted with lemons and turn them into lemonade, copies of the *Advertiser* were kept under a counter and displayed to supporters, especially matronly white women, with feigned outrage. His staff would ask, "Have you seen this?" One appalled woman from Anderson told Thurmond's campaign manager, William "Billy" Wilkins (three decades later the chief judge on the U.S. Fourth Circuit Court of Appeals), that he should load the trunk of her car with yard signs, brochures, and other campaign material. She told him, "I'll see that all of it gets distributed!"[6]

Authors writing about Thurmond have treated the subject gingerly, if at all. In her book, biographer Nadine Cohodas dismissed the story of the alleged black daughter as "a legend in the black community" that Thurmond had denied.[7] Robert Sherrill included a paragraph in *Gothic Politics in the Deep South* about "one of the most widespread political rumors I ever saw wrapped around a state: that Thurmond had paternal interest in a Negro girl." Sherrill added, "The odd part of it, to me, was that instead of crediting Thurmond with good faith for sending this legendary girl to college, many of the Negroes I talked with somehow seemed to hold it against him that he did not recognize her more authoritatively, although this would of course have been politically fatal."[8] Sherrill called the story "apparently without foundation" but later told a *Penthouse* gossip columnist that he believed it was true, but his publisher wouldn't allow him to write that.[9]

After Mims published his "Colored Offspring" headline, a farmer with a legal problem came into Edgefield to see his lawyer. Before they began discussing the matter at hand, the farmer mentioned that week's *Edgefield Advertiser.* He got agitated and denounced the headline as "the most scandalous thing" he'd ever seen. Then he added, "Of course, everyone knew Strom's people had trouble keeping help."[10]

James Felder, who preceded Tom Moss as state Voter Education Project director and won election in 1970 as one of South Carolina's first twentieth-century black legislators, explained the reaction at the time among African Americans to the rumors and the "announcement" of Thurmond and "the daughter." Felder said, "What black people resent is his messing around with one of our women and then going around knocking us."[11]

Durham Carter, a member of a group of black men and women who in the late 1940s had worked nights at the Wade Hampton Hotel, remembered, "We said, 'Damn, he sure got that right.'" While Thurmond was governor, this group remembered him frequently—often two or three times a week—checking into a room at the end of the day after leaving his office in the Statehouse across Gervais Street from the hotel.

Carter said, "My friends working the freight elevator were told by the night supervisor not to leave until the person visiting the governor came down. We couldn't leave until we brought down his black female guest. About a quarter of eleven, the freight elevator rang." Carter described the governor's visitor as "a light-complexioned, nice looking woman who appeared to be in her thirties."

He continued, "One of my friends got a job teaching in Edgefield County. He saw her there and knew she was the woman riding the freight elevator."[12]

Jerry Wilson, a café owner and politically active leader in Edgefield's black community, told at least three friends before his death that a car and driver was sent two or three times a week to pick up the woman and drive her to Columbia. Blacks in Edgefield who heard about the story believed the woman was Essie's mother, but Carrie Butler had been living in Pennsylvania since 1939 and had become critically ill. She received dialysis treatment and died in 1948 from kidney failure.

At a reception for Thurmond in Charleston in February 1972, feisty civil rights activist Victoria DeLee, her head wrapped in a colorful turban, drew more attention than anyone except the guest of honor. DeLee, of Dorchester County, had established credentials as an embattled but politically shrewd grass-roots leader. She had won 8,000 votes in a 1970 race for Congress as an independent candidate. DeLee had early viewed the state's white political leadership with distrust. She once hid a tape recorder under her kitchen table while she pressed a white legislator to promise to do more for the black community.

After trying other avenues, DeLee had turned to Thurmond for help securing a federal grant to establish a day-care center. She showed up at the reception to stand supportively at his side.

"I'm for the man who can get the job done, and Strom is getting the job done," she said.[13]

Slowly watching his hopes for higher office vanish, Zeigler dubbed Thurmond "Santa Claus in South Carolina and Scrooge in Washington." He had trouble raising enough campaign money to thwart the Republican power, spending $167,750 to Thurmond's $666,372.

In late October 1972, as the Senate campaign headed down the stretch, a handful of political reporters met Thurmond at 8:15 A.M. in downtown Columbia at Cogburn's Grill on Sumter Street, a few days after the well-publicized birth of Strom Jr. The senator had already visited a textile-mill shift and talked to a third-grade elementary school class.

At breakfast, he downed an eight-ounce glass of prune juice in one long gulp and then drained a glass of skim milk. With a knife and fork, he slashed three eggs over easy, the runny yolks yellowing the grits on a platter beside whole-wheat toast. He wolfed it all down as if on fast-forward, wiped his mouth with a paper napkin, and rose to shake hands with every patron and kitchen helper.

Soon after, at the state's largest shopping center, Strom shook hands nonstop, every third person or so congratulating him on his new baby boy. A young woman, obviously near the end of a pregnancy, teetered to maintain her balance and held the hand of a young daughter. "We're just trying to keep up with the Thurmonds," she declared admiringly.

An elderly male bystander nudged a reporter and said, "Ol' Strom. He's sump'n, ain't he?"

At an electronics plant in Lexington County later on, Thurmond's broad appeal was obvious. Plant workers thronged around to congratulate him on "that fine family." Two black female assembly line workers asked for his autograph, with one telling a reporter, "I think he's fantastic."

The next morning Thurmond flew to Anderson, the Upcountry town whose daily newspapers were unique in the state for consistently opposing him. Strom walked through the newsroom, shaking hands with anyone in sight. Uninvited, he strode into the editor's office to greet him.

Outside, he brushed aside his campaign manager's entreaty to return to the plane to be on time for his next appointment. "Let's go by the court-house," he said. Like a vacuum cleaner, he sucked it clean in minutes, shak-ing hands with everyone, whacking the stooped probate judge almost out of his chair with a strong slap on the back. "I remember when you used to room across the hall from me at Clemson," Thurmond told him.

In magistrate's court, a thin, sallow-complexioned mother stood with clasped hands and head down in front of the judge while her pubescent son squirmed in the witness chair as the defendant in a misdemeanor case. Without slowing down, Thurmond shook hands with the magistrate, the woman, the boy, and moved on. The startled woman turned to the magis-trate and said, "Din't know I was gon' get to shake Strong Thurmond's hand when I come here today."

After flying to Greenville and addressing a civic club, Thurmond made the half-hour drive by car to Spartanburg. By the time he arrived at Spar-tan Mills, one of the city's few unionized textile plants, it was dark. As the gate opened and workers streamed out at the end of a shift, Strom positioned himself in the middle, darting sideways back and forth like a crab, reaching out on either side to grab and shake almost every worker's hand.

At the bidding of the state's textile barons, Thurmond had moved ear-lier in the year to push President Nixon to fulfill a campaign pledge to limit textile imports from Japan and other countries in the Far East. Before Thurmond left Spartan Mills to continue a schedule that stretched until almost midnight, the president of the union local learned that he was on the premises. Because of his record on a broad range of issues supported by the AFL-CIO, the senator had a national image as a hated enemy of organized labor, and his Democratic opponent was the lawyer in South Carolina for the International Ladies Garment Workers Union. The union leader came over to let Thurmond know how he felt.

"Senator," he told him, "I want to thank you for what you've done in saving jobs for us on these textile imports. You've got our support."

Although he crushed Zeigler by winning 63 percent of the vote, Thurmond ran nine points behind Nixon in South Carolina. *Edgefield Advertiser* editor W. W. Mims got almost no votes as a write-in candidate.

Meanwhile, Nixon's attorney general John Mitchell wanted Thurmond loyalist Harry Dent to serve as President Nixon's national campaign manager for the 1972 campaign. Dent yearned for the job.

But White House chief of staff H. R. Haldeman vetoed the plan, saying that Dent was "too much of a Boy Scout." Dent, in fact, had been an Eagle Scout, and his straitlaced nature had already led to concerns among the band of Nixon's California operatives who were about to be ensnared in the biggest political corruption scandal in U.S. history. A break-in at the Democratic headquarters in the Watergate office complex—along with other well-orchestrated campaign "dirty tricks" and corrupt fundraising—helped ensure a Nixon victory in 1972 against Democratic Senator George McGovern, the darling of the party's left wing. Dent had refused several assignments in what became known as the Watergate scandal, but his peripheral involvement nonetheless tarnished his reputation.

Unlike most of his White House associates, Dent spent no time in jail. Watergate prosecutors got a misdemeanor guilty plea from Dent for shared responsibility in the failure to report a million-dollar campaign contribution for the 1970 off-year election. The incident involved a fundraiser depositing the money in an account about which Dent was not informed. U.S. district judge George Hart in Washington sentenced him to thirty days' probation and said from the bench, "It does appear to me that Mr. Dent was more of an innocent victim than the perpetrator."[14]

After the Nixon White House self-destructed, with the eventual impeachment and resignation of the president, Thurmond saw his own influence wane. With Nixon, he was a player, someone called in by the president to discuss policy. That never happened again.

At the Miami convention in 1968, Thurmond had promised Reagan he would support him next time. That "next time" came in 1976, after Nixon's resignation. Gerald Ford had assumed the presidency, and Dent had taken over Ford's Southern campaign. Reagan was challenging Ford for the Republican nomination.

Ten days before a crucial North Carolina primary, Dent and top Ford campaign aide Stuart Spencer met Strom and Nancy for dinner at the Joshua Tree in McLean, Virginia.

"Our suggestion was to have the senator call on Reagan to withdraw," Dent explained, "and if Reagan did not withdraw, then have the senator assist the Ford campaign in North Carolina."

Dent apparently believed the changed reality of Gerald Ford's presence in the White House as a Republican incumbent nullified Thurmond's pledge to Reagan at Miami Beach. He thought that Thurmond agreed that the party did not need a "fruitless bloodletting" among challengers, and that Ford, as White House occupant and with years of experience in Congress, would be the stronger candidate.

Before Dent left that evening, Thurmond asked him "to draw up the appropriate language for a statement by Thurmond to accomplish the end we sought," which to Dent indicated that he was considering backing away from supporting Reagan. But Dent soon learned once again the strength of his longtime boss's commitments. "Two days later," Dent later wrote, "the senator dropped the idea." Ford would go into North Carolina without Thurmond's support.

Reagan won over Ford in North Carolina with a 52–46 percent victory, energizing his campaign. Dent believed Thurmond's intervention on behalf of Ford would have made the difference.[15]

Thurmond remained quietly in the background at the hotly contested 1976 convention in Kansas City. Many believed that he wanted to support the sitting president, and Reagan had offended many of the most conservative Southern delegates by announcing before the convention that one of the more liberal Republican senators, Richard Schweicker of Pennsylvania, would be his running mate to balance the ticket. In the close contest in which Ford narrowly won the nomination, Thurmond quietly voted for Reagan.

Ford lost in November, with Democrat Jimmy Carter employing a shrewd Southern strategy and carrying all of the eleven former states of the Confederacy, except Virginia.

In presidential politics, Thurmond's political judgment appeared to be slipping.

In 1980, with Reagan again in the race, Thurmond instead gave his early support to former Texas Governor John Connally. Like Thurmond, Connally was a former Democrat who had switched parties. He had served in Nixon's Cabinet, but by 1980 had a sullied reputation after an acquittal in a bribery trial.

Thurmond backed Connally in the South Carolina primary, but Reagan overwhelmed the Texan, 79,549 to 43,113. Reagan's surprising victory had been orchestrated by former Thurmond campaign aide Lee Atwater, whose political savvy led to his appointment to the political operations shop of the Reagan White House. Although Atwater had worked both as a political consultant and an informal adviser for Thurmond, he never served on the senator's staff. While working for Reagan and later directing a brutally effective presidential campaign in 1988 for George Herbert Walker Bush against Massachusetts Governor Michael Dukakis, Atwater became nationally recognized as a shrewd political operative. Once asked whether he ever saw himself becoming a candidate, Atwater responded, "Oh no, not me. I don't want to go home and find my children crying when they come back from school."[16]

After the 1980 South Carolina primary, Thurmond gave wholehearted support to Reagan. "He and I rode around South Carolina for a week in a camper, visiting thirty-seven communities, and he was out campaigning hard. He gave it everything he could," said Congressman Carroll Campbell, Reagan's state campaign chairman and a future two-term governor, who cut his political teeth as a Thurmond aide.[17]

In 1988, Thurmond protégés Atwater and Campbell gave their support to Vice President George Bush, and Atwater—by that time, arguably the wisest and most cutthroat political operative in the nation—served as Bush's national campaign manager. Thurmond sided in the South Carolina presidential primary with his Senate ally, Robert Dole, the Kansas Republican whose wife was a close friend of Nancy Thurmond. Dole was wiped out by more than two to one, 94,738 to 40,265.

Although Atwater felt betrayed (he confided to an associate, "Strom Thurmond screwed me"), he continued to help Thurmond after the election. Named Republican national chairman by Bush, Atwater died in 1991 of brain cancer after expressing remorse over his campaign tactics. Without his top strategist, Bush lost reelection in 1992 to Bill Clinton.

Thurmond joined Governor Campbell's forces in the 1996 presidential primary for Dole, who got an important win in South Carolina in his race for the Republican nomination. Dole lost the general election.

DESPITE HIS MIXED RECORD on presidential politics, Thurmond over the years missed no opportunity to rebuild his South Carolina political base. In the early 1970s, with two vacant federal district judgeships in South Carolina, he offended state Republican leaders and puzzled South Carolina political analysts by naming a Democrat, Sol Blatt Jr., to one of them instead of longtime Republican activist Welch Morrisette. The other judgeship went to Robert Chapman, a former state GOP chairman with impeccable legal and family credentials and personal lawyer to Roger Milliken.

Judge Charles Simons, Thurmond's friend and former law partner, suggested the Blatt appointment.[18] Simons respected the younger Blatt's legal ability and correctly perceived that it would win Thurmond the undying gratitude and loyalty of Solomon Blatt Sr., his old enemy. Blatt's word meant the difference of several thousand votes in Barnwell County, and he influenced other small-county Democratic legislators whose local machines could translate into Thurmond votes.*

Strom seemed to get genuine pleasure from helping others and satisfaction in showing that he could help. It all bundled together with his role as politician—someone who knew how to deal with people, who liked to deal with people, and who helped people and related to them positively. In that sense, Thurmond was "incomparable," says Don Fowler, a political scientist by training who, as a state and national Democratic Party leader,

---

*Jack Bass, who wrote the foreword to a biography of Solomon Blatt Sr., ran for Congress as a Democrat in 1978. He got Blatt's support in the Democratic primary, handily winning Barnwell County. Co-author of *The Orangeburg Massacre*, the definitive account of the 1968 shooting at South Carolina State College, Bass expected solid black support against Republican incumbent Floyd Spence. He got that support everywhere except Barnwell County, where roughly one-fourth of the black vote went to Spence. A black undertaker in Williston, totally loyal to Blatt, had built a disciplined political organization. Blatt later

spent decades observing him in South Carolina, as well as many years lining up opposition at election time.

After Fowler became commanding officer of the 360th Civil Affairs Unit as an Army Reserve colonel, Thurmond in 1981 attended the unit's thirtieth anniversary of its founding. Thurmond had organized the 360th after completing his term as governor.

It was summer, and the seventy-eight-year-old senator—by then a retired major general in the Army Reserve—stood on the hot asphalt in Columbia and spoke for almost twenty minutes, denouncing the Communist menace as the troops sweltered. Afterward, he met Colonel Fowler's son, Donnie, and said, "My, my what a fine young man. If you ever want to be my page in Washington, let me know and I'll make sure it happens."

Fritz Hollings never made such an offer, and Thurmond called Fowler back a few years later, renewing the offer. As a high school senior, Donnie Fowler went up and became a Senate page for Thurmond in January 1985.[19]

The senior Fowler by then operated his own public relations and lobbying firm, and Thurmond was always happy to be helpful. He also had only token opposition from political unknowns in 1984 and 1990, winning reelection handily at the ages of eighty-one and eighty-seven.

Neill Macaulay, a Columbia dentist's son and adventurous graduate of The Citadel, first met Thurmond in 1956 while hitchhiking home from Central America. Thurmond, driving his Cadillac, thought the hitchhiker had "an honest face." He picked him up on Highway 78 west of Augusta, Georgia, and then stopped at his brother's house in North Augusta for Cokes and cookies before dropping Macaulay off on the highway to Columbia. Macaulay found Thurmond "sincere and gracious, and although I disagreed with him on almost every question of the day, I couldn't help liking him."

(*continued*) explained to Bass that his most important goal was the reelection of Strom Thurmond. Because Blatt lacked confidence that the black voters he controlled were sophisticated enough to effectively split their ballots by voting for a Republican for the Senate and a Democrat for the House, he passed the word they should vote for both Republican candidates. For Bass, the only difference was losing with 43 percent of the vote instead of 44 percent.

Four years later, Thurmond interceded when the State Department threatened to take away Macaulay's American citizenship. He had moved to Cuba and fought in the early days with Fidel Castro. The issue was whether he had done so voluntarily after January 1, 1959, in violation of American policy. Macaulay, already disenchanted with Castro, had submitted his resignation on January 1 to comply with the American edict, but the embassy in Havana charged otherwise.

Travis Medlock, a young lawyer who later became South Carolina's attorney general, represented Macaulay and called on Thurmond for help. Thurmond set up and attended a meeting in his office with Medlock and two State Department attorneys, saying only that he once picked up Macaulay as a hitchhiker and thought him a "nice fellow." After Medlock presented the evidence, the State Department allowed Macaulay to retain his citizenship.[20]

Early in the evening of October 30, 1980, a few days before the presidential election, a descendant of one of Charleston's old Huguenot families called Thurmond in Washington. He explained that an extremely close friend had been long-line fishing for sailfish with three companions beyond the Gulf Stream, about seventy-five miles out in the Atlantic. A large storm had caught them, radio contact was lost, and the Coast Guard had called off an aerial search after several days and refused to continue on grounds that little hope of survival remained.

Thurmond was aware of the story from press accounts. He said he would do something. Minutes later, he got in his car and drove to the home of the commandant of the Coast Guard. Before long, a Coast Guard officer in Miami called the family to say a search plane would be launched the next day. It turned out the sailing vessel had been cut in two by a freighter. The four men died, but the boat remains were recovered, and the tearful families at least felt peace in knowing they had exhausted every possibility of saving the young men.[21]

As the full effect of the civil rights revolution transformed the American South into a far more open society, Lonnie Hamilton of Charleston found himself in need of a favor from Strom Thurmond. Years earlier, Hamilton had driven with Thurmond's secret daughter, Essie, to Columbia to get gas money from her father. A trumpet player as a child for the touring jazz band of the Jenkins Orphanage, Lonnie couldn't study music as an undergraduate at South Carolina State College in the late 1940s because the subject was not taught then at the all-black institution.

He majored instead in industrial arts, and one of his jobs was working with a team in a tailoring class to make a two-piece suit for Governor Strom Thurmond—a traditional goodwill gesture to each new governor. Correspondence exists showing that Thurmond sent the suit back for alterations. Historian William Hine at SC State said Thurmond was not unique among governors in getting the alterations, but he was the only one who offered to pay for them.[22]

Hamilton's next contact with Thurmond came four decades later, in 1987. By then, in his second term as chairman of Charleston County Council, Hamilton needed approval by the navy for a solid-waste incinerator for the county. The contract agreement was stalled on the secretary of the navy's desk.

Someone told Hamilton, "Lonnie, why don't you talk to Strom Thurmond about it?" Hamilton remembered, "I had the county administrator call his office, and I spoke to Senator Thurmond." When Hamilton said he wanted to come to Washington about the matter, Thurmond said he would be in Charleston that Friday and to meet him at a Marriott hotel near the Charleston Naval Station. Hamilton walked in with the county's public works manager and attorney, explained the problem, and asked Thurmond if he could help.

Hamilton remembered, "He said, 'Get me the secretary of the navy on the telephone.' I didn't know how to get the secretary of the navy on the telephone. I said, 'Senator, you're going back to Washington. It can wait until Monday.' He called me back on Tuesday and said, 'It's signed.'"

Charlton deSaussure Jr., the young bond attorney handling the project's financing and scion of an old aristocratic Charleston family, said, "Mr. Hamilton, that's some kind of power."[23]

Thurmond had a special talent for winning loyalty. After Charles Wickenberg retired as executive editor of *The State*, his grandson Ben Cobb decided, for a third-grade assignment, to report on a biography of Senator John Glenn, the former astronaut. The odyssey that followed included a trip to Washington to meet with Glenn, who unexpectedly had to return to Ohio. Strom Thurmond stepped in, found out who the youngster was, and escorted him to meet Utah Senator Jake Garn, who had flown aboard a space shuttle. Ben then had his picture taken with Thurmond. In his thank-you note, Ben on his own initiative invited Thurmond to visit his school. He came in the fall of 1992, speaking to Ben's class and then to all the students.

After that, Ben Cobb was never afraid of meeting anyone. Thurmond told Ben's father, "For thirty years, I've been trying to get Wick to put up a picture of me in his office, and now he will."[24]

Thurmond didn't always get the desired results. A politically active South Carolina lawyer got Thurmond to accompany him in 1980 to meet with the director of the Environmental Protection Agency to consider a request to waive a regulation for a steel mill in Georgetown. Thurmond brought along a package of shelled South Carolina pecan halves as a token gift. The EPA official listened to a presentation of projected economic benefits for the community but refused to grant the waiver.

"We've got a new administration coming in," Thurmond told him bluntly, "and we'll replace you." With that, the senator picked up the pecans and left.[25]

STROM KNEW HOW TO APPEAR IN PUBLIC and how to conserve his time. Former Congressman Butler Derrick's home office in Aiken was located next door to Thurmond's. They had agreed to ride over together to Barn-well, roughly a half hour away, for a 10 A.M. ceremonial reception, with Thurmond furnishing the car and driver. As the hour approached, Derrick went to the senator's office to say it was almost time for the event itself to start. "If you don't get there late and leave early," Thurmond told him, "they think you don't have anything else to do."[26]

A notorious "backseat" driver, Strom on another occasion was riding from Columbia to Charleston, with a young male intern driver. "Faster," Thurmond would insist, and the cautious young man stepped a bit more firmly on the accelerator as he headed east on I-26.

Finally, after several repeats of the exchange, followed by a siren and revolving blue light from the rear, the driver pulled over. As a highway patrolman stepped from his car and walked toward them, Strom opened his door, stepped out, and glanced at his watch as he raised his arm to point at his driver. Before the officer could speak, an agitated voice barked at him, "He's driving too slow. I'm Strom Thurmond and I need you to get me to Charleston. Now!"

The startled lawman called headquarters in Columbia, motioned for Thurmond to climb in, and sped away.

However, on some matters, Strom did display a thin skin. Thurmond had been upset when, on the weekend his engagement to Nancy was announced, someone on the news desk at *The State* scurried to find a photo and ran on the front page a shot of Nancy in a bathing suit at a beauty pageant. Thurmond called publisher Ambrose Hampton, who called the general manager, who called executive editor Charles Wickenberg—and appropriate apologies were made. (Strom himself later came in to the newsroom, demanded to see all photographs of Nancy from the newspaper's files, obtained them from a young editor on duty, and removed all depicting her in a swimsuit.[27]) Thurmond said years later the news editor should have been "horsewhipped."[28]

Thurmond earlier had believed there was a conspiracy in *The State* newsroom because Lee Bandy was not writing stories on each of the senator's press releases. This time Thurmond traveled to Columbia and showed up at publisher Hampton's weekend lake cottage to complain. Strom brought copies of all his press releases and of Bandy's stories to prove his point.

Hampton turned the material over to Wickenberg, who had known Strom for a long time and was furious that Thurmond had not come to him with his concern. Wickenberg flew to Washington, met with Strom and Nancy and the senator's press secretary and bluntly explained, "Mr. Bandy doesn't work for you, Senator. He works for *The State*, and it's interested in news, not publicity." He made it clear that if the handouts were printed, they would be rewritten as news "in some not-so-self-serving form." Thurmond then understood.

"He wanted credit for every nickel the federal government turned over to South Carolina," Wickenberg said. "I was steamed when I got there, but I cooled off. Nobody raised their voices."[29]

THE ONE CASE of Thurmond providing "help" that proved genuinely embarrassing involved seventy-seven-year-old twin sisters from Barnwell County who called in 1971 to complain that Edgar Brown, the local political kingpin, was trying to take their land. The sisters never understood that Brown's office was routinely handling a legal matter for the state.

South Carolina law then required that any recipient of public welfare owning real estate had to give the state a lien on the property. The state took legal action after the person's death to recover the amount of aid received. The objective was to discourage poor people from seeking public assistance if they owned land they wanted to leave to heirs.

In this case, the sisters had inherited from an aunt 160 acres with a small house in which they lived. The aunt had received $4,955.72 in old-age assistance from the state—80 percent of it federal funds. The acreage included a family cemetery and had been owned by the family for generations.

Brown's office got involved by chance. The state attorney general's office rotated such cases in Barnwell County between the law offices of Brown and House Speaker Solomon Blatt. It was Brown's turn this time, and a young lawyer from his office, Thomas Boulware, went to see the two women and explain the situation. He pointed out there were twenty acres of virgin timber on the property, and the trees, if cut and sold for lumber, were worth enough to pay off the lien. He offered other suggestions, but the women were suspicious and believed that somehow, Edgar Brown was attempting to take their land. They valued the trees and did not want them cut. They explained their predicament to a relative, who suggested they contact Thurmond for help.

Strom was more than willing to assist them. Nancy, too. One of the sisters later wrote a cousin in Florida, "A very prominent person will own our famous place some day—U.S. Sen. Strom Thurmond paid the debts in full and gave us the privileges we asked for—what a friend."

The women, clad in ragged clothing, told Jack Bass and a fellow reporter that they had willed the property to Strom and Nancy Thurmond. But the reporters had a copy of courthouse records showing that, with payment of the lien, title had passed to Nancy Thurmond, and the two sisters retained a life estate. In other words, they could continue living in the house until they died. Thurmond's lawyer included a provision that the women could not cut or sell any timber. They insisted to the reporters, however, that they still owned the land, that they paid the taxes.

The women lived off the highway from Blackville to Barnwell, and the reporters drove to the county courthouse to check the tax records. Those records also listed Nancy Thurmond's name as owner after the deed was recorded. Her name was typed on the tax books, but then scratched through with a pen and the names of the two sisters handwritten in above it.

When asked about it by the reporters, the county treasurer explained that the women had sent him a "right nasty note" about not getting the tax notice and told him they also called the senator about it. The treasurer said someone in Thurmond's office returned the tax notice with directions "that it should be sent to the ladies." The taxes amounted to $78.30. The ladies paid them even though Nancy held title to the property.

Thurmond said he had not taken advantage of the women, that he offered to help them get a loan, but they refused. He paid the cost of installing running water and indoor plumbing in the house. The Thurmonds' purchase price amounted to $4,955.72, slightly more than $30 an acre. He acknowledged that no independent appraisal was made of the value of the property. Boulware estimated that comparable land in Barnwell County then was selling for $225 to $250 an acre.[30]

A cousin of the sisters, a large-scale peach farmer in Edgefield County and a contemporary of Thurmond's, told the reporters, "Ol' Strom's a rascal."

Soon after a story about the transaction was published in the *Charlotte Observer*, the South Carolina legislature quietly repealed the lien law. Thurmond announced publicly an offer to sell the property back to the two sisters, for what Nancy paid. The sisters, however, had no money.

Less than a year later, after one sister died, the timber was cut under a contract between Nancy Thurmond and the surviving sister, who received a payment of $2,000, divided into $1,000 for herself and $1,000 to be applied to debts of the deceased sister's estate.[31] There is no further public record related to the timber sale.

When Bass and his colleague met with Thurmond to ask him about the land purchase from the two sisters, he responded angrily about their "making something out of that" when he had an election coming up the next year. Thurmond told them he did not have any money, but that Nancy had some that she had saved from her year as Miss South Carolina.* He was already unhappy with articles Bass was writing about his changing image and outreach to black voters, a politically sensitive issue, and he called Bass "a skunk." But in keeping with Thurmond's philosophy of keeping no ene-

---

*Thurmond had received national attention in 1969 when *Life* magazine disclosed that he and Charles Simons had received higher payments than neighboring landowners for acreage condemned for highway I-20 near Aiken, but they were accused of no illegality. Thurmond had also purchased two lots across the Congaree River from Columbia

mies, he wrote Bass a friendly "Dear Jack" letter a week or so later that accompanied an official book of testimonials and tributes to "our good friend Mendel Rivers," the Charleston congressman who had died earlier that year.

As SOUTH CAROLINA'S FIRST BLACK CONGRESSMAN since 1897, James E. "Jim" Clyburn went to Washington after his election in 1992 with a priority goal. He intended to name a new federal courthouse in Columbia for Judge Matthew J. Perry, the state's first African American federal jurist. Clyburn got a seat on the Public Works and Transportation Committee, with an assignment to the Public Buildings and Grounds Subcommittee.

Clyburn introduced his bill. "It didn't cross my mind that anybody would object to this," Clyburn said. "Everybody liked Matthew Perry." He soon found himself in a clash with Thurmond.

The existing federal courthouse in Columbia was attached to the Strom Thurmond Federal Building, and someone told Clyburn, "The old man is upset." He found out that Thurmond was blocking the bill to name the new courthouse for Perry.

Clyburn then heard objections raised about naming the building for Perry while he was still on the bench, that it could cause a problem if any kind of scandal arose. "We just named the federal building in Aiken for Judge Charles Simons, Thurmond's former law partner," Clyburn said. "Nobody said a word about that. I was fit to be tied."

---

adjacent to a site that the South Carolina Highway Department later announced as the location for a new bridge across the river. Thurmond later sold the land to the Highway Department for what he paid, plus the prevailing rate of interest for the period he owned it. Four days after publication of the *Life* story, Thurmond purchased 1,668 acres in York County about sixteen miles from a proposed $60-million nuclear fuel reprocessing plant but immediately transferred the deed to the Strom Thurmond Foundation. (By 1992, a year in which Thurmond gave $398,000 in campaign funds to the foundation for scholarships, one of its officials reported it had provided 3,709 scholarships during thirty years of existence.) In 1989, Thurmond purchased thirty-nine acres near Columbia from South Carolina Electric & Gas Co. (SCANA) for $23,300 ($599 an acre) but sold it back later in the year to avoid the appearance of a conflict of interest after several real estate developers said the land was worth more than $100,000 and after an aide reminded the senator of a meeting he attended with federal highway officials and power company representatives to discuss a nearby proposed interstate highway interchange (*Life*, 1969; *The State*, undated clippings).

He resolved the matter when John Napier, a Republican and Thurmond loyalist who had once represented Clyburn's Sixth District, came by one day to ask for help on a matter. Before leaving, Napier asked if there was anything he could do for Clyburn.

Clyburn said yes, then issued a not-so-subtle threat. Based on his research, he explained that the current Strom Thurmond Federal Building was named by administrative edict of the Governmental Services Administration (GSA). Bills twice introduced in the House to name the building for Thurmond by statute had failed.

Clyburn told Napier that anything done by administrative edict can be undone by statute. Unless Thurmond removed his objection, Clyburn said he planned to introduce a bill to rename the current Strom Thurmond Federal Building for Perry.

Clyburn told Napier, "'It may not pass the Senate, but it will pass in the House. If the Senator can stand that embarrassment, it's all right with me.' He said, 'Oh, you wouldn't do that.' I said, 'Yes I would. Just watch me.'"

Clyburn asked Napier to pass that information to Thurmond and get a response over the weekend because Clyburn planned to introduce his bill on Monday. Clyburn got a call from Napier on Saturday, saying that Thurmond would remove his objection, provided the new courthouse was going to be a freestanding building.

"It always was a freestanding building," Clyburn said. "Anyway, that's how we got the building named." Construction on the Matthew J. Perry Federal Courthouse began in 1998. Clyburn was dedication speaker at the formal opening of the facility in spring 2004.

In fighting the battle to name the courthouse, Clyburn's research found twenty-three different entities in South Carolina named for Strom Thurmond. The official "Tributes" to Thurmond printed by the U.S. Government Printing Office lists these: Thurmond Hall at Winthrop College (1939); Strom Thurmond High School, Edgefield County (1961); Strom Thurmond Student Center, Charleston Southern University (1972); Strom Thurmond Federal Building, Columbia (1975); Strom Thurmond Center for Excellence in Government and Public Service at Clemson University (1981); Strom Thurmond Chairs and Scholarships (1981); Strom Thurmond Auditorium at University of South Carolina School of Law (1982); life-size statue erected on Edgefield town square by people of Edgefield County (1984); streets in several South Carolina cities; Strom Thurmond

Lake, Dam, and Highway, Clarks Hill (1987); Strom Thurmond Mall, Columbia (1988); has endowed fifty-two scholarships at forty-five colleges and universities, established the Strom Thurmond Foundation, which assists in educating 80 to 100 needy, worthy students annually; Strom Thurmond Soldier Service Center, Fort Jackson, Columbia (1991); Strom Thurmond Room, U.S. Capitol, 1991; Strom Thurmond Highway (Interstate 20 from the Georgia Line to Florence, South Carolina) (1992); Strom Thurmond Biomedical Research Center, Medical University of South Carolina (1993); Strom Thurmond National Guard Armory (1994). The list hadn't stopped growing, including the 1997 act of the legislature for a Strom Thurmond statue on the Statehouse grounds. The statue of a striding nine-foot Strom on a seven-foot pedestal—he personally approved all inscriptions—included his receiving the "Order of the Palmetto" awarded by governors (Jack Bass has one), but conspicuously missing is any reference to Thurmond's Dixiecrat presidential campaign.

After Clyburn did his research, he grew more determined about naming the courthouse for Judge Perry. "I don't think every damn building in the state has to be named for Strom Thurmond," Clyburn said. "I think the state has a real sickness about it."

Alone among South Carolina's congressmen, Clyburn demonstrated a willingness to challenge Thurmond. Thurmond had become the patron of South Carolina's six traditionally black colleges, but all six were located in the boundaries of the new black majority Sixth District after the 1990 census.

When a bill that provided funds for those institutions came up in the House, a colleague told Clyburn to leave it alone. Thurmond wanted to amend it in the Senate to increase funding for the South Carolina schools. "All six are in my district," Clyburn told him, "and you're telling me that I've got to wait for the great white father? Why don't you wait for your senator to do it? I said, 'Hell, I'm not going to do that. I'm going to amend this bill right here.' And I did, and we got it passed."

Clyburn continued, "I don't mind Strom Thurmond getting his just credit. But my staff works just as hard, and I think they deserve credit, too."[32]

A DECADE AFTER Strom Thurmond had called Jack Bass a "skunk" and followed with a friendly letter, Bass was developing a television course, *The*

American South Comes of Age, and he interviewed Thurmond in the president pro tem's Senate office. An aide asked if the senator could be helpful while Bass and his camera crew were in Washington. Bass, who had been repeatedly rebuffed in efforts to schedule an interview with U.S. trade ambassador William E. Brock, asked for assistance. Bass wanted to interview Brock, a former Tennessee senator and chairman of the Republican National Committee, about the party's "Southern strategy," which Brock viewed as a mistake. Thurmond made a telephone call.

The next morning, while a cameraman was attaching a microphone to Brock's lapel, he looked at Bass, smiled, and said, "You fellows know how to play the game."

CHAPTER 22

Mainstream Senator

As STROM THURMOND BEGAN TO SEEK maximum acceptance, he abandoned the harsh rhetoric that had generated controversy and made many hate him. Unlike George Wallace, Thurmond never admitted he was "wrong." But the code words "states' rights" began disappearing from his vocabulary. This new Thurmond reflected the diminishing sense of historic Southern grievance as the region turned its energies away from defending the social institutions that had stymied its economic growth and national political influence. Thurmond sought to become part of the consensus—at least the new Republican consensus of reducing the role of government (except when it meant announcing federal dollars for South Carolina). How history would judge him began to matter.

In the summer of 1973, a full year before Richard Nixon resigned as president because of the Watergate scandal, Thurmond declared at the Hampton County Watermelon Festival in Estill, "If the president and all those people working for him up there don't get their story straight and explain it to the American people, they're all through." Don Fowler remembered, "I almost dropped my teeth. And he was right. The most amazing of all of Strom's abilities is to read people and sense the public will. I think he has some sort of counter inside his soul, an intuition that is arithmetic. It's astounding."[1]

Thurmond in 1977 gave up his position as ranking minority member of the Senate Armed Services Committee to become ranking Republican on the Judiciary Committee. At the suggestion of other conservatives, he yielded on Armed Services to his good friend and fellow conservative Barry Goldwater and moved to block liberal Republican Senator Charles "Mac" Mathias of Maryland on Judiciary. If Republicans gained a Senate majority, it would mean Thurmond as chairman of Judiciary and Goldwater as chairman of Armed Services.

The next year, at age seventy-five, Thurmond met his most serious re-election challenge. He faced Charles D. "Pug" Ravenel, who in 1974 had

made one of the most spectacular political launches ever in South Carolina. Growing up in modest circumstances in Charleston, Ravenel had returned home at thirty-six with serious political ambitions and a financial
stake after a record as star quarterback at Harvard, White House Fellow,
and Wall Street investment banker.

He brought sizzle and fresh ideas to the 1974 Democratic primary for
governor, with good looks, youthful vigor, and a message of governmental
reform that he articulated with conviction. He took his message directly to
the voters with the most sophisticated TV campaign South Carolina had
seen. His campaign echoed the progressive themes of Thurmond's 1946
race for governor, taking on the political establishment.

But unlike Strom in 1946, Ravenel was not an experienced politician
whose father had served as mentor. Rather, he was like a beautiful cut of
wood not yet seasoned. He generated excitement in derailing two political
veterans, Lieutenant Governor Earle Morris and Congressman Williams
Jennings Bryan Dorn, to win the Democratic nomination. When Ravenel
referred to the overwhelmingly Democratic State Senate as a "den of
thieves," however, even its honest members took offense. Ravenel seemed
not to understand that he had impugned people's honor. The state's political establishment operated with its own unwritten rules and did not tolerate attacks on personal honor. He soon learned he was dealing with the pit
bulls of South Carolina politics. Ravenel found himself in a court fight
over whether as a candidate for governor he met the state constitution's
five-year residency requirement.

South Carolina remains unique in that the legislature continues to elect
judges. And, like Thurmond when he campaigned among colleagues forty
years earlier to become circuit judge, legislative service still provided the
usual path to a judgeship. The challenge to Ravenel came in a lawsuit filed
by Milton Dukes, a showman and part-time fundamentalist preacher who
cooked and sold pork barbecue for a living and once provided comic relief
as a candidate for governor. Funding for the lawsuit apparently came from
undetermined political opponents, with speculation centering on Dorn
supporters and Republicans.

The case came before state circuit judge Julius B. "Bubba" Ness, a former state senator and future state supreme court chief justice. He disqual-
ified Ravenel for failing to meet the residency requirement—a legally
vague issue that a person's intent helps determine, leaving a judge wide

room for discretion. Although Ravenel had sought and obtained an earlier ruling that seemed to clear that hurdle, Judge Ness ruled definitively. Ravenel appealed to the five white men on the state supreme court—former legislators all. They upheld Judge Ness, and the U.S. Supreme Court declined to overrule them.

The state Democratic Party's convention then reconvened and nominated Dorn in a squeaker over reform state Senator Dick Riley. Riley gave Dorn his full support. Although Dorn had developed a progressive record in Congress, he was linked politically and by style to the Democratic old guard that Ravenel had challenged. Facing this dilemma with his supporters, Ravenel said he would vote for Dorn but not endorse him, a move that further alienated the Democratic political establishment. In the confusion that followed, the Republican sacrificial lamb, Charleston oral surgeon and first-term State Senator James B. Edwards, got 52 percent of the vote to win election as governor.

Riley then became state campaign chairman in 1976 for Georgia Governor Jimmy Carter's presidential bid. For Riley's plans to run for governor in 1978, Ravenel presented a major obstacle that the White House helped remove.

The story is told in South Carolina that Pug Ravenel rode in from the Charleston airport in 1977 with Vice President Walter Mondale, who was making a ceremonial visit to the city. When Mondale suggested that he challenge Strom Thurmond in 1978, Ravenel said he planned to run again for governor, that he believed he had a lot to offer the people of the state. The story goes that Mondale then said, "But what about the people of the United States?" And Ravenel replied, "I never thought of it like that."

Ravenel did run against Thurmond, and Riley ran for governor—nosing out Dorn for second place in the first primary and then getting Dorn's support for a runoff primary victory against Lieutenant Governor Brantley Harvey Jr. Lee Atwater helped run Thurmond's campaign. A few days before the election, he confided that although polls indicated Thurmond's age made him vulnerable, most people didn't know he was seventy-five. "Pug tried to be coy by saying he wouldn't make age an issue," Atwater said, "but that didn't cut it."[2]

Strom moved his family to Columbia for the fall campaign. He looked vigorous on the campaign trail with his young children wearing T-shirts that read "Vote for my Daddy." Thurmond combated the age issue by projecting vim, vigor, vitality, and virility.

Strom, as usual, didn't debate his opponent. At one joint appearance with Ravenel, however, Thurmond asserted he would be embarrassed to ask people to vote for him for the U.S. Senate if he had never even been elected to a town council.

Ravenel's handling of his 1974 dilemma also worked against him. County courthouse Democrats—the sheriffs, clerks of court, and other local elected officials who influenced their friends and neighbors and who had been loyal to Bryan Dorn four years earlier—remembered Ravenel's failure to endorse Dorn. And they ridiculed Ravenel as a liberal New Yorker.

Riley got 60 percent of the gubernatorial vote against Republican Congressman Ed Young. But in the Senate race, Thurmond, who outspent Ravenel $2,013,000 to $1,134,000, got 56 percent of the vote.

Unlike Governor James Edwards, who developed political skills and personal relationships as a state senator after an unsuccessful race for Congress, Ravenel seemed unwilling to serve a political apprenticeship. After losing to Thurmond, he ran for Congress from the Charleston area and lost. Looking back a quarter century later, Ravenel vividly recalled one voter telling him, "Listen, Pug, I agree with you on the issues, but Strom really helped me out by getting my wife instant access to a hospital when she was really sick, and I can't forget that." Ravenel understood. "I completely sympathized with that voter's position. Our polling showed something like 78 percent of South Carolina voters had had a favor done for them directly or for a family member—something like getting a family member in the military home for a funeral. The quality and duration and constancy of his constituent service trumped any issues that may have weakened him. He was very, very politically astute. And he had Lee Atwater running a tremendously successful 'get out the vote' operation."

Ravenel also quickly learned the extent of Thurmond's fabled refusal to keep a political enemy. On Christmas after the 1978 election, Thurmond called Ravenel's campaign treasurer at home, saying, "Nancy and I were sitting beside the fire and wanted you to know we were thinking about you and your wife and wanted to wish you a merry Christmas." Although some recipients of such calls viewed them cynically, Ravenel said his treasurer was both astonished and touched.

Two years later, as associate secretary of commerce in the Carter administration, Ravenel visited Thurmond and told him of his readiness to help any South Carolinian who needed assistance from the Department of Commerce. Thurmond subsequently called on behalf of a Greenville company that was blocked from receiving compensation for work performed under contract with the Soviet Union because of sanctions Carter had imposed after the Soviet invasion of Afghanistan. Ravenel had it moved "from the bottom of the pile to the top of the pile and got it approved" after a review found the claim was entitled to an exemption.[3]

Ravenel later helped organize a federally insured savings and loan and received help from Thurmond in cutting through Washington's red tape.[4] His business ventures, however, developed serious financial difficulties, and his political dreams flamed out.

Back in Washington, Thurmond began his fifth term in office as ranking Republican on the Judiciary Committee as Chairman Ted Kennedy expanded its staff with young liberal lawyers after taking over in 1979 following the retirement of Senator James O. Eastland of Mississippi. As Thurmond's relationships with blacks and behavior toward them changed to conform to new political realities, so did his attitudes. During the Carter administration, when about forty blacks were nominated to the federal district and appellate courts, Thurmond voted for every single one. When Kennedy accused him in November 1979 of holding back approval of several liberal nominees in an attempt to speed approval of some conservative appointees, Thurmond warned that Kennedy had better not bring up Thurmond's position on black nominees. "I have leaned over backward to approve every one of the black judges," he told the Judiciary Committee."[5]

Thurmond's position and committee assignments would only improve, including an elevation to Judiciary chairman, as Ronald Reagan swept in a Republican Senate majority with his crushing defeat of Jimmy Carter in 1980. When Strom introduced Ronald Reagan at an overflow rally that year in the Clemson University field house, Reagan got a glimpse of the Thurmond mystique.

At the Reagan rally, retired head football coach Frank Howard first introduced Thurmond, then seventy-seven. A legend in the state for both his coaching record and his dry rustic humor, Howard paid tribute to the late Jean Crouch Thurmond and told of her connections to Clemson. Then he alluded to Strom's virility and spoke of his winning the heart of young Nancy Moore.

Howard then deadpanned, "And I'm proud to announce that this morning in Edgefield, a very important event took place—Strom's third wife was born." The audience howled, Thurmond beamed, and Reagan looked puzzled—then sensed it was politically safe to join in the laughter.[6]

Thurmond was in his glory. As both president pro tempore of the Senate and chairman of the Judiciary Committee, he proclaimed himself to reporter Marilyn Thompson, who was covering him at the time, as "the third most powerful man in the world."[7] Thurmond seemed to be basking in his newfound power. He slashed Judiciary's budget by more than $1 million and pared the staff from 207 to 134, dismissing many of the liberal staff members Kennedy had hired. The committee's respected chief counsel, Emory Sneeden, contended that an oversized staff had felt compelled to "justify its existence with needless hearings and legislation."[8] In an unusual move, Thurmond placed two conservative non-lawyer senators, Jeremiah Denton of Alabama and Charles Grassley of Iowa, on the committee, making Denton chairman of the new Security and Terrorism Subcommittee.

President pro tem of the Senate was a largely honorific position, but it did indeed put Thurmond third in the line of presidential succession, behind the vice president and Speaker of the House. Thurmond understood that the title and imposing office in the Capitol that went with it provided the power of prestige; he formally opened the Senate each day and made special key-chain souvenirs for visitors, decorating them with his name and title, "President Pro Tempore."

Still, Thurmond was not an insider in the Reagan White House. He got no advance notice when Reagan picked William Rehnquist as chief justice to succeed Warren Burger, but Thurmond happily presided over the confirmation process for Reagan's conservative jurists. As Judiciary Committee chairman, he guided Sandra Day O'Connor, the first woman nominated to the Supreme Court, like the father of the bride, shielding her from tough questioning and escorting her to receptions. On September 25, 1981, the Senate confirmed her unanimously.

HARRY DENT AND LEE ATWATER had handpicked a pair of bright, young, and self-confident staff assistants. University of South Carolina Law School honor graduate Dennis Shedd and newspaper reporter Mark Goodin became a team to rival in influence Dent and Buzhardt two decades earlier. With Thurmond's higher visibility, they replaced his gaudy plaid jackets with distinguished-looking dark suits. They moved him in the direction of moderation and sensitized him to the idea that addressing professional women at committee hearings as "pretty ladies" offended them. Although Thurmond had always supported the Equal Rights Amendment, he had difficulty understanding that professional women wanted to be treated the same as their male counterparts, whom he did not welcome to the committee as "handsome men."[9]

Shedd and Goodin grasped that South Carolina had been transformed in the half century since Thurmond first ran for political office. It was now part of the booming South Atlantic region, with economic growth spurred by progressive leadership from governors such as Hollings, Russell, McNair, West, and Riley, who improved public schools, raised technical skills, and enhanced state universities while actively courting higher-paying industries. Freed by the civil rights revolution, they included blacks in their new equation, resulting in an expanded workforce that created broader markets for goods and services.

Between 1965 and 1988, South Carolina's population grew by 40 percent, from 2.5 million to 3.5 million, compared with 27 percent for the United States as a whole. The newcomers included retirees and service workers at the coastal developments that followed the environmentally conscious lead of Hilton Head, as well as upwardly bound younger people who moved in to participate in the state's expanding economy. African Americans no longer felt a need to leave the state after high school in search of better jobs and more freedom. As part of the changing social mores, younger people remained single longer and women expected to work—many in white-collar jobs away from the traditional textile and apparel industries.[10]

Shedd and Goodin recognized that to attract new voters, Thurmond needed to demonstrate that he accepted these new realities. Despite the reaching out to blacks that Thurmond had been attempting in various ways for a decade, he still seemed not to understand that blacks often welcomed a large and interventionist federal government as their agent of social change. Although he continued to vote against programs and policies designed to assist black communities, his announcement of grants for them, his acceptance of the social change that flowed from the civil rights movement, and the general softening of his image meant he no longer aroused their determined opposition. He began attracting a growing trickle of black votes. Even Modjeska Simkins expressed an approving recognition of the new Strom.

Thurmond's defining moment during his six years as Judiciary Committee chairman came in the 1982 debate over extending the Voting Rights Act. Thurmond had said after Reagan's sweep that he wanted to abolish the act. He had bitterly opposed it in the past and still resented that Section Five, the preclearance section, applied only to states with a history of discrimination.

A 6–3 Supreme Court ruling in the spring of 1980 on a case from Mobile, Alabama, mobilized civil rights organizations across the country. The Supreme Court decided in the Mobile case that plaintiffs in Section Two cases, which outlawed discriminatory election systems nationally, must prove a discriminatory "purpose" rather than effect. Thurmond had reason to be pleased with the record of Richard Nixon's Supreme Court appointments. All four Nixon appointees—Warren Burger, Harry Blackmun, William Rehnquist, and Lewis Powell—voted with the majority in the Mobile case. To prove discriminatory intent would be almost impossible. An editorial in a Birmingham, Alabama, newspaper quipped that perhaps dead legislators could be subpoenaed to testify.

Nowhere did the Mobile decision hit more directly than Edgefield County. Black leadership there came from Thomas C. McCain, an Edgefield County resident for thirty years with a master's degree in math from the University of Georgia. When he paid his filing fee in 1974 to run for county council, the Democratic Party refused to put his name on the ballot. He filed a complaint with the Justice Department.

He and others had already filed a lawsuit protesting the "Rebels" nickname for Edgefield's Strom Thurmond High School athletic teams and the waving of the Confederate battle flag and playing of "Dixie" at school events. They also sought to rename the school. The case was resolved with a compromise to stop waving the flag and playing "Dixie," practices that almost all public high schools across South Carolina discontinued after integration. McCain filed other suits to end discrimination in selecting grand juries and to end segregation of prisoners on chain gangs.

Under Section Two of the Voting Rights Act, McCain in 1975 challenged the at-large system of electing county councils. He got help from the American Civil Liberties Union regional office in Atlanta. Finally, in April 1980, District Judge Robert Chapman issued a strongly worded opinion that found "racial discrimination in all areas of life, with bloc voting by whites on a scale that this court has never before witnessed." In striking down the at-large system and replacing it with single-member districts, Chapman said, "the law requires that black voters and candidates have a fair chance of being successful in elections."[11]

When the Mobile opinion came down weeks later, Chapman withdrew his order. Over the next year, Thurmond moderated his opposition, saying he could vote for a watered-down version of the Voting Rights Act if all provisions were applied nationally. It was an impractical solution. In practice, it would mean every election law change from every state, including those with no history of discrimination, would have to be reviewed by the Justice Department, overwhelming the enforcement mechanism.

On June 28, 1981, as a strong bill was working its way through the Democratic-controlled House, South Carolina native Jesse Jackson joined hundreds of black protesters at a rally in Edgefield, telling them, "We don't want to dominate, we want to participate." The crowd marched by the Strom Thurmond High School and past the historic law office where Thurmond had first met his secret black daughter, Essie Mae. In perfect harmony, the crowd sang "Ain't Gonna Let Strom Thurmond Turn Me 'Round" as it marched, gaining national publicity designed to hurt Thurmond's image.

Two days later, a group of South Carolina blacks met with Thurmond in Washington. They included Jackson, McCain, and state Representative James Felder. Thurmond asked McCain, "What church do you pastor?"

McCain answered, "This is Tom McCain, Senator."

Thurmond replied, "I thought you were in Ohio." McCain, who was completing a doctorate in educational administration at Ohio State University, smiled that Strom was keeping tabs on him.

Jackson pleaded with Thurmond to commit his support for the Voting Rights Act, but the group found Thurmond more interested in talking than listening, telling them how he got rid of the poll tax as governor and defending his record as someone who always supported any qualified person's right to vote.[12] Whatever Thurmond was thinking, he kept it to himself.

Civil rights groups mobilized an all-out effort both to extend and to strengthen the Voting Rights Act. They especially wanted to overcome the Supreme Court's ruling in the Mobile case. The Reagan administration indicated opposition to the bill but displayed little interest in shaping it.

By early 1982, Thurmond indicated a willingness to reconsider his position. He talked to Armstrong Williams and agreed to meet with a group of prominent black Republicans who supported the Voting Rights Act. Williams remembered, "Strom showed me all these letters from racists, using the 'N' word and everything. He said, 'I want you to convince me I should support it.'"

The chief lobbyist for the Voting Rights Act's extension was Armand Derfner, a top civil rights lawyer who had moved to his wife's hometown of Charleston. She was related to Judge J. Waties Waring. Another key draftsman for the bill was Laughlin McDonald, the ACLU's Southern regional director in Atlanta and a South Carolina native. He and Derfner had been involved in McCain's civil rights litigation in Edgefield County, with McDonald a central figure in challenging the county's at-large voting system.

Meanwhile, Thurmond's staff quietly advised him that the hard-liners writing the letters would be with him politically whatever he did, that the bill was going to pass anyway, that a vote for the bill would improve his image with moderate white ticket-splitters, and that his vote would help shape how history would judge him.

By the time McDonald appeared as a lead witness before Senator Orrin Hatch's Constitution subcommittee, Thurmond's public position remained unchanged. He had opened the hearing by asserting that his past opposition to the voting rights law had been based on the mechanics of the statute. That position, he emphasized, "must not be interpreted as opposition to the right to vote itself." As committee chairman and a subcommittee member, Thurmond led off the questioning of Laughlin McDonald. Knowledgeable observers, expecting a grilling, got a surprise:

"Mr. McDonald," Thurmond asked, "do you live in Atlanta?"

"Yes, I do, Senator."

"I know the McDonald family in South Carolina," Thurmond continued. "They originally came from Winnsboro. Some moved to Chester, some to Greenwood, some to Columbia. Heyward McDonald is a state senator down there now."

"Yes sir, he's my cousin," McDonald said.

"Who was your father?"

"Tom McDonald from Winnsboro."

"Tom is your father?"

"Yes sir."

Thurmond told him that Tom McDonald had been a good friend.

"I know he was, Senator."

"We've tried cases together. And I had the pleasure of appointing your mother to the state hospital board. She is a very lovely woman."

"And nothing has ever pleased her any more in her life, I might add, Senator, than that appointment. She speaks about it often to me."

"I just wondered if you were connected with the McDonalds there," Thurmond said, "because they are all very fine people and friends of mine."

"Well, I appreciate that, Senator Thurmond."

"I have no questions," Thurmond added. "Thank you." With that, Hatch turned on his microphone, commenting, "I knew Senator Thurmond was a legend in his own time, but I didn't realize he knew everyone in the South." The audience laughed, and laughed even louder when McDonald commented, "I think he just got my vote when I move back to South Carolina."

Tom McCain testified that Edgefield County's at-large election system and record of voting on racial lines provided a textbook example of why the Voting Rights Act was still needed and why the Supreme Court ruling in the Mobile case needed easing. It wasn't proportional representation he was seeking, McCain explained, but a plan that gives blacks "a chance of electing someone."[13]

While Thurmond was holding out for a weak bill, Republican Majority Leader Robert Dole got interested in passing something stronger. He seemed to have only one concern, asking if Rowan County, North Carolina, where Elizabeth Dole grew up, was among the forty of North Carolina's 100 counties that the act covered. The answer was no, and it was full speed ahead for Dole, who believed in fairness and the right to vote, had a vision of the Republicans still being the party of Lincoln, and was thinking about running for president.[14]

Dole and Kennedy worked out compromise language for Section Two, essentially incorporating the language the Supreme Court had used in an earlier case, *White v. Register*. It outlawed election systems that had a discriminatory result but provided specific criteria based on "the totality of the circumstances."

As the compromise neared final agreement, Dole asked Ralph Neas, the head of a Washington civil rights coalition, to meet with Thurmond and

two other reluctant Republicans. Thurmond mentioned that South Carolina's black mayors had not taken a position on the bill and that he planned
to meet with them in a few days. With that tip, Neas alerted Armand
Derfner. He spoke to several black leaders back home, including Mayor
Charles Ross of Lincolnville, moving away from its origins as an almost
all-black community near Charleston whose roots dated back to Reconstruction. The dozen or so mayors scheduled to meet with Strom almost
all represented hamlets with populations of less than 1,000.

When Thurmond met with them to make the case for his weakening
amendment, he faced a barrage of questions from fully briefed inquisitors.
Although Thurmond and three of the other seventeen Judiciary Committee members opposed the compromise, he agreed to forward it to the full
Senate.

There, Fritz Hollings took on North Carolina Republican John East, a
former college professor who grew up outside the South. East attacked the
bill for treating one state differently from another and claimed he'd never
seen a bill come before the Senate "so ill-conceived and so badly flawed."
Hollings said that East's remarks against the bill "completely disregard the
historical practice and experience of his backyard and my backyard over
the many years." He spoke passionately, telling East that it wasn't a case of
the law treating the states differently—the essential Thurmond argument.
"The states treated the people differently," Hollings asserted. "That is
where you cannot understand and see what I see."

He continued, "If this debate is going to continue on as though a
bunch of technical nuts got together in the Judiciary Committee and reported an ill-conceived and so badly flawed law, someone has to give the
hard, bitter experience of the past thirty years, and even years before that,
where the official policy, practices, conspiracies, societal habits, customs,
mores and what-have-you said, 'No, you're not going to come in the door.'"

Hollings cited the Edgefield case. He pointed out Judge Chapman's
finding that white bloc voting prevented black candidates from being considered on their merits. He called Chapman "a pedigree Republican, not a
white-flight Republican." To Hollings it was "not easy or a happy thing to
get up and tell of this particular history, but unless we can speak honestly
and realistically and objectively of what we have learned from our experiences, then we are not going to be able to vote intelligently on this particular matter."

South Carolina Governor Riley had written to the Judiciary Committee supporting the House bill. He pointed to South Carolina's progress, with fifteen blacks in the legislature and another fifty-eight in "significant county offices." Riley then asked, "Should we pat ourselves on the back for a job well done? I think not. That we have achieved great strides is without question; that we have met the task of eradicating the blight of discrimination from our election process is just not true."

The next day, Thurmond expressed resentment that Hollings had singled out Edgefield with no mention of "the positive and decent character of its citizens." Even if true, he said, the allegations no more indicted "all the people of Edgefield County" than a school discrimination case in Boston, Detroit, or Cleveland "is a comment on all the citizens who live in these cities." He proudly pointed out South Carolina's progress and criticized Hollings for focusing "almost entirely on negative aspects of our state and its citizens in the past. . . . The implication that we in South Carolina are dealing with the issue of voting rights in any way other than a proper manner is simply inaccurate and without foundation."[15]

At bottom, the Thurmond-Hollings debate reflected the same themes that would reverberate within the Supreme Court as it moved further to the right, with the conservatives arguing that any individual case of discrimination should be remedied but overlooking the history of discrimination against African Americans as a class. (This theme would come alive in the 1990s during debates over affirmative action, the role of judicial remedies, and public policies designed to overcome the effects of past discrimination.)

In the end, Thurmond expressed "concerns" about the bill but said, "I must take into account the common perception that a vote against the bill indicates opposition to the right to vote and, indeed, opposition to the group of citizens who are protected under the Voting Rights Act." When his turn came to vote on the legislation, Thurmond answered, "Aye."

By late summer of 1983, Thurmond had eliminated any serious opposition for his reelection in 1984. President Reagan came to South Carolina and helped raise $300,000 in one night. Thurmond got endorsements from the black mayors who had met with him to discuss extending the Voting Rights Act (and much more) and from progressive Democratic Mayor Joe Riley of Charleston (Thurmond had helped secure $14 million for Riley's revitalization of the city's business district), and fund-raising help from former Democratic Governor McNair. Richard Riley and Congressman Butler Derrick, potentially his major Democratic challengers, bowed out.

Among those voting for Thurmond that fall was Tom McCain, who told *Washington Post* reporter Bill Peterson he did so because of Thurmond's vote extending the Voting Rights Act. "When [Thurmond] changed his philosophy, I figured he deserved my thanks," McCain said.[16]

Although stories were beginning to appear suggesting that the eighty-one-year-old Thurmond's age had caught up with him, he got two-thirds of the vote, a pattern he essentially repeated in 1990. Each time he spent more than $1.5 million against political unknowns who spent less than $10,000.

He was still "taking exercise" every day, a routine of calisthenics that emphasized stretching, working with weights, and riding a stationary bicy-cle—and swimming once or twice a week. And he maintained his healthy diet. "I don't think it's a question of age," he said, "as it's a question of what kind of shape you're in."[17] But he was slowing down, and his atten-tion shifted gradually in his remaining years primarily to South Carolina issues and keeping the folks back home happy.

Back in Edgefield, blacks finally got single-member districts, elected a 3–2 majority on county council, and appointed Tom McCain as county ad-ministrator. One of his first goals was to get the county Department of Social Services out of the courthouse basement. Naturally enough, he went to Thurmond, who got a $100,000 grant for a new building from dis-cretionary funds in the Department of Health and Human Services.[18]

ON THE ARMED SERVICES COMMITTEE, Thurmond played a key role in the passage of the Department of Defense Reorganizations Act of 1986. Committee chairman Barry Goldwater and ranking Democrat Sam Nunn of Georgia faced determined opposition from the Joint Chiefs of Staff and the Department of Defense. The military services opposed a unified de-fense structure. The navy especially sought to retain an independent status.

The committee was split 10–9 in favor of the legislation, with Republi-cans opposing it 7–3 and Democrats supporting it 7–2. Among Republi-cans, only Thurmond and William Cohen of Maine, who would become secretary of defense under President Bill Clinton, supported Goldwater.

The Department of Defense expected Thurmond, given his conser-vatism and long history of support, to oppose reform and attempted to recruit him to their side. Although the Department of Defense was targeting Thurmond, Goldwater never doubted he would keep his commitment, but Nunn was concerned that he might waver. Nunn later said the battle within the committee during its first days "was as fierce as it gets." He called the rock-solid nature of Thurmond's support under enormous pressure absolutely critical. One scholar concluded, "After the first week, when Senator Thurmond's support did not waver and their majority held, it was clear that Goldwater and Nunn would be able to report some kind of bill out of committee."[19] Nunn said, "I had learned not to rely on every senator's commitment, but Strom Thurmond was solid."[20]

WHEN DEMOCRATS REGAINED CONTROL of the Senate in 1987, Thurmond gave up the Judiciary chairmanship to Democrat Joseph Biden of Delaware. Forty years younger than Thurmond and a man whose interest in politics was sparked in large part by the civil rights movement, Biden as ranking Democrat had forged a good relationship with Thurmond by promising never to do anything to undercut him. Thurmond reciprocated.

In a tribute to Thurmond upon his breaking the record on May 25, 1997, as the longest-serving senator, Biden said, "His word is his bond, and each of us—even the most partisan of political opponents—knows that through the heat of political debate, regardless of the intense pressure that may be upon him, Strom Thurmond can be trusted to keep that word; not when it's politically possible or expedient, but always."

The tributes paid by many senators that day seemed perfunctory, but Biden's was longer and more passionate. He further asserted that Thurmond's "political longevity lies . . . deep within Strom Thurmond himself. It lies in his strength of character, his absolute honesty and integrity, his strong sense of fairness, and his commitment to public service. None of those things are skills which you learn; they are qualities deep within you which, when people know you well, they can sense. That is the secret to Strom Thurmond's success."[21] Biden's tribute made a deep and lasting impression on Thurmond. Years later, the older senator would request that his junior colleague speak for him one last time.

WITH MUCH OF HIS FIERCENESS by now replaced by grandfatherly affability, those less knowledgeable about Thurmond began to question his innocence and his mental soundness.

At the 1986 confirmation hearings following Ronald Reagan's nomination of Justice Rehnquist for chief justice, Jeffrey Levi, the executive director of the National Gay and Lesbian Task Force, testified in opposition. He appeared at a late-night hearing along with representatives of Americans United for Separation of Church and State and the chairman of the National Abortion Rights Action League.

Under questioning from Biden, then ranking Democrat, Levi expressed special concern about Rehnquist's vote in *Bowers v. Hardwick*, a 5–4 decision that upheld Georgia's statute criminalizing any act of sodomy.

Thurmond asked about Levi's claim that 10 percent of American adults are predominantly homosexual, saying he was "shocked to hear that if that is true." Levi attributed the figure to the Kinsey Institute (other studies suggest a much lower number), and then the following colloquy took place:

THE CHAIRMAN: Does your organization advocate any kind of treatment for gays and lesbians to see if they can change them and make them normal like other people?

MR. LEVI: Well, Senator, we consider ourselves to be quite normal, thank you. We just happen to be different from other people. And the beauty of the American society is that ultimately we do accept all differences of behavior and viewpoint.

To answer the question more seriously, the predominant scientific viewpoint is that homosexuality is probably innate; if not innate, then formed very early in life. The responsible medical community no longer considers homosexuality to be an illness but rather something that is just a variation of standard behavior.

THE CHAIRMAN: You do not think gays and lesbians are subject to change? You do not think that they could change?

MR. LEVI: No more so, Senator, than heterosexuals.

THE CHAIRMAN: You do not think that they could be converted to be like other people in some way?

MR. LEVI: Well, we think we are like other people with one small exception. And, unfortunately, it is the rest of society that makes a big deal out of that exception.

THE CHAIRMAN: A small exception? That is a pretty big exception.

With that, other senators tried to suppress laughter, and Levi gamely replied, "Unfortunately, society makes it a big exception. We wish it would not, and that is why our organization exists."

The witnesses and a handful of supporters left, stunned at Thurmond's remarks, which seemed to ridicule a witness at a hearing. One of them told Levi, "You should have said, 'Thank you, Senator,' then go kiss him on the lips."[22]

Thurmond was then eighty-three, and a staffer later insisted that the senator was not baiting the witness, that like others of his generation, Strom knew little about homosexuality and that his questions were only an effort to learn more. It was reminiscent of what law clerks said about Eleventh Circuit Court of Appeals Judge Frank M. Johnson, who wrote the lower court opinion that the Supreme Court reversed in *Bowers v. Hardwick*. The law clerks detected a generational gap as he talked about "finding a cure" for homosexuality before ruling the Georgia sodomy statute unconstitutional.[23]

Examples of this unself-conscious curiosity abound. For example, Thurmond decided in 1983 to support the bill making Martin Luther King's birthday a national holiday after gauging audience reaction during a speech at Voorhees College, an Episcopal-related, historically black institution in Denmark, South Carolina. Tom Moss set up the appearance and accompanied Thurmond.

Thurmond initially opposed the bill because of the cost of adding another recognized national holiday. By the time he got to Voorhees, his doubts centered on whether Dr. King was the right black leader to honor. In his remarks, Thurmond mentioned George Washington Carver and Booker T. Washington—whom Strom as a child had heard speak in Edgefield. But cheers and applause filled the auditorium when he said the name Martin Luther King Jr. For Thurmond—fifteen years after King's death—it was a revelation. His knowledge of King had come primarily from FBI director J. Edgar Hoover and his notorious effort to discredit the civil rights leader. As he always had, Thurmond absorbed reality through his pores, and he told the Voorhees audience that he would support the King holiday. Back in Washington, he told his staff about mentioning King's name and the auditorium "going wild."[24]

On another occasion, a Mormon member of his staff explained to Thurmond the Mormon belief that God had written the Book of

Mormon and presented it as divine revelation to a tribe of North American Indians. Thurmond asked, "Could they speak Hebrew?" She accepted it as a serious question. It was: Thurmond associating God with the Hebrew Old Testament and asking how the tribe that received the Book of Mormon was able to read it. (When Morris Amitay directed the American-Israel Public Affairs Committee (AIPAC), the so-called Jewish lobby, Thurmond in conversation with him referred to Israelis as Israelites.[25])

Most experienced politicians develop either a forthrightness with the press that serves them well or a glibness that offers protection. But Thurmond's earnestness seemed to scare his staff into overprotecting him, especially around savvy national reporters. Because Thurmond was in fact generally well informed on issues he cared about, this overprotection did not serve him well.

For example, when the *Washington Post* assigned Robert G. "Bob" Kaiser in the late 1970s to cover the Senate, he set out immediately to meet and interview all 100 senators. It took almost a year to get to see Thurmond. Four aides sat in. Kaiser felt the aides were clearly there to get rid of the reporter for the *Washington Post* as quickly as possible. Thurmond was unresponsive, and to Kaiser, who went on to become managing editor, "he seemed out of it, even then."[26] The interview lasted about ten minutes.

But Nina Totenberg, Supreme Court correspondent for National Public Radio, got a far different impression of Thurmond in a 1981 interview. For a magazine profile as he was taking over as Senate Judiciary Committee chairman, she wrote, "A personally delightful, courtly Southern gentleman, Strom Thurmond is often misunderstood. People who don't know him often underrate his intelligence, his political canniness and his energy."[27]

As Strom headed into the twilight, he would face a personal challenge more devastating than any yet in his long life, and he would close his political career as he had lived it many years before—with a bit of controversy.

PART THREE
A Life Revealed

CHAPTER 23

"My Baby Is Dying"

On the evening of April 13, 1993, Democratic Lieutenant Governor Nick Theodore was reading the directions on some medication as his highway patrolman driver pulled out of the Eckerd's drugstore parking lot onto Harden Street in Columbia's busy Five Points area. With its restaurants and coffee shops, the spot is a place of heavy evening foot traffic near the University of South Carolina campus.

Theodore heard a dull thud. He looked toward the street and saw a car stop. A distraught woman driver got out, ran toward his car, and shouted through the window, "I didn't mean to hit her. She stepped in front of my car."

Theodore's driver, James Peppers, had looked directly at the accident, less than twenty feet away, as the speeding northbound car struck a young woman walking across the street. Her head smashed into the windshield and she then pinwheeled into the air, limbs flying, and crashed down again on her head. The northbound car had seemed to come from nowhere, Peppers later estimating its speed at forty-five miles per hour.

As Peppers called for help, Theodore jumped out of the car, dashed over to the unconscious young woman, removed his jacket, and placed it over her as protection against shock. She had been walking across the street from a boyfriend's apartment to buy a chess set at Eckerd's.

The driver of the northbound car, Corrinne Koenig, called her lawyer, Henry McMaster. He was chairman of the South Carolina Republican Party and a former U.S. attorney for the state, a patronage job that had been arranged by Strom Thurmond. McMaster lived only a few blocks away and interceded for his client with the police, who waited almost two hours before administering a blood alcohol test.

A wallet in the victim's purse identified her as Nancy Moore Thurmond, Strom and Nancy's oldest child. Theodore had gotten to know her as his favorite waitress at Al's Upstairs, a pasta restaurant across the Congaree River, and had attended her twenty-second birthday party a few weeks earlier. He knew Strom Thurmond was in Columbia because both men had attended a ceremonial event earlier in the day.

Within ten minutes, Theodore and his driver followed an ambulance that rushed the victim, still unconscious, to Richland Memorial Hospital. A few minutes later, Theodore located Senator Thurmond and told him there had been a serious accident, then called the senator's estranged wife in Aiken. The ninety-year-old Thurmond arrived quickly. "He had his faculties," said Theodore, who remained at the hospital until 2 A.M., after the distraught mother had arrived. Strom Jr., a twenty-year-old student at the University of South Carolina and close to his sister, learned of the accident soon after it happened and rushed to the hospital.[1]

Hours later, Thurmond called Chris Simpson, a former press aide then working in media relations for USC, and asked him to take charge. Simpson closed off the hospital floor, called in two of the senator's Columbia office secretaries to man phones, and set up press briefings. Upon learning the victim's identity, McMaster joined the Thurmonds at the hospital and withdrew from the case.

Early the next morning, Vice President Al Gore called Thurmond. Gore's own son had almost been killed a few years earlier when hit by a car after a Baltimore Orioles baseball game. Soon afterward, President Bill Clinton called and asked about Nancy Moore's condition. A grieving Strom Thurmond told him, "My baby is dying."[2]

She died within hours without regaining consciousness.

A beauty queen like her mother, Nancy Moore was only a month away from graduating with honors from the university. She had quit her waitress job two weeks earlier to prepare for the upcoming Miss South Carolina pageant, where she was to represent Aiken. She had been modeling for years and was an instructor for a local modeling agency. She was also sole proprietor of Designs by Nancy, a business specializing in designer jewelry. She intended to enroll in law school and pursue a career championing children's causes.

Tests showed Koenig, thirty-six, had a blood alcohol count of .16 almost two hours after the accident. Anything .10 or higher is enough in South Carolina for a driving under the influence conviction. Koenig, a native of Spokane, Washington, was a consultant for people seeking alcohol permits. She had previously worked for a private attorney who was former chairman of the state Alcoholic Beverage Control Commission.

For Thurmond, a teetotaler for much of his life, the accident was a grim prophecy come true. From his earliest days as a schoolteacher, he had railed against the danger of alcohol, preaching abstinence as a key to healthy living. In the Senate, he pushed for higher taxes on alcohol and stronger warning labels on bottles. In 1982, during a spirited floor debate in the Senate on his proposal to increase the tax on alcoholic beverages, he concluded, "drunk driving is responsible for the most common form of violent death in the nation."[3]

When young Nancy's body was brought to the funeral home in Aiken, Strom Thurmond joined her mother to view the battered face of their precious first child in her coffin. They had already agreed to donate her organs to help others, a way of honoring her before the burial in the Thurmond family plot in Edgefield.

At the funeral service at the First Baptist Church in Aiken, Strom Thurmond broke down crying. Many staffers had never seen him cry before. Now they saw Strom Jr. stretch his arm around his father to comfort him. Later, the three surviving children stood with their parents, shaking hands with hundreds who came to express condolences. To an intimate of the senator, the children displayed an adult understanding of their role in a public family. The event seemed to him—with much of the Senate and Gore, the Senate's presiding officer, there—almost like a dress rehearsal for Strom Thurmond's funeral.[4]

At Willowbrook Cemetery in Edgefield, a family friend had arranged for the purchase of adjoining land from a neighbor's backyard to add to the Thurmond family plot, making it the largest there. On either side of the daughter's grave sit pink marble benches. On one of them is inscribed:

Suffer the little children
to come unto me,
for of such is the kingdom of heaven.

Inscribed on the other is:

Precious Nancy Moore
Our love for you endureth forever
Mommy and Daddy
Nancy and Strom Thurmond

Both felt a special closeness to her. Nancy Thurmond later described how her namesake "called me sometimes ten or twelve times a day. We looked alike. We talked alike. She was my best friend in this world."[5] When Strom held the newborn Nancy in his arms in 1971, photographs showed him beaming, his usually gruff demeanor transformed. He was almost always like that in her presence.

The State published a letter to the editor memorializing the young woman. "Not Nancy, the daughter of a prominent U.S. senator," wrote one of her professors, Gene Stephens at the USC College of Criminal Justice. "Not Nancy, the dazzling beauty queen. But Nancy, the wonderful, caring, concerned human being."

> I knew Nancy as a student and as a friendly, easy-to-talk-with young lady whom I recommended for law school a few weeks ago.
>
> To my knowledge, Nancy never sought special consideration, as she well might, but instead used the opportunities prominence brought to serve others. While maintaining a high grade point average and enjoying the best of college life, she gave tirelessly of her time to the sick and needy—particularly children—and to countless community service projects.
>
> Whereas I feel that the privileged and wealthy have an obligation to serve others with a portion of their time and money, I'm sure Nancy never saw it as an obligation. She saw it as a pleasure and gained enormously from the experience.
>
> While we are deeply saddened, there is one thought that should give us all comfort: Nancy Thurmond packed a lot of quality living into her twenty-two years on this earth.[6]

THE MORNING AFTER THE ACCIDENT, Circuit Solicitor Richard "Dick" Harpootlian, the state prosecutor, personally went out and began interviewing witnesses. Clearly, Koenig had been drinking heavily, but he needed details to present a strong case to a jury.

"She'd been to four bars that night, and I interviewed every bartender as to how much she had to drink. I had her obtaining nine to twelve beers over a three-hour period prior to getting into the car and hitting her.

"I found that one of the national experts on blood alcohol extrapolation happens to be at the Medical University of South Carolina in

Charleston, so we were going to use him. Sixteen is what she read two hours after the accident." The expert was prepared to testify it would have been a minimum of twenty-two at the time of the accident.

"She did not appear to be drunk," Harpootlian continued, "but our expert would testify that somebody who drinks a lot every day can mask it, especially when the adrenaline hits from having this kind of trauma."[7]

There was some irony to Harpootlian's role in the case. More than two decades earlier, as editor of Clemson's student newspaper, the *Tiger*, Harpootlian had written scathing editorials about Thurmond and had run every humiliating picture of him that he could find, including one with Thurmond's cheeks bulging with a closed mouth chomping on pork barbecue. Harpootlian and a handful of like-minded Clemson student journalists—Marilyn Thompson's brother, Jim Walser, among them—then descended on Columbia and launched an alternative weekly, *Osceola*. Modeled after the progressive *Texas Observer*, it likewise reviled Thurmond while providing depth reporting on politics and public affairs.

Harpootlian, who in 1998 became state Democratic chairman in South Carolina, said:

> Politically, I've never been on the same side of the fence as him and did not know him except in the political context. You know, in my perspective he was a segregationist, pro-war, very conservative, all those sorts of things that didn't mesh with my idea of what we ought to be doing in this country.
>
> I probably talked to him no more than ten minutes in my life up until the point at which he and Nancy came to me to decide whether the woman that hit and killed his daughter should be prosecuted.
>
> Immediately it was a sort of sentiment out there that this woman would not have been prosecuted had she not hit Strom Thurmond's daughter. Rumors started flying that this Thurmond girl was jaywalking, that she was drunk, that Koenig had been roughed up. I mean it was just awful. It was amazing how public opinion shifted to Koenig. I was shocked that it shifted that way.

Harpootlian ordered an autopsy so there would be no dispute over whether Nancy Moore had been drinking. The report revealed a zero blood alcohol content. Several months passed before the solicitor's first in-depth meeting with Strom and Nancy Thurmond.

Harpootlian said:

What amazed me about him was that he was alert, that he was articulate, that he had a grasp of some of the more arcane legal principles and the difference between felony DUI [driving under the influence] and reckless homicide. I forgot he was a state court judge back in the '30s and '40s. The elements of crime haven't changed much, so he knew a lot more than any other victim's parents knew that I've dealt with on these kinds of cases.

As we went through the process, it became obvious to me that we were going to have a hell of a time getting a jury that would be fair to me. Koenig was just very adept in promoting the concept that she was somehow being strung up because she had killed Strom Thurmond's daughter.

Because Harpootlian declined at the time to comment on the details of the accident to insure a fair trial, the press had limited information that did not include Koenig's high speed at the time of the accident. Although the .16 blood alcohol content was reported, it was placed in the context of drinking "several beers" instead of the nine to twelve that Harpootlian confirmed. What the public read after the accident implied that the speed of the car might have been less than twenty-five miles per hour, that the victim was jaywalking, and that the driver didn't see her until too late. Harpootlian recalled being shocked in hearing a number of potential jurors say they thought the defendant was being singled out.

Thurmond and Nancy for a couple of weeks were in and out of my office every day. They acted just like any other victim's father and mother I ever dealt with except they were much more understanding, more willing to get the thing resolved than most parents. And Strom—Nancy had to be a little firm with him from time to time because he was used to the '30s and '40s where people got twenty-five years. Reckless homicide carries five years. Felony DUI carries up to twenty years.

It took him a while to grasp the fact that public opinion wasn't in his favor. Initially, he wanted to hang her. If it had been my daughter, I would have wanted to hang her.

In addition to the high speed and drinking, an examination by the solicitor's office of Koenig's car indicated that the front beam lights were aimed too low, giving limited forward vision. Police were ready to testify that Koenig told one of them she drank a beer before the accident, another that she drank two, and another that she drank three—compared with the nine to twelve that the bartenders said they saw her consume.

But Harpootlian had doubts about getting a felony DUI conviction because it would have required proof that Koenig had also been speeding. Harpootlian wasn't sure whether he could prove with legal certainty that the speed limit in the dense shopping area at Five Points technically was only twenty-five miles per hour—as posted a block north of the accident—rather than forty-five miles per hour, the limit by state law for unposted areas in a municipality. There was also the jaywalking by the victim, which Koenig's trial lawyer, John Hardaway, would have stressed in arguing that the wreck was an "unavoidable accident."

But the real problem, Harpootlian thought, was the sympathy Koenig had generated. If the victim had not been Strom Thurmond's daughter, Harpootlian was convinced he could have convicted the driver on felony DUI, with at least a fifteen-year sentence. "Being Strom Thurmond's daughter cut against us," he said. "Jurors were telling me that. All it takes is one juror to hang it up."

Harpootlian located personal records relating to past behavior by Koenig, and Judge Ralph Anderson considered, in a closed hearing, whether they could be admitted as evidence. "If these records came in," Harpootlian later explained, "our job would be much easier."

When Anderson ruled them admissible, the parties negotiated a tentative plea bargain, one that would seal the records. Harpootlian discussed the plea issue with the Thurmonds and they finally agreed. "They did not want to be perceived as using his stature in the state as somehow to punish somebody more than they would be punished normally," Harpootlian said. "They wanted Koenig to be punished in some way, and the fact was that she was going to jail. Thurmond just looked at me and said, 'You do what you think is right.'"

"I said, 'Well, Senator, I think my best estimate of the right thing to do is to show some mercy and get it over with right now. She's going to jail.' Mercy meant to me to put an end to it."

Koenig entered a guilty plea to involuntary manslaughter, but not until after testimony on September 1 in open court and an offer by Harpootlian to accept a guilty plea with no sentencing recommendation to the judge. In the courtroom, Harpootlian routinely followed his practice of inviting the family to sit in a row of chairs behind the prosecutor's table. Strom Jr. and Julie joined Strom and Nancy. The youngest son, Paul, was at a tennis academy in Florida. The senator's twin younger sisters, Mary Tompkins and Martha Bishop, also joined them.

Thurmond rejected any notion he was there to pressure the court. "That's not the purpose at all," he told reporter Lee Bandy. "Here is a father whose daughter was killed by a drunk driver exceeding the speed limit."

Bandy could see "the hurt and pain in their eyes as they were forced to relive that horrible night of April 13." But Thurmond, the war hero, tried to minimize the emotional toll. "Of course, this is a tough time. But it hasn't gotten me down," he told Bandy. "All through life, you have matters that come up you have to deal with. And this is one of them."

The Thurmond family showed little emotion as a sobbing and remorseful Koenig entered the guilty plea in open court and said, "I'm so sorry." Nancy Thurmond bit her upper lip. A letter from her, read to the court, said, "The silent and vicious killer in this case was alcohol" and expressed hope it would serve to educate others about alcohol's dangers.[8]

After agreement on the guilty plea, Judge Anderson asked the still crying Koenig, "Do you still want to go forward?"

"Yes, sir."

"In your heart and soul, are you guilty of involuntary manslaughter in the death of Nancy Thurmond?" The courtroom fell silent.

"Yes, sir."

Harpootlian told Anderson that agreeing to a plea bargain was not an easy decision. "There is no joy in what we do here today," the solicitor said. "There is no feeling that the Thurmonds will leave here satisfied, happy, with what occurred. . . . What we hope we leave the courtroom with is a sense that justice was done."

The judge imposed a sentence of two years in prison, plus five years' probation. He also required that Koenig receive substance-abuse counseling.[9] Columbia's most influential TV station, WIS, broke into its programming with the verdict and transmitted its feed live to other NBC affiliates statewide.

Thurmond had told Bandy he would be relieved when the trial ended. It would allow him to look forward again. "I believe in the Bible, in God, in the future, in eternal life. And that's what keeps us all going," he said.[10]

Looking back four years later, Harpootlian said:

Strom was taken aback that his stature didn't cut for him in this case, that it cut against him. I still shake my head about it. I mean here's Strom Thurmond, the beloved Strom Thurmond's daughter killed by a drunk driver and the perception out there was that somehow this woman was being prosecuted because she killed Thurmond's daughter rather than being guilty. It was the weirdest thing I've ever seen.

He was just a stand-up guy, and I can't say enough good things about him. I still don't agree with much of what he does politically, but I know there is a guy that has a sense of values. He really agonized over what's the right thing to do, and the relationship between him and Nancy was fascinating.

He actually listened to her, took her advice. He initially said she's got to get at least ten years. Nancy said, "Strom, that's not what's important. What's important is that something positive comes out of this. If she'll plead guilty and goes to jail, then we ought to live with it." She felt Nancy's death could be used for something positive, against drunk driving; it shouldn't turn into a political circus.

I left and when I came back she and Strom were sitting on the couch together and holding hands. It wasn't "Senator and wife" or "Senator and estranged wife"; it was mom and dad figuring out what to do. That was just it. Not what I expected.

They were like any other family I ever dealt with except they were a lot calmer and a lot nicer and a lot more considerate of me and what I have to go through than any other family I have had to deal with.

Strom Jr. just wanted to kick somebody's ass. What do you expect of a twenty-year-old? His sister is dead, and she was very close to him. Again, that's natural. That's what you see with every one of these families. I've dealt with too many people whose families are in trauma and who don't have a good foundation; you watch them disintegrate.

That's what I figured would turn into a nasty scene—with Nancy and Strom separated and the daughter dead and the political overlay, but it never did. They really behaved like champs.

And I think it was real. I think whatever their relationship is, it's a real one. I don't know why they are separated. I don't know why they are not living together, but they got along very well. They worked it together. They had the kids come in to talk to them for a while about what was going to happen. There was a mom and dad trying to get through this thing together, and that was sort of amazing to me.

At one point before the trial, Harpootlian said, "Thurmond and I were having a very back-and-forth two lawyers talking about elements of crime. That particular moment I came to the realization that this guy got where he got because he's a smart son-of-a-bitch. He's like a young guy in an old guy's body."[11]

Koenig, paroled after serving almost a year in jail, later was charged with violating her parole. After a hearing on August 29, 1996, that called for her to undergo four months of daily drug testing, she said she wanted to leave South Carolina. "I'm a spectacle for the state," she told a reporter, complaining she could get nothing more than a minimum-wage job. "People think I've forgotten. I live this accident every day."[12]

Two days after Koenig's hearing, and a little more than three years after her daughter's death, Nancy Thurmond was charged with drunken driving and speeding by an Aiken police officer. Her first response, when asked for her driver's license, was to pull out a wad of money and arrange it in front of the officer. The incident was videotaped from the arresting officer's patrol car.

After losing her balance during a sobriety test and refusing to stand on one foot or take the Breathalyzer test, she was arrested and spent the night in the Aiken County Jail. The next morning, she posted a $418 bond.

The senator issued a statement a few days later, saying, "My family and I deeply regret this and pray she will handle it in a responsible manner."[13]

Nancy immediately entered an out-of-state treatment center. She forfeited the bond, losing her license and getting sentenced to perform community service. Roughly a year after her daughter's accident, she had acknowledged her problem with alcohol in letters to friends, including Bandy. He quoted from it a month after her arrest: "In an effort to face this issue openly and honestly, and hopefully to strengthen my own journey toward sobriety and recovery, I wish to acknowledge this progressive and fatal disease with all of its ramifications, beginning with my powerlessness over alcohol and the unmanageability of life around it."

She asked for prayers and "God's grace, not just for myself, but for all those who continue to suffer in silence from addictive disease."14 Some language in her letter is almost identical to that found in Alcoholics Anonymous literature.

Three months after her arrest, Nancy for the first time publicly acknowledged a twenty-year battle with alcoholism and prescription diet pills. She said she had been "clean and sober" for the three months since her arrest. She went public after a speech at Clemson by former Senator George McGovern. He talked about his daughter, Terry, who died after a long struggle with alcohol. Nancy told reporter Dottie Ashley of the *Post and Courier* in Charleston, "I want people to know how I feel about my alcoholism and how I know that I, too, could have killed someone just as my own child was killed."

Nancy had never tasted alcohol until soon after marrying Strom, who had begun privately drinking an occasional glass of wine on the advice of his doctor. Curious, Nancy decided one night to have her own glass of wine. After her first sip, she said, "I immediately threw up in my plate, right there in front of everyone. Strom, always the Southern gentleman, covered my plate with his napkin and just pretended nothing had happened!" Her allergic reaction was symptomatic of a certain type of alcoholism.

"Strom was always very busy and he did not confront me per se with my addiction. But when I told him I needed some help, he was very receptive. But, of course, Strom was famous as a health advocate and [considered] a teetotaler and for him to be saddled with a drunken wife just didn't make sense—it just didn't add up."

She talked about the stress as a senator's wife who had four children in less than five years. She said Strom was a devoted father, but his career kept him busy. Nancy found herself staying home alone with the children more often at night.

"I was a very quiet drunk," she told Ashley. "I never felt that I caused any trouble or got loud or obnoxious or embarrassed anyone."

In the 1970s, she began taking diet pills prescribed to help lose weight after the births of her children and became dependent on amphetamines. "Because I was so hyper from the pills, often I just couldn't get to sleep, and so I would have a glass of wine to block out tiredness."

She became despondent and her self-esteem diminished. Further, "I was using wine as a sleeping potion, and over the years I became more and more clandestine about my drinking. . . . My most deeply felt sense of loss is that I have to realize that I was not the mother I intended to be, or that God intended for me to be."[15]

After the Associated Press distributed the story statewide in South Carolina, *The State* editorialized, "This is a brutally harsh self-assessment—probably much too harsh. It would have taken an unusually strong person to navigate a marriage with a huge age gap (forty-four years) in the glare of national media and with constant demands on a husband whose public life she had to adopt as her own—not to mention raising four children born close together. But the Nancy Thurmond South Carolinians remember so well and appreciate is a gracious woman who gave generously of her time to public fund-raising efforts by multiple organizations throughout the state. We admire her for her openness and her courage."[16]

If a mother is to be judged by the reputation of her children, Nancy Thurmond was quite successful. Many who knew Strom Jr. as a young man use the words "sensitive," "quiet," and "reserved" to describe him. An undergraduate English major, he finished at the University of South Carolina Law School in 1998, a few months before his marriage in September to Heather Gail Holland, who graduated a year behind him at both Aiken High and USC. He returned to Aiken to work as a lawyer in the solicitor's office before his career was advanced by a move from his father in his final year in the Senate.

When it was diagnosed that Julie, the second daughter, suffered from a severe form of diabetes, family associates said both parents responded with attention and concern. Julie graduated from the College of Charleston and returned to Washington. She worked in the private sector, saw her father regularly, and sometimes accompanied him at official functions. She joined him in 1997 on a trip he made to China as president pro tem of the Senate just before his ninety-fifth birthday. She later married and remained in Washington.

Paul Thurmond was captain of the Vanderbilt University tennis team in 1998, his senior year. As an athlete he was an academic all-SEC (Southeastern Conference) selection all four years. He made the Dean's List, majoring in human and organization development. He was also involved off the court with such activities as tutoring public school first graders in reading. He entered law school at USC in 1999. He graduated three years later and went to work in Charleston as a prosecutor in the solicitor's office.

Thurmond, in response to an interviewer's question, once said he would like his sons to enter politics "only if that's what they want."[17] A family friend said both young men "handle themselves well" around people and had the qualities to succeed if they ever chose to seek elective office. Many in South Carolina believe they will.

In the year after Nancy's arrest, she had begun to see Strom a bit more, even attending Washington events with him. In the fall of 1997 she let friends know that she had been "clean and sober" for a year. Later, after her children developed families of their own, Nancy visited each of them regularly. But she continued to grieve over the loss of Nancy Moore and to visit her grave often.

CHAPTER 24

"Alive and Serving"

In 1995, at the age of ninety-three, Strom Thurmond was already the oldest person ever to serve in the Senate. But against the advice of most of his wisest aides, he set out to do what he knew best—campaign for election. Election to this, his eighth term, and if he were to complete the term, would mean a stint in office that would carry him through his 100th birthday.

Harry Dent, by this time largely retired from politics and devoting himself to a lay ministry, weighed in early with his disapproval, as did the senator's trusted former press secretary, Mark Goodin, a Lee Atwater protégé. "You don't have to prove anything," Goodin counseled at a lunch. "You have served well and admirably. I would hate to see your career end with a bitter campaign waged over the age issue that might be a squeaker that you could lose."

"He thanked me, but it was clear he wasn't happy," Goodin recalled. Instead, Thurmond took heart in the advice of another trusted associate who told him that even though a majority of South Carolina voters would prefer he not run, they would still vote for him if he did.

After making his decision to run, Thurmond met again with Goodin and asked him to go to South Carolina and assess his campaign organization. Reluctantly, the loyal Goodin agreed to go. He had left Thurmond's office after seven years to work with Vice President Dan Quayle, but he revered the elderly senator, whom he regarded as the most "un-venal, un-cynical person I've ever known."

Goodin returned from South Carolina with grim news. "Do you want the unvarnished truth?" he asked Thurmond.

"Give it to me straight."

"I've seen better campaigns for a high school student council race. There's no organization." A long pause followed.

"Will you run it? Will you fix it?"

Goodin agreed to set up the campaign on a volunteer basis, provided he had absolute control, and to find a competent manager. He knew Thurmond balked at placing that much control in one person, but Strom agreed.

By the end of 1995, the campaign had raised barely $100,000, a "ridiculously low amount," Goodin recalled. He hit the phones and within two weeks had raised a couple of hundred thousand dollars from his corporate clients. He kept Cindy Carter, "the best political organizer I ever knew. She helped bring the campaign back to life." To manage the campaign, Goodin reached out to Tony Denny, former executive director of the state Republican Party.

He hired political fund-raiser Maxie Haltiwanger as finance director for $8,000 a month and told her she would earn every penny.

Thurmond had never before paid such a hefty salary, and when Goodin told him about it, he exclaimed, "Eight thousand dollars a month!"

"You said I would have full authority," Goodin said.

Thurmond bit his lip, "We have a lot of confidence in you."

Goodin understood. "He meant, 'You better deliver.'"

The first order of business was to bump the strongest potential opposing candidate, Secretary of State James Miles of Greenville, from challenging Thurmond in a GOP primary. Miles was the only statewide Republican officeholder who had not endorsed Thurmond, and Goodin suspected that Miles was running a nascent campaign. Goodin put on the pressure to dry up Miles's campaign contributions.

On a day when Miles was out of state, Goodin denounced him at a press conference for not endorsing the senator, stressing that giving money to Miles meant opposing Thurmond. He said that anyone who had contributed to Miles under the illusion that they were supporting a future campaign against Fritz Hollings should ask for their money back.

Goodin encouraged people to write letters to the editor. In Greenville, Goodin brought Dan Quayle in for a fund-raiser and set up a huge Thurmond rally at the conservative Bob Jones University, where more than 7,000 people packed the assembly hall. At the annual Silver Elephant dinner in Columbia, the major fund-raiser for the state GOP, Young Republicans at each door pasted "I'm for Strom" stickers on the several thousand attendees. In his remarks, "Strom said nice things about Miles—classic Strom Thurmond," Goodin said. Soon afterward, Miles endorsed the senator.

A much weaker contender, state Representative Harold Worley, a Myrtle Beach developer, spent $600,000 of his own money challenging Thurmond in the Republican primary. Worley called Thurmond "simply too old" to serve. Worley got 30 percent of the vote, carrying only his home county of Horry, and a third Republican candidate got 9 percent.

With the primary out of the way, Thurmond bided time while the Democrats found someone willing to challenge a Senate institution. Richard Riley, the popular former two-term governor and Clinton secretary of education, considered and rejected the idea. So did Fifth District Congressman John Spratt.

Thurmond ended up facing Elliott Close, forty-three, a wealthy but politically inexperienced great-grandson of textile magnate Elliott White Springs, founder of Springs Industries. Although he avoided mentioning it in his campaign, Close was also a brother-in-law of Clinton's White House chief of staff, Erskine Bowles.

Thurmond had not debated an opponent since Olin Johnston in 1950. Following Goodin's strategy, he saw no reason to change that tactic now. "I told him," Goodin said, "We're making history. Nobody your age has run before. We have to keep excitement out of this race. That means no mistakes, and that means, 'Don't take chances.' I make a mistake and it's because I'm tired; you make a mistake and it's because you're old."

Thurmond hit the campaign trail like a man half his age, shaking hands in his exuberant style from barbecue restaurant to barbecue restaurant and courthouse to courthouse.

Close spent $944,000 of his own money in a chaotic campaign that went through three different managers. His timing often seemed off. A week after he pointed out that his family's mills had never laid off workers during the depression, the company closed three mills and laid off 850 workers.[1]

Close attempted to focus on Thurmond's age and rumors of his infirmity with ad lines like: "Is Strom Thurmond still up to the job? Vote for our future, not for our past." In one of his few direct encounters with Close, Thurmond engaged in chitchat, telling the younger man that he had attended the 1928 Democratic National Convention with his grandfather. Close said afterward, "Actually, it was my great-grandfather."[2] Strom seemed to neutralize the issue by asserting, "It would take my opponent sixty years to catch up with what I can do in the next six years. . . . He's got the money, but I've got the experience."

Staff writer Kevin Sack reported in the *New York Times*, after two days on the campaign trail with Thurmond, "Polls show that the vast majority of

South Carolinians believe it is far past time for him to retire. . . . But the polls cannot accurately measure the profound affection felt in this state for Mr. Thurmond. . . . Despite their concerns about his abilities, many South Carolinians just cannot bring themselves to turn the old man out."

Sack also wrote about Esther Hunter, an eighty-one-year-old black woman who showed up at a campaign stop at Gene's Restaurant in the town of Union "to thank Mr. Thurmond for the condolence letter he sent when her husband died in 1993."

> It mattered little that it was a form letter, no different from thousands of others sent to survivors over the years by Mr. Thurmond's staff. Nor did it matter that Mr. Thurmond was once one of the South's staunchest segregationists.
>
> "He sent me this fine letter when my husband died," Mrs. Hunter said, clutching a wrinkled page. "You can't pay attention to everything you hear. People say, you know, he didn't like black people. But he knows I'm 100 percent black and he sure did pay me respect. You have to praise the bridge that carries you across."[3]

In addition to his own money, Close raised almost another million, which Thurmond's strategists interpreted to mean the wealthy challenger, apparently unwilling to invest more of his own fortune, lacked confidence. From the primaries through the election, Thurmond outspent Close $2,632,682 to $1,913,574.

On election night, Thurmond joined Goodin for dinner and to wait for returns. He seemed resigned to whatever might happen. "If they turn me out, they turn me out," the senator said.

But Goodin knew differently. "I think he would have been hurt," he said later. "Heartbroken."[4]

Thurmond won with 53 percent of the vote—with 44 percent for Close and 3 percent for minor candidates—and apparently survived because no better-qualified Democratic challenger came forward. Reporter Lee Bandy concluded that Thurmond had "dodged the bullet," with the senator's campaign aides privately conceding that either Riley or Spratt could have beaten him.[5]

Proudly, Thurmond called the skeptical Harry Dent at home. "Harry, I won, didn't I?" the senator asked rhetorically.

"Yes, Senator, you sure did," Dent replied.

"Guess what I'm doing."

"What?"

"I'm writing a $250 check for your ministry," Strom said.

Dent and his wife, Betty, were born-again Southern Baptists, associates of the Reverend Billy Graham. They had written an "inspirational" book, *Right vs. Wrong: Solution to the American Nightmare*. Even Strom, who acknowledged he almost never read a book, read this one. Their energies went to serve their lay ministry, the name of which seemed particularly appropriate for the aging senator.

They called it: "Laity: Alive and Serving."

On May 25, 1997, Thurmond set another record, becoming not only the oldest but also the longest-serving senator in U.S. history. He broke the record held by Democrat Carl Hayden of Arizona, who had served forty-one years, ten months and eleven days before his death in 1969. Thurmond returned to Edgefield County, where he gave the main speech for the town of Johnston's centennial celebration eight miles from his birthplace. His sister Mary sat in the front row. "People often ask me how I want to be remembered," he said, and then answered, "honest, patriotic and helpful."

Speakers from across the state's political spectrum praised him, including Tom McCain and black state Representative William Clyburn, whose House district included Johnston. If their presence on the program represented change, the bare smattering of black faces in the audience reflected continuity, a feeling that this Sunday afternoon function somehow did not really include the African Americans who made up more than half of Johnston's population.

Thurmond's niece, Mary T. Freeman, wrote a poem to observe the milestone that reflects his family's pride and affection for him:

STROMMY

Your life is one of service.

Your good influence has reached wide and far.

Today you set a new record as you capture that highest star.

For the longest senatorial service ever

you humbly take your bow.

To the record books you now go

For folks to read about and think, "Wow!"
Your family takes much pride in you. We love you for who you are.
The warm and caring "Strommy" who's most always "up to par."
Strong in mind and body
determined to succeed,
mingling with other folks of fame
you didn't neglect your neighbor's need.
God bless you now and always
for the many achievements you have made and give you grace and
more time to serve as you continue to "make the grade."

BACK IN WASHINGTON, however, Thurmond showed increasing frailty. A staffer accompanied Thurmond anywhere he went on Capitol Hill, but Thurmond said he was still riding his Exercycle every morning and swimming weekly. After graduating from Vanderbilt University in 1998, his son, Paul, moved in with him for a year, which he later called the "best thing I ever did."[6]

Administrative Assistant Robert J. "Duke" Short, a former FBI agent, and his wife had Thurmond come over for at least one meal every weekend.[7] As Thurmond aged, Short's power grew enormously, causing some concern among Thurmond's colleagues. A fellow senator on the Armed Services Committee complained that Short "gets him up in the morning and puts him to bed at night and basically guides him through the day. Everything is sort of in the area of protecting Senator Thurmond."[8]

The national media focused on how heavily scripted Thurmond's remarks now often seemed to be, suggesting that Duke Short was calling most of the shots as Thurmond faithfully showed up to cast his votes. But Lee Bandy of *The State* pointed out, "When Strom was much younger, I would go to the committee hearings and Strom always read what was written for him on the 4x5 cards," Bandy observed. "He didn't ask a question that wasn't already written for him."[9]

And yet, even in his nineties, Thurmond had his moments. On July 22, 1998, the fiftieth anniversary week of Thurmond's Dixiecrat acceptance speech, the Senate Armed Services Committee rejected the nomination of Daryl Jones, a jet pilot, lawyer, and Florida legislator who would have been the first black air force secretary. Thurmond was the lone Republican to support Jones. Critics, including a former Air Force Reserve squadron commander, had accused Jones of lying about why he stopped flying jet fighters. They charged him with attempting to pressure enlisted reservists to buy Amway products from him and collecting flight pay after he stopped flying.

The charges were detailed during a nine-hour hearing, broadcast on C-SPAN, in which Jones offered troubling explanations. Jones at first said he voluntarily decided to stop flying to work a desk job. But it turned out that his squadron commander had grounded him over safety-related issues, forcing him to either appeal or stop flying. He also exaggerated his amount of flight time.

Jones's supporters, including other squadron members, argued that some of the complaints about him were motivated by racial animosity. White pilots resented him, suspecting that his race had won him a spot in the unit. Jones, however, denied encountering racism in the squadron.[10]

Thurmond jumped to Jones's defense. While other senators shifted uncomfortably, he questioned the nominee's wife about whether she wanted him to have the job and whether she loved him. Then, in a staff-written statement he read before the final vote, Thurmond cited "media accounts, rumor campaigns, and personal attacks" in an effort to "raise doubts about the integrity, character, and ability of Daryl Jones." But, he continued, "In each and every matter, Mr. Jones offered a plausible, credible, and believable explanation concerning the matters in question."[11]

Thurmond made clear his intention to stand by Jones. He recognized Jones's exceptional achievement in overcoming an unprivileged background to compile what Thurmond called an "admirable" record.

In contrast to his assertion a half century earlier that even the army lacked the force to break down segregation, Thurmond stood alone among fellow Republicans in supporting a black Southerner to be the civilian leader of the Air Force. And yet, the vote was a clear sign of Thurmond's lost influence. A committee chairman, he was unable to persuade a single fellow Republican to vote with him.

The outcome allowed Thurmond to have it both ways politically. He went on record in support of a black nominee. But with Jones's nomination rejected, there was no blame to bear from those who might have been outraged had Jones been confirmed.

AFTER CASTING HIS 15,000TH VOTE, only the second senator in history to have reached this milestone, following Robert Byrd of West Virginia's

15,000th vote in May 1998, Thurmond in September of that year stepped down as chairman of the Armed Services Committee. His stewardship of that committee, which he had inherited from the lawyerly Democrat Sam Nunn of Georgia, had come under fire. One witness said that in private meetings Thurmond alternated from being "the slickest politician I ever saw" to appearing overwhelmed by details, totally dependent on his aides and focused on the funding of South Carolina military installations to the exclusion of weighty national security issues.[12]

A few years earlier, after the fiftieth anniversary celebration and memorial of the D day landing at Normandy in 1994, Senator Paul Coverdell of Georgia told the Senate that Thurmond did not attend because it conflicted with the high school graduation of his youngest son, Paul. Some members chuckled at the nature of their ninety-one-year-old colleague's dilemma. A much younger fellow senator who had attended the memorial events at Normandy came up to Thurmond afterward to tell him what a wonderful occasion it had been and that it was unfortunate he had been unable to attend.

Jabbing a forefinger in his younger colleague's chest, Thurmond said, "Son, I was there when it counted."

THE IMPEACHMENT HEARINGS of President Bill Clinton proceeded behind closed doors in January 1999, as did most of Thurmond's consultations about the votes he would have to cast. His advisers saw how uncomfortable he was with the proceedings. Clinton stood accused of lying to a grand jury about an affair with White House intern Monica Lewinsky after a long, excruciating investigation by a special prosecutor. It took several weeks before Thurmond's public statement was published in the *Congressional Record*.

> Mr. Chief Justice, the vote I cast on the articles of impeachment was one of the hardest votes that I have had to make in all my years in the United States Senate, not that I do not think I made the correct decision. While I am saddened that we had to make the judgment we made in this impeachment trial, each of us had a duty to undertake this task, and I do not shirk from duties . . .
>
> The purpose of impeachment is not to punish a man. It is not a way to express displeasure or disagreement with a President or his policies.

Impeachment is a mechanism designed to preserve, protect, and defend the Constitution, the Country, and Office of the Presidency. My primary concern, from the first day of this scandal, was the impact it would have on the Office of the Presidency.

This case is not about illicit conduct or even about not telling the truth about illicit conduct. Instead, the case is about two activities. The first is whether the President intentionally made false statements under oath to a Federal grand jury, to the Judiciary of the United States. The second is whether the President obstructed justice before a United States District Court and a Federal grand jury, again to the Judiciary of the United States.

In the end, Clinton was acquitted of both charges. The perjury charge against him was defeated 55–45, and the obstruction-of-justice charge brought an even 50–50 split along party lines.

Thurmond resolved his dilemma as he had so many times in his career. As he had once told Essie in explaining the Dixiecrat campaign, he had to do what it took to "keep his constituents happy."

When the time came for Thurmond to vote on Clinton, he followed the lead of the others in his party. As the clerk called the roll, Thurmond raised his voice and shouted, "Guilty. Guilty."

For his careful attention during the Clinton impeachment trial, Thurmond received notice. *New Yorker* writer Jeffrey Toobin, a Harvard Law graduate who had worked as an associate for independent counsel Lawrence Walsh, wrote, "Throughout the long days, only a single senator emerged as a perfect model of unwavering attentiveness—ninety-six-year-old Strom Thurmond of South Carolina."

After the first day of the trial was shortened so the Senate could troop to the House chambers in the Capitol to hear Clinton give a rousing State of the Union address, Thurmond moved toward the front of the ceremonial receiving line to greet the president and the first lady, Hillary Rodham Clinton. Toobin described what happened:

The president and first lady greeted Strom Thurmond with smiles and handshakes. As they later described the scene to a friend, they heard Thurmond say, "You're two turds."

"Pardon?" said the president.

"You're two turds," the senator repeated.

As Thurmond moved through the line, the Clintons exchanged perplexed looks with each other, baffled by the hostility they had engendered, and continued shaking hands. It wasn't until late in the evening that they realized that they had failed to understand the ancient senator through his soupy South Carolina accent.

They'll never get two-thirds, Thurmond had said. *They'll never get two-thirds.*[13]

He was referring, of course, to the constitutional requirement for a two-thirds vote of the Senate for impeachment in order to remove Clinton from office. The final vote ended up far short of two-thirds. Some political observers in South Carolina believed the vote was due to a political commitment to help fellow South Carolinian Lindsey Graham, one of the House managers serving as prosecutors in the impeachment trial. (Graham was elected senator in 2002 as Thurmond's successor.)

ALTHOUGH THURMOND HAD BEGUN appearing to many in Washington as an irrelevant relic, the wine industry learned otherwise. Six months after the Republican effort to impeach Clinton fizzled, there was Strom on the July 31, 1999, cover of *Wine Spectator* magazine, which designated him "Wine's Public Enemy #1." In breathless prose, the cover page declared in large type:

> For almost two decades, Senator Strom Thurmond
> has waged a relentless campaign against wine, using
> warning labels, tax proposals and parliamentary
> maneuvers. Find out why he wants to continue his
> crusade, and why every wine lover should be fearful.

What so aroused the ire of the wine industry was Thurmond's applying his still acute political acumen to an apparent deal cut by the Wine Institute, the trade organization of California's dominant wine industry, and Secretary of Treasury Robert Rubin to add two new labels to wine bottles that would call attention to what the magazine called "the health benefits of moderate wine consumption."

Five months before *Wine Spectator*'s cover story, Thurmond responded by introducing three bills as warning shots to both Rubin and the wine industry. One would triple the excise tax on wine, adding 60 cents a bottle to the cost, with the revenue—estimated at $7.9 billion over a decade—earmarked for research and treatment for alcohol abuse. A second would remove wine from regulation by the Treasury Department's Bureau of Alcohol, Tobacco, and Firearms (ATF) and move it to the Food and Drug Administration, an agency that the magazine said "could take a more antialcohol stance." The third would block ATF's little-noticed approval of the new labels. Rubin had apparently signed off on them without consulting Thurmond, who in 1988 had been responsible for the health warning labels on wine bottles—in its limited way, perhaps his major piece of legislation.

Thurmond also demanded a federal investigation, charging that the Wine Institute had "conspired" with others to get the health benefits of moderate alcohol consumption included in the 1995 federal dietary guidelines, the basis for the proposed new labels. The Wine Institute's frustrated Washington lobbyist characterized Thurmond's actions as "punitive, mean-spirited and vindictive."

As Rubin was preparing to leave the Cabinet and return to Wall Street, Thurmond placed a senatorial "hold" on three nominations to fill key positions at the Treasury Department. Thurmond withdrew his blocking of the appointments after Rubin said his department would hold public hearings about the placement of any future health-related statements on wine labels. In 2004, five years later, such labels still remained unapproved.[14]

DESPITE THE APPEARANCE that his marriage had almost totally fallen apart, he talked almost every day by telephone to Nancy, hundreds of miles away in Aiken. From time to time, there was speculation that he wanted her to succeed him in the Senate and was preparing to step down in order to give her the job.

Earlier, after Democrat Jim Hodges was elected governor in 1998 and asked whom he would appoint if a vacancy occurred, he said it would be someone uninterested in more than filling the remainder of Thurmond's term. One of the more bizarre episodes occurred in the fall of 2000, a month before Strom's ninety-eighth birthday, when Nancy Thurmond visited Governor Hodges at the Statehouse and played a videocassette of Strom announcing he was resigning from the Senate and saying he would like her to fill the seat. One confidential source says that Hodges, who would have appointed any interim successor, was "stunned" by Nancy's presentation of the tape, that he mostly listened, but made it clear there was no vacancy and therefore no reason for him to discuss the matter.[15]

The story broke three months later with an article in *The State* that came from Thurmond political insiders wanting to squash the idea. Days later, Thurmond issued a statement saying he had no intention of stepping down.

Time then speculated in its March 5, 2001, issue that Hodges still might appoint a Republican, even though a Democrat would switch party control in the Senate. A few months later, *Newsweek* cited political allies of the governor as suggesting that he might like to make history—and improve the state's image—by appointing the first African American senator from the South since Reconstruction. In the end, of course, it didn't matter. Thurmond served out his full term.

In a rare interview about their marriage, Nancy told *Washington Post* reporter Kevin Merida that Thurmond "did not want to go forward with the divorce at all. And I think in his heart he wanted me to be happy and so he was willing to go along with the separation. . . . I just don't think he really felt that he wanted that as part of his life [or] legacy." Thurmond had cut her free without a divorce, she said, to pursue life independently with people her own age.

But Strom, in a great-grandfatherly way, managed to show his continued interest in women. After Hillary Clinton's election in 2000 to the Senate from New York, Thurmond greeted her on the first day with a big hug and later would stop by her desk to give her a piece of candy.

In one of his last bold moves, Thurmond also used his influence to position his twenty-eight-year-old son, Strom Jr., as U.S. attorney for the state of South Carolina and in effect, to launch his political career. The younger Thurmond had tried only a handful of cases, and his appointment in 2001 by President George W. Bush at the senator's request caused grumbling both at home and in Washington. The controversy called to mind the similar appointment of young Strom's grandfather, Bill, almost nine decades earlier, a stubborn triumph of patronage by Senator Pitchfork Ben Tillman.

Strom Jr. announced in December 2004 that he would resign effective January 20, 2005, exactly three years after taking office. He left with high praise from veteran staff prosecutors in the office and an image of maintaining a low public profile and demonstrating that he could handle the job. He joined a law firm in Aiken as a partner, expressed uncertainty about running for office, and at thirty-two stimulated wide speculation in South Carolina that he—and his brother—would at some point become a formidable political force in the state. In the summer of 2004, Strom Jr. had become the father of Strom Thurmond III.

In 2001, the senator's health became a national issue as the Senate became a 50-50 body between Democrats and Republicans, with Vice President Dick Cheney holding a tiebreaking vote and a Democratic governor in South Carolina who would appoint a replacement should Strom pass away. The *New York Times Magazine*, in an article titled "Strom in the Balance," said that his age had "in sum, made Strom Thurmond powerful." The article quoted Thomas Mann of the Brookings Institute, who said, "Strom takes on an importance individually because of his possible departure that he has never had as a member of the Senate."[16]

The news media began to hone in on Thurmond's career, providing an opportunity for him to reflect back on his successes and mistakes. But those anticipating a possible late-life apology for his segregationist years soon learned they would get no such satisfaction.

Four decades after his July 1948 Dixiecrat speech, when he had declared "there's not enough troops in the Army to force the Southern people to . . . admit the Negro race into our theaters, into our swimming pools, into our homes and into our churches," Strom Thurmond told an interviewer, "I don't have anything to apologize for. I don't have any regrets. I may have said some things that I could have left off, because I favor everybody receiving equal treatment. Race should not enter into it. It's merit that counts. The States' Rights Party addressed a legitimate issue in 1948 America—whether our states should surrender power to the federal government."[17]

George Wallace, Thurmond's rival as a symbol of segregationist resistance, had said, "We were wrong."[18] Thurmond was never willing to say that, denying even that he had run a racist campaign. Yet defense of white supremacy was the heart of the Dixiecrat movement. His campaign poster in South Carolina, with a huge headline, "Now Is the Time to Fight," at the top, proclaimed, "Join the fight to defeat the FEPC and the abolition of segregation . . . and to protect States Rights."

Thurmond seemed to vacillate between stands of—"no regrets" and "I may have said some things that I could have left off." Wallace may have had far more for which to apologize. But he did apologize, and he did it forthrightly. Thurmond did not. Tom Turnipseed, a key figure in Wallace's presidential campaign who years later acknowledged and repudiated his own racism, said Thurmond remained "a racist in denial. I've been there, and I know."[19] When it came to race, Strom wanted to cross back over the Rubicon without getting his feet wet.

IT MAY BE BECAUSE of his thin record of legislative accomplishments that Thurmond's legacy has received little scholarly attention. However, his impact on American history, politics, and policy was extraordinary.

His Dixiecrat campaign helped transform the South from a political backwater to a major force in American politics. First, it returned race to a central place in electoral politics in the South for more than two decades. Second, it tore loose the South's allegiance to the Democratic Party, marking a break from the Democratic "solid South" that had endured for more than seven decades, and accelerated the development of a competitive two-party system in which Republicans have become dominant.

Thurmond's 1964 switch to the Republican Party reinforced the race-based "Southern strategy" that the Goldwater movement had already begun, and it accelerated GOP growth in the region. In a 1981 interview while he was a member of the Reagan White House political staff, Lee Atwater gave a frank exposition on that strategy in an interview:

ATWATER: You start out in 1954 by saying "Nigger, nigger, nigger." By 1968 you can't say "nigger"—that hurts you. Backfires. So you say stuff like forced busing, states' rights, and all that stuff. You're getting so abstract now [that] you're talking about cutting taxes, and all these things you're talking about are totally economic things and a by-product of them is [that] blacks get hurt worse than whites. And subconsciously maybe that is part of it. I'm not saying that. But I'm saying that if it is getting that abstract, and that coded, that we are doing away with the racial problem one way or the other. You follow me—because obviously sitting around saying, "We want to cut this," is much more abstract than even the busing thing *and* a hell of a lot more abstract than "Nigger, nigger."[20]

In 1968, Thurmond's decisive roles, first in blocking confirmation of Abe Fortas as chief justice and then both in getting Richard Nixon the Republican nomination and thwarting much of George Wallace's threat to Nixon in the South during the general election, had enormous consequences. The result was Nixon's appointing four justices, including new Chief Justice Warren Burger and Associate Justice William Rehnquist, who succeeded Burger and helped turn the court more sharply to the right. And the 1968 election set the template for Republican control of the White House during twenty-four of the next twenty-eight years.

Alex Sanders—a former legislative leader, state appeals court chief judge, and college president who ran unsuccessfully in 2002 as the Democratic candidate against Lindsey Graham for Thurmond's seat—recalled that when school desegregation was coming into effect in the late 1960s, he and other progressives in the legislature "caught hell" trying to prepare the public for the inevitable. "Strom Thurmond made it much worse by misleading statements about the law and generating false hopes. Hell—I had my car shot into. He changed his position on race when it no longer got him votes. That's all part of his legacy."

When Sanders ran for the Senate, however, he avoided any attack on Strom (who had endorsed Graham). When CBS correspondent Leslie Stahl provided ample opportunity during a *60 Minutes* interview for Sanders to criticize Thurmond, barely a month before Strom's 100th birthday, Sanders told her, "I have to be very careful not to offend Senator Thurmond. If I offend him, he might come back in six years and run against me."[21]

BY THE TIME OF HIS LAST CAMPAIGN, and his last term in office, Strom Thurmond had become the grand old man of South Carolina politics. As former Clemson political scientist Charles Dunn put it, "This is the most traditional state in the Union. We don't have a history of turning people out to pasture." Those who endorsed Strom's past political stands could continue to admire his place in their history. Many who opposed those stands appreciated the softening effects of time on Thurmond's image and his abandonment of racial politics. With so many years and so much water under the bridge, that he continued to represent the people of South Carolina seemed to many constituents something they could count on remaining unchanged.

Armstrong Williams said South Carolinians had come to regard Thurmond as a link with fading traditions, even as divinely inspired. "They say, 'The Lord must have saw fit for him to live so long.' It's mystical, mythical."[22]

CHAPTER 25

"Blind, but Now I See"

IN OCTOBER 2001, at a time when the nation was still reeling from the September 11 disaster, a frail Strom Thurmond crumpled dramatically to the Senate floor and his colleagues hovered protectively around him, fearing the worst. Like a tottering grandfather presiding over a long-running family reunion, Thurmond by the age of ninety-eight commanded respectful and tender treatment from both sides of the aisle, and most senators refused to indulge publicly in the escalating debate about Thurmond's health or his competence for office. He continued to hold a near perfect voting record, unsteadily guided into the chamber by aides. But Thurmond's well-publicized tumble marked the beginning of what one irreverent Web site dubbed "The Thurmond Death Watch." Anyone who knew the senator's spunk and legendary determination realized that surely he would not give up the ghost so easily. Without public mention, an EMS team in an ambulance was stationed outside the Capitol—just in case.

Thurmond quietly took up residence at Walter Reed Army Hospital just outside Washington, which provided essentially an assisted-living suite, still clocking days extending his record of longest-serving and oldest senator. He needed to be watched around the clock, and his staff had given up after frustrated efforts to find a male sitter who could tolerate Thurmond's fitful sleep and middle-of-the-night roaming around his Virginia condominium. That December 5, Senate leaders Thomas Daschle (D–SD) and Trent Lott (R–MS) paid tribute to Thurmond on the occasion of his ninety-ninth birthday, bringing a standing ovation on the Senate floor. Lott lauded Thurmond as "an example and an inspiration to all of us. He has been a tremendous servant for the people of South Carolina. I have known very few people in my life more dedicated to their job and to the people they represent."

Lott called attention to Thurmond's natty dress and bright necktie, and Thurmond played to his image as incurable ladies' man. He announced to the chamber amid loving chuckles, "I love all of you men, but you women even more."

A year later, a much grander party unfolded on Capitol Hill in celebration of Thurmond's 100th birthday. Thurmond arrived from Walter Reed in a wheelchair, only to be serenaded by a sultry Marilyn Monroe impersonator. His daughter Julie confided that she was pregnant, due to deliver on July 4. The White House issued a statement by George W. Bush that said, "God bless you, Strom. The nation and I are grateful for your life of service."

The party attracted many political luminaries who praised Thurmond's contributions to public life, including former Majority Leader Bob Dole (R–KS), who called Thurmond the "patriarch" of the Senate who had shown an "extraordinary example of service." The tone of the ceremony was so loving and deferential that few seemed to notice the potentially incendiary nature of remarks made by then majority leader Lott. Lott's comments, which were carried on C-SPAN, ignited a debate on racial politics unlike anything seen in the United States since the 1960s. The ensuing outcry over Lott's insensitivity not only forced him from the Senate leadership but also resurrected bitter feelings and racial division over Thurmond's 1948 Dixiecrat campaign and lifted that episode from the footnotes of history back into the day's headlines.

Speaking from notes, the Mississippi Republican said, "I want to say this about my state. When Strom Thurmond ran for president, we voted for him. We're proud of it. And if the rest of the country had followed our lead, we wouldn't have had all these problems over the years, either."

There were audible gasps and silence among the crowd gathered at the Capitol ceremony, but over the next twenty-four hours, major media did not mention the remark. Lott's comments instead ignited a firestorm on Internet political blogs, illustrating for the first time the immense, new-found power of web chatter on the American political system. It took five days for major media to catch up with, and further extend, the fallout.

The first blogger to pick up on Lott's remarks, on December 6, was the liberal Joshua Micah Marshall, who called them "just another example of the hubris now reigning among Capitol Hill Republicans." The comments also merited mention in abcnews.com's increasingly influential *The Note*.

The political staff at the *Washington Post* scrambled to catch up. On December 7, national reporter Thomas Edsall wrote a short story in the *Post* about the comments. These same Web sites and other news sources began to pore over the language from Strom's 1948 campaign with a level of attention the campaign had not received in years. Perhaps not in South Carolina, but many Americans, a people famously forgetful of their own history, were shocked that the man they had come to think of as colorful but harmless had once run such a vigorous and effective racist campaign for the presidency. By Monday, December 9, conservative bloggers had picked up on the theme, with critical comment. Asked about it the next day, a Lott spokesman said, "Senator Lott's remarks were intended to pay tribute to a remarkable man who led a remarkable life. To read anything more into these comments is wrong."

But Bush White House speechwriter David Frum, on his own blog, predicted the long-term impact. "I cannot help thinking that this story is not over—that Republicans will hear Lott's words quoted at them again and again in the months to come." Another conservative wrote, "Lott's comments were dumb. Morally, they were indefensible."

Vacationing in Key West, Florida, Lott formally apologized to anyone offended by his "poor choice of words" about "discarded policies of the past." But others checked clip files for similar comments, such as one that quoted Lott in 1980 while campaigning for Ronald Reagan with Thurmond, "You know, if we had elected this man thirty years ago, we wouldn't be in the mess we are today."

On December 12, President George W. Bush elevated the decibel level about the issue. He told an inner-city group in Philadelphia, "Any suggestion that the segregated past was acceptable or positive is offensive, and it is wrong. Recent comments by Senator Lott do not reflect the spirit of the country." He noted that Lott had "rightly" apologized.

Lott apologized again the next day, on Black Entertainment Television, asking forgiveness for his "grievous mistake." But two days later, the *Washington Post* quoted a "senior administration official" as saying, "He didn't do what he needed to do." In endorsing affirmative action on BET, Lott offended Senate Republicans who contend racial quotas or preferences violate civil rights laws.[1]

The intense controversy proved too powerful for Lott to regain his footing. On December 19, freshman Senator Bill Frist of Tennessee— clearly with White House support—said he would accept the job of majority leader should it become available. Although he remained in the

Senate, Lott stepped down from his leadership position the next day. Years after the fact, the fire that Strom had spread so effectively and later avoided so carefully had claimed a different Southern senator as its victim.

A month later, on January 19, 2003, Thurmond presided over the Senate for the final time. From the podium, he read in a weak voice, "The Senate stands adjourned." He lifted up his hands, a gesture he had made in so many speeches in so many campaigns, and declared, "That's all."

THURMOND RETURNED TO EDGEFIELD to live out his final months, which is how he wanted it. Bettis Rainsford created a special assisted-living suite in the local hospital where Strom's family could visit him frequently. He went peacefully, with none of the drama that had defined his political career, on June 26, 2003, at age 100. His family surrounded his bedside. Hours before his death, daughter Julie arrived from Washington with her newborn son, delivered four days earlier by C-section, but by then her father was in a coma and never saw her child.

TRUE TO FORM, Thurmond had planned his funeral in detail, with pomp and ceremony befitting a Senate titan. His plans included lying in state in South Carolina's Statehouse rotunda, with a horse-drawn caisson then slowly carrying his casket four and a half blocks past silent sidewalk crowds to Columbia's spacious First Baptist Church—site of the signing 142 years earlier of the Ordinance of Secession, which resolved that South Carolina would lead the South out of the Union and into the nation's bloody Civil War. Strom had chosen the music, the speakers, and his hometown Baptist minister to perform the religious rites. Afterward, the hearse drove at high speed for more than an hour to Edgefield for final burial at Willowbrook Cemetery beside his daughter, Nancy Moore.

Thurmond had once told Harry Dent that he wanted him to give his funeral eulogy, adding, "Unless I have to give yours." But by the time of his death, Harry Dent had faded tragically into advanced Alzheimer's. Thurmond chose for his main eulogist, unannounced, the liberal Democratic senator from Delaware, Joseph Biden, who acknowledged surprise at his role. *Washington Post* staff writer David Von Drehle called it Thurmond's "last laugh—for what else could explain a Northeastern liberal's presence?" And yet there was a brilliance to this final touch by a political master. Biden, who had made his own failed bid for the presidency, had bonded with Thurmond in their days together on the Senate Judiciary Committee. Strom sensed that Biden, an especially talented public speaker, would be capable of talking sensibly about Strom's politics and empathetically about him as a man, that he was the perfect choice to reflect Thurmond's astute building of alliances, regardless of party affiliation, and that he was the right person to give a full, rounded, and warm send-off. Biden would make a moving speech that both addressed and transcended politics. Three thousand mourners, including several hundred African Americans, packed into the church as Biden, sometimes directly addressing Strom's family in the front row, just to his left, began his tribute:

> Strom Thurmond was the only man whom I knew who in a literal sense lived in three distinct and separate periods of American history, and lived what would have been considered a full life in each of those periods, particularly in his beloved South.
>
> Born into an era of essentially unchallenged and unexamined mores of the South, reaching his full maturity in an era of fully challenged and critically examined bankrupt mores of his beloved South, and living out his final three decades in a South that had formally rejected its past on race—in each of these stages, my observation—and I was only with him the last three decades—Strom represented exactly where he came from.
>
> There's an old hymn that includes these lyrics: "Once to every man and nation comes the moment to decide/In the strife of truth with falsehood, for the good or evil side/Then it is the brave man chooses while the coward stands aside."
>
> No one ever doubted Strom Thurmond's physical courage. You've heard much written about it. Not fifteen years ago I was reminded of this. I was coming across to vote in the Senate and going up the escalator, and a fellow who apparently had held a longtime grudge against Senator Thurmond, a tourist, literally interposed himself between me and Strom and said . . . "If you weren't so old, I would knock you . . ." And I immediately stood between them. And Strom literally took off his coat and said, "Hold my coat, Joe."
>
> (LAUGHTER)
>
> Swear to God.
>
> And I looked at him and said, No, no, no, no, no, no.
>
> And with that, he went down and did twenty-five pushups.
>
> (LAUGHTER)

He had to be eighty-eight, eighty-seven. He stood up and looked at the man, he said, "If you weren't so young, I'd knock you down."

(LAUGHTER)

Strom Thurmond was also a brave man, who in the end made his choice and moved to the good side.

I disagreed deeply with Strom on the issue of civil rights and on many other issues, but I watched him change. We became good friends. I'm not sure exactly why or how it happened, Nancy, but you know we did. And Fritz could never figure it out. Neither could I . . .

(LAUGHTER)

But I do know that friendship and death are great equalizers, where our differences become irrelevant and the only thing that is left is what's in our heart.

I went to the Senate emboldened, angered and outraged at age twenty-nine about the treatment of African Americans in this country, what everything that for a period in his life Strom had represented.

But then I met the man. Our differences were profound, but I came to understand that as Archibald MacLeish wrote, "It is not in the world of ideas that life is lived: Life is lived for better or worse in life."

Strom and I shared a life in the Senate for over thirty years. We shared a good life there, and it made a difference. I grew to know him. I looked into his heart and I saw a man, the whole man, and tried to understand him. I learned from him, and I watched him change oh so suddenly.

Like all of us, Strom was a product of his time. But he understood people. He cared for them. He truly wanted to help. He knew how to read people, how to move them, how to get things done. I'll never forget we went down to see President Reagan. He and I had the Thurmond-Biden crime bill. And we sat in a room with President Reagan and with Ed Meese, Jim Baker, and William French Smith, the attorney general, and Strom started to try to convince the president to sign onto our bill, and he turned to me and he said, "Joe, explain it to them." So I did my little bit, and it looked like the president was coming along.

And I swear to the Lord in the Lord's house this is a true story, and with that, as Ed Meese . . . thought the president might be convinced, Ed Meese stood up and said, "Mr. President, time to go, time to go." And with that, the president very dutifully looked—not dutifully, but very respectfully— looked over and said . . . "He said I have to go." And he had his hands on the table, and the president went to get up like this, and Strom grabbed his arm and pulled him back down in his seat.

(LAUGHTER)

I never saw anybody do that to a president.

(LAUGHTER)

And the president—true story—the president looked very sternly at Strom, and Strom said with his hands still on his arm, he said, "Mr. President, when you all get to be my age you'll understand you've got to compromise."

(LAUGHTER)

And the president then was about seventy-five years old.

Strom knew America was changing, and that there was a lot he didn't understand about that change. Much of that change challenged many of his long-held views. But he also saw his beloved South Carolina and the people of South Carolina changing as well, and he knew the time had come to change himself. But I believe the change came to him easily. I believe he welcomed it, because I watched others of his era fight that change and never ultimately change.

It would be humbling to think that I was among those who had some influence on his decision, but I know better. The place in which I work is a majestic place. If you're there long enough, it has an impact on you. You cannot, if you respect those with whom you serve, fail to understand how deeply they feel about things differently than you. And over time, I believe it has an effect on you.

This is a man, who in 1947, the *New York Times* ran a lead editorial saying, "Strom Thurmond, Hope of the South," and talked about how he had set up reading programs, got better books for separate but equal schools. This is a man who was opposed to the poll tax. This is a man who I watched vote for the extension of the Voting Rights Act. This is a man who I watched vote for the Martin Luther King holiday. And it's fairly easy to say today that that was pure political expediency, but I choose to believe otherwise. I choose to believe that Strom Thurmond was doing what few do once they pass the age of fifty: He was continuing to grow, continuing to change.

His offices were next door to mine in the Russell Building, or more appropriately mine were next to his. And over the years, I remember seeing a lot change, including the number of African Americans on his staff and African Americans who sought his help.

For the man who will see, time heals, time changes, and time leads him to truth. But only a special man like Strom would have the courage to accept it, the grace to acknowledge it, and the humility in the face of lasting enmity and mistrust to pursue it until the end.

There's a personal lesson that comes from a page in American political history that is yet unwritten, but nevertheless, it resonates in my heart. I mentioned it on the floor of the Senate the other day. It's a lesson of redemption that I think applies today, and I think Strom, as he listens, will appreciate it.

When I first arrived in the Senate, in 1972, I met with John Stennis, another old Southern senator, who became my friend. We sat at the other end of this gigantic, grand mahogany table he used as his desk that had been the desk of Richard Russell. It was a table upon which the Southern Manifesto was signed, I am told. The year was 1972.

Senator Stennis patted the leather chair next to him when I walked in to pay my respects as a new young senator, which was the order of the day. And he said, "Sit down, sit down, sit down here, son." And those who serve with him know he always talked like this.

And he looked at me and he said, "Son, what made you run for the Senate?"

And like a darn fool I told him the exact truth . . . I said, "Civil rights, sir." And as soon as I did I could feel the beads of perspiration pop out of my head and get that funny feeling. And he looked at me and said, "Good, good, good." And that was the end of the conversation.

(LAUGHTER)

Well, eighteen years later . . . we'd become friends.

I saw him sitting behind that same table eighteen years later, only this time in a wheelchair. His leg had been amputated because of cancer. And I was going to look at offices, because in my seniority, his office was available as he was leaving.

I went in and sat down and he looked at me as if it were yesterday and he said, "Sit down, Joe, sit down", and tapped that chair. And he said something that startled me. He said, "Remember the first time you came to see me, Joe?" And I shook my head, I didn't remember. And he leaned forward and he recited the story.

I said to him, "I was a pretty smart young fellow, wasn't I, Mr. Chairman?" He said, "Joe, I wanted to tell you something then that I'm going to tell you now. You are going to take my office, aren't you?" And I said, "Yes, sir, Mr. Chairman."

And he ran his hand back and forth across that mahogany table in a loving way, and he said, "You see this table, Joe?" This is the God's truth. He said, "You see this table?"

And I said, "Yes, sir, Mr. Chairman." He said, "This table was the flagship of the Confederacy from 1954 to 1968." He said, "We sat here, most of us from the Deep South, the old Confederacy, and we planned the demise of the civil rights movement."

Then he looked at me and said, "And now it's time: it's time that this table go from the possession of a man against civil rights to a man who is for civil rights."

And I was stunned. And he said, "One more thing, Joe," he said. "The civil rights movement did more to free the white man than the black man."

And I looked at him. I didn't know what he meant, and in only John Stennis fashion, he said, "It freed my soul; it freed my soul."

Strom Thurmond's soul is free today. His soul is free. The Bible says, Learn to do well, seek justice, relieve the oppressed, judge the fatherless, plead for the widow, come now and let us reason together, though your sins may be as scarlet, they shall be as white as snow.

Strom, today there are no longer any issues to debate, there's only peace, a patch of common ground, and the many memories that you've left behind.

For me, those memories are deeply personal, and they will stay with me as long as I live. Strom Thurmond stood by me when others didn't, and when it was against his political interest to do so.

I had been accused of something terrible, in my view, on the eve of the Bork nomination. I gathered the entire Senate, I was then chairman, the entire Judiciary Committee, and I said to Democrats and Republicans alike, I will stand aside as chairman so it will not affect this proceeding.

And [looking at the Thurmond children] the first man to jump to his feet was your father, and he said, "No."

And I said, "Well, let me explain." He said, "You don't have to explain anything to me. You're my chairman."

And with that, everyone ad seriatim stood up, but Strom Thurmond was the first man on his feet—did not seek a single explanation for what I had been accused of.

And clearly, when partisanship was a winning option, he chose friendship, and I'll never forget him for it. I was honored to work with him, privileged to serve with him, and proud to call him my friend. His long life may well have been a gift of his beloved God, but the powerful and lasting impact he had on his beloved South Carolina and on his nation is Strom's legacy, his gift to all of us. And he will be missed.

The British essayist William Hazlett once wrote, quote: "Death conceals everything but truth, and strips a man of everything but genius and virtue."

It's a sort of natural canonization.

The truth and genius and virtue of Strom Thurmond is what I choose and we all choose to remember today. To Nancy, to Strom, to Julie, and to Paul, to all his friends, the people of South Carolina who knew him so well and love him so much, America mourns with you. I mourn with you.

For I knew Strom well. I felt his warmth as you did. I saw his strength as you did. I was the beneficiary of his virtues, as you were. And I'll miss him as you will, as we all will.

He lived a long and good life. And I know that today a benevolent God has lifted his arms to Strom. I just don't know what Strom is saying to that benevolent God, because you know he's saying something.

So I say, Farewell, Mr. Chairman. We stand in adjournment until we meet again.

WHEN THE CASKET HAD ARRIVED outside the church, a military band played "The Battle Hymn of the Republic," and inside, an orchestra accompanied a huge choir in royal blue robes singing the hymn, "How Great Thou Art." In Edgefield for the burial, the retail area around the square virtually shut down, as shop owners joined most of the town's other citizens—at least the white ones, and some of the black—to walk the few blocks to Willowbrook Cemetery. They stood or sat on the hill that wound around and looked down at the burial site, their final silent good-bye during the rites and the lowering into the ground of the coffin, not far from his daughter Nancy Moore.

It was the end of the service in Columbia, however, as the coffin was borne up the aisle, that Strom seemed to have chosen for a redemptive statement about his Dixiecrat rhetoric and his record of adamant opposition to civil rights in the two decades that had followed. A bagpipe played a tune written two centuries earlier.

"Amazing grace, how sweet the sound, that saved a wretch like me," say the lyrics written by a repentant slave-ship captain. "I once was lost but now am found. Was blind, but now I see."

Strom Thurmond's life on earth had ended, but as he had predicted, more of the story remained.

CHAPTER 26

Breaking the Silence

Not long after Strom Thurmond's death, the phone began ringing at Essie Williams's low-slung house on Chesley Avenue in Los Angeles. Gambling that the senator's death might finally unlock his deepest secrets, reporters from numerous national news outlets pounced on Williams to pursue the ancient rumor that she was Thurmond's illegitimate daughter. Politely, in a soft motherly voice, Williams stonewalled even the best of them. The rumor was simply not true, she repeatedly insisted. Thurmond was nothing more than an old family friend.

Just after Thurmond's 100th birthday party and Trent Lott's infamous comments, the matter gained new life when *Washington Post* columnist Colby King, an African American, wrote a poignant piece suggesting that Essie was the "uninvited guest" at Thurmond's celebration. King's column recounted Marilyn Thompson's efforts to prove that Thurmond had a secret black daughter. Williams had declined to respond to King's phone calls seeking comment. The piece attracted international attention when it became part of a submission of Colby King's columns that was awarded a Pulitzer Prize.

In the months after Thurmond's death, the most tenacious attempt to force a confession from Williams came from two dogged women producers for television anchorman Dan Rather and CBS's popular investigative program, *60 Minutes II.* Mary Mapes, who is white, and her partner, Dana Roberson, who is African American, had become fascinated by the legend of Strom Thurmond's black daughter. Along with the King column, they had researched a detailed chapter about Williams in the 1998 Jack Bass and Marilyn Thompson biography, *Ol' Strom*, and an earlier report in 1992 by Thompson in the *Washington Post* Style section. The Texan Mapes, known for her unrelenting doggedness, calculated that CBS had the best chance of winning "the get," television lingo for a hotly sought exclusive. "The story made our hair curl," she said. "We loved it." If they stuck with it, she believed that she and Roberson could convince Williams that the time had come to finally tell the truth.

Like private detectives tracking an unfaithful spouse, Mapes and Roberson quietly flew to Los Angeles, rented a car, and tracked down the Williams home. From time to time over the course of several weeks in the summer of 2003, they would approach the house and ring the doorbell, only to be rejected by Ms. Williams, her daughter Wanda Terry, or Jason Terry, Wanda's handsome, muscular grandson, who gave them a thrill by coming to the door in gym clothes, only to make excuses for his grandmother. All of them, as Mapes said later, had the "deadpan act down cold." Mapes would call from a cell phone and sometimes reach Ms. Williams, who was always friendly but would cut short the conversation as soon as Mapes began pursuing the Thurmond connection. Once, Wanda Terry met the producers in the driveway, according to Mapes, and berated them, "My mother doesn't know anything about Strom Thurmond. It's a bunch of Internet crap."

Undeterred, Mapes and Roberson made three trips to Los Angeles over the course of several months, developing an ever more intimate telephone relationship with Williams. They sent floral tributes in increasingly gargantuan sizes; they had food delivered from a trendy restaurant partly owned by Essie's favorite movie star, Denzel Washington. They tried every journalistic trick, using phone calls from Rather to reinforce the pressure. Separately, they consulted Thompson at the *Washington Post* and Bass at the College of Charleston, looking for new strategies.

One day, Mapes thought she had a breakthrough when she talked with Ms. Williams by telephone about the importance of setting straight the historical record, stressing that she had an obligation to future generations of black Americans. Normally an extremely composed and reticent woman, Williams began to cry. "I have my grandchildren and children to worry about," she sobbed. Williams suggested that she had never told her children the truth. Mapes believed she was on the verge of a confession, but then, as usual, Williams ended the conversation.

Finally, in late summer, after Mapes suggested to Williams that she talk the matter over with her children, the *60 Minutes* team backed off and moved on to other assignments. Mapes was convinced that Williams was on the verge of disclosing her secret, but the team simply could not sit outside her doorstep forever.

By mid-December 2003, Marilyn Thompson had taken a leave from the *Washington Post* to battle cancer. She was recovering from a round of chemotherapy when the telephone rang at her bedside. Her *Post* colleague Jeff Leen was on the line.

"A lawyer in Los Angeles is trying to reach you," Leen said. "He said he represents someone named Essie Mae Washington-Williams. He says she's holding a press conference next week to tell the world her story."

Thompson bolted upright in the bed. "Are you kidding me?" she said.

Thompson had first approached Williams in 1984, carrying two letters retrieved from Thurmond's gubernatorial archives that acknowledged the receipt of money in 1947 and 1950. Thompson thought the letters constituted a "smoking gun," proof that the senator had secretly supported a young black woman during the height of his segregationist years. She had tracked Essie's life in Orangeburg, South Carolina; Savannah, Georgia; and Coatesville, Pennsylvania, finally locating her in Los Angeles. But Williams had flatly denied that Thurmond was her father, using many of the same rehearsed lines that she told Mapes during discussions twenty years later.

Thompson jotted down the telephone number for attorney Frank Wheaton of Compton, California, an agent for sports figures. When she reached him en route to an afternoon golf date, Wheaton laid out the bare details. Williams had retained him to help her orchestrate a press conference in South Carolina in which she would acknowledge that Thurmond was, indeed, her father. She hoped to use the press conference to launch a book or movie deal that Wheaton had been asked to negotiate, a deal that he believed would be worth at least seven figures.

Wheaton said he had sought out Thompson because of her years of work on Thurmond and her knowledge of South Carolina. He said that Williams distinctly remembered her from the 1984 interview at her Los Angeles school office. She believed she had been treated respectfully, Wheaton said. He said they had tracked down Thompson to consider whether she might make a suitable author for Williams's biography.

Thompson could not believe her good fortune, but the prospect of a book project did not have nearly the appeal of a more immediate newspaper scoop. Thompson convinced Wheaton that if Williams would give the *Washington Post* her first exclusive interview for publication in the Sunday edition, the story would make international news and galvanize the press conference that Wheaton hoped to hold the next week.

Normally, Thompson would have jumped on an airplane to do the interview in person, but her health would not permit it. So Wheaton arranged for a conference call. Thompson did the interview from her bedroom office, with Wheaton, Williams, and Wanda Terry on the line.

The interview lasted over an hour, allowing Thompson to fill in many of the gaps in her knowledge of Williams's life story. There were still many holes, and Wheaton interrupted Williams several times to warn her not to give away too much, to "save something for the book."

Thompson was most intrigued by Williams's possible financial motivation. She had always believed that Thurmond's financial support of Williams during her college years was intended to buy her silence, since he could not afford exposure while building a political career espousing segregation. Williams testily dismissed this line of reasoning. She portrayed Thurmond as a beneficent figure, refusing even to entertain the notion that he may have been paying her money to keep her quiet.

Clearly, however, more was going on behind the scenes. After watching her father's funeral on a video sent to her by a South Carolina friend, Williams soon learned that she and her heirs were not mentioned in Thurmond's will, which left his assets to his wife and three surviving white children. Wheaton had written a letter on her behalf in September to the Thurmond family attorney, Mark Taylor—a copy of which was sent to Strom Jr.—asking that Essie be recognized as an heir with access to the will. The letter had gotten no response. The Williams family had turned to Wheaton for help.

Meanwhile, Wheaton—unlicensed to practice law in either South Carolina or California (he had an Indiana license)—had asked a number of South Carolina lawyers to associate with him. He ran into concerns about taking on the Thurmonds, especially with Strom Jr. now the U.S. attorney for the state. Finally, Glenn Walters of Orangeburg, an African American graduate of SC State University and the University of Virginia School of Law, agreed to work on the matter. Colleagues warned him of the risk of taking on such a powerful family, but he believed Williams deserved the best representation he could offer. To declare Essie an heir to Thurmond would have the legal effect of establishing parentage and providing access to the will, but would not necessarily entitle her to a share in the estate. Walters researched South Carolina estate law and prepared the necessary court papers for an order to exhume Strom's body and provide DNA testing, should that prove necessary.

Meanwhile, Williams and Wheaton prepared for a return to South Carolina to hold a press conference that would also get the family's attention. Wheaton confided to Thompson that Williams would do whatever was necessary to press her claim, up to and including exhumation. The prospect of unearthing a freshly buried South Carolina legend under such circumstances was apparently designed to force action by the Thurmond family.

In writing her story, Thompson also discovered details of Williams's troubled finances. Margot Williams, a *Washington Post* researcher, found an early 2003 bankruptcy filing by Williams that revealed debts to department stores and lending institutions and included two loans received during the 1990s from the U.S. Small Business Administration. One of the loans had been forgiven, the agency reported, but a spokesman told Thompson that such action was not unusual. The agency declined to release details of the loans, citing privacy restrictions, and Wheaton said he knew nothing about them. Essie Williams later told reporters that she had run into financial trouble only because she took on debt for others. She deeply resented Thompson's inquiries.

Thompson's story was slated for the morning editions of the *Post* on Sunday, December 14, but a condensed version of the story was released on Saturday for the *Post* Web site, washingtonpost.com, and for dissemination on the *Post* wire service.

As soon as the story was put to bed and there was no danger of being scooped, Thompson, with permission from her editor, contacted Mary Mapes to tell her that Williams had given the *Post* an exclusive interview and was set to tell the world who she was at a press conference the next Wednesday. The two reporters—print and television—had developed a relationship and shared an appreciation for the dimensions of Williams's story. Mapes leaped into action, contacting Wheaton to finally snare the television exclusive. She also sent Thompson a dozen long-stem red roses on behalf of the *60 Minutes* crew. "Congratulations on the scoop of a lifetime!" the card read.

Meanwhile, Mapes started the wheels turning at CBS. Rather prepared to fly to Los Angeles, but the breaking news early Sunday morning of Saddam Hussein's capture in Iraq kept Rather from traveling. Mapes arranged instead for Ms. Williams and a full entourage, including Wheaton, Wanda Terry, her son, and a longtime friend of Wheaton's, to fly to New York for an interview on Monday for the upcoming Wednesday evening edition of *60 Minutes II*. Wheaton demanded deluxe treatment for the group on CBS's tab and also negotiated for paid airfare and accommodations for the trip to Columbia, South Carolina, in preparation for the Wednesday press conference. The room service bill alone ran into the thousands, causing some grumbling at CBS. But in return, Wheaton agreed to keep Williams sealed off from other television networks until after her public announcement.

Meanwhile, things were popping in South Carolina. On Saturday, as Thompson's story was disseminated nationally by the *Washington Post–Los Angeles Times* News Service for use in Sunday newspapers across the nation, Strom Thurmond's youngest son, twenty-seven-year-old Paul, was getting married that night in Charleston and leaving on his honeymoon. After the astounding story showed up on the wire, at least one local reporter wanted to go to the wedding and get a reaction, but a wise editor said no.

In Aiken, thirty-one-year-old Strom Thurmond Jr. and his mother huddled with a few confidants to develop the family's response to Essie's announcement. He did not return calls seeking comment for the *Post* story. The tentative plan called for neither denying nor confirming Williams's claim, in effect saying she was entitled to believe what she wanted to believe.

Carried internationally, Thompson's *Post* piece also ran under front-page banner headlines in South Carolina newspapers, stunning many of the state's citizens. Tens of thousands of Strom loyalists felt especially numb. Some whites had experienced less shock but became deeply interested in the story, and many blacks felt vindicated at the full public acknowledgment of a story well known in their communities, but little known among whites outside of Edgefield County. Across the country, responses ran the gamut from surprise to outrage and even to glee among some of those who had never liked Strom's politics and were now happy to see his reputation take a hit from beyond the grave. Other Strom critics were more philosophical about the matter and took the announcement as a reminder of the complicated nature of race and politics in the South. Among some of Thurmond's most prominent and staunchest supporters, the initial news of Essie's claim met with disbelief. For example, Congressman Joe Wilson called her story "unseemly" and a "smear" on Thurmond's image.

But the Thurmond family was carefully gauging the reaction. Young Strom Thurmond Jr. took charge. His appointment two years earlier by Bush at his ailing father's behest had met with considerable skepticism in both the state and national press, and critics had questioned both the clear nepotism and his qualifications to hold such a prestigious legal post. His handling of this matter would be closely watched as a sign of his political savvy. On Monday, December 15, the day Essie was being interviewed for *60 Minutes II,* Strom Jr. issued a statement on behalf of the Thurmond family. It acknowledged "Ms. Essie Mae Washington-Williams' claim to her heritage" and expressed hope it "will bring closure for Ms. Williams."

Young Thurmond told reporters, "As far as emotions or how I feel, I feel good because that's a feeling you get from doing the right thing." He also said he once had a conversation with his father about reports of the relationship some ten years earlier, after Thompson's 1992 story in the *Washington Post.* "I asked about this, and he didn't tell me whether she was or whether she wasn't [his daughter]. I did not ask again."

He added that before "these very interesting headlines" on Sunday morning, the story had never "really been discussed among members of my family. My mother, brother and sisters and I have very limited personal knowledge of this."

In taking the initiative as family leader and reaching out to Williams, young Strom had not only done the "right thing" in openly acknowledging the validity of Essie's claim, but also the smart thing. His response drew wide acclaim, doused the public and press speculation, and provided an opening for him and his brother, should either or both seek elective office, to reach out to the African American electorate of their state.

Walters later called young Thurmond's handling of the matter "a class act—he hit it right on the head."[1] Thompson persisted, disclosing that Thurmond's nephew, the chief U.S. bankruptcy judge in South Carolina, had secretly delivered payments to Essie Mae. Judge Thurmond Bishop acknowledged the role.

In the Palmetto state, the word "heritage" is loaded with special meanings and values. For Essie, her recognition by the Thurmond family resulted in an unprecedented place of acceptance, respect, and recognition between both black and white South Carolinians for any person of similar background—that became her heritage.

Williams had already said she waited until after her father's death before coming forward in order to protect his reputation and standing while he was alive. Her announcement, Strom Jr. said, left his father's image unchanged. "His legacy is secure to me. I loved him last week, and I love him this week, and I miss him." He expressed appreciation for Essie's kind words about their father, and further, for understanding her desire to confirm her heritage for her children. "Everyone has a right to know their heritage," he said.[2]

For her part, Williams seemed gratified by the family's acknowledgment. "I'm happy and very much surprised," she said.

As expected, Williams's press conference at the Adams Mark Hotel ballroom in Columbia attracted news crews from all over the nation and the world. Wheaton presided as impresario. When he finally made a fanfare call for Williams, she walked alone from behind a door on the side into the spotlight, limping from recent knee replacement surgery to address more than 200 journalists. After a sentence or two introducing herself, her face relaxed and she said in a calm, clear voice: "My father's name was James Strom Thurmond."

She spoke of her background and her four children, thirteen grandchildren, and four great-grandchildren. "Their lives are meaningful and important in American history," she said. "There are many stories like Sally Hemings and mine. The unfortunate measure is that not everyone knows about these stories that help to make America what it is today."

She told of her father's continued communication and financial support after his election to the Senate, her many visits to him in Washington, where all his staff "knew exactly who I was. I knew him beyond his public image."

She then said why she had waited so long to come forth.

> Throughout his life and mine, we respected each other. I never wanted to do anything to harm him or cause detriment to his life or the lives of those around him.
>
> My father did a lot of things to help other people, even though his public stance appeared opposite. I was sensitive about his well-being and career and his family here in South Carolina.
>
> It was only at the urging of my children and Senator Thurmond's passing that I decided that my children deserve the right to know from whom, where, and what they have come. I am committed in teaching them and

helping them to learn about their past. It is their right to know and understand the rich history of their ancestry, black and white.

At this juncture in my life, I am looking for closure. I am not bitter. I am
not angry. In fact, there is a great sense of peace that has come over me in
the past year. Once I decided that I would no longer harbor such a great
secret that many others knew, I feel as though a tremendous weight has
been lifted.

She added, "At last, I feel completely free."

In response to a question about her father, she said, "I certainly never
did like the idea of his being a segregationist, but that was his life."

The question that may have caused the largest stir came not from a reporter but from a white woman in the audience, seated in the back of the
room. She asked Ms. Williams if she would like her name added to those
of Thurmond's other children on the base of his statue on the Statehouse
grounds. "I would like that very much," she said.

Afterward, State Senator John Courson, who had raised private funds
and presided over the dedication ceremony for the statue, told an Associated Press writer, "I was totally surprised about the revelations." He added,
"I think Ms. Williams handled it very well. She's obviously a very classy
lady."

In his story, *Washington Post* staff writer Darryl Fears quoted Jack Bass,
who attended the press conference, saying, "The most important thing to
me is what it means in terms of tearing away the veil of secrecy shrouding
these types of relationships. Across the South, many black people are
aware of their white ancestry, even though they don't know the parents.
But white people never talk about it. White people are going to be stunned
by the emotional content of this."

After later learning he was there, Williams sent word to Bass that she
would like to see him after she rested. She greeted him pleasantly in the
lobby, recalled his coming to her house six years earlier and being rebuffed,
and said, "I'm glad that now we can talk." (He did learn on that 1997 visit
that her first great-grandchild was about to celebrate a second birthday,
that Strom had become a great-great-grandfather.)

That Wednesday night, after the press conference, Williams spoke to
the nation on *60 Minutes II*, adding details previously unknown. She told
about taking her infant first child, at six months, to Washington so her

father could see his first grandchild. "He didn't see the others until they were older," she said, when she took them to meet him when he was speaking at a church in Los Angeles.

"And he was elated," she told Rather. "He was glad to see them because they were teenagers. He thought I had a lovely family. He always thought that I was a lovely person. That's why he was helpful to me, because he felt like I deserved it."

She explained that the only Thurmond family members who knew about the relationship were Strom's sister, Mary Tompkins, and his nephew, Judge Bishop, an attorney who handled Strom's financial arrangements with Essie. She also explained that she knew she could not talk about the relationship, "without harming him. . . . And I think that would totally have changed the history."

Rather changed the subject to speculation that "this woman's coming forward is . . . all about the money."

She responded, "It is not about the money. There is no money. We are not making any claims." But she wanted "the acknowledgment" that Strom Jr. had given the day before. "It was nice to have that. And I had wanted to write about this. And I had started it but I hadn't completed what I was doing." Wheaton was already working on a book deal and a TV movie of the week.

She repeated that her coming forth was not about money, but when pressed by Rather, she said she had once asked Thurmond about a report that he was worth several million dollars. Although he mentioned owning property, "He didn't elaborate on it. But I mentioned that I read it. And of course, things he didn't want to talk about he quickly got away from the subject."

She said the amount of money that she had received from Thurmond over the years "helped me quite a bit," but she did not "want to go into figures." She said she had a good retirement, however, with her Social Security income and from teaching twenty-seven years in the Los Angeles Unified School District, which also provided full health insurance benefits. "So financially I'm fine."

She added that she was never pressured to keep quiet, but she found efforts by journalists and others seeking to get her to talk a burden, including her knowledge that fellow students from college days had talked about it. "That's the burden I feel that I've gotten rid of."

She believed her relationship with Strom had brought him to the point that Joe Biden had spoken about at Thurmond's funeral, where "change came to him easily."

"With me being his daughter," she said, "I do feel it might have softened some of the ways that he felt about other people. And that's why I think he did the many things that he did to help other black people. . . . He wanted me to know that he was doing positive things, in spite of the segregation."[3]

By the end of the week, Essie had met Strom Jr. and Nancy, her stepmother young enough to be her daughter. Nancy spoke to Essie about her own deep feelings of loss about both her daughter and her husband, from whom she apparently never separated emotionally. Essie would soon have dinner with both of them at Strom Jr.'s home in Aiken.

STROM REMAINED A HERO TO MANY. "From a moral standpoint, yes, what happened was wrong," Roberta Combs told the *New York Times.* Combs, the national president of the Christian Coalition and a South Carolinian, said, "That's not the traditional family. That's not how it's supposed to be. But we're not going to sit around today and criticize Strom. He's helped so many people. He's touched so many lives."

Others, including notable University of South Carolina historian Dan Carter, an award-winning biographer of George Wallace, responded differently. "After all the rage at Bill Clinton for having an affair," Carter said, "I'm always waiting for conservative icons like this who stand for family values to get creamed for their indiscretions. It never happens."[4]

If South Carolinians were still numb, many in the rest of the country continued to be fascinated, some puzzled, and others outraged. After the *New York Times* quoted a Thurmond niece that the revelation was "a blight" on the family, the newspaper's editorial page columnist Brent Staples declared Thurmond "a mercenary character." He wrote that as an abandoned child, Ms. Washington-Williams "decided that a fraction of a father who met her in back rooms but disowned her in public was preferable to no father at all."[5] Another African American columnist, Californian Earl Ofari Hutchinson, faced a far more personal challenge. As Essie's story was breaking, he wrote in a column for an Internet site that he would have to deal with the fact that his eight-year-old and two-year-old granddaughters, Essie's great-granddaughters, are now known to be Strom Thurmond's great-great-granddaughters. The older child had already asked Hutchinson about Thurmond. "Segregation, states rights and conservatism, the things he championed, are alien concepts to her," Hutchinson wrote, so he simply told her he was "an important Southern senator."

"But she deserves to know the full truth." When she's old enough, he added, "I'll tell her that Thurmond did more than any other Southern politician to resuscitate a moribund Republican Party in the South and transform it into a conservative force in national politics."

A female law professor in the Midwest wrote an article about Strom, suggesting that his affair with Carrie Butler could have constituted statutory rape. A careful editor at the *Nation* called Bass in verifying the story. He asked if they had checked out when the statutory age of consent in South Carolina was changed from fourteen to sixteen. He added that the relationship had apparently continued for many years, with Carrie Butler having sufficient intimacy to easily arrange for Judge Thurmond to meet his daughter when she was fifteen. The article was not accepted for publication.

AT THE TIME STROM JR. ANNOUNCED the family's acknowledgment of Essie's claim, he told a reporter that his father's will was inviolate. "I have no intention to alter my father's wishes," he said. "His will is the controlling document."[6] After her memoir, *Dear Senator*, was released in January 2005, Wheaton told several reporters that there may be a challenge to Thurmond's will. A major South Carolina newspaper reported that Wheaton claimed there were reports describing Thurmond as one of the larger landowners in the state. He cited no evidence.[7] Weeks later Ms. Williams terminated the services of Wheaton, issuing a statement declaring as "false" and "unauthorized" his statements indicating her interests in pursuing claims against the Thurmond estate.

THURMOND BISHOP, THE NEPHEW who handled the financial transactions, was the son of Mary Tompkins's twin sister, Martha. As a teenager in the 1950s, Bishop had visited his uncle often and developed a close relationship with Jean Thurmond, whom he considered "like a big sister to me."

In the years following her death, while a student at The Citadel, where he played varsity tennis, and later in law school, Bishop spent weeks every summer with his uncle in Washington, in the early years watching him bury himself in work at the office at night. "Such work served as an outlet to him."

Bishop said that in 1968, after he became a lawyer, "My uncle asked me to be facilitator for getting funds to Essie," telling him "not to tell anyone." Strom had handled the transactions himself earlier, on Essie's visits to Washington. After Bishop took over, money was paid once or twice a year. Funds initially came from property Thurmond owned, but when it failed to produce the expected income, the property was sold and Bishop put the money from the sale in a trust fund.

In the early years, payments ranged roughly from $600 to $1,500, twice a year. Over time they got larger, ranging from $1,500 to $2,000. Bishop estimated that altogether she received more than $100,000, which in terms of inflated 2004 dollars would be several times that.

Initially, as a means of shielding the transactions from scrutiny, there was a system Strom had established and Bishop continued of sending the money together with a promissory note for her to return. After a year or two, the promissory note would be returned, marked "paid in full." Over time, Bishop discontinued the use of promissory notes. "It was never intended for her to pay back the money," he said.

According to Bishop, Strom chose not to include Williams in his will because he had never told Nancy and their children about her. The senator set up generous trust accounts for his children, Strom Jr., Paul, and Julia, splitting up his real estate holdings in Aiken and Union counties and other assets. Around the same time, in 1998, he stopped making payments to Essie. He set aside $30,000 that she would receive over the next three years as her legacy.

Most of the assets in his will, Bishop said, consisted of pensions from the Senate, Social Security, and the Army Reserve. They could go only to Nancy as an eligible survivor.

Thurmond initially wanted Bishop to personally meet with Williams and turn over funds in cash, but he says they met only once, at the airport in Columbia. She turned down an offer for dinner with him or to spend the night, saying she had to return on the next flight in order to take care of her children. Bishop told her that he would arrange to send the funds to her in the future. Her re collection is that they met subsequently at the Atlanta airport, but Bishop says he never made such a trip from his home in South Carolina.

She would call every six to nine months, telling him how much she needed. "I never initiated a call to Essie," Bishop said. "I would wait to hear from her. I never got the impression of extortion or that she would ever do anything to hurt him. I have high regard for her."

Bishop compares his uncle's "belonging to the people of South Carolina" with that of "a priest belonging to God."[8] In addition to the funds provided through Bishop, Strom apparently continued to hand over envelopes filled with cash, often $100 bills, to Essie on annual trips she made to his Senate office in Washington. Although Essie has declined to specify the total amount Thurmond provided her in cash payments over more than a half-century, she told the authors it was "less than a million."[9]

In 2000, after Essie became unable to travel because of knee surgery, her daughter Wanda flew to Washington on her mother's behalf, briefly meeting her grandfather. Despite his impaired hearing, she found him mentally alert. "You look just like your mother," he told her. She passed on her mother's good wishes and returned to Los Angeles with funds from him.

Thurmond's top aide, administrative assistant Duke Short, sat in on the meeting. Wanda Terry recalled Short pulling her aside during the visit to applaud her mother's ability to keep a secret and asking, "How has she managed to go all these years without saying anything?" Short later denied this conversation.

ESSIE'S PASTOR, Madison Shockley, went to see her after her announcement to offer counsel. She made it clear she didn't want to hurt Thurmond. "She didn't see any benefit in it," he said. As the pastor saw it, "Clearly, she was not a front-line civil rights activist or she would have done anything to expose him. But would you really expect someone to go to war with their father? That is a pretty heavy thing to ask."[10]

Although Essie's oldest son, Julius, a Seattle transit worker, maintained a self-imposed silence after the announcement, his siblings were more open.

"This was a grandfather that you didn't see," said Ronald Williams, an emergency room physician in the state of Washington. "When you grow up with a grandfather that you don't see, that you don't really hear from and you know that they exist, it's almost like God or something. You know it's there, but you don't have any immediate contact. You don't question." A registered Republican, he spoke proudly of his grandfather and expressed regret he was not closer to him. In a playful jest, he added, "I got Thurmond back. I married a white girl."[11]

Monica had long ago forgiven her grandfather for his political stances. Working with agent Wheaton, Wanda assumed the role of her mother's business manager in negotiations for a book deal and paid speaking engagements. Some publishers were put off by Wheaton's demands for a high advance, but she found a receptive audience with Judith Regan, who, ironically, would be publishing Senator Trent Lott's memoir in the same season. Wheaton's discussions with Thompson about a book project broke down after the *Post* article appeared. Among other issues, Williams and her daughter Wanda were upset that Thompson had included information about the bankruptcy filing and had raised questions about whether Thurmond's payments constituted hush money. Williams believed that her personal finances were not relevant to the story. She wanted her book to be written in her own words, the autobiography of a loving and appreciative daughter.

AFTER THE SHOCK OF THE INITIAL STORIES, the Thurmond family's acceptance of Essie and her own winning style brought her the kind of attention in South Carolina of which she could only have dreamed.

On February 28, Williams spoke in Columbia to an audience of 450 at a sellout $50 fund-raiser banquet to provide student scholarships for Allen University, the historically black school founded in 1870 by the African Methodist Episcopal Church and named for AME founder Richard Allen. Black city councilman E. W. Cromartie presented her with a key to the city.

At the banquet, she characterized her father as a strong advocate of education and said, "My mission and my goals are simple. I want to make a difference in the lives of young people and children. Education offers a key."

She expressed hope that her life story might generate more communication among blacks and whites. "One of the things that I would like to see come out of this is better relationships between the races," she said. "Believe me, we need that."[12]

Bruce Elrod, whose grandmother was Strom's first cousin, owned both nationally distributed Lost Gold Records and a partnership interest in the Confederate States Mint, which makes commemorative replicas of coins of the Confederacy, with a dollar from each one going to the Sons of the Confederacy. He worked out an arrangement with Wheaton, whom Elrod said shared costs with him as an equal investor in the project, and Essie to make bronze (\$20), silver (\$39), and gold (\$575) coins with Essie's likeness on one side. They were sold for the first time at Allen. According to Elrod, roughly one-third of the income will go to the Essie Mae Washington-Williams Foundation for need-based college scholarships.[13]

Essie returned to South Carolina to receive an honorary doctorate from South Carolina State University on May 7 in what became a whirlwind weekend that included a royal visit to Edgefield and an hour-long chat with Strom Jr. in Columbia, who stopped by to visit at her hotel.

At SC State, she was cited for "her commitment to learning" in a citation declaring, "She has embarked upon the task for educating a nation." Her daughter Wanda, watching the presentation from the president's box above the seats of the school's football stadium, told a companion, "I never would have believed something like this would be possible."

The next day the two of them traveled to Edgefield, where Bettis Rainsford escorted them. After getting the invitation, Ms. Williams checked with Thurmond Bishop, who told her that Rainsford was "all right." It was Essie's first visit to Edgefield in the sixty-three years since the introduction to her father in 1941.

She visited her father's grave for the first time and toured his birthplace. Essie introduced Wanda to her great-aunt, Strom's sister Mary Tompkins, who died two months later.

The town's two weeklies both ran front-page articles with photographs. In the *Advertiser*, a three-column photo showed Essie and Wanda in front of a framed depiction of a horse-drawn covered wagon and the words, "Trailing Your Ancestors." The caption under the photo read, "As the sign in background suggests, Essie Mae Washington-Williams and her daughter Wanda Terry were indeed 'trailing their ancestors' during a visit to Edgefield this past Saturday."

The *Advertiser* noted that one response to Essie was "her lack of pretense." She seemed to charm them all. Tom Baughman, publisher of the *Citizen-News*, called her "a very nice Lady." He believed there was no imminent change in the "ingrained" black and white relations in the area, but said on both sides of Thurmond's family, "The way it was handled softened the truth enough that it added to the legend."

Suzanne Mims Derrick, the editor of the *Advertiser*, believed the visit by Ms. Williams and the reception given to her would ultimately have "some healing effect" on the community.[14]

The following weekend, Ms. Williams visited Charleston for an event featuring her that was designed to raise money for a minority journalism program. A Saturday morning newspaper account of a Friday press conference characterized her as "showing a reserved dignity." The article quoted Wheaton on her relationship with Nancy Thurmond: "Mrs. Williams is like a mentor to Nancy. Mrs. Thurmond calls very frequently, and Mrs. Williams speaks to her probably as she would another daughter."[15]

At lunch that day she met her half brother Paul at his suburban home, over a two-hour lunch that Nancy had prepared for the three of them. "We chatted a good while and had a very nice afternoon," said Paul, a lawyer working in the solicitor's (district attorney) office as a prosecutor. "It was a very nice conversation," he told a reporter.[16] The visit was followed by a downtown carriage ride for Essie and a guide, which Nancy arranged but did not join.

That evening she spoke in North Charleston at an imposing brick Baptist church with a black congregation and clergyman. Mayor Keith Summey greeted her and presented a key to the city. "The oldest child of J. Strom Thurmond," he said, "is working to make race relations more meaningful to all South Carolinians."

Although the church was less than half full, the audience responded attentively, many coming forward after her talk to greet her. One man stood and said, "Oh, you just make me feel so proud." A black woman in Charleston, however, said a few days later, "So what? I know a hundred stories like that."[17]

A few weeks later, back in Los Angeles, Mrs. Williams worked with others in that city's South Carolina State alumni chapter to raise $4,000 in scholarship funds for the school.

On July 1, exactly a year after Strom Thurmond's funeral—and after the Thurmond family had signaled its approval to the legislature—the name Essie Mae was chiseled in the granite monument on the Statehouse grounds below those of Nancy Moore, J. Strom Jr., Juliana Gertrude, and Paul Reynolds. There was no ceremony, but a story and large photo received prominent front-page display the next morning in *The State.*

The Charleston *Post and Courier* commented in an editorial, "What also should be recorded for posterity is what a remarkable woman Essie Mae Washington-Williams is in her own right." Calling her "a model of decorum," the newspaper added, "Mrs. Williams hasn't refused the spotlight, but she has chosen her appearances and her words carefully. She has been so impressive that the Legislature's endorsement of the proposal to add her name to the Thurmond monument was a foregone conclusion. It was, of course, her due. But her fine character has made it a particularly satisfying event."[18]

THE DAY AFTER ESSIE'S NAME went on the Thurmond monument, Frank Wheaton hit a press bonanza, a six-column headline on the National Report page of the *New York Times*, "Thurmond's Biracial Daughter Seeks to Join Confederacy Group." The story was illustrated by a five-column photo of the two of them with Wanda and her son, taken at her Columbia press conference more than six months earlier.

The article opened by stating Mrs. Williams "now wants to join the United Daughters of the Confederacy (UDC), an organization of female descendants of soldiers who fought for the South in the Civil War."[19]

The only quote attributed to Mrs. Williams, in a statement released by Wheaton in her name, said, "It is important for all Americans to have the opportunity to know and understand their bloodline. Through my father's line, I am fortunate to trace my heritage back to the birth of our nation and beyond. On my mother's side, like most African-Americans, my history is broken by the course of human events."

Her interest in the two organizations stemmed from different sources. At the Allen University event where Bruce Elrod first sold coins with her likeness, he had talked to her about the advantages of joining the UDC, saying that it would change the course of history. Elrod also talked up the idea with Wheaton, whom the *New York Times* quoted as saying one of Essie's sons would join the Sons of Confederate Veterans, an organization in which Elrod plays an active role.

Before Wheaton gave the story to the *New York Times* as an exclusive, the UDC's California director, Rhobie Reed-Curtis, called Essie at home, but she was busy at the time and never returned the call. The newspaper quoted Reed-Curtis as saying, "She has an ancestor, and just like anybody else, if they can document it with the proper paperwork, that's all there is. If people want to put more to that, I can't."

The president general of the UDC, Patsy Limpus, said she knew of "several" blacks in her organization, which claims 170,000 members.

Almost a month after the *Times* story, Ms. Williams said she had neither joined nor asked to join either the UDC or the Daughters of the American Revolution (DAR), but added, "I may do so. I need to find out about organizations." She continued, "I didn't know so many black men had been killed in the Civil War in the South. Lots of blacks were involved in that war—and in the American Revolution, too."

Curiosity about the story reverberated both nationally and in South Carolina, where June Wells, a former national leader of the UDC, told the *Post and Courier*, "I would be very hesitant right now to talk about that one subject." Another leader of the group in Charleston said she knew of no local black members of the Daughters of the Confederacy.

But state Senate Majority Leader Glenn McConnell, active in Sons of Confederate Veterans and owner of CSA Galleries store, a major retailer of Confederate memorabilia, said he was "delighted" by the news that Ms. Williams might be joining the UDC. "She'll find a welcome home," he said. "We're not a racist organization. She can become a bridge between the majority community and the minority community."

Marvin Dulaney, director of the Avery Research Center for African-American Life and Culture at the College of Charleston and former chairman of the Department of History, said, "I don't know what to think. Let's just say I wouldn't do it. Traditionally, those organizations have excluded African-Americans."

Dulaney said he had recently learned he was eligible to join the Sons of Confederate Veterans because a slave ancestor had been taken to at least two Civil War battles by his master, "but I know, in reality, that my grandfather wasn't there by choice. It was that he had to be there. Since I have a choice, I don't want to join the Sons of Confederate Veterans."[20]

The *New York Times* columnist Brent Staples wrote that Ms. Williams's very public claim to the Thurmond legacy "has consciously transformed her family's story into a penetrating lesson in the history of race in the early South."

"White patriarchs who trafficked in racism by day and sired black children at night are an archetype in the history of the South, where white and black families have always been more closely related by blood than many whites care to admit. The final public outing of Mr. Thurmond was viewed with amusement in black communities across the country.

"But amusement turned to perplexity," he said, with the announcement that she would embrace her white heritage by applying for membership in the United Daughters of the Confederacy. He concluded, however, that the "reality of a socially complex, mixed-race South—with whites and blacks closely related by blood and mutually complicit in slavery—disappeared from public view as the country adopted simplistic formulations of the racial past.

"The drama unfolding between the daughter of a black woman born in the shadow of slavery and a white family with deep Confederate roots seems the perfect window through which to revisit the subject. If that is what Ms. Washington-Williams intended, she has served a useful purpose for us all."[21]

Unlike her interest in the United Daughters of the Confederacy, Essie's curiosity about joining the Daughters of the American Revolution arose from a call to Wheaton made by Maurice Barboza, a nephew of Lena Santos Ferguson, a black woman whom the DAR rejected for membership in 1980. She was admitted in 1984 after a four-year legal battle. Her nephew helped her found the Black Patriots Foundation. Mrs. Ferguson died in 2004, and Ms. Williams expressed regret she never had the chance to meet her.

Barboza added to the story two weeks after the Staples column by writing in detail in a co-authored *New York Times* op-ed column about what he called the DAR's "troubling" behavior in following his aunt's court settlement, which had required historical and genealogical research to discover and identify more black soldiers.

"When the lists are complete," the columnists said, "many people whose families assimilated into white society and cloaked their African heritage may learn, for the first time, of their complicated history. . . . Every American, regardless of color, must realize that the past is not pretty, linear, or easily explained."[22]

Mrs. Williams expressed special interest in the Black Patriots Foundation, which is raising $14 million for a monument in Washington, a project she intends to support. Two months after the initial article in the *New York Times*, after taking time to find out more about both organizations, she said it was her intention to join both the UDC and the DAR.

Meanwhile, Governor Mark Sanford had quietly sent word to her that he would like at some point to host a dinner for her and the South Carolina Thurmond family.

Ms. Williams seemed to take it all in with an air of tranquillity. Later she said, "The outreach by the public has amazed me. Everyone has been trying to be helpful." A few months after her meeting in Charleston with Nancy and Paul, however, her relationship with the Thurmond family did not seem to have advanced much further. "I'm not closely in touch with them," Essie said, adding, "They've all been very nice." 23

IN SOUTH CAROLINA, the end of enforced racial segregation four decades earlier had opened a new era in social relations. The first generation of children who attended integrated public schools today are parents of schoolchildren.

In telling the story of one of the state's oldest and most deeply rooted plantation families, Edward Ball's award-winning book, *Slaves in the Family*, helped launch a dialogue about black-white family relationships. The book involves a dozen families, only two of which were interracial. Ball has said that members of those families divided in their response to the book, but curiosity tended to replace initial fear among whites and sarcasm among blacks after the taboo of silence was broken. The question became, "Can we talk to them?"

"Dozens of times at book signings," Ball recalled, "it happened that people said they had suspicions of black relatives and, after the book, it would be easier and less dangerous to confront."24

Even before Essie broke her silence, South Carolinian John S. Rainey picked up on the central theme of Joe Biden's eulogy that "time changes." Rainey—a University of Virginia law graduate serving as chairman of the state's Board of Economic Advisors and linked by early-eighteenth-century South Carolina forebears to a web of similar elites who dominate the state's traditionalist culture—contended that Thurmond had set an example of changing with grace and dignity.

"With this great gift," Rainey wrote in an op-ed column sent to leading newspapers in the state and that suggested a theme of reconciliation, "We should be able to continue to emerge from the divisions of the past to a more enlightened, healed society where, at long last, we can finally separate and lay to rest the oppression that has been so tragically linked with courage and honor and has comprised the burden of Southern history. For us, too, time can heal; time can change."25

A PLAY, *Strom in Limbo,* opened in South Carolina in late 2004 with extensive press coverage in the state and positive reviews. Written by New York native David Zinman, a retired Associated Press writer and New York native now living in South Carolina, the drama depicts Strom demanding a trial after he is turned away from Heaven's gates and then getting a hearing before a celestial court. Witnesses at the trial range from Sue Logue to Essie Mae Washington-Williams. The judge is Martin Luther King Jr. Suzanne Derrick attended the opening of the play and reported positively on it for the *Edgefield Advertiser,* but expressed doubt that Edgefield as a whole was ready for a local production. The play focuses on and leaves open the question of whether Thurmond's change from segregationist to racial moderate had been a real change of heart or simply a matter of political survival. The broader moral question underlying the play is how responsible individuals are for the choices they make.

Thurmond's debilitation at the end of his record U.S. Senate career helped persuade Fritz Hollings to retire two years later on January 2, 2005, a day after turning eighty-three. U.S. Representative Jim Demint, a conservative Republican, succeeded him. For South Carolina, it meant going in two years from senators in each party with a combined eighty-four years of seniority to (for the first time since Reconstruction) two Republicans with a combined two years of seniority.

A few months before his retirement, Hollings described to *Washington Post* reporter Peter Carlson what doddering old senators looked like when they'd hung around too long. He mentioned "poor Strom in his wheelchair" and added, "You lose your effectiveness. I've been elected seven times, and now it's time to go home." Unlike Thurmond's thin record of legislative achievement, Hollings not only protected and expanded the food stamp and related programs, but he created ocean protection laws and agencies, shaped port and airport security legislation, and established long-term environmental protection for more than 100,000 acres of fragile marshlands along the South Carolina coast.

Although acknowledging his support of segregation as a political necessity when he got elected as governor at thirty-seven, Hollings reminisced about serving in 1952 on the state's legal team that argued the case for school segregation before the Supreme Court in 1952 at an early stage of

Brown v. Board of Education. He heard an opposing lawyer say, "How in the world can you ask them to serve in the front lines in Europe and when they come home, ask them to sit in the back of the bus?" Hollings said, "As a veteran, that struck me. I realized that just ain't right."

Sociologist Herbert Blumer, in an essay published in 1965, "The Future of the Color Line," discussed the "inner" line of separation, the question of equal social status. Writing about it at a national level at the peak of the civil rights movement, Blumer said, "Its presence can be noted most clearly among the whites who are willing to accept Negroes as having equal social status yet who are not disposed to admit them into intimate and private circles, represented by social sets, cliques, private clubs, friendship sets, family circles, courtship, and marriage."[26]

But even that inner circle has begun to bend. For example, the *Post and Courier* in twenty-first-century Charleston frequently includes photographs of blacks attending predominantly white social events. In Edgefield, the *Advertiser*'s "Students of the Month" photograph for the final installment in the 2003–2004 school year at Strom Thurmond High School depicted four in each class: eight white females, five black females, two black males, and one white male. Although biracial marriages in the state remain uncommon, especially among the upper class, they happen. When they do, most families adjust to the new realities, especially after children are born.

Hastings Wyman, an Aiken native who writes and publishes "Southern Political Report," a biweekly newsletter, observed in early 2004 that the responses of the Thurmond family, "which contrast sharply with the late Thurmond's earlier denials when the rumor received publicity, may be a sign of the times in today's South. Today, for an aspiring politician, even a Republican, to exhibit racist behavior, even in such a touchy subject as interracial sexual relations, is bad form. This suggests a little-noticed but real change in the views of many Southern whites toward blacks."

He continued,

In a few more decades, there may well be a large population of biracial young people in the South. If their older white relatives grimace at their young kin's skin color, their older black family members may be chagrined to see their flesh-and-blood taking pride in the Confederate soldiers as well as the civil rights activists in their mixed-race past. That Strom Thurmond

... should be a symbol—and indeed one of the catalysts—of this change is one of the great ironies of our time.[27]

As Wyman recognized, this will not occur overnight, but breaking the silence begins the process. A month or two after Mrs. Williams came forward, a black man in a county seat town passed on the street a white man of prominence he had known forever, greeted him, and for the first time boldly asked, "When is the family reunion this year?" Among white family members, word was quickly passed that the event was canceled. The question is whether, as Edward Ball has suggested, curiosity will replace fear after the silence is broken, and whether curiosity will lead to action.

Historian Orville Vernon Burton of the University of Illinois believes Carrie Butler will take a place in the American imagination equal to that of Sally Hemings. This South Carolina native, whose groundbreaking *In My Father's House Are Many Mansions* is a classic work about Edgefield as a place central to understanding the mystique of Southern history and culture, said: "In both cases . . . they become mythical characters that are part of a past that helps us create who we are. This woman from Edgefield we don't know much about will take on historic proportions."[28]

Although her relationship with her father included an occasional clandestine hug, in the end both Strom and Essie acknowledged that emotionally it was less than fulfilling. Armstrong Williams told *GQ* writer Robert Draper that Thurmond "told me, 'I'm sure I contributed to the racism. And I'm sure it hurt her in the process.' And because of what he was and what he'd bought into, he couldn't spend time with her and her kids. He felt he had robbed himself. It was a regret he had in life."[29] In *Dear Senator,* Essie wrote, "he and I never so much as sat down together for a meal. We had never said, 'I love you' to each other. We had never confronted the reality of our relationship."

Thurmond knew that when Essie's story came out, it would be bigger than anything in his life. The way his family handles it may make it one of the most significant parts of his legacy. However the future of the color line evolves in South Carolina, it will be different because of Strom Thurmond's children—all of them.

Notes

INTRODUCTION: THE PERFECT STROM

1. Marilyn Thompson telephone interview with Armstrong Williams, May 2004.

2. Jack Bass telephone interview with Butler Derrick, July 24, 1998.

3. *Charlotte Observer*, October 29, 1972.

4. Bass interview with Dennis Shedd, August 11, 1997.

5. Bass confidential interview, August 1997.

6. Sam Nunn to Bass, 1998.

7. *New York Times Magazine*, October 6, 1968, p. 85.

CHAPTER 1: THE BOLDNESS OF AN EDGEFIELD MAN

1. W. W. Ball, *The State That Forgot: South Carolina's Surrender to Democracy* (Indianapolis: Bobbs-Merrill, 1932), p. 22.

2. Ibid.

3. The ten governors are named on a stone marker on the courthouse square: Andrew Pickens (1816–1818), George McDuffie (1834–1836), Pierce Butler (1836–1838), James H. Hammond (1842–1844), Francis Pickens (1860–1862), Milledge L. Bonham (1862–1864), John C. Sheppard (July–December 1886), Ben Tillman (1890–1894), John Gary Evans (1894–1896), and J. Strom Thurmond (1947–1951). Many of their family names still command respect in Edgefield County.

4. *New York Times Magazine,* October 6, 1968.

5. Orville Vernon Burton, *In My Father's House Are Many Mansions* (Chapel Hill: University of North Carolina Press, 1985), p. 336, note 2.

6. Eleanor Mims Hanson, *The Edgefield Advertiser and Its Editors* (Edgefield, SC: Edgefield Advertiser, 1980), p. 2.

7. James G. Banks interview with Strom Thurmond, July 1978, Southern Oral History Project, University of North Carolina at Chapel Hill, p. 8.

8. *Citizen-News* and *Edgefield Advertiser,* May 12, 2004.

9. Modjeska Simkins to Jack Bass, circa 1973.

10. Bass interview with W. W. Mims, March 11, 1998.

11. Mims letter to Jack Bass, July 17, 1971; *Edgefield Advertiser*, October 14, 1970 and August 4, 1971.

12. Bass interview with Derrick, op. cit.

13. *Edgefield Advertiser*, October 11, 1972.

14. David Bonderman letters to Jack Bass, April 23, 1998, April 29, 1998; W. W. Mims letter to Jack Bass, May 7, 1998; Bass interview with Mims, March 11, 1998.

15. Op. cit.

16. Bass interview with W. W. Mims, Edgefield, South Carolina, June 4, 2004.

17. Mims interview with Thompson, circa 1981.

18. Thompson interview with W. J. Bryan Dorn, circa 1981.

19. Banks interview, Southern Oral History Project, p. 26.

20. Burton, *In My Father's House*, p. 139.

21. Ibid.; Carol K. Rothrock Bleser, ed., *The Hammonds of Redcliffe* (New York: Oxford University Press, 1981), pp. 11–12; Drew Faust, *James Henry Hammond and the Old South: A Design for Mastery* (Baton Rouge: Louisiana State University Press, 1982), pp. 86–88, 314–317.

22. Bass interview with Sameera Thurmond, June 4, 2004.

23. Burton, *In My Father's House*, p. 292.

24. Ibid., pp. 297–301.

25. Ibid., p. 94.

26. Benjamin Ryan Tillman, *Struggle of 1876: How South Carolina Was Delivered from Carpetbag and Negro Rule* (1909), speech at Redshirt Reunion at Anderson, South Carolina. Also see *Edgefield Advertiser*, February 12, 1936.

27. Burton, *In My Father's House*, p. 290.

28. Francis Butler Simkins and Robert H. Woody, *South Carolina During Reconstruction* (Chapel Hill, NC: University of North Carolina Press, 1932), p. 564.

29. David Bruck, "Strom Thurmond's Roots," *New Republic*, March 3, 1982, p. 16.

30. Simkins and Woody, *South Carolina During Reconstruction*, pp. 185–187.

31. Burton, *In My Father's House*, p. 227.

32. *The Clansman* was the second book in a trilogy Dixon wrote about Reconstruction. Tillman may well have been a source, but Dixon's biographer, Raymond Allen Cook, reported that he sifted through more than 5,000 pamphlets and books for source material (Raymond Allen Cook, "Thomas Dixon: His Books and His Career," Ph.D. diss., Emory University, 1953, pp. 79–80).

33. Mays at dinner in his honor given by Dorn in 1979, attended by Bass.

34. Bass telephone interview with Carlanna Hendrick, biographer of John Gary Evans, July 26, 1998.

35. Burton, *In My Father's House*, p. 238.

36. Ibid., pp. 199, 276.

37. Joel Williamson, *The Crucible of Race: Black-White Relations in the American South Since Emancipation* (New York: Oxford University Press, 1984), pp. 80–81.

38. James G. Banks, preface to Ph.D. diss., "Strom Thurmond and the Revolt

Against Modernity," Kent State University, 1970, p. 4, copy in possession of the authors.

39. W. J. Cash, *The Mind of the South* (New York: Vintage Books, 1941), p. x.

CHAPTER 2: "I HAVE GOOD GENES"

1. Thompson interview with Strom Thurmond, December 22, 1980.
2. Banks interview, Southern Oral History Project, p. 7.
3. Ibid.
4. Thompson interview with C. Granville Wyche, July 18, 1981.
5. *Edgefield Advertiser*, account of coroner's inquest, March 25, 1897.
6. Ibid.
7. Ibid.
8. *Edgefield Advertiser*, April 7, 1897.
9. Ibid., August 11, 1897.
10. Ibid.
11. Thompson interview with Strom Thurmond.
12. *Edgefield Advertiser* accounts of 1902 campaign.
13. Thompson interview with Allen George Thurmond, circa 1981.
14. Banks interview, Southern Oral History Project, p. 1.
15. Thompson interview with Allen George Thurmond, op. cit.
16. Banks interview, Southern Oral History Project, p. 2.
17. Thompson interview with Thurmond, op. cit.
18. Ibid.
19. Alberta Lachicotte, *Rebel Senator* (New York: Devin-Adair Company, 1966), p. 128; Bass telephone interview with Harry Dent, March 27, 1998.
20. *Edgefield Advertiser*, 1912.
21. Thompson interview with Thurmond, op. cit.
22. Banks interview, Southern Oral History Project, p. 17.
23. Personal correspondence, Gubernatorial Papers, Thurmond Historical Records, Special Collections, Clemson University.
24. Banks interview, Southern Oral History Project, pp. 29–30.
25. Ibid.
26. *Atlanta Journal and Constitution*, April 23, 1995.

CHAPTER 3: "THE COMMENDABLE EFFORTS OF MR. THURMOND"

1. Banks interview, Southern Oral History Project, p. 37.
2. *McCormick Messenger*, April 3, February 7, and May 8, 1924.

3. Ibid., November 28, 1923.

4. *Edgefield Advertiser*, contemporary accounts, 1924.

5. Banks interview, Southern Oral History Project, p. 37.

6. *Edgefield Advertiser*, contemporary accounts, 1926.

7. Thompson telephone interview with Bruce Elrod, May 2004.

8. Robert Draper, unpublished manuscript. Bass interview with Bettis Rainsford, op. cit.

9. Frank G. Roberson, *What Is the Conclusion of the Whole Matter?* (North Augusta, S.C., FGR Publications, 2004), pp. 59–77; Bass interview with Willie Adams, August 9, 1998.

10. Thompson interview with Thurmond, op. cit.

11. Thompson interview with T. A. Logue, July 24, 1981.

12. Banks interview, Southern Oral History Project, p. 40.

13. Thompson interview with Thurmond, op. cit.

14. Ibid.

15. *Edgefield Advertiser*, February 1930.

16. Bass interview with Clem McIntosh, whose father was a principal in Edgefield County when Thurmond was county superintendent of education.

17. *The State*, Columbia, South Carolina, circa 1930.

18. Thompson interview with Modjeska Simkins, February 26, 1981.

19. Thompson interview with Thurmond, December 22, 1981.

20. Bass interview with Harry Dent, Columbia, South Carolina, June 26, 1997; Thompson interview with J. Fred Buzhardt, circa 1981.

21. *Edgefield Advertiser*, contemporary account, 1930.

22. Joseph C. Ellers, *Strom Thurmond: The Public Man* (Columbia, SC: Sandlapper Publishing Co., 1993), p. 33.

23. *Edgefield Advertiser*, undated clipping.

24. Letters to the Editor, *The State*, January 12, 1933.

25. Ball, *The State That Forgot*, pp. 281–282.

26. Solomon Blatt to Bass, circa 1970.

27. Bass interview with Edgar Brown, January 1967.

28. Thompson confidential interview, circa 1981.

29. *Saturday Evening Post*, October 8, 1955, p. 120.

30. Thompson interview with confidential source, circa 1981.

31. Thompson confidential interview, circa 1981.

32. Williams, a Democrat, told the story publicly at the investiture of his daughter-in-law as a federal judge, appointed by a Republican president while Thurmond chaired the Senate Judiciary Committee (confidential source who attended the investiture).

33. Thompson interview with Roy Powell, circa 1981.

34. Thompson interview with Mims, op. cit.

35. James Banks interview with Strom Thurmond, 1979, copy in possession of the authors.

36. Ibid.

37. Bass interview with Willie Adams, August 9, 1998.

38. Bass interview with Modjeska Simkins, circa 1982.

39. Bass interview with Adams, op. cit.

40. Ellers, *Strom Thurmond*, pp. 38–39.

41. Banks interview, Southern Oral History Project, p. 43.

42. Thompson interview with Robert Figg, circa 1981.

43. Thompson interview with Solomon Blatt, June 1981.

44. Ibid.

45. *Anderson Independent*, January 16, 1938.

CHAPTER 4: CIRCUIT JUDGE JAMES STROM THURMOND

1. Banks interview, Southern Oral History Project, p. 43.

2. Bass interview with Harry Ashmore, June 7, 1997, Athens, Georgia.

3. Bass telephone interview with Joel Williamson, February 14, 1998.

4. Bass telephone interview with Thomas A. Pope, May 15, 1998.

5. Thompson interview with Robert Figg, June 9, 1981.

6. Stephen Nettles letter to J. Strom Thurmond, January 3, 1940, pointing out that Judge G. Duncan Bellinger had spoken out against the Klan recently in Spartanburg and suggesting that Thurmond do the same (Strom Thurmond Historical Records, Special Collections, Clemson University).

7. *News and Courier* (Charleston), Associated Press story, January 9, 1940.

8. Interview with Colden Battey, December 31, 2004.

9. *News and Courier*, contemporary account, 1938.

10. Ibid., December 8, 1938.

11. *Anderson Daily Mail*, February 22, 1939.

12. Ibid.

13. David Bruck, Outlook section, *Washington Post*, April 26, 1981. This article was the longest ever to run in the Outlook section of the newspaper.

14. Ibid.

15. Bruck, *Washington Post*.

16. Thompson interview with Billy Coleman, June 2, 1981.

17. Bruck, *Washington Post*.

18. Thompson interview with Thurmond, op. cit.

19. Bruck, *Washington Post*.

20. Thompson interview with Thurmond, op. cit.

21. Bruck, *Washington Post.*

22. Ibid.

23. Ibid.

24. Ibid.

25. Ibid.

26. Thompson interview with Thurmond, op. cit.

27. Bruck, *Washington Post.*

28. Ibid.

29. Ibid.

30. Thompson interview with Thurmond, op. cit.

CHAPTER 5: THE JUDGE'S WOMEN

1. Judge G. Duncan Bellinger, *State v. Joe Frank Logue,* order denying a new trial, October 25, 1943, p. 129, 104 S.C. 1H.

2. Trial transcript, *State v. Joe Frank Logue,* 204 S.C. 171, pp. 57–58, 74.

3. Lachicotte, *Rebel Senator;* Ellers, *Strom Thurmond,* p. 65.

4. Associated Press, December 12, 2004.

5. Bass interview with Essie Mae Washington-Williams, July 20, 2004; Thompson interview, December 10, 2003.

6. Bass interview with Essie Mae Washington-Williams, July 20, 2004; Thompson interview December 10, 2003, *The State,* September 13, 2004.

7. Trial transcript, *State v. Joe Frank Logue,* 204 S.C. 171, pp. 50–51.

8. Bass interview with a retired officer of the South Carolina State Law Enforcement Division (SLED) who had worked with Joe Frank Logue when he trained the bloodhounds for SLED after his sentence for electrocution was commuted.

9. Lachicotte, *Rebel Senator,* p. 7.

10. T. Felder Dorn, *The Guns of Meeting Street* (Columbia: University of South Carolina Press, 2001), p. 127.

11. Bass interview with Charles Simons, Aiken, South Carolina, August 13, 1997.

12. Undated newspaper clipping.

13. The depiction of events not otherwise cited, including dialogue, is recreated from the trial transcript, *State v. Joe Frank Logue,* 204 S.C. 171; *State v. Bagwell et al.,* No. 15461, Supreme Court of South Carolina, November 9, 1942; and *State v. Logue,* No. 15613, Supreme Court of South Carolina, January 19, 1944.

14. Bass interview with Randal Johnson, Columbia, South Carolina, at home of Modjeska Simkins, circa 1980.

15. Dorn, *The Guns of Meeting Street,* pp. 256–257.

16. Ibid., pp. 57–58, 258–259.

17. Bass telephone interviews with retired SLED agents, April 29, 1998.

18. Bass interview with confidential source.

CHAPTER 6: "SO MANY NARROW ESCAPES"

1. Banks, 1979 interview with Thurmond, p. 17.

2. *Edgefield Advertiser*, June 17, 1942.

3. Alva Lumpkin letter to Bass, July 28, 2003.

4. Primary account from Civil Affairs Section II, *Civil Affairs Takes the Field*, Military Series, Box 4, "Civil Affairs 1943–1944," Special Collections, Clemson University Libraries, Clemson, South Carolina; augmented by Banks 1979 interview with Thurmond, pp. 17–21.

5. Undated 1945 article from *The State*, interview with Lieutenant Colonel Thurmond just before his release from active duty, after the end of the war.

6. Letter from Thurmond to J. F. Ouzts, printed in *Index-Journal*, September 14, 1944.

7. *The State*, December 28, 1944.

8. Banks, 1979 interview with Thurmond, p. 19.

9. Dale Rosengarten and Ron J. Menchaca interview with Strom Thurmond, for Jewish Heritage Project, Charleston, South Carolina, October 11, 1996.

10. Ibid.

11. Banks, 1979 interview with Thurmond, p. 21.

12. Thompson interview with Figg, June 9, 1981.

13. Thompson interview with Jules Brunson, July 16, 1981.

CHAPTER 7: PROGRESSIVE OUTLOOK, PROGRESSIVE PROGRAM, PROGRESSIVE LEADERSHIP

1. Thompson interview with Blatt, June 1981.

2. Bass interview with Ashmore, op. cit.

3. Personal letter, April 29, 1946, Historical Papers of Strom Thurmond, Strom Thurmond Institute, Clemson University.

4. Bass interview with John C. West, Hilton Head Island, January 2, 1998.

5. *News and Courier*, July 24, 1946; Associated Press, Columbia dateline, August 13, 1946.

6. *Sun* (Baltimore), Associated Press story, December 8, 1946.

7. *The State*, September 8, 1946.

8. *Sun* (Baltimore), Associated Press story, December 8, 1946.

9. Thurmond Historical Papers, Strom Thurmond Institute, Clemson, South Carolina.

10. *New York Herald Tribune,* April 20, 1947. The article was written by reporter Earl Mazo, who had grown up in South Carolina.

11. James McBride Dabbs letter to Strom Thurmond, February 22, 1947, Gubernatorial Papers, Thurmond Historical Records, Special Collections, Clemson University.

12. *Atlanta Journal,* May 23, 1947.

13. *New York Times,* May 23, 1947.

14. Nadine Cohodas, *Strom Thurmond and the Politics of Southern Change* (New York: Simon and Schuster, 1993), p. 112.

15. *Elmore v. Rice,* F.Supp. 516 (D.C.S.C. 1947).

16. *Anderson Independent,* September 16, 1947.

17. "Let's Look at '48," address by J. Strom Thurmond at panel discussion over radio station WHAS, Memorial Auditorium, Louisville, Kentucky, October 2, 1947, Special Collections, Robert Muldrow Cooper Library, Clemson University.

CHAPTER 8: "MY DARLING JEAN"

1. Thompson interview with Thurmond, op. cit.

2. Thompson interview with Wilma Smith, circa 1980.

3. *Saturday Evening Post,* October 5, 1955, p. 121.

4. Most of the material in this chapter not otherwise credited comes from Lachicotte, *Rebel Senator,* pp. 10–29.

5. *The State,* October 12, 1947.

6. Associated Press, October 16, 1947.

7. Strom Thurmond–Jean letters, Thurmond Historical Records, Special Collections, Clemson University.

8. Eugene Patterson letter to the author, February 14, 1998.

CHAPTER 9: "DEAR SIR"

1. Strom Thurmond historical collection, Strom Thurmond Institute, Clemson University, Clemson, S.C.; *Washington Post,* August 4, 1992; *Ol' Strom: An Unauthorized Biography of Strom Thurmond* (Longstreet, 1998), p. 278.

2. Bass interview with Maceo Nance, Orangeburg, South Carolina, October 4, 1997.

3. Bass interview with Matthew J. Perry, July 20, 1997.

4. Bass telephone interview with Perry, June 24, 1997; Thompson telephone interview with Perry, December 2003.

5. Bass interview with Emma Casselberry, Orangeburg, South Carolina, October 4, 1997.

6. Thompson interview with Essie Mae Williams, Los Angeles, circa 1984.

7. W. Lewis Burke and William C. Hine, "The South Carolina State College Law School," in *Matthew J. Perry: The Man, His Times, and His Legacy* (Columbia: University of South Carolina Press, 2004), p. 31.

8. Ibid., pp. 33, 34.

9. Tinsley Yarbrough, *Judicial Enigma: The First Justice Harlan* (New York: Oxford University Press, 1995), pp. 10–14, 141.

10. Bass confidential interview.

11. Bass telephone interview with Joel Williamson, February 2, 1998.

12. The relationship between the Richard Thurmond of Ripley, Mississippi, and Strom Thurmond's family is remote. Although Strom Thurmond referred to his ancestor "John Thurmond of Virginia, who fought in the Revolutionary War, then moved to Georgia, and finally established his family in South Carolina," a Thurmond family genealogist in Georgia believes the senator was mistaken. Frank Parker Hudson of Atlanta, while working on the manuscript for *Thurmans and Thurmonds of Early Georgia*, concluded that the Revolutionary War service of the John Thurmond who was Strom Thurmond's great-great-great-grandfather consisted of "driving cattle for thirty days" in Albemarle County, Virginia. Hudson believes the misinformation resulted from a faulty account by an earlier family researcher based on family lore and hearsay rather than on public records. Hudson's research indicates that the John Thurmond ancestor of Strom Thurmond left Virginia in 1784, two years after the Revolutionary War ended, and moved directly to Edgefield County, South Carolina, purchasing land there in 1784. He had brothers who went to Georgia. His brother Benjamin's daughter, Nancy Thurmond, married John Thurmond's son William, Strom Thurmond's great-great-grandfather. William Thurmond was born in 1761 in Virginia and was the son of John Thurmond and his first wife, Molly (or Mally) Dickerson. Strom's great-grandfather was John Thurmond, the son of William Thurmond. The great-grandfather was born in Edgefield County on May 1, 1794, and his son, George Washington Thurmond, was born November 12, 1819. He had one son, Jasper, by his first wife, and Strom's father, John William (Will), was born twenty-four years later on May 1, 1862, the youngest child of George W. Thurmond and his second wife, Mary Jane Felter of New Orleans. Jasper Thurmond was the father of Herman Talmadge's mother, which made her a half first cousin of Strom, and made Herman (who served as governor of Georgia and subsequently U.S. senator) and Strom half first cousins, once removed). George Washington Thurmond died April 11, 1904, when he was eighty-four. An expanded genealogy prepared by Marie Crockett Mims of Edgefield, locates the earliest Thurmond ancestor living in America as Edward Thurman in Virginia in 1660, the son of John Thurmond, Jr., who was born in England in 1630. The list of surnames included in the ancestry of J. Strom Thurmond includes

the following: Aldridge, Alexander, Anderson, Ashley, Bland, Broadnax/Brodnax, Brooks, Bruce, Burton, Cain, Carmarden, Cheatham, Church, Cogan, Coggin, Cooper, Day, DeLaughter, Dickerson, Felter, Forbes, and Goode, Harris, Henderson, Holloway, Knowles, Lewis, Macon, Massie, Morecroft, Morris, Moss, Pace, Poythress, Reynolds, Sharpe, Strom, Taylor, Thurmond, Wassher, and Woodward.

13. Burke and Hine, "The South Carolina State College Law School."

14. Thompson interview with Randall Johnson, circa 1981.

15. Thompson telephone interview with Essie Mae Washington-Williams, December 2003.

16. Bass interview with Lonnie Hamilton, May 23, 2004.

17. Bass telephone interview with Essie Mae Washington-Williams, July 30, 2004.

18. Ibid.

19. Bass telephone interview with Knoetta Goodwin Judkins, April 19, 1998.

20. Bass telephone interview with Rosa Lee Torrey, April 18, 1998.

21. Bass interview with Julie Washington Nance, April 25, 1998.

CHAPTER 10: DIXIECRAT

1. Thompson interview with Thurmond, December 22, 1980.

2. November 1, 1948, address over ABC; original in Gubernatorial Papers, Thurmond Historical Records, Clemson University.

3. Banks, 1979 interview with Thurmond, pp. 29–30.

4. Cohodas, *Strom Thurmond*, p. 137.

5. *The State*, Associated Press story, December 31, 1947.

6. Patterson letter to Bass, op. cit. Gene Patterson followed Ralph McGill as editor of the *Atlanta Constitution* and later became managing editor of the *Washington Post* and then editor of the *St. Petersburg Times*.

7. Clark Clifford memorandum for the president, November 19, 1947, quoted in Cohodas, *Strom Thurmond*, p. 129.

8. Clark Clifford memorandum for the president, August 17, 1948, quoted in Numan V. Bartley, *The New South* (Baton Rouge: Louisiana State University Press, 1995), p. 78.

9. *The State*, January 30, 1948.

10. *New York Times*, February 3, 1948.

11. Fielding Wright inaugural address, January 19, 1948, Jackson, Mississippi, quoted in Cohodas, *Strom Thurmond*, p. 126.

12. Strom Thurmond speeches, quoted in Cohodas, *Strom Thurmond*, p. 132.

13. *Atlanta Journal*, February 8, 1948.

14. W. L. Daniel memo to Strom Thurmond, February 19, 1948, in Gubernatorial Papers, Thurmond Historical Records, Clemson University.

15. Cohodas, *Strom Thurmond*, p. 135.

16. *New York Times*, February 24, 1948.

17. *Charleston Evening Post*, Associated Press story, March 18, 1948.

18. Bartley, *The New South*, p. 78.

19. Cohodas, *Strom Thurmond*, pp. 128–143.

20. *Greenville News*, April 6, 1948.

21. Ibid., Associated Press story, April 23, 1948.

22. *New York Times*, May 11, 1948.

23. Ibid.

24. Thurmond Historical Records, Special Collections, Clemson University.

25. Bass telephone interview with William Winter, May 5, 1998.

26. Patterson letter to Bass, op. cit. When Governor Thurmond vetoed an appropriations bill in 1947 that included a $4,500 annual salary increase for the governor, the legislature overrode the veto. Although funds were appropriated, Thurmond refused to accept the pay increase for all of his term.

27. *Greenville News*, May 26, 1948; *Columbia Record*, May 28, 1948.

28. Proceedings of 1948 Democratic National Convention, Records of the Democratic National Committee, Harry S. Truman Library, Independence, Missouri.

29. Lachicotte, *Rebel Senator*, p. 43.

30. Quoted in Bartley, *The New South*, p. 87.

31. Cohodas, *Strom Thurmond*, p. 177.

32. Thompson interview with Modjeska Simkins, 1980.

33. *Baltimore Afro-American*, August 24, 1948.

34. Bass telephone interview with Essie Mae Washington-Williams, July 2004.

35. Lachicotte, *Rebel Senator*, p. 45.

36. Bass telephone interview with Robert Lipshutz, May 26, 1998.

37. *New York Times*, United Press story, July 19, 1948.

38. *Christian Science Monitor*, July 19, 1948.

39. *Washington Evening Star*, July 21, 1948.

40. *The State*, August 2, 1948.

41. Thompson interview with Figg, June 9, 1981.

42. Thompson interview with Donald L. Fowler, circa 1981.

43. John McCray, "The Need for Changing," *The Lighthouse and Informer*, April 19, 1949.

CHAPTER 11: CAMPAIGN OF THE CENTURY

1. Bass confidential source.

2. Typed manuscript, dated April 10, 1947, of a speech for delivery to a Democratic audience in Atlanta, Olin D. Johnston Papers, South Caroliniana Library,

University of South Carolina, quoted in "Defending the Faith: The 1950 U.S. Senate Race in South Carolina," master's thesis, Luther Brady Faggart, University of South Carolina, 1992.

3. Talmadge to Bass, June 2, 1998; Dorn to Bass, October 1974.

4. Thompson interview with Roy Powell, July 1981.

5. Thompson interview with W. J. Bryan Dorn, September 13, 1981.

6. James Lever letter to Byrnes, April 15, 1950, Byrnes Papers, quoted in Faggart, "Defending the Faith," p. 25.

7. Cohodas, *Strom Thurmond*, p. 201.

8. Thompson interview with Reverend I. DeQuincey Newman, circa 1981.

9. Thompson telephone interview with McCray, circa 1980; confidential source, circa 1980.

10. Kari Frederickson, *The Dixiecrat Revolt and the End of the Solid South, 1932–1968* (Chapel Hill: University of North Carolina Press, 2001), pp. 209–215.

11. *The State*, June 10, 1950.

12. Ibid., June 9, 1950.

13. Ibid., June 21, 1950.

14. Thurmond advertisement, circa 1950, Johnston Papers, cited in Faggart, "Defending the Faith," p. 51.

15. *News and Courier*, June 28, 1950.

16. *The State*, July 5, 1950, and June 30, 1950.

17. Ibid., June 23, 1950; *Rock Hill Evening Herald*, June 23, 1950.

18. *The State*, June 24, 1950.

19. Bass interview with Dent, op. cit., 1997; *News and Courier*, June 27, 1950; Faggart, "Defending the Faith," p. 163; Cohodas, *Strom Thurmond*, p. 211.

20. Faggart, "Defending the Faith," pp. 114–115.

21. *News and Courier*, July 7, 1950.

22. Faggart, "Defending the Faith," p. 107.

23. Workman to Greenville newspaperman Judson Chapman, July 9, 1950; and *News and Courier*, June 23, 1950, cited in Faggart, "Defending the Faith," p. 5.

24. Official election returns reported in *The State*, July 19, 1950.

25. Robert Sherrill, *Gothic Politics in the Deep South* (New York: Ballantine Books, 1969), p. 242.

26. Bass interview with Simons, op. cit.

27. See Faggart, "Defending the Faith," p. 252, note. He cites Steven F. Lawson, *Black Ballots: Voting Rights in the South, 1944–1969* (New York: Columbia Univesity Press, 1976), pp. 54, 134. According to Lawson, 35,000 blacks voted in the 1948 Democratic primary in South Carolina, a year after an estimated 50,000 were registered.

28. Banks 1979 interview with Thurmond, pp. 28–29.

29. Dent, op. cit., 1997.

30. Jean Thurmond to Strom Thurmond, August 9, 1949, and Strom Thurmond to Jean Thurmond, August 15, 1949 and August 27, 1949, Strom Thurmond Historical Records, Special Collections, Clemson University, Clemson, South Carolina.

31. Dent, op. cit., 1997.

CHAPTER 12: "STRUM THORMOND"

1. Bass interview with Charles Simons, op. cit.; Thompson interview with Strom Thurmond, December 22, 1981.

2. Ashley Halsey Jr., *Saturday Evening Post,* "Dixiecrat in Washington," October 8, 1955, pp. 32–33; *Augusta Chronicle,* October 18, 1951.

3. Thompson interview with Bryan Dorn, September 13, 1981; William Jennings Bryan Dorn and Scott Derks, *Dorn: Of the People* (Columbia and Orangeburg, SC: Bruccoli Clark Layman and Sandlapper Publishing, 1988), pp. 157–159.

4. Sherrill, *Gothic Politics in the Deep South,* p. 248.

5. Thompson interview with Bryan Dorn, September 13, 1981; William Jennings Bryan Dorn and Scott Derks, *Dorn: Of the People: A Political Way of Life* (Orangeburg, SC: Bruccoli Clark Layman and Sandlapper Publishing, 1988), pp. 155–158.

6. Thompson interview with William J. Prioleau, circa 1982.

7. Ibid.

8. Thompson interview with Alex McCullough, February 8, 1982.

9. Bass telephone interview with Charles Wickenberg, March 5, 1998.

10. Thurmond letter to Thomas R. Waring, December 20, 1954, Waring correspondence files, South Carolina Historical Society, Charleston.

11. Bass interview with Strom Thurmond, February 1, 1974, Bass-DeVries Collection, Folio A166, Southern Historical Collection, University of North Carolina at Chapel Hill.

12. Thurmond letter of December 20 to Waring, op. cit.

13. *News and Courier,* September 8, 1954.

14. Bass telephone interview with Dolly Hamby, March 5, 1998.

15. William D. Workman Jr., *The Bishop from Barnwell: The Political Life and Times of Edgar Brown* (Columbia, SC: R. L. Bryan Company, 1963), p. 256.

CHAPTER 13: HARD TIMES

1. Strom Thurmond historical collection, Strom Thurmond Institute, Clemson University, Clemson, S.C.; *Washington Post,* August 4, 1992; *Ol' Strom: An Unauthorized Biography of Strom Thurmond* (Longstreet, 1998), p. 278.

2. Essie Mae Washington-Williams and William Stadiem, *Dear Senator: A Memoir by the Daughter of Strom Thurmond* (New York: HarperCollins, 2005), p. 148.

3. Bass telephone interview with Essie Mae Washington-Williams, July 28, 2004.

4. Thompson telephone interview with Frank Cain, May 28, 2004.

5. Washington-Williams and Stadiem, *Dear Senator*, p. 154.

6. Bass telephone interview with Williams, op cit.

7. Ibid.

8. Ibid.

9. Thompson telephone interview with Ronald Williams, May 18, 2004.

10. Thompson telephone interview with Monica Williams Hudgens, May 25, 2004.

11. Thompson telephone interview with Ronald Williams, op. cit.

CHAPTER 14: RAMBUNCTIOUS DEMOCRAT

1. Thompson interview with McCullough, op. cit.

2. Ibid.

3. Robert Sherrill, *Gothic Politics in the Deep South* (New York: Ballantine Books, 1969), p. 256.

4. *The State*, November 25, 1989, quoting former administrative assistant Dennis Shedd.

5. Bass telephone interviews with Ellie Beardsley and Missy Britt Barkdoll, March 1998.

6. Bass interview with Dent, op. cit., 1997.

7. Lachicotte, *Rebel Senator*, p. 120.

8. Bass interview with West, op. cit.

9. Lachicotte, *Rebel Senator*, p. 126.

10. Bass interview with Dent, op. cit., 1997.

11. Glenn to Bass, circa 1973.

12. Bass interview with Dent, op. cit., 1997.

13. Jack Bass, *Porgy Comes Home* (Columbia, SC: R. L. Bryan Co., 1970), p. 32.

14. Bass telephone interview with Charles Wickenberg, Timmerman's executive assistant, who witnessed the meeting, May 31, 1998.

15. Early drafts of "Origin of the Southern Manifesto," Special Collections, Cooper Library, Clemson University, Clemson, South Carolina.

16. Merle Miller, *Lyndon, An Oral Biography* (New York: Putnam, 1980), p. 187.

17. Special Collections, Robert Muldrow Cooper Library, Clemson University, four drafts of the Southern Manifesto and undated, unsigned two-page docu-

ment, "Origin of the Southern Manifesto"; *Congressional Record*, 84th Cong., 2d sess., vol. 102, pt. 4, pp. 4515–4516, 4461–4462.

18. Bass interview with Ashmore, op. cit.

19. Dan T. Carter, *The Politics of Rage: George Wallace, the Origins of the New Conservatism, and the Transformation of American Politics* (New York: Simon and Schuster, 1995), p. 86.

20. Jack Bass, *Unlikely Heroes* (New York: Simon and Schuster, 1981), p. 65.

21. Jack Bass and Walter DeVries, *The Transformation of Southern Politics* (Athens: University of Georgia Press reissue, 1995), quoting Jim Johnson, p. 92.

22. Ibid.

23. Ibid.

24. Ibid., p. 347.

25. *New York Times*, July 8, 1957, p. 15.

26. Stanley Morse letter to Strom Thurmond, July 16, 1957; W. J. Simmons letter to Strom Thurmond, July 22, 1957; Morse letter to Thurmond, March 31, 1964; Stanley Fletcher Morse papers, South Caroliniana Library, University of South Carolina, Columbia.

27. Grass Roots League, Inc., Research Bulletin No. 2, October 1, 1954, "Truth About Supreme Court's Segregation Ruling"; Grass Roots League Fact-Finding memo "C," January 1961, and memo "F," August 1962, Stanley Fletcher Morse papers, South Caroliniana Library, University of South Carolina, Columbia.

28. See Taylor Branch, *Parting the Waters* (New York: Simon and Schuster, 1989), p. 403, and *Pillar of Fire* (New York: Simon and Schuster, 1998), pp. 27–28, 526–531; David Garrow, *The FBI and Martin Luther King, Jr.* (New York: W. W. Norton, 1991), pp. 54–59, 78–85.

29. *Charlotte Observer*, Hoke May column, September 1, 1957.

30. Quoted in Roscoe Drummond column, *New York Herald Tribune*, September 10, 1957.

31. *Atlanta Constitution*, August 31, 1957.

32. Bass interview with Herman Talmadge, Lovejoy, Georgia, June 2, 1998.

33. Lachicotte, *Rebel Senator*, pp. 140–156.

34. Bass interview with Simons, op. cit.

35. Harry Dent, *The Prodigal South Returns to Power* (New York: John Wiley and Sons, 1978), p. 61.

36. Bass interview with Dent, op. cit., 1997.

37. Ibid.

38. *Charlotte Observer*, Associated Press story, May 22, 1960.

39. *Columbia Record*, September 2, 1960.

40. Associated Press, May 27, 1961.

41. United Press International, July 4, 1962.

42. Associated Press, May 22, 1960.

43. Thompson interview with Dent, December 13, 1982.

44. Ibid.; Bass interview with Dent, op. cit., 1997.

45. Former state representative David Taylor to Bass, 1973.

46. George Rogers, *The Encyclopedia of Southern History* (Baton Rouge: Louisiana State University Press, 1980).

47. *News and Courier*, December 31, 1962.

48. Bass, *Porgy Comes Home*, p. 7.

49. *News and Courier*, December 31, 1962; January 23, 1963; *The State*, January 9, 1963; *Charlotte Observer*, January 22, 1963.

50. Cohodas, *Strom Thurmond*, p. 335.

51. Pete Strom to Bass, 1970.

52. Hollings to Bass, 1968.

53. Stanley Morse letter to Strom Thurmond, August 3, 1963; Thurmond letter to Morse, August 19, 1963, Caroliniana Library, University of South Carolina.

54. Branch, *Parting the Waters*, pp. 861–862.

55. Cohodas, *Strom Thurmond*, pp. 348, 435.

CHAPTER 15: THE REPUBLICAN ROAD

1. Bass and DeVries, *Transformation of Southern Politics*, pp. 23–24.

2. Ibid., p. 27.

3. *Charlotte Observer*, January 26, 1963.

4. Lachicotte, *Rebel Senator*, p. 220.

5. *Charlotte Observer*, July 27, 1963.

6. United Press International, August 25, 1963.

7. Jack Bass, *Unlikely Heroes* (Tuscaloosa: University of Alabama Press edition, 1990), p. 146.

8. Cohodas, *Strom Thurmond*, p. 349.

9. Thompson interview with Ralph Yarborough, 1982.

10. Bass-DeVries interview with Strom Thurmond, February 1, 1974.

11. Bass interview with Dent, op. cit., 1997.

12. Bass interview with Dent, op. cit., 1997; and Thompson interview with Dent, op. cit.; Lachicotte, *Rebel Senator*, pp. 229–235.

13. Thompson interview with Dent, op. cit., 1997.

14. Ibid.

15. Thompson interview with Donald Fowler, circa 1981.

16. Ibid.

17. Ibid.

18. Bass interview with Dent, op. cit., 1997.

19. Dent, *The Prodigal South*, p. 77.

CHAPTER 16: "AND YOU REFUSE TO ANSWER THAT?"

1. George Christian to Bass, 1974.

2. Laura Kalman, *Abe Fortas: A Biography* (New Haven: Yale University Press, 1990), p. 337. This book is heavily drawn on for Fortas's biographical background.

3. Ibid., p. 328.

4. Strom Thurmond, *The Faith We Have Not Kept* (San Diego: Viewpoint Books, 1968), p. 15.

5. James Banks to author, July 1998.

6. *Slaughterhouse* cases, 83 U.S. 36 (1873), p. 82.

7. *Santa Clara County v. Southern Pacific Railroad*, 118 U.S. 395 (1886).

8. *Scott v. Sanford*, 60 U.S. 393 (1857).

9. Thurmond, *The Faith We Have Not Kept*, p. 15.

10. After Johnson left the presidency, he told former *Atlanta Constitution* editor Gene Patterson that the editorial caused Fortas not to be confirmed. Patterson letter to Jack Bass, July 6, 1998.

11. Kalman, *Abe Fortas*, p. 37.

12. Ibid., pp. 340–341; Cohodas, *Strom Thurmond*, pp. 393–394.

13. Cohodas, *Strom Thurmond*, pp. 394–395.

14. Kalman, *Abe Fortas*, pp. 350–357, and Cohodas, *Strom Thurmond*, pp. 395–396; *Washington Post* cartoon, September 8, 1968, cited in Cohodas; footnote reference, Kalman, *Abe Fortas*, chap. 16, and Bass telephone interview with Harold Burson, April 6, 1998.

CHAPTER 17: "NIXON'S THE ONE"

1. Bass interview with Tom Turnipseed, Columbia, South Carolina, March 10, 1998.

2. Dan Carter, *The Politics of Rage* (New York: Simon and Schuster, 1995), p. 329.

3. Ibid., quoting the *Los Angeles Times*, November 4, 1962.

4. Carter, *Politics of Rage*, pp. 196–215.

5. Dent, *The Prodigal South*, p. 91.

6. Carter, *Politics of Rage*, p. 330, citing Lewis Chester, Godfrey Hodgson, and Bruce Page, *An American Melodrama: The Presidential Campaign of 1968* (New York: Viking), p. 445.

7. Carter, *Politics of Rage*, p. 329, citing *Miami Herald*, August 7, 1968.

8. Clarke Reed to Bass, circa 1989.

9. Dent, *The Prodigal South*, p. 100; *Charlotte Observer*, August 8, 1968.

10. Dent, *The Prodigal South*, p. 101; Oberdorfer to Bass during taxi ride at the convention.

11. Dent, *The Prodigal South*, p. 102.

12. Ibid., pp. 105–110; Bass interview with Dent, op. cit., 1998.

13. Ibid.

CHAPTER 18: "AMAZEMENT AND WONDER"

1. Bass interview with Talmadge, June 2, 1998.

2. *The State*, July 12, 1965.

3. *The State*, December 12, 2004 (from Thurmond Historical Collection, Clemson University).

4. Bass interview with Lee Bandy, June 24, 1997.

5. Thompson interview with Thurmond, December 22, 1981.

6. Dent, *The Prodigal South*, pp. 111, 116–117; Bass interview with Dent, op. cit., 1997.

7. *Charlotte Observer*, December 30, 1968.

8. Bass telephone interview with Dent, 1998.

9. Nina Totenberg, *Parade* magazine, February 15, 1981.

10. Jack Bass, *Charlotte Observer*, January 19, 1969.

11. *Washington Post*, December 22, 1981.

12. Bass confidential interview.

13. John Monk, *The State*, October 14, quoting the *New Yorker.*

14. *Washington Post*, April 8, 1996.

15. Bass confidential source.

16. *The State*, October 17, 1988.

17. Bass interview with Lynda Robb, July 1997.

18. *New York Times Magazine*, October 23, 1994; *The State*, October 22, 1994.

19. *The State*, Associated Press story, November 8, 1996.

20. *The State*, October 27, 1996.

21. Thompson interview with Thurmond, op. cit.

22. Bass confidential interview, July 1997.

23. *The State*, February 5 and April 14, 1989.

24. Bass confidential interview, July 1997.

25. *The State*, March 21, 1993.

CHAPTER 19: "TIME FOR CHANGE"

1. *Charlotte Observer*, January 10 and 14, 1969.

2. Ibid., April 29–30, 1970.

3. Bass and DeVries, *Transformation of Southern Politics*, p. 261.

4. Bass interview with William Want, October 2004.

5. *Congressional Record*, Senate, June 9, 1969, p. 15203.

6. *New York Times* and *Washington Post*, June 10, 1969.

7. AFL-CIO official to Bass, 1970.

8. Tom Wicker, *One of Us: Richard Nixon and the American Dream* (New York: Random House, 1991), pp. 496–498; Bass, *Unlikely Heroes*, 1st ed., pp. 318–323.

9. Ibid., p. 23, quoting *Baltimore Sun*, December 14, 1969.

10. *Alexander v. Holmes County Board of Education.*

11. Bass and DeVries, *Transformation of Southern Politics*, p. 262.

12. Ibid., pp. 262–263.

13. *Charlotte Observer*, October 31, 1970.

14. Bass and DeVries, *Transformation of Southern Politics*, pp. 262–263.

15. Ibid., p. 47.

16. Thurmond Historical Records, Clemson University (cited in *The State*, October 3, 2004).

17. Ibid.

18. Bass and DeVries, *Transformation of Southern Politics*, p. 272.

19. Bass-DeVries interview with Thurmond, Washington, D.C., February 1, 1974, Southern Historical Collection, CB#3926, A-166, University of North Carolina at Chapel Hill.

20. Ibid.; Bass interview with Dent, op. cit., 1997; and Bass interview with Thomas Moss, Columbia, South Carolina, March 10, 1998.

21. Bass telephone interview with Matthew J. Perry, June 24, 1998; Thompson telephone interview with Perry, May 31, 2004.

22. Bass interview with Lee Bandy, Columbia, South Carolina, June 24, 1997.

23. Bass interview with Nance, op. cit.

24. Bass interview with Griffin Bell, Jacksonville, Florida, August 3, 1979.

25. Bass interview with Armstrong Williams, Washington, D.C., July 1997.

26. *Washington Post*, March 9, 1995.

27. Armstrong Williams syndicated column, December 2003.

CHAPTER 20: LIFE IN CALIFORNIA

1. *Los Angeles Times*, January 25, 2004.

2. Thompson telephone interview with Ronald Williams, May 18, 2004.

3. *Ebony*, March 2004.

4. *The State*, December 17, 2003.

5. Lauren Markoe, Knight-Ridder newspapers, January 18, 2004.

6. Ibid.; Tavis Smiley interview with Essie Mae Washington-Williams, January 9, 2004.

7. *Los Angeles Times*, Features, January 25, 2004; Thompson interview with Madison Shockley, May 2004; Bass interview with Essie Mae Washington-Williams, August 2004; Madison Shockley, newspaper column, December 26, 2003.

8. *Los Angeles Times*, op. cit., January 25, 2004.

9. Thompson telephone interview with Monica Hudgens, December 2003.

10. *Los Angeles Times*, January 20, 2004.

11. *Seattle Post-Intelligencer*, December 20, 2003.

12. *Seattle Times*, January 19, 2004.

13. *Seattle Post-Intelligencer*, December 20, 2004; *Los Angeles Times*, January 20, 2004; Thompson interview with Monica Hudgens, May 31, 2004.

14. Correspondence filed at Strom Thurmond Institute, Clemson University; Thompson telephone interview with Ronald Williams, May 18, 2004.

15. *Los Angeles Times*, Features, January 25, 2004.

CHAPTER 21: PLAYING THE GAME

1. Bass confidential interview.

2. Bass interview with Dent, op. cit., 1997.

3. Bass interview with West, op. cit.

4. Bass interview with Dent, op. cit., 1997.

5. Bass interview with Bettis Rainsford, Edgefield, South Carolina, March 12, 1998.

6. Bass conversation in 1972 with William Wilkins, Thurmond campaign manager.

7. Cohodas, *Strom Thurmond*, p. 481.

8. Sherrill, *Gothic Politics in the Deep South*, p. 244.

9. Bass telephone interview with Sharon Churcher, spring 1992.

10. Bass confidential interview, October 1974.

11. Felder to Bass, fall 1969.

12. Bass telephone interview with Durham Carter, July 21, 1998.

13. *Washington Post*, February 27, 1972.

14. Harry and Betty Dent, *Right vs. Wrong: Solutions to the American Nightmare* (Nashville: Thomas Nelson Publishers, 1992), pp. 5–6.

15. Dent, *The Prodigal South Returns to Power*, p. 26.

16. Bass conversation with Lee Atwater, circa 1986.

17. Thompson interview with Carroll Campbell, 1982.

18. Bass interview with Simons, op. cit.

19. Bass interview with Donald Fowler, February 6, 1998.

20. Neill Macaulay, *A Rebel in Cuba* (Chicago: Quadrangle Books, 1970), pp. 182–194.

21. Bass interview with Dan Ravenel, July 2004.

22. William Hine to Bass, May 1998.

23. Bass telephone interview with Lonnie Hamilton, December 21, 1997.

24. Bass interview with Tom Cobb, Ben's father, June 1998.

25. Bass telephone interview with James Moore, July 12, 1998.

26. Bass telephone interview with Derrick, op. cit.

27. Bass interview with confidential source.

28. Thompson interview with Thurmond, December 22, 1981.

29. Bass telephone interview with Wickenberg, March 5, 1998.

30. *Charlotte Observer,* May 23, 1971.

31. See Recording Book 13-H, pp. 338–339, Barnwell County Courthouse, Barnwell, S.C. 1; Bass interview with West, op. cit.

32. Bass interview with James Clyburn, February 1, 1982.

CHAPTER 22: MAINSTREAM SENATOR

1. Bass interview with Fowler, op. cit.

2. Atwater to Bass, October 1978.

3. Bass interview with Charles D. (Pug) Ravenel, November 2004.

4. On Thurmond help for Ravenel, Bass confidential source, August 1997; "Thurmond Outspent," *The Almanac of American Politics 1980,* p. 794; other information, Bass as participant-observer (public affairs coordinator for 1974 Bryan Dorn for governor campaign; Democratic candidate for Congress in 1978).

5. *American Lawyer,* January 1981, p. 21.

6. Interview with Howell Raines, who covered the event for the *New York Times,* May 14, 1998.

7. Thompson interview with Thurmond, 1981.

8. Thompson interview with Emory Sneeden, March 1981.

9. Cohodas, *Strom Thurmond,* p. 461.

10. *Almanac of American Politics 1988,* p. xxxix; *Almanac of American Politics 1990,* p. xxv.

11. Civil Order No. 74-281, U.S. District Court for the District of South Carolina, Greenwood Division.

12. Bass telephone interview with Thomas C. McCain, July 15, 1998.

13. Cohodas, *Strom Thurmond,* pp. 470–472.

14. Bass telephone interview with Armand Derfner, July 12, 1998.

15. Cohodas, *Strom Thurmond,* pp. 473–478.

16. *Washington Post,* "New Fortunes of 'Rebel' Politics," February 25, 1985.

17. Cohodas, *Strom Thurmond,* pp. 484–485.

18. Bass interview with McCain, op. cit.

19. Colleen Marie Getz, "Congressional Policy Making: The Goldwater-Nichols Defense Reorganization Act of 1986," Ph.D. diss., Yale University, May 1998, pp. 202–207.

20. Nunn to Bass, May 1998.

21. Strom Thurmond, Tributes, in the Congress of the United States (Washington: U.S. Government Printing Office, 1997), pp. 43–44.

22. Bass confidential source, May 1998.

23. Jack Bass, *Taming the Storm* (New York: Doubleday, 1993), p. 424.

24. Bass confidential source, March 1998.

25. Bass telephone interview with Morris Amitay, July 28, 1998.

26. Bass interview with Robert G. Kaiser, July 14, 1997.

27. *Parade*, February 15, 1981.

CHAPTER 23: "MY BABY IS DYING"

1. Bass interview with Nick Theodore, July 1, 1998.

2. Bass confidential source, June 1998.

3. *Congressional Record*, July 22, 1982.

4. Bass confidential interview, June 1967.

5. *Post and Courier*, December 1, 1996.

6. *The State*, April 18, 1993.

7. Unless attributed otherwise, Richard Harpootlian's comments in this chapter are taken from a Bass interview with Harpootlian, June 25, 1997.

8. *The State*, September 2, 1993.

9. Ibid.

10. Ibid.

11. Ibid.

12. Ibid., August 30, 1996.

13. Ibid., September 8, 1996.

14. Ibid., October 5, 1996.

15. *Post and Courier*, December 1, 1996.

16. *The State*, December 4, 1996.

17. James Banks interview with Thurmond, 1976.

CHAPTER 24: "ALIVE AND SERVING"

1. *Almanac of American Politics 1998*, p. 1,271.

2. Bass confidential source, May 1998.

3. *New York Times,* October 24, 1996.

4. Bass telephone interview with Mark Goodin, July 30, 1997.

5. *The State,* November 10, 1996.

6. Paul Thurmond to Bass, August 2004.

7. R. J. "Duke" Short to Bass, July 1997.

8. *Washington Post,* April 8, 1996.

9. Lee Bandy to Bass, July 1998.

10. *New York Times,* July 23, 1998.

11. Opening Statement by Senator Strom Thurmond (R–SC), Senate Armed Services Committee, July 22, 1998.

12. *Washington Post,* April 8, 1996.

13. Jeffrey Toobin, *A Vast Conspiracy* (New York: Random House, 1999), pp. 374, 379.

14. *Wine Spectator,* July 31, 1999, pp. 38–44.

15. Bass interview with confidential source, October 2004.

16. *New York Times Magazine,* April 20, 2001, pp. 58–61.

17. *The State,* July 12, 1998.

18. *American South Comes of Age* video, University of South Carolina and South Carolina Educational Television, 1987, program 14, "The Emerging South."

19. Bass interview with Tom Turnipseed, op. cit.

20. Alexander Lamis, ed., *Southern Politics in the 1990s* (Baton Rouge: Louisiana State University Press, 1999), p. 8.

21. Bass interview with Alex Sanders, November 22, 2004; Sanders discussion paper, Joan Shorenstein Center, Harvard University, November 2004.

22. *New York Times Magazine,* April 20, 2001.

CHAPTER 25: "BLIND, BUT NOW I SEE"

1. *The Almanac of American Politics 2004,* p. 902.

CHAPTER 26: BREAKING THE SILENCE

1. Bass telephone interview with Glenn Walters, August 10, 2004.

2. *The State,* December 16, 2003.

3. CBS transcript, "Part IV: Williams on Thurmond," *60 Minutes II,* December 17, 2003.

4. Week in Review, *New York Times,* January 4, 2004.

5. Brent Staples, *New York Times,* December 26, 2003.

6. *The State,* December 16, 2003.

7. *Post and Courier*, January 29, 2005.

8. Bass interview with Thurmond Bishop, July 20, 2004.

9. Bass interview with Essie Mae Washington-Williams, February 21, 2005.

10. Thompson interview with Madison Shockley, May 17, 2004.

11. *Seattle Post-Intelligencer*, December 18, 2003; *Pittsburgh Post-Gazette*, December 20, 2003; Thompson interview with Ronald Williams, May 31, 2004.

12. *The State*, February 29, 2004.

13. Bass telephone interviews with Bruce Elrod, July 31 and August 16, 2004.

14. *Edgefield Advertiser*, May 12, 2004; *Citizen-News*, May 12, 2004. Rainsford, Baughman, and Derrick quotes from Bass interviews, June 4, 2004.

15. *Post and Courier*, May 22, 2004.

16. Ibid.

17. Bass notes from attending the event.

18. *Post and Courier*, July 3, 2004.

19. *New York Times*, July 2, 2004.

20. *Post and Courier*, July 6, 2004.

21. *New York Times*, July 17, 2004.

22. Ibid., July 31, 2004.

23. Essie Mae Washington-Williams to Bass, July 29 and August 22, 2004.

24. Bass telephone interview with Edward Ball, June 11, 2004.

25. John S. Rainey, *Post and Courier*, September 23, 2003.

26. Herbert Blumer, "The Future of the Color Line," in *The South in Continuity and Change* (Durham: Duke University Press, 1965), p. 336.

27. *Southern Political Report*, January 5, 2004.

28. *The State*, September 13, 2004.

29. Draper, unpublished manuscript, op. cit.

Acknowledgments

We are indebted first to Strom Thurmond for living a life whose richness, longevity, and historic impact combine to make it worth telling. His voice is present throughout this book. Second only to him is his daughter, Essie Mae Washington-Williams, who provided much detail about the six decades of their complicated black-and-white relationship. We applaud her decision in 2003 to finally, after years of denial, tell the truth about her relationship to her father.

In 1998 Jack Bass and Marilyn Thompson co-authored *Ol' Strom: An Unauthorized Biography of Strom Thurmond*, which provided background information for this new book. Williams' decision to acknowledge her relationship with Thurmond sent us back to the archives illuminate the relationship between the South's staunchest segregationist in the 1940s and his illegitimate black child.

Jack Bass covered Thurmond between 1963 and 1973 as a South Carolina-based political writer for *The State* and the *Charlotte Observer* who also served as correspondent for a number of national publications. This critical decade included Thurmond's switch to the Republican Party, his kingmaker role in Richard Nixon's winning the 1968 republican nomination for president, and Thurmond's central role in that campaign. This period also covered Thurmond's second marriage and the start of his becoming a family man, and it marked the beginning of his reaching out politically to black South Carolinians.

Marilyn Thompson conducted extensive interviews in the early 1980s, first in preparation for a series on Thurmond for *The Columbia Record*. Thurmond gave her access to his gubernatorial papers at the South Caroliniana Library at the University of South Carolina where she first discovered correspondence with Essie Washington, a student at the all-black South Carolina State College, and then the married Essie Williams. At the urging of Thurmond protégé Lee Atwater, she began research on a Thurmond biography and wrote more than twenty chapter drafts for an unpublished book manuscript. She owes a debt of gratitude to her former editors, Thomas McLean and Gil Spencer, and to her editors at *The Washington Post*, especially executive editor Leonard Downie, In many ways, her book became a family project, with help from her former husband, the late Robert W. Thompson Jr., her sister Leigh Myzk and her sons, Cory and Andrew.

Caroline Stone, the editor of *The Tiger*, Clemson University's student newspaper, provided invaluable assistance by gathering documents from the archives of the Strom Thurmond Institute at Clemson University.

In addition, historian James G. Banks and Thurmond biographer Nadine Cohodas both generously provided transcripts of many hours of interviews with Thurmond. She also made available extensive additional research material collected for her book, *Strom Thurmond and the Politics of Southern Change.* Banks wrote a 1970 dissertation on Thurmond at Kent State University—"Strom Thurmond and the Revolt Against Modernity"—that stands out as a scholarly study of his career to the point.

Special appreciation is due the archivists at the Strom Thurmond Institute at Clemson University, the South Caroliniana Library and the Modern Political Collection at the University of South Carolina, the South Carolina Historical Society, and the Southern Historical Collection at the University of North Carolina at Chapel Hill. Joe Cross of the U. S. C. Law School Library staff provided especially valuable assistance in locating court records.

Emily Newman at *The Charlotte Observer* and Dargan Richards at *The State* in Columbia, S.C., were especially helpful in providing access to the rich archives of those two newspapers. Other valuable assistance came from researcher Ginny Everett at the *Atlanta Journal-Constitution,* managing editor Clint Bowie of the *Edgefield Advertiser,* and researchers Margot Williams and Alice Crites at *The Washington Post.*

Special thanks to cartoonists Robert Ariail of *The State,* Doug Marlette of the *Tallahassee Democrat,* and Roger Harvell of the *Greenville News* for use of their work.

The College of Charleston provided research and administrative support for this project to Bass as a member of the faculty there.

At PublicAffairs, we thank publisher Peter Osnos for his oversight of the book's creation, our dedicated editor David Patterson and managing editor Robert Kimzey.

Literary agent Ron Goldfarb encouraged this project from its inception and performed professional responsibilities with efficiency and dispatch.

Most of the scores of persons interviewed are mentioned in footnotes throughout the book. Special thanks among them goes to Harry Dent, for sharing insights developed from an intimate relationship with and knowledge of Strom Thurmond that dates back to his 1950 Senate campaign.

Among those who read and commented helpfully on portions of the manuscript are Dan Carter, Orville Vernon Burton, Allen Tullos, Laura Kalman, James G. Banks, and Jack Nelson. Nathalie Dupree, the wife of Jack Bass, provided useful critiques of the manuscript as it developed and spousal support replete with a breadth that only fellow authors can fully appreciate.

Index